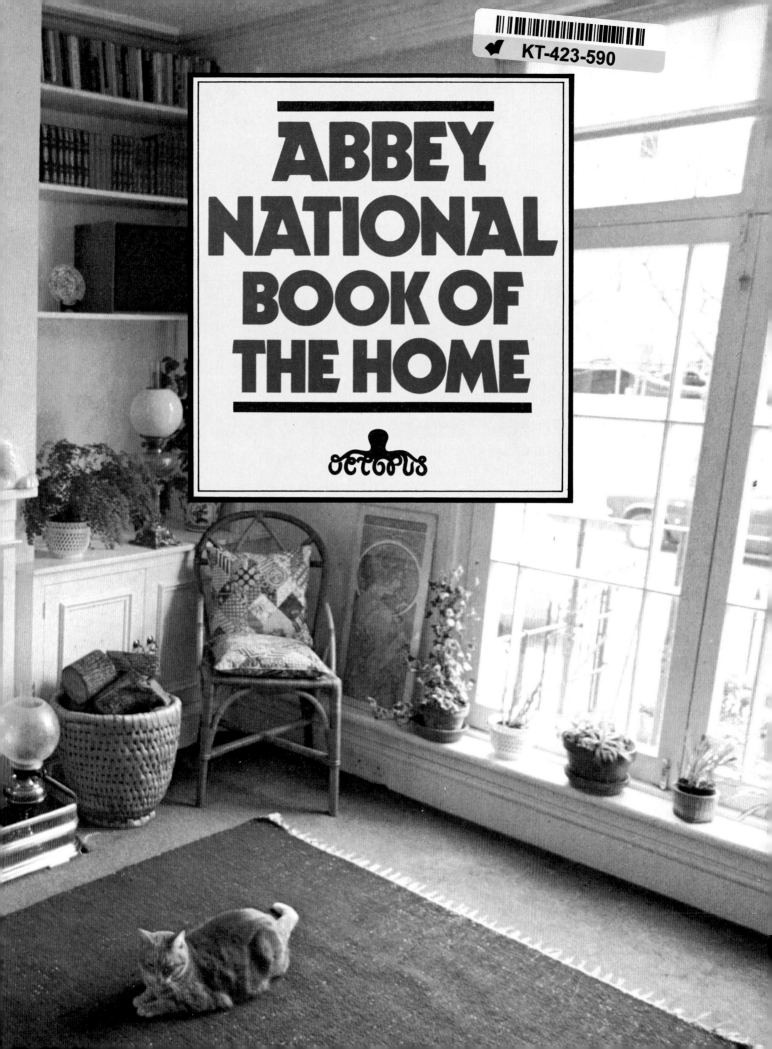

ABBEY NATIONAL BOOK OF THE HOME

OCTOPUS

CONTENTS

First published 1982 by
Octopus Books Limited
59 Grosvenor Street
London WIX 9DA

© 1982 Octopus Books Limited

ISBN 0 7064 1725 9

Produced by
Mandarin Publishers Limited
22a Westlands Road,
Quarry Bay, Hong Kong

Printed in Hong Kong

A PLACE TO LIVE
Abbey National Building Society

MAKING A HOME
Jill Blake

HOME DESIGN
Jill Blake

HOME DECORATING
Jill Blake

A PLACE TO LIVE

Finding the right property, whether to purchase or to rent, is a major undertaking for most of us. The aim of this survey is to provide a guide through the whole process, pointing out the possible pitfalls and advising you how to avoid them.

We begin by studying the choice between renting or buying your home and the factors which should be taken into account when deciding where to live.

We then take you through the various stages of house purchase and explain the role of financial institutions, surveyors, solicitors and estate agents. Throughout we have attempted to answer technical points in as straightforward a way as possible.

The survey ends with a guide to insuring your home, and your legal obligations to your neighbours.

FIRST CONSIDERATIONS

WHETHER TO BUY OR TO RENT

The main factor in deciding whether to rent or buy is generally one of cost. It is usually, but not always, cheaper to rent than to buy, although the continuing decline in the supply of rented accommodation available can make it very difficult to find (see *Renting*). The financial considerations fall into two categories – 'one-off costs' and 'regular payments'.

One-off costs. When *renting* accommodation, such costs are relatively small. It is quite usual for new tenants to pay a deposit (as security for the landlord in case of damage to fixtures, fittings or contents during the period of occupation) plus some rental in advance.

In the case of unfurnished rented accommodation, which is relatively rare these days, you may also need to purchase essential items of furniture and household equipment.

When *buying* a property, these non-recurring costs are much greater. A deposit of up to 10 per cent of the value of the property (this can be even more in times when mortgage funds are in short supply), will almost certainly be required. There will also be building society inspection fees, the cost of your own private survey, if you decide to have one, and legal expenses. As with unfurnished rented accommodation, if this is your first home, you will probably also need to budget for essential items of furniture and household equipment.

Regular payments. Recurring expenditure for rented accommodation will vary considerably, depending on the terms of the letting but, as a broad indication, the following items must be budgeted for:
1. Rent, and possibly rates.
2. Heating and lighting.
3. Service charge or repairs and maintenance costs, depending on the terms of the letting.
4. Travel costs to and from work.
5. Any other regular expenses e.g. telephone bills, if applicable.

If you have bought a property the outlays will differ quite considerably. A typical breakdown might be as follows:

1. Mortgage repayments – net of tax relief on the interest element.
2. Heating and lighting.
3. Repairs and maintenance costs, including private roads where applicable.
4. Travel costs to and from work.
5. Regular bills such as telephone.
6. Life and property insurance premiums.
7. Rates (both local authority and water/sewage).
8. Ground rent and service charges if the property is leasehold.

Having considered both initial outlay and running costs, the decision whether to rent or to buy is also heavily influenced by longer term factors. Owning property is likely to be an excellent investment and serve as a hedge against inflation, whereas payment of rent is an irrecoverable expense which can be expected to increase broadly in line with inflation. Unless you anticipate being extremely mobile, there is little doubt about the long-term financial advantages of buying rather than renting.

CHOOSING AN AREA

Another great advantage of *buying* a house is that, within the limits of financial resources, you are free to choose the area or district. Often, however, it is undertaken in something of a hurry and under pressure, perhaps due to a change of job which necessitates moving to a different part of the country at short notice. Remember,

HOME BUYER'S BUDGET PLANNER

RENT–KEEP	£	

REGULAR BILLS

Electricity		
Gas		
Rates		
Water Rates		
Telephone		
TV Rent		
	£	

HOUSEKEEPING	£	

TRAVEL & TRANSPORT

Commuting		
Road Tax		
Car Insurance		
Car Maintenance		
Petrol		
	£	

OTHER COMMITMENTS

Clothing		
Leisure		
Credit		
Holidays		
	£	

TAKE HOME PAY	£	

EXISTING COMMITMENTS

Rent		
Regular bills		
Housekeeping		
Travel & Transport		
Other commitments		
Total	£	
Balance	£	

HOUSE PURCHASE PRICE £

Deposit		
Solicitor's fees		
Surveyor's fees		
Total	£	

Existing savings		
Mortgage required		

MONTHLY MORTGAGE REPAYMENTS £

Left: explore the area to see if it will meet all your requirements: proximity to employment, transport, shops, schools, entertainment and so on.
Above: whether buying or renting property, it is helpful to set down your income and regular outgoings before committing yourself to any major expenditure.
Right: the advertisements in local estate agents' windows are a good guide to the property prices in a particular area

the purchase of a house, once done, cannot easily be undone without a large measure of inconvenience and cost.

Convenience. Careful consideration should be given to the chosen area, the proximity of shops, schools, employment and transport. Explore the area in general, not just to decide whether you like it but to see if it will provide for all your requirements.

Notice whether the houses in the vicinity are well cared for. Do they have garages or parking areas or is there likely to be much street parking, car washing and maintenance on the road rather than in drives or garage forecourts?

Proximity to public transport could mean the difference between having to drive to the shops, or taking children to school, and being able to live without a second or even a first car. So check the standard of service – availability *and* regularity. Similarly, visit the local shops to see if they suit your needs and purse.

Consider also the siting of the property. If the house is at the top of a hill, it's likely to mean a lot of strenuous walking and is not going to be suitable for a disabled or elderly person. A property on a main road could well be affected by heavy traffic – noise, vibration likely to cause structural defects, and lack of privacy are all possible disadvantages. If you have young children it could also be very dangerous.

Check the proximity to such noise-producing establishments as a sports club, public house, school or cinema. It may be wonderfully convenient to have them within walking distance, but quite another matter to have them within earshot!

Advice and information. Visit the local planning authority and ask about the area. Study the town map and ask the Planning Officer about schemes planned for the town in general. In this way you will be forewarned of any planning schemes which would 'blight' the neighbourhood in which you are interested. You will find out, too, about any redevelopment schemes or traffic management proposals which could eliminate kerb side parking within a reasonable distance of the house.

Apart from newspapers, there are many other possible sources of information. Many local councils have information or publicity officers who may be able to answer your questions or send you town guides and other useful publications.

Priorities. Naturally, a younger couple will have different priorities to those of retired people. The former will probably be vitally interested in the availability of pre-schooling, primary and secondary schools, recreation facilities and the like, while older people may be most concerned about the proximity of shops and public transport.

House buyers should first consider their minimum requirements so far as the number of rooms and the floor space are concerned. Obviously, a couple with three children would not consider a house or flat with one bedroom and, conversely, an older couple, having retired or nearing retirement, would probably look for accommodation of more modest size, say with just one spare bedroom for visitors.

If these decisions are made at the outset you will avoid unnecessary and abortive inspections and reduce the risk of being tempted into buying something unsuitable. Also remember that overheads generally relate to size and to the number of rooms except in the case of a flat, where overheads tend to be higher.

It is surprising how many people ignore these very important points, so sit down and make your own check list. The hour or so this takes will be time well spent.

FINDING A PROPERTY

It is possible that a friend or acquaintance may put you in touch with a prospective seller but there are other ways of setting about the task.

Property pages of the local newspapers are a good source of information (they will also include details of the major estates developed by the big house builders). To make sure that you don't miss an issue, arrange with the local papers to have a copy sent to you each week.

Estate agents can also save you a great deal of time and effort. Not only do they have offices in practically every high street but they carry extensive advertising in local papers throughout the year, and their sale boards appear in front gardens throughout the country.

Most people can tell you what an estate agent does but not everyone realizes that the estate agent is acting on behalf of the seller and is obliged to put forward the best points of a property and obtain the best price on behalf of his client. The seller pays the agent a fee for a successful sale so you, as the buyer, will not have to pay for any service.

An estate agent is not necessarily qualified professionally and does not offer any guarantee that his description of a property is accurate. He certainly does not pass comment on the fitness of the structure, even if qualified to do so.

Tell him what you are looking for, in what price range and the financial limits to which you can go, and he will try to satisfy your requirements. But the maxim of *caveat emptor*, 'let the buyer beware', should be constantly borne in mind.

As a prospective buyer you are not obliged to rely on one particular estate agent and you should look at the availability of properties as shown in the windows and advertisements of as many local agents as possible.

PRICES

In looking around, you can get a good idea of the prices applicable to various types of property in different areas. Prices vary so much even between one area of a town and another – and more so between towns and regions of the country – that it is impossible here to give reliable long-term guidance. The best possible guide is the advertisements in local papers and in the estate agents' windows.

Many people prefer a new house but older properties should always be thoroughly investigated, as it is frequently possible to obtain better value on an older house.

WHAT TO LOOK FOR IN A PROPERTY

Obviously, your first inspection of a property will concentrate on whether it meets

your basic requirements. Does it have the required number of living- and bedrooms and so on? Having found the place that meets this initial minimum it is sometimes easy to become starry-eyed about the property and miss many of its drawbacks.

When to look. Most houses look at their best on a balmy summer's day with sun streaming through the windows, so be wary about your feelings if you're doing your house-hunting in the summer. If you like the feel of a particular property on a cold, wet winter's day, however, there's a good chance you won't make a rash choice. Also in cold, wet weather it is most likely that the heating system will be functioning, giving you an opportunity to note its effectiveness or otherwise. And in any event, never assume that because there are the requisite number of radiators throughout the property, the system functions efficiently. Check that it does!

Fuel, heating. Ask what type of fuel the heating system uses. There are differences between the cost of oil, electricity, gas and solid fuel, not to mention problems of delivery or supply. Also, it is going to be expensive to change from one system to another if your preference is, say, for gas

where the existing boiler burns oil. Check the hot water system too – run the hot tap to see if it is delivering hot, not tepid, water. Also check that both hot and cold water taps run clean. Discoloration could indicate a rusting storage tank and pipework.

Damp. Look out for damp patches on ceilings and walls. These are obvious pointers to a leaking roof or broken rainwater pipes and gutters or perished pointing to the brickwork. Are there areas of lighter wallpaper or 'tide marks' above the skirting boards? These are sure signs of rising damp.

Timber defects. Are the floors springy, with large gaps under the skirting boards and the carpets or linoleum firmly fixed down? This could indicate timber defects, but such faults are not always easy for the layman to detect, and it is therefore advisable to seek an independent surveyor's report once you have decided on a particular property. It could save you a great deal of money (see *Structural survey*).

Power. Look for adequate electrical power points and check whether they are of the modern square pin type, although

It is unlikely that your search for a suitable property will lead to the discovery of a street quite like this one, but it does give an idea of the enormous range on the market! Consider the options very carefully before making a firm decision

this is not an infallible pointer to the age of the wiring. Ask to look in the meter cupboard where it is often possible to see new wiring running into the fuse boxes.

Services and rates. Check whether all the main services run into the house. An 'all electric' house may have a gas point still laid onto an old meter position which the owner has removed. It is far cheaper to reconnect to an existing supply than to have a new supply run in from the road or from even farther away.

If the house is in semi-rural or rural surroundings check whether it is connected to the main sewer. If not, it may have a septic tank system of drainage or cesspool which has to be emptied periodically – another possible inconvenience and a costly item. Find out exactly what is involved.

Ask how much the General, Water and Sewage rates are, how much the heating system costs to run and, if the property is leasehold, how much the ground rent is and whether any service charges are applicable.

Insulation. Find out if the loft is properly insulated and if the cavity walls have been insulated by foam or other filling and by whom, and whether there is a guarantee applicable (although usually the owner will be only too happy to volunteer such information). Check any double glazing. Are the units sealed? Note any signs of condensation.

If it is an old house, ask about any timber treatments or damp courses which may have been inserted, how long ago, and what guarantees go with them.

Check for subsidence, due to any form of mining in the district. Ascertain the responsibilities, if any, of relevant authorities.

General condition of property. What is the general state of decoration throughout the house? If it is not to your taste, can you afford to change it quickly; if not, will you be able to live with it? More important, what is the state of the plasterwork, doors, window frames, skirting boards and staircases? Replastering, and replacing damaged wood is a costly business.

Space. Imagine yourself living in the house. Will your furniture fit in? Don't be deceived by the apparently large areas available when a house is empty. Ask for the measurements of the various rooms. Better still, take your tape measure along and ask if you may measure them for yourself.

Layout. If any rooms have two or more doors, are they so positioned that draughts could be a problem? Or will they make the placing of furniture difficult?

Is the layout of the house convenient e.g. is the bathroom reasonably near the bedrooms? Is there a separate lavatory, or is the only one in the bathroom? Is there a separate dining-room so that you do not always have to eat in the kitchen? Such considerations may not worry *you* too much – but they can take on a new significance when you have guests.

It may be that at the present time your children are young and can be put together in one room, but think a year or two ahead. Are they going to need separate bedrooms then, and if so, are other bedrooms available?

Other considerations. Ask the vendor whether he intends to leave the carpets,

curtains and other items; bear in mind that fittings screwed or otherwise permanently fixed to walls and floors may be fixtures and thus are properly part of the structure and should not be removed.

Consider too, whether they are appropriate to your needs. It is one thing, for instance, to inherit lots of well-designed and well-constructed storage units, and quite another to have the task of dismantling and disposing of flimsy, unwanted units and making good the walls.

Find out which way the property faces. A north-facing living room or kitchen, where a housewife may spend a lot of her time, is likely to be cold and dismal if it gets no sun at any time of the day.

If it is a terraced house, do neighbouring properties have extensions which could seriously obstruct light?

Obviously, common defects in other similar houses nearby may well affect the one you are looking at. Old slated roofs, for instance, which are gradually being replaced by new covering materials, could point to the need for repairs to your potential home.

If there is a garden is it of a practical size for your needs, which of the boundary walls are your responsibility, and what is their present state of repair?

Any of the structural aspects touched on here should properly be dealt with by a professionally prepared structural survey but they can be used as initial guidelines and bear on a decision whether or not to proceed further with a particular property.

FLATS – WHAT TO CHECK

In the case of flats, how thick are dividing walls, or floors and ceilings? Try to make your visit on a weekday evening when neighbouring flats are most likely to be occupied and you can assess possible noise disturbance.

If the flat is at basement level, how much natural lighting can you expect – particularly on dull days? The placement of windows, their number and size are all relevant factors. Also, if there is on-street parking, how many of your windows could be obstructed by parked cars and, worse, large vans?

When budgeting, remember that not only will the annual outgoings include the mortgage payments and rates but also the

Left: possible noise disturbance is one of many considerations when buying a flat. Right: building societies have been helping people to buy their own homes since the late 18th century

ground rent and a possible service charge, and perhaps costs for central heating, garage and even porterage. Take particular care to check the general condition. You may be liable for major repairs which could be very costly if the block has not been maintained properly in the past.

In the case of converted flats, and certainly with freehold flats, approach your building society before proceeding too far towards buying such a property to check whether they will accept it.

This is by no means an exhaustive catalogue of points to look for but rather a guide to potential problems. If you make your own checklist, which takes into consideration your own set of priorities, the chances are you will avoid many of the pitfalls which can trap the unwary.

MAKING AN OFFER

Another advantage of dealing through an estate agent is the avoidance of any unpleasant haggling over price direct with the vendor.

The purchaser should have a clear and precise understanding with the agent as to what an offer for a property includes. A written confirmation of the price should be obtained from the estate agents, giving details of all items included with the property. This will range from light fittings, curtains and carpets, to outhouses such as greenhouses and sheds, and even garden plants, shrubs and trees. This written list will avoid any disputes later on and will be of great help to your solicitor.

Whatever happens, *do not* sign any documents agreeing to purchase; no reputable agent will press you to do so. If you put in an offer, be certain to state that it is 'subject to contract'. But of course, you must go to your solicitor and set matters in motion as soon as possible (see *The home buyer and the law*). When you are quite satisfied that your prospective purchase is progressing smoothly do, as a courtesy, tell the other estate agents so that they can remove you from their mailing lists.

FINANCING THE PURCHASE

Completion of the house purchase process is quite simple for anyone able to pay cash. Provided that the vendor is not involved in a series of sale and purchase transactions, each depending on the other (known as a 'chain') it is just a matter of arranging to pay the purchase price through your solicitor when requested, so that the conveyance can be completed and the title deeds passed on to you for safe keeping.

Unfortunately few of us are in the happy position of being able to purchase a home outright, so here we explain how to go about raising the finance.

Homeloan. If you are a first time buyer, you may be able to raise some money through a government scheme known as 'Homeloan'. Under this scheme you contract to save for at least two years through a building society, bank, national savings or other approved scheme. Depending on the amount saved, you receive a tax-free bonus of up to £100 and a loan of £600 which is interest-free for up to five years. There are other restrictions and you have to fill in a special form before you start saving. A leaflet entitled *Homeloan* and giving full details is available from any participating savings organization or from a post office.

Building societies. The first building societies were set up in the late 18th century both to help people acquire their own homes and to provide a convenient savings medium. The societies received 'subscriptions' from their members and used the money to acquire land and property via loans to other members. In some cases the aim was political, for the ownership of property was the only means by which a man could gain the right to vote. Thus the franchise could be extended by encouraging home ownership.

By the late 19th century, the societies had lost any political aims and existed purely as savings and home loan institutions. Since then they have expanded rapidly as mutual, non-profit making institutions, owned by the members.

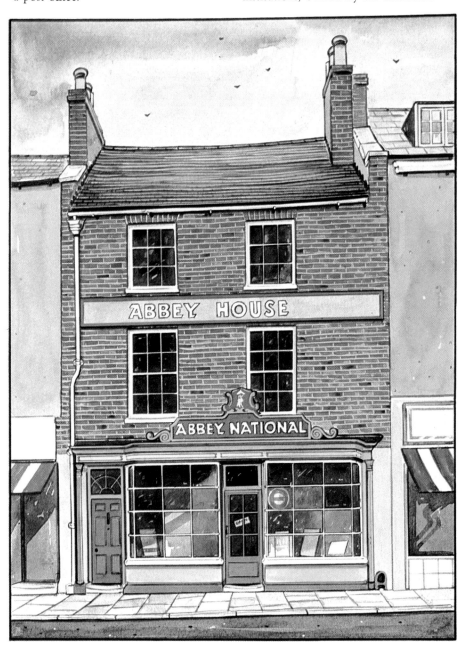

Most building societies adopt a policy of providing loans to investors first so it is worth becoming an investing member as far ahead as possible.

Societies will consider properties of most types and ages but where a property is of unusual construction, design or character, such as converted flats or maisonettes or properties not in a residential area, there may be complications. If the tenure is leasehold (see *Leasehold*), generally the lease must have at least 30 years to run at the end of the mortgage term.

Depending on availability of funds, some societies may be prepared to lend rather larger amounts than usual but a higher rate of interest normally applies to such loans. Often, when a borrower is not able to obtain a sufficient loan from a building society, insurance companies will provide a 'topping-up' second mortgage.

All the major, and most of the smaller, building societies belong to the Building Societies Association. This body recommends the interest rates relating to both investments and mortgages and represents the interests of member societies to government.

Building societies have to be satisfied that prospective borrowers can afford the monthly payments on the loan and generally the income of each individual applicant, whether the sole or one of two joint applicants, is divided into 'principal income' and 'secondary income'.

This division is made irrespective of the sex of the applicants but according to the nature of the income.

The principal income may be defined as the income of the highest earner, which is likely to rise in the future.

Secondary income is normally defined as any additional income of a less permanent nature which can be expected to be available indefinitely in support of, or until, the 'principal income' has increased equivalently.

How much a society will grant depends on their individual lending policy, but as a rough guide most will make an advance of up to two and a half times the principal income, plus the secondary income. For instance, if a couple earn £6,000 and £4,000 with the larger amount being the 'principal income', the maximum advance most societies would consider would be £6,000 × 2½ = £15,000 plus £4,000 giving a total of £19,000.

A normal basic loan would provide up to 80 per cent of the purchase price or valuation (whichever is the lower) but this percentage may be reduced where the property is old, higher priced, or where

there are other features which suggest that the security warrants a lower basic advance.

It may be possible to obtain a higher advance of up to 95 per cent, or in some cases 100 per cent of the purchase price or valuation (whichever is the lower), if additional security is provided. The simplest form of additional security is a 'single premium insurance guarantee policy' arranged by the building society.

CHECKLIST OF STAGES IN HOUSE PURCHASE

Talk to the branch manager of your Building Society, Bank or other source of mortgage, to discuss the type of home you want and to determine how much you can expect to borrow towards that end.

Find the house/flat that you would like to buy – remembering to look not only at the property but at its surroundings. See main text for points to consider.

Make an offer 'subject to contract', then complete a mortgage application without delay and submit with a valuation fee.

Also, it is advisable to contact a surveyor and arrange for your own private survey. On the strength of his report, it may be possible to arrange a lower purchase price to enable you to carry out essential repairs, so it is well worth the cost.

The mortgagee (body providing mortgage) will obtain a valuation report and if everything is all right will send you a mortgage offer.

Respond to this offer as quickly as possible – having first considered your own surveyor's report and determined whether or not you wish to proceed.

Consult a solicitor in readiness for the next stage – the exchange of contracts – at which point you will need to pay the deposit.

Arrange and confirm your moving-in date, and arrange for both the connection of services and removals.

On completion day, the mortgagee will send a cheque to your solicitors and the property is yours.

Local authorities. Like building societies, local authorities lend only for the purchase or improvement of property for owner occupation. Although they tend to alter their interest rates rather more frequently than building societies these rates are generally higher and loans are usually made on a capital repayment basis (see *Types of mortgage*).

Funds available through local authorities have declined in recent years and may be restricted to certain types of property.

Banks. In the past banks were involved mainly in granting second mortgages and bridging (short-term) loans and did not normally grant first mortgages. However, banks have now become much more active in the supply of funds for the housing market. This applies to the big high street banks as well as the Trustee Savings Bank and a number of so-called 'trusts', many of which are off-shoots of American companies.

Most of these banks charge a higher rate of interest than the building societies though this is not always the case. They still account for only a small share of the total market.

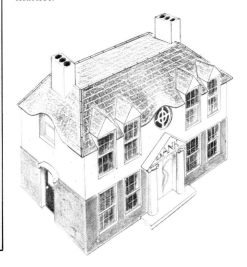

Insurance companies. Some life insurance companies will lend funds for the purpose of house purchase on first (main) mortgages where the advance is repaid by means of an endowment policy issued by the company. Although an advance would not normally exceed 80 per cent of the property valuation, companies are sometimes prepared to make loans up to perhaps £50,000 on larger properties. However, the interest rate is almost always higher than that charged by building societies.

A number of life insurance companies also make funds available to 'top-up' a shortfall which may arise between the loan

from the other main source, such as a building society, and the total borrowing required. Because it is generally the policy of building societies to distribute their funds to assist as many people as possible, the amount available from this main source could be less than the purchaser requires.

If you need to borrow, say, £24,000 and a building society will advance £19,000, a life insurance company may be willing to 'top up' the advance by lending the remaining £5,000.

The *top-up loan (second mortgage)* would be repayable to the insurance company by means of an endowment policy and the interest rate would usually be higher than that charged by a building society. When considering the amount to be advanced the company would take into account the type of property, and the applicant's financial status. In addition, the company would probably stipulate that the *first*, as well as the *second* mortgage must be arranged in conjunction with a combination of either endowment non-profit, endowment with-profit or low cost endowment policies (see *Insurance*).

Finance companies. Although finance companies may provide funds for first and second mortgages, their interest rates are generally much higher than the sources already mentioned and they will only lend over a fairly short term, at most about 15 years.

Their usual method of calculating interest is on a fixed balance whereas most building societies charge interest on the balance outstanding at the end of each year.

Private loans. A private loan or mortgage can be arranged with a friend, relative or employer, possibly at a reduced rate of interest. Solicitors would normally prepare a document defining the terms of such a mortgage – a sensible safeguard against the possibility of later misunderstandings or disputes.

TYPES OF MORTGAGE

Potential borrowers should first see their building society manager or whoever is to make the loan and discuss the type of mortgage best suited for them.

Repayment mortgage. This involves payment of a monthly instalment of both interest and capital necessary to repay the loan within the term of years originally agreed. These instalments may have to be adjusted if a change in the interest rate (whether an increase or reduction) occurs. Your building society will inform you at the relevant time.

If you decide on a repayment mortgage, do not forget to consider taking out mortgage protection insurance, details of which are given under *Insurance*.

During the early years of the mortgage, nearly all the monthly instalments are interest and you may find that even after four or five years, you have paid off as little as £400 or £500, but the tax relief is at its highest during this time.

Endowment mortgage. In this case the loan is repaid by the proceeds of an endowment policy issued by an insurance company. The policy provides a sufficient amount to repay the mortgage in one lump sum either on a specified future date or upon earlier death. The premiums on the endowment policy are paid to the insurance company and interest on the loan (not repayment of capital) is paid to the building society or other lender.

Throughout the period of the mortgage the capital balance outstanding remains constant. If the mortgage is arranged with a building society then the interest rate charged on an endowment type mortgage is often a little higher than that made under the repayment system. Most major insurance company policies are acceptable, but check with the building society or other lender before committing yourself.

The types of policies suitable as a means of repaying the mortgage are:

Endowment non-profit. A fixed sum of money (the sum insured) is paid either at a fixed future date to coincide with the mortgage term or upon the earlier death of the person insured.

Endowment with profits. The policy is similar except that by paying a higher premium the policy owner participates in the profits made by the insurance company.

Apart from there being a guaranteed sum sufficient to repay the mortgage an element of saving is introduced by means of the bonuses paid by the insurance office.

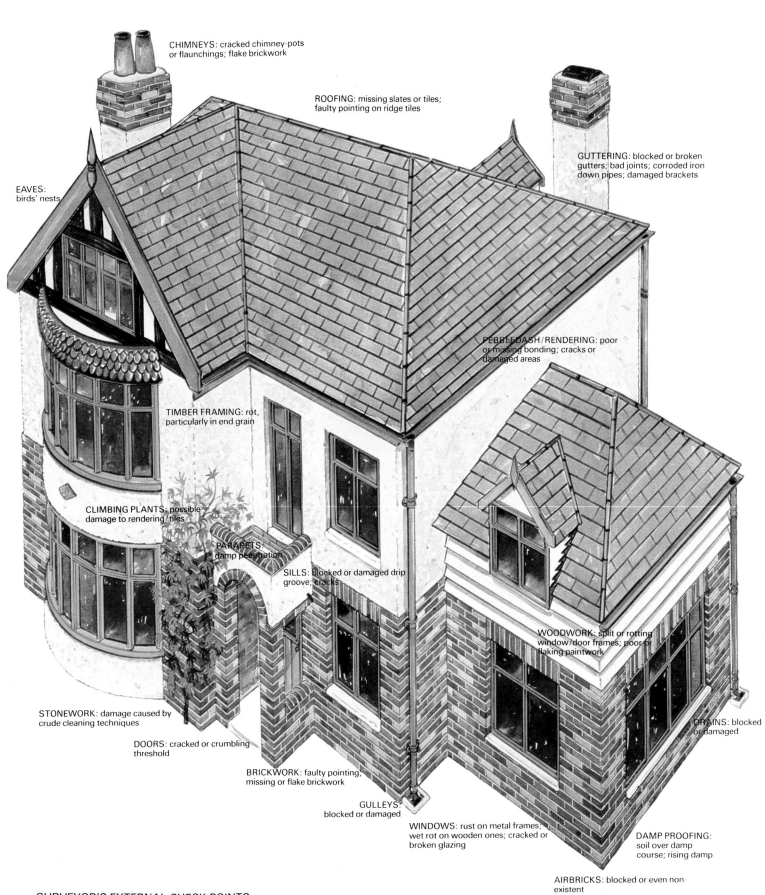

CHIMNEYS: cracked chimney-pots or flaunchings; flake brickwork

ROOFING: missing slates or tiles; faulty pointing on ridge tiles

GUTTERING: blocked or broken gutters; bad joints; corroded iron down pipes; damaged brackets

EAVES: birds' nests

PEBBLEDASH/RENDERING: poor or missing bonding; cracks or damaged areas

TIMBER FRAMING: rot, particularly in end grain

CLIMBING PLANTS: possible damage to rendering/tiles

PARAPETS: damp penetration

SILLS: blocked or damaged drip groove; cracks

WOODWORK: split or rotting window/door frames; poor or flaking paintwork

STONEWORK: damage caused by crude cleaning techniques

DOORS: cracked or crumbling threshold

DRAINS: blocked or damaged

BRICKWORK: faulty pointing; missing or flake brickwork

GULLEYS: blocked or damaged

WINDOWS: rust on metal frames; wet rot on wooden ones; cracked or broken glazing

DAMP PROOFING: soil over damp course; rising damp

AIRBRICKS: blocked or even non-existent

SURVEYOR'S EXTERNAL CHECK-POINTS

Low cost endowment. This form of policy is a combination of an endowment-with-profits policy to cover part of the loan, and a form of term insurance for the balance. The insurance company builds into the policy an assumption that bonuses on the endowment portion will accumulate during the period of the policy so that when the proceeds of the policy become available at the end of the term, the basic endowment sum insured, together with bonuses, should be sufficient to repay the mortgage.

The assumed bonuses are assessed at a conservative level below the amount of current bonus so, provided the bonuses exceed the assumed rate, upon maturity of the policy there would be a surplus available to the policy owner after repaying the mortgage advance. In the event of earlier death, the guaranteed sum available would be sufficient at least to repay the mortgage.

There are advantages and disadvantages to consider when arranging a mortgage in conjunction with an endowment policy. Tax relief is normally deducted by the insurance company from the premium of most life policies providing that the policy is arranged to cover the life of oneself or one's spouse. Policies can be taken out so as to cover the joint lives of both husband and wife when the proceeds from the policy are paid in the event of death of either person.

One disadvantage is that the term of the mortgage cannot be extended if interest rates go up.

Option Mortgage Scheme. Whichever type of mortgage is selected, you will have to decide whether or not you wish the mortgage to be included in the Option Mortgage Scheme. (Bank and finance company loans are excluded from this.)

Given that a house is one of the most important expenditures you are ever likely to make, it is advisable to have a structural survey carried out. Opposite you will see just how many factors have to be checked. A trained surveyor will detect defects or possible future sources of trouble that the untrained eye might fail to see

This scheme came into effect from 1 April, 1968, and its purpose is to assist house buyers with moderate incomes who pay little or no tax. The rate of interest paid is reduced by a government subsidy to the building society or local authority to give a benefit comparable to that otherwise provided by tax relief.

Building societies operate this scheme in accordance with government legislation and a local branch of the building society or the local authority office will provide the details.

Paying the mortgage. Having organised your loan, don't forget to make your payments regularly! For convenience, these can normally be paid through a bank standing order.

If, through some misfortune such as unemployment or illness, you find you are having difficulty making the payment, do arrange a meeting with your bank or building society manager as soon as possible. He should be able to re-arrange the payments to meet your circumstances and, in some cases, may be able to suspend payments altogether for a while. He will also be able to advise you on help you are entitled to claim from the Department of Health and Social Security.

Banks and building societies do not like to start legal action for re-possession of properties, and only do so as a last resort. However, borrowers who build up arrears without any explanation eventually force the lender to take this step, albeit reluctantly.

THE SURVEYOR

The surveyor plays an important role in the process of buying and selling a house. Where the property is being purchased with a mortgage loan the surveyor has two main but quite distinct functions: *a) the building society inspection* and *b) valuation.* By law, a building society must have a property *inspected* by a qualified surveyor, who then advises the society as to its value and suitability for security against the intended loan.

The surveyor is not required to and does not carry out a structural survey (see next section). The applicant pays for the inspection when applying for the mortgage with the amount based on a sliding scale.

The purpose of the *inspection* is to give the building society a valuation and, depending upon the individual society's requirements, various other information and observations. Until 1980, building societies and banks treated the report as a

privileged document, produced for their purposes only, but now there is a growing tendency – at least on the part of the major societies – to issue the report to mortgage applicants. In many cases the valuer informs the society of essential and other repairs which he feels will be necessary to maintain the property and protect the value and financial security.

The undertaking of any such repairs or alterations may be stipulated as conditions of an offer of mortgage. However, where reports are still confidential the society concerned is under no obligation to pass on to you knowledge of any or all the items of repair suggested by the surveyor, even though you, as prospective purchaser, will have to pay for the inspection. Nor is the society obliged to, and often does not, pass on other information and opinion presented in the report.

It follows that the issue of a list of repairs to be carried out as a condition of mortgage or merely for information is not necessarily a comprehensive list. Nor is it an implied guarantee of the property's fitness in general or in particular.

For these reasons, such an inspection falls considerably short, both in fact and in law, of a structural survey and even if societies in general decide in future to release their previously confidential valuation reports, an intending buyer should still seriously consider the desirability of having an independent structural survey carried out.

More than one million homes change hands annually and in most cases purchasers do not take any independent professional advice on the condition of the house they intend to buy. Many assume that if the building society approves the mortgage, then the house is free from defects. This could be a very costly – even disastrous mistake.

A *valuation* is *not* a structural survey; the structure is not examined in depth and the valuer does not necessarily detail all the defects from which a property suffers. The valuer will take into account the age and nature of the building and there are various apparent defects which will influence the value of a property but others cannot be detected without substantial and, in some cases, specialist in-depth investigation.

STRUCTURAL SURVEY

The object of having such a survey is basically to find out if the house has any structural faults and thus help you to decide whether or not you want to go ahead with the purchase. With all houses, especially pre-1939 properties, a sensible buyer must seriously consider the situation. Obviously, with a newly-built house, which has the benefits of the N.H.B.C. (National House Builders' Council) backing, there is far less risk of major costs having to be borne by the first purchaser due to serious structural defects appearing during the initial 10 years of the property's life.

However, even in such cases, possible problems and the inconvenience involved in having defects put right should not be discounted and a structural survey could forewarn of trouble ahead. In any case, second purchase rights to redress do not extend to structural defects apparent at the time of purchase and which should have been reported by the previous owner or have been revealed by a survey.

It should be borne in mind also that building societies will not generally lend on any new property without an N.H.B.C. Certificate unless the construction has been supervised by a qualified surveyor or architect, acting for the purchaser.

Costs. Unlike building society inspections, there is no scale of fees for structural surveys and they will vary considerably, depending on the type, age, size and design of the property under consideration and indeed between one surveyor and another. It is always a good idea to seek a quotation from two or three individuals or firms, and you should always be quite clear in specifying just how detailed you expect the survey to be.

A structural survey will not be cheap and at the time of writing you would be hard pressed to get even a small, two-storey terraced property inspected for less than £100 while the average semi-detached and detached houses will command a fee of between £100 and £200 or more. It may be possible to effect a saving by arranging for the surveyor who carries out the building society inspection to do so in conjunction with a structural survey. Some societies will agree to this arrangement – but check that the surveyor is on the society's approved panel before committing yourself.

The saving by this arrangement is relatively small. It will usually be conditional on the surveyor being able to carry out the structural survey at the same time as the valuation and it may entail waiting for the latter until the surveyor can arrange his appointments to accommodate the much longer time involved in carrying out a structural survey. Remember, there are no set fees for structural surveys, so one is

completely in the hands of the surveyor in assessing the 'saving'.

Warning. There is much danger in the 'quick look by a friend' approach. A look around by someone who is involved in building, and may indeed be very competent in his own line of business, can lead to a false sense of security and major defects being overlooked because insufficient time has been spent in seeking out their probable sources. Many a friendship has foundered on this particular rock.

Advantages. There are several advantages in having a structural survey.
Objectivity. The surveyor will view a property with an unbiased and objective mind. He will not be influenced by the furnishings or by the décor (although he will note the condition of the decorations) and he will not be emotionally involved in the social and financial pressures surrounding the purchase.
Expertise. He will employ his considerable experience and knowledge of building construction to appraise the whole building from roof to foundations and provide a list of any repairs, improvements and

renovations he considers necessary and desirable, together with the likely cost.
Advice. Your surveyor should also offer advice on the future liability for repairs, faults in design, layout or construction and give his opinion as to probable marketability in the foreseeable future, if and when it becomes necessary to sell.

A copy of the list and cost of any repairs can be presented to the vendor via the agent with a possibility that the purchase price can be reduced by negotiation.

Interpreting the report. A structural survey report can appear to be a mournful catalogue of doom and disaster. The surveyor has an obligation to present the facts of the situation and list all the defects and shortcomings which he has been able to find – that is what he is being paid to do and is accountable for to you, his client. However, do not automatically reject the property, since much anxiety can be alleviated in many cases by asking the surveyor for a personal interview to discuss the report. He can then be asked to expand upon particular points.

A surveyor can, of course, only see and report on those things which are capable of

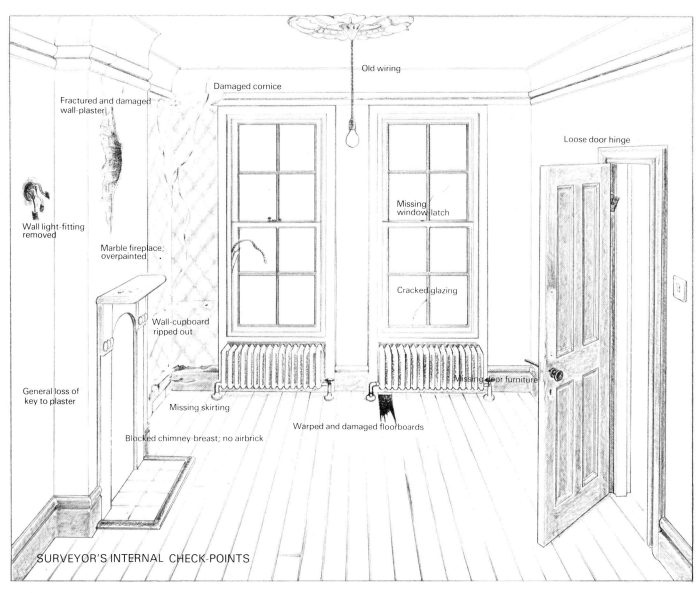

Old wiring

Damaged cornice

Fractured and damaged wall-plaster

Loose door hinge

Wall light-fitting removed

Missing window latch

Marble fireplace; overpainted

Cracked glazing

Wall-cupboard ripped out

General loss of key to plaster

Missing door furniture

Missing skirting

Warped and damaged floorboards

Blocked chimney-breast; no airbrick

SURVEYOR'S INTERNAL CHECK-POINTS

Left and above: a good surveyor will assess any shortcomings and defects found outside and in, and give an authoritative opinion

being seen. He cannot possibly inspect areas of the property which are hidden and inaccessible. He can and must, however, use his skill and experience to deduce certain conclusions which could follow upon matters of fact.

For instance, he cannot see under wooden floors if the owner refuses to allow either the fitted carpets to be lifted or boards to be removed. However, he can warn that dry rot could be present in such a floor if air vents have been blocked by soil and a rainwater pipe is soaking the brickwork.

A surveyor will comment upon – although not usually test – drains, electrical circuits, plumbing or central heating systems. He will, if requested and for an appropriate charge, arrange for such tests

to be done. A formal valuation will usually also incur an extra fee.

Surveyors are individuals and expertise and opinions vary. Consequently, no two surveyors will necessarily pass the same comments, least of all in the same way. However, a good surveyor will be precise and concise in his reports and, most of all, he will provide an authoritative opinion and reach a definite conclusion if one can be reached.

As a buyer, you should expect to find 'saving clauses' in a survey report so far as concealed parts of the structure are concerned. But what is unforgivable is a verbose and woolly report which contains so many *caveats* or qualifications that its overall effect tends to be not only misleading but meaningless. A survey report should leave the purchaser in no doubt as to the wisdom or otherwise of proceeding with the purchase.

Since mid-1981 it has become possible

to arrange for a report which falls between the building society report and a full structural survey.

CHOOSING A SURVEYOR

Unlike a doctor, a solicitor, or an architect, anyone can set himself up and call himself a 'surveyor', so it is prudent to seek out a properly qualified person. Such a person will either be a member of the Royal Institution of Chartered Surveyors and entitled to use the letters F.R.I.C.S. (Fellow) or A.R.I.C.S. (Professional Associated) after his or her name, or a member of the Incorporated Society of Valuers and Auctioneers (I.S.V.A.).

If you have difficulty finding a qualified surveyor, contact the R.I.C.S., 12 Great George Street, London SW1P 3AD or the Incorporated Society of Valuers and Auctioneers, 3 Cadogan Gate, London SW1X 0AS. They will give you particulars of members who practise in the area.

THE HOME BUYER AND THE LAW

Having decided which house to buy, agreed a price with the seller and raised the finance – probably through your building society – the next step is to make sure that the house or flat is legally transferred into your name. It is no use committing yourself to the biggest purchase of your life, only to find a few weeks later that you had no legal right to it in the first place.

We start by looking at the legal procedures which have to be completed and then discuss the need to employ a solicitor.

CONVEYANCING

The term 'conveyancing' will occur frequently in this section. It covers not only the actual documents transferring the 'title' (or ownership) of land – which, of course, includes the buildings on it – from one person to another, but also the enquiries, searches, contracts, and other documents used in connection with such a transaction.

The conveyance is the document by which the title to land is transferred. It will actually be called a 'conveyance' when the title being transferred is unregistered and a 'transfer' when the title is registered. (For definitions see the *Registration of land*).

FREEHOLD AND LEASEHOLD

When you purchase a property your interest or 'estate' in that property will be *freehold* (often described in conveyancing documents as 'fee simple') or *leasehold*. A freehold means that you are the absolute owner of the property. Originally it was an estate of inheritance, being the most extensive interest a person could hold from the Crown.

Leasehold. With a leasehold interest, you will occupy the property under a lease as the tenant and the landlord will own the freehold. Leases can be for a period (usually called 'the term') of only a few years or for as much as 999 years. Long leases, for periods of 99 years or over, provide for a low ground rent to be paid. This may be only £20 or £30 per annum, although the modern practice is to provide for several increases over the period of the lease.

The lease will contain covenants regulating what you can and cannot do. For example, covenants as to the use of the property as a dwelling and governing what alterations and additions require the landlord's consent. When a property held on a long lease is sold, the purchaser will pay to the outgoing tenant a 'premium' which is the purchase price for the remainder of the lease.

If your house has a long lease, you may have the right to purchase the freehold under the Leasehold Reform Act 1967. Your solicitor will advise you on this.

Most *flats* are let on long leases, the reason being to ensure enforceability of covenants in the lease (such as for repair and insurance) against other tenants in the same block. The individual leases usually provide that, in addition to the ground rent, the tenants will pay a 'service charge' to cover the costs involved in maintaining the structure of the building and any common services and amenities.

Freehold. There are *freehold* flats as well as leasehold flats. It is claimed that freehold flats cause particular problems concerning enforceability of covenants and many building societies do not look favourably on them, so if you wish to buy a freehold flat ask your solicitor to make sure that the legal documents are acceptable to your building society *before* proceeding.

REGISTRATION OF LAND

In the case of unregistered land, the title to the property will consist of the title deeds. These will be the previous conveyance and any other documents recording any transaction affecting the property over a period of at least the last 15 years.

Registered land is land where the title is registered at the Land Registry. As long ago as 1862 it was felt desirable to record the titles of properties throughout England and Wales in a register and compulsory registration was introduced in 1897.

The system. Compulsory registration of land now applies in most parts of the country and the Chief Land Registrar hopes that the whole of England and Wales will be subject to compulsory registration by about 1985.

When your property is registered, you receive a Land Certificate which is a copy

There may be additional legal implications when buying a new property. If you ask the builders to do work not included in the basic specification, agree the extras in writing to avoid disputes later

22

of the register entries, recording your interest as owner and all the various covenants, rights and other matters affecting the property.

The object of the Land Registration system is to maintain a record of the ownership of property in a simple form which avoids re-examination of the Deeds on successive sales, and to guarantee the security of the owner's title – the register's accuracy is guaranteed by the State.

Upon purchase of a property that happens to be in an area of compulsory registration, land with an unregistered title must be registered for the first time at the Land Registry. This process is one that is normally carried out by the purchaser's solicitor.

THE CONVEYANCING PROCEDURE

We now look at certain aspects of the conveyancing procedure in England and Wales in more detail from the point of view of first the buyer and secondly the seller of the property.

Making an offer. Having found a property to buy, you will make an 'offer' to purchase. 'Offer' is used here in its technical, legal sense, since the creation of a binding contract requires an offer and an acceptance plus consideration (in this case the purchase price). You are perfectly free to make an offer which is less than the 'asking price'. You may feel that the asking price is somewhat high in comparison with similar properties in the neighbourhood, or you may wish to negotiate a reduction as the result of a structural

survey report showing that you are going to have to spend money to put the property into a satisfactory state of repair.

It is very important that in any correspondence with the vendor or the estate agents, you should refer to an offer as being made 'subject to contract'. The inclusion of these important words will ensure that there is no binding contract between you and the vendor at this stage. You will clearly not want to commit yourself until you have obtained a mortgage and possibly had a structural survey carried out, and until your solicitor has made the relevant searches and other enquiries about the property.

Occasionally a vendor or his estate agent may wish you to pay a preliminary deposit as a gesture of good faith. There is no reason why you should make such a payment before exchange of contracts. Therefore, the best advice is to resist such a request. Clearly, if the seller is adamant, you will have to decide whether to comply, if you are very keen to purchase the property. Your solicitor will again be able to advise on this. You should certainly not pay the main deposit before signing the contract.

The contract. The vendor's solicitors will prepare a draft contract and submit it to your solicitor for approval. A degree of uniformity and standardization of the form of contracts now exists and there are sets of standard conditions. These seek to balance and to regulate the rights and remedies of both vendor and purchaser up to and including the completion date.

The two most common sets of standard conditions are the National Conditions of Sale (first published around 1902) and the Law Society's Conditions of Sale (first published in 1926) although local Law Societies often use their own variations of these conditions.

At the initial interview with your solicitor you will normally be asked into whose names the property will be put. If you are purchasing jointly e.g. as husband and wife, then you can own the property as 'joint tenants' or 'tenants in common'.

As 'joint tenants', if one of you dies the deceased party's share will automatically pass to the surviving joint tenant and this is the case even though there is a provision to the contrary in any will. The reverse is the case with a deceased 'tenant in common' when his or her share passes under the will as part of the estate and does *not* automatically pass to the surviving tenant in common.

Incidentally, do not be alarmed by

reference to 'tenants' in the context of joint ownership as this is used in a technical legal sense here and does not mean that you are simply a tenant of the property.

Most contracts for new properties on new estates provide for a fixed price being paid. Some contracts, however, provide for an increase in the purchase price to cover increased costs incurred by the builder; such contracts need very careful consideration as a rapid escalation in costs can throw your financial calculations into confusion. Sometimes it is possible to negotiate a ceiling to any such increases. Your solicitor will advise you.

If you request the builders to carry out works that are not included in the basic specification, make sure that they are agreed in writing with the builder, also recording the date when they are to be completed and when payment is to be made. It is not advisable to pay any money for such extras until contracts have been exchanged.

Sometimes the contract will provide for instalments ('stage payments') of the purchase price to be paid as the building work progresses. If this is the case first check with your building society to see whether they will allow the mortgage advance to be paid in instalments.

Exchange of contracts. Once the form of the contract has been agreed, this will be prepared in duplicate and the buyer and seller each sign a copy. These copies are then exchanged and at that point there is a binding contract between the parties.

A deposit is paid at the time of exchange of contracts and it is the buyer's responsibility to insure the property from this date. The contract will refer to a completion date which is normally some four weeks from the date of exchange of contracts.

In the case of properties on new estates, where the property is not complete at the time of exchange of contracts, the completion date will normally be within a set period, for example, within 14 days, from the date when the property is completed by the builder. Do bear in mind that the completion date on your sale may have to be based upon the builder's estimate of when the property you are purchasing will be ready (plus a few extra weeks that you may add as a safety margin).

The deposit. While contracts are being prepared, it is up to the buyer to arrange funds for the payment of the deposit – normally 10 per cent of the agreed purchase price. This is paid when contracts are exchanged. If you are buying for a second time you will need to arrange bridging finance. This can be arranged through a bank.

If the vendor asks you to pay a larger deposit than 10 per cent this should certainly be resisted but your solicitor will be able to advise you about this.

If you are obtaining a 95 per cent mortgage, it may be possible to negotiate a reduction in the deposit from 10 per cent to 5 per cent.

The object of the deposit is to safeguard the seller in the event of your not completing the purchase in accordance with the contract. In such circumstances, one remedy open to the vendor is to seize the deposit and sue you for the balance of the purchase price. The deposit therefore acts as a powerful incentive to abide by the terms of the contract.

The deposit will normally be held either by the vendor's solicitor or the estate agents, as 'stakeholders'. This ensures that the deposit will not be paid over to the vendor until the purchase is completed and in the meantime it is held in trust on behalf of both parties. The stakeholder cannot pass the money on to the vendor without the purchaser's written permission.

Sometimes the deposit will be held by the solicitors or estate agents as *agents for the vendor*, which means that the vendor can require the deposit to be paid to him or her before the completion date. If this happened, it could cause difficulties should you wish to recover the deposit where, for example, the vendor fails to complete the sale to you or a defect is found in the title to the property. Nevertheless, there are occasions when the vendor will insist that the deposit is held by his or her solicitors or estate agents as agents for the vendor, particularly in the case of a new estate where the builder wishes to use the deposit to reduce his outgoings as quickly as possible. The matter should be discussed with your solicitor who will advise you of the legal implications and of any problems that might arise.

In the case of new estates, the builder may ask you to pay a preliminary reservation deposit, expressly for the purpose of holding the price for a set period. This is not an unusual practice but do make sure that the deposit is returnable to you, should your purchase not proceed. Where an estate agent is involved in selling the plot for the builder, you should pay the reservation deposit to the agent, to be held by him as stakeholder. Your solicitor will need to know the amount paid.

From contract exchange to completion. At the time of exchange of contracts the vendor's solicitors will send to your solicitors an abstract of the title (a precis of the information contained in the

Above left: once contracts have been exchanged there is a binding contract between the parties.
Below: make sure that you have the keys in good time for moving in

title deeds, or photocopies of the deeds). The title of the property will then be checked by your solicitor, who will prepare and submit his report on the title to your building society with a request for the mortgage advance to be sent to him. The conveyance and mortgage will be prepared and signed and the final searches made prior to completion.

Things to do. While your solicitor is dealing with the legal work you will have plenty to organize. Here is a checklist:
1. Contact two or three removal contractors to get estimates (see also *Moving in*).
2. If you wish to take over the telephone, notify both the vendor and British Telecom without delay.
3. If the property has oil-fired heating, check whether there will be any oil left in the tank, negotiate a price for this and arrange for fresh supplies. This is obviously important in winter time.
4. If you have a building society share account or bank deposit account, you may need to give notice of withdrawal, so that you can arrange to place funds with your solicitor in good time for completion.
5. Give careful consideration to the question of keys. There have been cases where the vendor has left all the keys with his

solicitors who have offices a long way from the property, causing the buyer to spend several frustrating hours making frantic telephone calls to establish the whereabouts of the keys and then obtain them.

You could arrange with the vendor that one key should be left with the next door neighbour (make sure that he or she will be at home on the day) or, alternatively, with a local firm of estate agents who have handled the sale. The estate agents will release the keys on hearing from your solicitor that the matter has been completed (make sure that your solicitor knows of the arrangement and has the estate agents's phone number).

From the seller's point of view, there is a risk in leaving the key with a next door neighbour when, for example, the purchase is not completed on the due date. Nevertheless, the vast majority of purchases proceed smoothly on the appointed day, and the alternative is to cause considerable disruption in the removal arrangements, particularly where there is a whole chain of purchasers, all moving on the same day.
6. Visit the property and establish with the vendor if there are any other loose ends to be tied up prior to the completion date.

Fixtures and fittings. A frequent cause of disagreement between vendor and purchaser concerns fixtures and fittings at the property. Generally speaking, *fixtures* are included with the property as they are permanently annexed to it. *Fittings*, on the other hand, will not generally be included as there is no such annexation. There can, however, be difficulties when deciding what is and what is not a fixture so it is sensible to prepare a comprehensive list for your solicitor showing the items that the seller intends to leave at the property and those that are to be removed.

New properties. With a new property, wherever possible during the period between exchange of contracts and completion monitor the progress made by the builder. Timing is difficult if you are able to obtain only a provisional date from the builders for completion of the property. You will, therefore, need to leave removal and delivery arrangements until the last minute.

Inspection. Following receipt of the builder's provisional estimate for completion, formal notice will be given to you or to your solicitors that the property is completed. It is essential at this point to make an immediate inspection, to ensure that it is satisfactorily completed. Here are some of the things to check:

1. Test the central heating.

2. Make sure all the doors and windows open and close properly, and can be locked securely.

3. Check that the taps, lights and socket points work.

4. See that the lavatories flush and the bathwater runs away properly.

There are likely to be one or two items that are not entirely satisfactory. If these are not major problems they can probably be dealt with by an undertaking given by the builder to sort them out after you have completed the purchase. Ideally, however, there should also be a deduction (called a 'retention') from the purchase money of an amount equal to the value of the outstanding items. This retention is likely to act as a spur to the builder as it will not be paid to him until the work is completed. Should the builder not carry out his obligations within a predetermined 'reasonable time', the retention can be used to pay someone else to complete the work.

Outstanding items can cause a lot of ill-feeling as builders are often reluctant to give priority to remedying defects when they are dealing with other properties on the site at the same time. It will be up to you to 'pester' the builder in order to make sure that he does comply with the undertaking given at completion, and if you have no success and there is no retention, your solicitor will have to take steps to enforce the undertakings.

You should be very wary indeed of accepting undertakings by the builder to complete any substantial outstanding works without a retention – particularly when your plot is the last on the estate and the builder has left the site. It may be very difficult to persuade him to return under these circumstances.

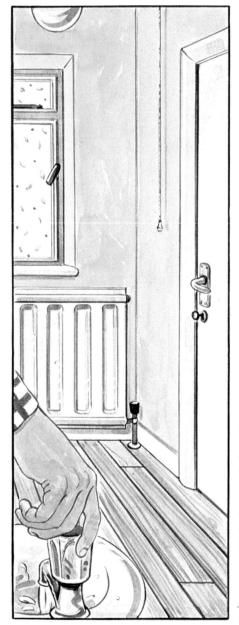

Left: items to check in a new property.
Above right: agree in writing any fixtures, fittings and other items to be left at the property to avoid misunderstandings

If the builder asks you to sign a certificate stating that you are satisfied that the property has been completed, it is advisable to discuss the certificate with your solicitor before signing.

Your building society's surveyor will make a final inspection and the society will not release the mortgage advance unless the surveyor is satisfied that the property has been adequately completed. However, he will only be looking at the property to see that it provides adequate security for the mortgage advance, so your view and his view as to whether the property is completed may differ.

The electricity, gas (if appropriate) and telephone authorities should be contacted

so that the property is connected up as soon as possible after it is completed.

Protection. In the case of a newly built property, a 'House Purchaser's Agreement' will normally be entered into. Basically, the builder agrees to put right any defects which occur within an 'Initial Guarantee Period' of two years and which are due to his non-compliance with the National House Builders' Council's (N.H.B.C.) building and design requirements. Defects due to normal shrinkage and drying out are excluded. In addition to this there is normally insurance cover under the N.H.B.C. Scheme which means that the builder's liability during the Initial Guarantee Period is guaranteed by the N.H.B.C. (subject to a maximum figure). From the third to tenth years after the insurance cover is in force you are protected against a structural defect causing major damage. Broadly speaking, this is a defect which affects the load-bearing structure of the property. The N.H.B.C. will accept responsibility only where damage has occurred, and providing that the damage necessitates extensive repair work and is not covered by the normal household insurance policy.

Most building societies need to be satisfied that a new property will have the benefit of such an Agreement and insurance cover before granting a mortgage.

Completion. By the completion date specified, your solicitor should have received satisfactory results to all his searches and he will then complete the matter by paying over the balance of the purchase price to the vendor's solicitors in exchange for the transfer or conveyance and the other title documents. These are then sent to the building society or other lenders where a mortgage is involved.

SOLICITORS

All the discussion on conveyancing has assumed the use of a solicitor. You are, of course, free to deal with your own conveyancing, without the services of a solicitor, but there are pitfalls for the unwary particularly in the case of leases for flats. And you should remember that buying a house or flat is probably the biggest single financial transaction with which you will have to cope.

Most people use a solicitor, who has had to undergo a legal training. Every solicitor must also have an insurance indemnity policy that will help safeguard you in the unlikely event that you have to sue him for negligence, and in addition, a solicitor's conduct is governed by the Law Society. The disciplinary committee of the Law Society can fine or suspend a solicitor from engaging in further practice where he has been guilty of misconduct.

Finding a solicitor. Most firms of solicitors will deal with conveyancing. Many people will go to a particular firm on the personal recommendation of a friend or neighbour.

There are lists of solicitors in the telephone book but if you have any particular difficulty, write to the Law Society, at Law Society's Hall, Chancery Lane, London WC2. They will provide names and addresses of solicitors in your area who will be able to deal with the conveyancing work.

Once you have selected a firm of solicitors, telephone or write to them and arrange an appointment to discuss the whole matter.

Legal executives. It may be that the person who sees you will not be a solicitor but a legal executive i.e. a member of the Institute of Legal Executives who has undergone a course of training and examinations. He or she will work under the supervision of a solicitor and if you have any cause for complaint about the conduct of the matter, you should ask to speak to a partner in the firm.

In your own interests, give your solicitor as much information as you can about the property. He will probably not be able to go and see it for himself and will therefore rely upon both you and the replies to his enquiries addressed to the vendor's solicitors.

Charges. At the time of your initial discussion with your solicitor you should raise the question of how much the conveyancing work will cost.

How the fees are made up. Before 1972, solicitors charged a scale fee based on the price of the property and whether or not the title was registered or unregistered. In 1972 the Solicitors Remuneration Order eliminated the scale and solicitors were left

free to charge a fair and reasonable fee having regard to certain factors.

These include the complexity of the matter, the difficulty or novelty of the questions raised, the skill, knowledge and responsibility involved, the time spent and the number and importance of the documents prepared or examined, the location where the business is transacted, the amount or value, whether the title is registered or not, and, finally, the importance of the matter to the client.

In addition there will be the search fees, out-of-pocket expenses, Stamp Duty and probably Land Registry Fees.

Overcharging. If you are dissatisfied with the solicitor's bill you can ask him to obtain a Remuneration Certificate from the Law Society. This will state whether the charge is considered to be fair and reasonable or, if it is not, what is a fair and reasonable sum. If you still feel unhappy then, you may apply to the Court to have the bill assessed (the technical term is 'taxed') by the Supreme Court Taxing Office. If such an application is made later than one month from the date you receive

the bill the Court will normally still allow a 'taxation' to take place if it considers it reasonable in the circumstances.

If you wish to query an account, do so before making payment or you will lose your right to request a Remuneration Certificate and, after twelve months, the right to apply for a taxation of the bill.

Building society panel. Most firms of solicitors are on the panels of the major building societies, and therefore the building society that makes a mortgage offer to you will also instruct your solicitors to act for the society in order to ensure that a proper title is obtained and a valid mortgage created over the property.

A separate charge will be made by the solicitors for acting for the building society and this, too, you will have to bear. If your solicitor is not on the panel of the building society making an advance, another solicitor will be instructed by that society which will mean an increase in costs. There are scales of mortgage charges recommended by both the Council of the Building Societies Association and the Law Society to building societies and solicitors.

INSURANCE

Once you have exchanged contracts on a property it is prudent to insure the structure against damage. This insurance will involve payment of an annual premium. Normally, the building society or other lender involved with the property purchase will make the necessary arrangements to insure the dwelling. If the property is leasehold it is possible that the freeholder or his agent will make these arrangements. You will have to pay the premium. Below we discuss what building insurance and other insurances cover.

BUILDING INSURANCE

What is covered. The building policy covers loss or damage to the structure by disasters or misfortunes (commonly known as 'perils'), listed on the policy – for example, fire, explosion, theft, storm, flood and burst pipes.

Terms of individual policies may vary but 'the buildings' are normally defined as the dwelling including foundations, central heating and sanitary fittings, fitted kitchen and bedroom units, loft insulation and decorations. Any garages, greenhouses, outbuildings, drives, paths, walls, permanently installed swimming pools, gates, fences and hedges are also included, but some risks are not. See *What insurance does not cover.*

Additional expenses. If the buildings are damaged by one of the perils listed on the policy a claim can be made for expenses incurred in connection with the reinstatement of the property, such as architect's and surveyor's fees, and the cost of removing the debris and shoring up the house.

Cost of alternative accommodation. Most policies cover the cost of alternative accommodation if it is necessary to move out of the property while repairs are being carried out.

If the house is let, a claim can be made for loss of rent incurred during the period of reinstatement. However, the amount that can be claimed for alternative accommodation and loss of rent is limited to 10 per cent of the total sum insured.

Accidental damage. Accidental damage to wash hand basins, sinks, baths, lavatory pans (but not toilet seats), underground pipes, drains, cables, glass in windows, doors or greenhouses is covered but the extent to which it is covered may vary from policy to policy.

Owner's liability to the public. The standard household policy normally extends to cover the insured against all sums for which he or she would become legally responsible to pay as owner (not as occupier of the building) for injuring others or damaging their property because of the insured's negligence to maintain the property in good repair. For example, if old and broken guttering came crashing down on a neighbour's car, provided that the claim involved you as the owner, it would be covered under the terms of the policy. However, claims of this nature are most often made against an owner-occupier as occupier of the property and as such are usually dealt with under the contents insurance policy.

What insurance does not cover. It is normally the responsibility of the property owner to keep the building in good repair. Buildings insurance does not cover damage due to normal wear and tear – for instance, the garage door falling off its hinges due to lack of maintenance. Neither does the policy cover damage from such things as dry rot or woodworm.

Some of the perils listed do not apply to all parts of the property. Storm and flood damage to fences and gates is normally excluded under most policies. It is also common to exclude damage resulting from bursting of pipes or escape of water,

malicious persons or theft or attempted theft, leakage of oil, breakage of glass and sanitary fittings when the property has been left unfurnished for a period longer than 30 consecutive days. Alternatively, in some policies these restrictions apply where the house has been left unoccupied for a period in excess of 30 days.

The costs necessary to prove a claim are not covered under the terms of the policy. This is particularly important in complicated cases such as subsidence as it is often necessary to appoint specialists where this type of damage has occurred.

Excesses. Insurers try to keep administration costs to a minimum and one way of doing this is by making you responsible for a specified amount of any claim, thus reducing the number of small claims to be processed. Examples of these are damage caused by storm, flood, escape of water,

malicious persons, falling trees or impact damages. Such amounts are known as 'excesses'; the amount and perils to which they will apply will vary from insurer to insurer.

Most policies have large excesses in respect of damage caused by subsidence, heave or landslip. This, again, will vary but it is normally calculated as a percentage of the total cost of rebuilding the house if it were totally destroyed; most policies specify a *limit* to the excess claimable.

It may be possible to remove some of the excesses by payment of an additional premium. Your insurance company will give you details.

All risks building insurance. A number of insurers grant wider cover than that normally included under the household policy and will insure most types of accidental damage to the buildings. Such

additional cover is considerably more expensive than standard cover.

How much insurance? It is normally a requirement of a household policy that the buildings should be insured for full reinstatement cost: that is, the cost of rebuilding the property including outbuildings should it be totally destroyed. This figure must not be confused with the market value as there is likely to be a difference between the two. Generally speaking, the cost of rebuilding a house is likely to be much higher than the market value of the property.

The mortgage lender will normally stipulate a minimum sum insured. They may also provide advice and guidance as to what the property should be insured for during the period of the loan. However, the final responsibility for ensuring that the property is insured for the correct

amount rests with the owners and it is wise to update this figure annually.

Index linking. The sums insured on most policies are index linked, so that the sum insured is changed automatically when there is a variation in house building costs. This system is only suitable for properties of standard construction (brick or stone walls with a slated or tiled roof).

A base figure is used to which an index, usually the one prepared by the Royal Institution of Chartered Surveyors, is applied. This table is published in the magazine *Building* each month. Provided that the base figure is correct there should not be any question of under-insurance.

The adequacy of the sum insured should be checked regularly and in this respect the British Insurance Association publish a *Guide to Insurance for the Home Owner* which gives the average cost of building various types of housing in different areas of the country. The leaflets are updated periodically and are available free from the British Insurance Association, Aldermanbury House, Queen Street, London EC4N 1TU.

Choosing your policy. Policies will vary, but there are three main types by which claim settlements are determined. *1. New for old.* Under this type of policy the full costs of repairing the house will be paid up to the total sum insured, provided that the house has been kept in good repair, and the sum insured is adequate. There will be no deductions for wear and tear, either for the cost of repairs to the structure or in respect of redecoration. *2. Indemnity.* In the event of a claim under an indemnity policy the insurers will pay out sufficient money to restore the property to the condition it was in before the damage occurred. Some deduction for wear and tear will usually be made. For example, if a room which had been decorated some three years previously was damaged by fire, the insurers would not pay the full cost of redecorating it because the old decorations are being replaced by new ones. In effect, you may be asked to pay half the cost of redecorating on the basis that the decorations were halfway through their expected life.

If the structure (walls or roof) which is of a more permanent nature, is damaged, you may get the whole cost of rebuilding provided that the property has been kept in good repair.

Left and above: make sure that you are insured against possible major disasters

3. Average clause. Some policies contain an average, or self-insurance, clause. Under this, the claim will be met provided that the sum insured is adequate. However, if there is under insurance the amount paid will be scaled down accordingly. For example, where a person makes a claim for £4,000 and the property is insured for £10,000 but should be insured for £20,000, the insurance company will pay out only £2,000 on the basis that the house was under insured by 50 per cent.

Claims. If you have to make a claim, contact the insurers, mortgage lender (if applicable), insurance adviser or broker as soon as possible after the damage has occurred. If the property is leasehold it may be necessary to contact the freeholders or their agents. Give as many details as possible, including the policy number and a brief summary of the incident.

It will be necessary to complete a claim form sent to you by the insurers and to get estimates of the costs of repairs. Reinstatement work should not be authorized until the insurers approve the claim, other than emergency repairs needed to prevent further damage. The insurers may send a representative along to assess the damage and consider whether the buildings are properly maintained and insured.

CONTENTS INSURANCE

Contents such as furniture, carpets, curtains and personal belongings should be insured. If you rent items such as televisions, you may be required to insure them by the rental company.

The same principles apply to contents insurance as to building insurance with regard to the sums insured, the range of perils covered, and claims settlement. Index-linking is also available – in this case it is the consumer durables section of the Retail Price Index (R.P.I.) that applies. The premium rates are higher for contents insurance and vary in different parts of the country. The most expensive areas include Central London, Liverpool and Glasgow.

Valuables. Where valuables are included in the total sum insured for contents the insurers will require to know the total value of articles (listed in the policy) if

they exceed a certain limit, which is normally one-third of the total sum insured. Most insurers consider articles made of gold, silver or other precious metals, jewellery and furs as valuables for this purpose. Some would also place pictures, curios and other works of art, collections of stamps, coins or metals in this category.

It is also normal for the insurers to set a limit for the value of each individual precious item, usually 5 per cent of the total sum insured. This figure can vary between insurers.

Cash. There will usually be a limit to the amount of cash which may be covered, or alternatively cash will not be covered against theft unless there is a physical break-in at the property.

Television. It is common for the contents policy to cover accidental damage to television sets in addition to the damage caused by the usual range of perils. Portable television sets are normally excluded from this type of cover.

Because the policy wording can differ so much, check the policy details carefully so that you are fully aware of the limitations, and if in doubt about any clause ask for a clear explanation.

All risks cover. It is normal to include items of value such as jewellery, furs, 'Hi-fi' equipment, under this section of the policy which covers loss or accidental damage to these articles both in and away from the property. The extra protection provided under this type of policy attracts higher premiums and, again, residents of

Central London, Liverpool and Glasgow pay the highest rates.

OTHER INSURANCES

There are various other specific types of insurance which may not apply to everyone and are not normally covered under contents or property policies.

Contents of deep freezer. This covers the food stored in domestic deep freezers against deterioration due to temperature change caused by breakdowns, accidental damage to the freezer or failure of the temperature control device. Variations in the type of cover are available.

Caravan insurance. This covers loss or damage to the caravan and equipment and third party liability up to an agreed limit. Additional cover is available for loss or hiring charges for bookings already made and for the cost of alternative accommodation if the caravan cannot be lived in after an insured loss.

Small boats. Cover for loss or damage to the boat, equipment and trailer usually has a limit on the total value for this type of craft. There is a limit on the overall length of the craft and also the age. These limitations will vary.

Sporting equipment. This covers damage or theft of equipment anywhere.

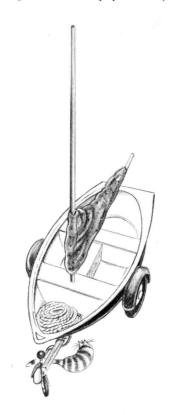

It takes a very long time and a considerable financial outlay to fully furnish and equip your home, so it makes sense to insure it adequately. Make an inventory of all your possessions, not forgetting to include books, records, cassettes and tapes, mirrors, pictures, cameras and all those other treasured items that make your home uniquely yours. Consider just how much it would cost to replace it all – it may well add up to much more than you ever anticipated

INSURANCE PACKAGES

It may be possible to include several forms of insurance – sometimes including motor insurance – under one policy, which simplifies the payment of premiums. However, where there is a mortgage on the property, the lender may not allow the building insurance to be included in the package. Some insurers allow a discount where the total premium is fairly large and most provide a facility to pay by instalments.

MORTGAGE PROTECTION

Apart from a form of endowment policy used as a way of repaying an advance, other types of insurance can provide a means of repaying a mortgage or meeting the out-goings in the event of death or incapacity. The types of insurance described here may also be suitable for any person whether or not there is a mortgage in force.

The objective is to provide dependants with sufficient financial resources to maintain their standard of living in the event of loss or reduction of income. The total family income should be taken into account when calculating the level of insurance benefits required. Benefits are paid in the form of a lump sum or regular periodic payments.

In all cases the amount of the premium depends upon the age and health of the person insured and the length of time that the insurers are to be at risk.

Whole life. This provides for a lump sum to be paid on death. The premiums are payable throughout the period of the policy or can cease at a predetermined date. A policy can be either with or without profits, but a with-profits policy costs more.

Term insurance. The sum insured is payable if death occurs within the period of the policy but no amount is payable upon survival of the term. An advantage of this policy is that it provides a large

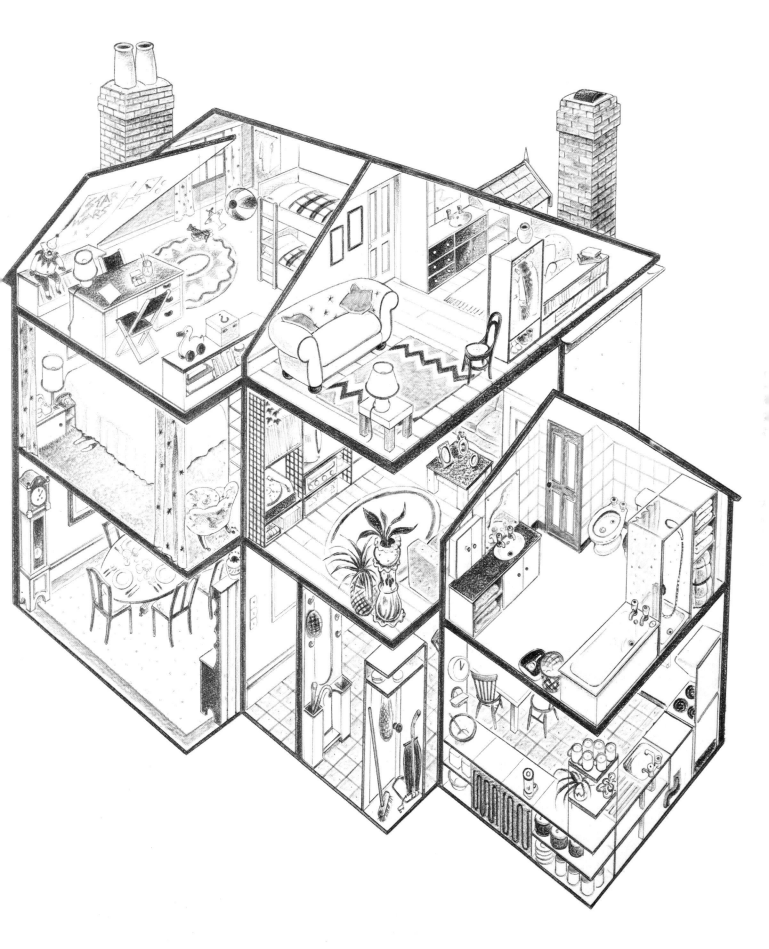

amount of cover for a relatively small outlay. There are three types of term insurance:

1. Decreasing term insurance. This provides for the sum insured to decrease by a predetermined amount over a period. The policy can be adapted for mortgage purposes, so that the sum insured is sufficient to cover the reducing balance outstanding on a repayment mortgage. However, to maintain full cover if interest rates increase, the mortgage repayments should be adjusted so as not to extend the loan term.

2. Level term. A policy where the amount of cover remains unchanged for the specified term.

3. Convertible term. A policy for a stated period which has an option to convert to another policy, say, whole life or endowment policy.

Family income benefit. A Family Income Benefit policy provides that, following the death of the insured person, a series of periodic payments are made for the remainder of the policy term. The regular payments are helpful contributions towards the costs of running a household, especially if there is a family to support.

PERMANENT HEALTH INSURANCE

This is not strictly life insurance. The policy provides that by paying an annual premium, the policy holder would receive a regular, defined income, during a period of incapacity and while being unable to earn a living. Cover ceases however when the insured reaches a specified age. The benefits are also restricted to a proportion of normal income. The policy is suitable for anyone who is employed or self-employed.

A factor when calculating the premium is the period which elapses before a claim is made. The premium would be less if benefits were not required until a period of six months incapacity has elapsed, than for a deferment of one month. An attractive point is that the insurer cannot refuse to renew the policy even if the health of the insured has deteriorated in the meantime.

PERSONAL ACCIDENT

This policy provides benefits in respect of accidents that can happen to anyone, such as slipping on ice and breaking a leg. It can also be extended to cover illnesses. The benefits may provide for a lump sum as well as income benefits. The lump sum is specified in the policy and is paid either on death, permanent disablement, or for the loss of an eye or limb. Income benefits are paid at periodic intervals, say monthly, during disablement.

Whereas a permanent health policy cannot be cancelled by the insurers regardless of the change of health, a personal accident policy can be amended at renewal by insurers. The benefits on the policy are limited to a specific period, whereas under a permanent health policy benefits are paid until incapacity ceases or upon reaching a predetermined age.

THE LAST STAGES

MOVING IN

Now that the house or flat is yours you can think about moving in. There are obviously checks to be made, some of which may differ according to whether you are moving into a new building or an older property.

Services. At least one week (preferably two) before moving in, arrangements should be made with the various services – electricity, gas, telephone, water and local authority – either to connect supplies or to give notification of intended occupancy, and the date of taking possession. At the same time, arrange for termination of whatever services applied at the previous address. Notification of your new address

should be sent to friends, relatives and all necessary contacts, as appropriate.

Removals. If you are being moved by professional removers, try to obtain estimates from three different companies. Make sure that you know exactly what the estimate covers. For instance, if the removers provide insurance cover against damage or loss throughout all stages of the removal they may prefer to do all packing and unloading.

Depending on the amount to be moved, you may be able to cope with a small self-drive hired van – companies operating such services usually advertise in the local press. For a do-it-yourself move, be sure to organize yourself well in advance.

You may be able to hire packing cases along with the van. If not, collect some heavy-duty cartons – often, local supermarkets or stores are quite happy to let you have these if you can arrange to call when they have had an unpacking session. If packing breakable items, wrap them carefully and check that the bottom of the carton is strong enough to support the load. Label every box with its contents as you pack.

On removal day pack a large flask of tea or coffee or, alternatively, a kettle and teapot or a coffee percolator plus a saucepan, mugs, spoons and plates in one clearly labelled box, and in a second pack coffee, tea, sugar, milk, sandwiches, soup and other essential foodstuffs so that you

MOVING IN CHECKLIST

When you've set the date for moving in, you will have to arrange a lot of things so that the move goes smoothly. This checklist will help:

ELECTRICITY AND GAS
Final meter readings at current home. Have vendors arranged for final readings? Ask them not to have supplies disconnected. If supplies have been disconnected, arrange for them to be reinstated on moving-in day.

COOKER
If you are taking your cooker with you, arrange for disconnection as near as possible to moving day, if possible at the same time as the final meter reading. Arrange connection of cooker in new home.

TELEPHONE
Arrange for final bill to be made up to the day on which you move out. If new occupants do not require the phone, arrange for disconnection.
Make sure that the line to your new home is not disconnected or, if a new line is required, arrange for installation as early as possible since there may be a delay.
Make sure that the vendors have requested a final bill.

REMOVALS
If you are doing it yourself you will probably need to hire a van, and packing cases. Make sure that the van will be available on the day. If using a removal company make sure that they have confirmed the date and time of arrival at your present accommodation. New furniture for your home could be delivered on the day you move in, or soon afterwards. Check to see if this is possible.

WATER AND GENERAL RATES
If you already pay rates, let the local authority know that you are moving out. Advise your new Rating Authority that you will be the owner from the moving-in date.

You should let the following people know about your change of address:
Doctor/Dentist/Optician
Bank
Insurance Company
Credit Card Company
Television rental company
Television Licence Authority
Vehicle Excise Authority
Driving Licence Centre
Vehicle Insurance Company.

Remember, for a small fee the Post Office will arrange to redirect mail to your new address. Ask them for the requisite form.

don't have to search frantically for them on arrival at the new address.

Plan in advance where all furniture will be placed – or, at least, the heavier items. What an experienced removal man makes light work of may well prove rather too much for you to move again later. Make a room by room plan and label each item of furniture with the floor, room and position in which it is to be placed. This will save you (and professional removers) a lot of time. Give the removers one copy and keep a second for yourself.

Try to arrange for young children and/or family pets to stay with relatives or friends on removal day. It can be a tiring business and the fewer distractions for you the better.

Fixtures and fittings. On taking occupation you should check that any fixtures and fittings in the property or garden which were intended to remain have, in fact, been left at the property (see *Fixtures and Fittings*). If not, notify your solicitor without delay.

Defects. If the property is new the builders will usually want to be notified of any minor defects within the first few weeks of occupation. These will usually be put in order by the builders without charge. Any major defects should be notified to the National House Builders' Council (see *The home buyer and the law*).

THE HOME OWNER AND THE LAW

Ownership of property carries with it certain rights against and obligations towards owners and occupiers of neighbouring property. It is not possible here to give an exhaustive list of the home-owner's rights and responsibilities, but here are a few rights and obligations likely to be of practical importance to you; some are also likely to apply to rented property.

Boundaries. Be warned. Boundaries, their demarcation, ownership and repair can cause unnecessary friction between neighbours.

Many title deeds do not have a plan attached to them showing the extent of the property. If there is a plan, any measurements shown may have been recorded a number of years before and the physical boundaries may have changed somewhat since then. If your property is registered at the Land Registry, the filed plan – that is the plan at the Land Registry showing the extent of your property – will be on a scale of 1/1250. This is not very large and may not be of much assistance to you. It is only intended to assist the Land Registry in the identification of land.

Should a dispute arise with your neighbour over the position of a boundary fence or wall, a bit of common sense is required. The title deeds may well not resolve the dispute, particularly if it is only a matter of a few inches or centimetres (yes, there have been disputes over such small discrepancies). The only likely result of such a dispute will be wasted lawyers' fees and, perhaps, protracted litigation.

If, following an examination of the title deeds, you discover that the boundary or boundaries of your property appear to be in the wrong place, it may be too late to do anything about it anyway. Subject to certain requirements being satisfied, if the situation has persisted for at least 12 years then, under the Limitation Act 1939, title to the land in dispute may have been conferred on your neighbour.

1. *Ownership*. The title deeds may indicate which boundaries belong to you. The conveyance plan may have 'T' marks on the boundaries indicating ownership and this is a common practice on new estates. Some boundary walls and fences may be party walls or fences, belonging jointly to you and your adjoining neighbour.

It is customary to build brick walls and close boarded fences so that the 'piers' and upright supports are on the land of the

Establish which of the boundary walls are your personal responsibility

owners. If they were not then a trespass would be caused by their positioning on a neighbour's property. Accordingly, if the supports are positioned on your side of the boundary this is an indicator (but no more) that the fence or wall belongs to you.

Ownership is clearly important where, for example, you wish to raise the height of a boundary wall. If the wall belongs to your neighbour or is a party wall owned jointly by you both then, generally speaking, you will only be able to raise such a wall with your neighbour's consent. There are special rights and obligations concerning party walls in London under the London Building Acts. The District Surveyor in your local borough can advise you.

2. *Maintenance*. The title deeds may indicate who is responsible for the maintenance of boundary walls and fences. As a

general rule, if you own the boundary in question it is likely that if repairs become necessary the obligation will fall upon your shoulders. In the absence of any specific mention of a repairing obligation you may still be liable for injury to your neighbour or damage to his or her property resulting from the state of disrepair of a boundary wall or fence belonging to your property.

Rights of way. If you enjoy the benefit of a right of way (you may see this described as an 'easement') serving your property, such a right may be restricted to pedestrians only or may include vehicle traffic as well. A right of way does not mean that you own the land over which the right of way passes but only a right to pass over the surface of that land. You may be responsible, perhaps jointly with others, to

contribute towards the upkeep and repair of the surface.

A right of way does not normally give a right to park vehicles on the land concerned in the absence of any specific mention of such a parking right being granted to you.

Covenants. A 'covenant' is, in essence, an obligation contained in a deed. If you hold your property under a lease, this will contain various covenants both to pay the rent and any service charge and also covenants which prevent you from carrying out any alterations or additions to the property without the landlord's consent, regulating the use that can be made of the property and stipulating that various rules made by the landlord as to common amenity areas should be observed. Always ask your solicitor to supply you with a copy of the lease and keep the copy for future reference.

Where you are the freeholder there may be covenants restricting the erection of new buildings without the consent of a neighbour or restricting you from parking a caravan at the property. Sometimes these covenants were imposed many years ago. Your solicitor will be able to advise you whether they are enforceable against you.

Obviously, it is in the best interests of all concerned that relations between neighbours are amicable, and it is always best to discuss any possible areas of contention *before* they get out of hand. Legal proceedings are costly, can be protracted and, even if you win the case, you've probably let yourself in for a 'cold war' that could continue indefinitely. Not a pleasant prospect.

Nuisance. Unlawful interference with a person's use or enjoyment of land, or some right over or in connection with land may constitute a private nuisance. As is probably well known, if the branches of a neighbour's tree project over your land you are entitled to lop off the offending branches without reference to your neighbour since the branches will be causing a trespass or a nuisance. But do raise the matter with your neighbour beforehand and don't forget to return any fruit or other produce hanging from the branches because you must not appropriate what is severed.

Stenches, smoke and the escape of effluent may amount to a private nuisance. However, the law does not take into account abnormal sensitivity and it would be very difficult to obtain any legal remedy (such as an injunction) to restrain a nuisance which is temporary and occasional only.

It is perhaps worth mentioning here that the lighting of fires in the garden is normally the subject of a local by-law governing the hours when the fire can be lit. Your local authority should be able to advise you about any by-laws affecting your particular area.

RENTING AND SHARED OWNERSHIP

RENTING

If you don't buy your own home, the alternative is to rent. However, there is a limited and decreasing supply of rented accommodation particularly in the private sector. Alongside the boom in home ownership has been an exit from rented accommodation of the private landlord who has found it increasingly difficult to make a reasonable return on his investment following a series of Rent Acts which have reduced his ability to raise rents in line with inflation.

Local authority renting. The largest proportion of rented accommodation is in the public sector provided by local authorities, though cutbacks in spending and the sale of council properties have reduced the total amount.

Not that this accommodation has ever been easy to come by. In most cases, local authorities have long waiting lists with priority decided by need. Most operate a points system – the more dependants an applicant has, the more points and the higher priority. Even then this will not guarantee a home; many families have to wait years in order to acquire a council house.

Housing associations and societies. A limited amount of rented accommodation is also available through housing societies and associations. These are non-profit making bodies which provide housing either through co-ownership or cost rental. In some cases, they operate as charitable trusts and provide accommodation for people with special needs. Public funds are available through the Government sponsored Housing Corporation to 'registered' associations while these also qualify for tax concessions and benefits under the Rent Acts.

A recent development has been the sponsoring of housing associations by some building societies.

Further information can be obtained from the National Federation of Housing Associations, 30/32 Southampton Street, London WC2E 7HE, or the Housing Corporation, 149 Tottenham Court Road, London W1P 0BN.

Special needs. There may be a need, either by yourself or relatives, for special housing – for the disabled and the elderly for instance. This sort of accommodation is provided by local authorities, housing societies and charities. Most local authorities will have details of all such accommodation so it's certainly worth approaching them.

Private sector. As we have already indicated, there is not much long-term rented accommodation available in the private sector. Some houses can be found for short periods of a year or two where, for example, the owner is abroad on business. In addition, there are bed-sitters

Right: an inventory of the contents of rented property safeguards the interests of both landlord and tenant.
Below: those with special needs might find it worthwhile to approach their local authority

and flats but most of this is purely short-term accommodation.

It is always worth contacting estate agents to see if they have anything on their books. However, the best source is generally the small advertisements in local newspapers. Buy the early editions and if you see a likely property, follow it up without delay – the competition will be fierce.

RENTING – WHAT TO CHECK

Many of the considerations for renting a specific property are the same as those for purchasing, though defects in the structure are likely to be the responsibility of the owner or landlord. It is important to check the condition of decoration and, in the case of furnished accommodation, the furniture. A written inventory should be agreed with the landlord, to avoid any likelihood of a disagreement and the loss of your deposit when you leave.

RENTING AND THE LAW

Because of the complexity of the law it is not possible here to give much useful advice as to the operation of the Rent Acts beyond the suggestion to take further advice should you need it! Your local Citizens' Advice Bureau or neighbourhood Law Centre will be able to guide you

on such matters. For more serious matters, a solicitor will be able to provide you with full legal help and advice.

SHARED OWNERSHIP

The concept of shared ownership was designed to meet the needs of those unable to purchase because of price escalation but who wish to become owner occupiers rather than housing association or local

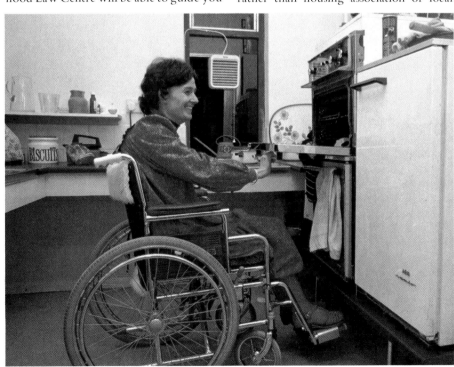

authority tenants. They can afford a proportion of the cost of the property and their share in any capital appreciation.

Initially, purchasers buy a long lease at whatever premium they can afford. This is effectively their 'share', although they will have the rights and responsibilities of full owners and be treated as such. They pay a rent to the landlord on the 'share' they have not acquired. Later, as their financial circumstances permit, the terms of the lease allow them to increase their 'share' by paying additional premiums, or to purchase outright.

In essence, the original finance can come from three sources:
1. Non-repayable housing association grant via the Department of the Environment and the Housing Corporation usually in the order of 40 per cent of cost.
2. A long-term mortgage from a local authority, usually about 10 per cent.
3. The balance from the sale to individuals of leases representing half the value of the property upon which they raise personal mortgages. This is where the building society can assist.

The Housing Act 1980 made it possible for the housing association grant to be paid to registered housing associations where part of the equity is to be sold. The buyer need not necessarily find any capital in that (provided he can afford the repayments) the building society can often grant an advance to cover the whole of his share.

SELLING A PROPERTY

As with buying a house, selling can be done in several ways.

SELLING PRIVATELY

Especially if time is not of the essence, some people advertise their properties in the newspapers and succeed in selling privately.

There are problems when one does sell privately but the prospect of saving the fee payable to an estate agent is spur enough for many to try to go it alone. You should bear in mind, though, that in choosing a purchaser you may be forced to ask him embarrassing questions relating to his financial standing. Do not forget either that agents can be very helpful to prospective purchasers in finding a mortgage. Also, most agents provide a free valuation and if you err in valuing the house this can all too easily offset the advantage of not having to pay an agent's fee. You may, in fact, undervalue it very substantially if you have not made a really close study of the property market.

ESTATE AGENTS

Many agents, in addition to the safeguards mentioned above, are also members of recognized professional societies and those who are must conform to a strict code of conduct in the interests of both seller and the buyer. Also, the Director General of Fair Trading will be able to prohibit an estate agent from engaging in business if the Director General considers there are grounds for considering the agent unfit to do so.

It can be advantageous to give one agent sole responsibility for selling for a short period of say one or two months, after which you can always bring in further agents if a purchaser has not been found. Some agents offer a reduction in their charges for the privilege of sole agency and will obviously have more incentive to make a special effort, knowing that they are not in direct competition with other agents. Fees normally vary between $1\frac{1}{2}$ and $2\frac{1}{2}$ per cent of the final house price but, since the abolition of scale fees, one has to shop around to find the best available deal. The fee is normally payable when a purchaser has been found and the sale has been completed. Be very careful about signing any document concerning the fee, and about advertising costs. If the property is to be advertised in the national press the agent may require an extra fee. Always establish at the outset what advertising the agent is planning to do within the scope of his fee.

Most estate agents will visit the house to take details, including measurements of all rooms. From this they will draw up a detailed description, often with a photograph, which they will circulate to potential buyers. They will also usually present the property in their regular advertisement in the local paper.

PUTTING THE HOUSE ON SHOW

Whether you decide to sell privately or through an agent, you will obviously want to make the house look its best for potential purchasers. A few hours spent clearing up and making sure the garden appears presentable will make your property look more desirable.

Remember, there is nothing more frustrating (and possibly off-putting) for a prospective buyer than to call by appointment to see the property and then not be able to gain admittance. Try to make sure that someone responsible is *always* there to let people in and show them around. This applies to evenings and weekends too, as many would-be buyers can only call at such times.

When showing potential purchasers around give clear, concise answers to avoid misunderstanding. Evasiveness may cover up a small fault but is likely to lead to acrimony and trouble at later stages of the transaction.

Once someone has made a firm offer for the house you should take it off the market. If other people still want to look over the property, you can let them do so but you should make it quite clear that the house is already 'under offer' and that the best you can do is to give the latecomers 'first refusal' should the original buyer drop out prior to exchange of contracts.

THE LEGAL PROCESS

Having agreed a price with your buyer, you should notify your solicitor so that work can begin on the preparation of contracts. You should be ready to answer any questions which the purchaser's solicitors may ask. Once the investigations and enquiries have been carried out, you will be required to sign the contract ready for the next stage which is the exchange of contracts.

From contract exchange to completion. Once contracts have been exchanged, the period before completion is a busy time for the vendor. The water, gas and electricity suppliers together with the British Telecom for the telephone and the rates authority will have to be contacted so that accounts can be obtained and settled up to date of completion. If you have paid an account for a period which extends beyond the completion date then you can forward the relevant receipts to your solicitor who can arrange for an apportionment and refund to be made at the time of completion.

If the property is held on a long lease, the last receipt for the ground rent and service charges must be forwarded to your solicitor who will usually need to produce this for the purchaser's solicitors.

Your solicitor will at this time be answering any queries he may be asked by the buyer's solicitor relating to the title. Your responsibility will be to make removal arrangements in good time.

PDO 81-728

MAKING A HOME

When you become a person of property, it does not necessarily mean that you automatically own a home. Bricks, mortar and a water-tight roof may provide you with shelter from the elements, but the property will not be a real home until you have tailored it to fit your family, furnished and decorated it to your taste and added those individual touches which turn a house into a home. Before you begin making major alterations or, indeed, seemingly minor ones, it is very important that you understand the basic structure of your property and how the various services work. Once you have this knowledge at your fingertips you will know precisely what you can or cannot do to improve your home.

STRUCTURE AND SERVICES

BASIC BUILDING MATERIALS.

Recent developments in the building industry, and others in the pipeline, may well revolutionize house construction in the next 25 years, but as most of us buy a ready-built property (or one in the process of being built), it is more than likely to be constructed of conventional materials.

The anatomy of a traditionally-built house can be explained as follows. The 'skeleton' consists of three main lines of structure – the front and back walls and the central internal partition or spine. These are restrained by being connected to the side walls and/or party walls, which in turn are restrained by the front and back walls and the internal spine. All of these walls are also restrained by the floors and roof, which 'tie' the walls back to strength, so walls 'return' at right-angles. Without the horizontal support by the floors (which are themselves supported by timber or, occasionally, metal joists) the walls would be prone to buckling along their length. The roof connects the front and back walls of the house and ties the side walls to each other by means of purlins and battens.

Walls. *Exterior walls* will most usually be of brick, concrete blocks or stone, all of which are put together in the same way – with mortar or 'bonding agent' which holds them firm. This can be the weakest part of the structure and exterior walls of older properties built in this way may need repointing (replacing the mortar), to prevent damp penetrating and causing gradual deterioration of the property. In many older houses, the exterior walls are solid and therefore strong, but heat loss is high (see *Insulation*). The exterior walls of modern buildings are more likely to be *cavity walls* – two 'skins' with a cavity in between which can be filled with insulating material. Wall ties mortared into the joints hold the two skins together, the inner skin carrying the weight of the floors and the outer edges of the roof trusses.

This type of wall may be *rendered*, or partially rendered – that is, another surface is used to cover up the basic building material. This surface may be smooth (cement rendering); slightly textured

(rough cast); or heavily textured (pebble dash – when stone chippings are added to the basic rendering material). It is usually painted with masonry or gloss paint to make it more decorative. Some Georgian, Victorian and Edwardian properties have partial decorative rendering (called *stucco*), usually combined with brick or stone.

Many other materials used in exterior

walls are ethnic in origin – locally produced/mined flint, slate and so on. Timber-framed structures are braced for maximum strength and may be combined with 'wattle and daub' (as in really old country cottages and houses) or clad with timber, usually overlapped and frequently called 'weatherboarding' – there are modern simulations in plastic and metal.

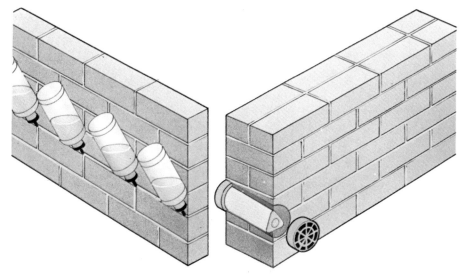

Some exterior walls or part of an exterior wall can be tile hung.

In modern houses (post 1900) a damp-proof course (d.p.c.) is built into the exterior walls. This consists of a layer of bituminous felt inserted into the course of the brickwork, 15 cm (6 inches) above ground level and should never be covered with earth, plants or rendering. In older properties, there may not be a d.p.c. and if there is a problem with rising damp it may be necessary to install one. This can be done by silicone injections, siphonage, electro-osmosis, 'tanking', or by the even more drastic treatment of cutting into the mortar and inserting a new damp-proof course of lead, copper, bitumen-impregnated hessian or asbestos, or special polythene sheet. This is definitely a job for the professional builder or d.p.c. expert, and many offer a 20–25 year guarantee – make sure that you engage a reputable firm.

Party Walls are those which separate two properties. They are likely to be solid in an older house, so unfortunately act as a sounding board for noise. You can convert them to a 'cavity wall' by battening insulation board, wall board or wood cladding to the existing party wall. For extra insulation, roof insulating material can be inserted behind the battens.

Interior Walls can be made of brick, stone, concrete slabs, breeze block etc. and be of solid or cavity construction. They may also be load-bearing. If alterations are planned which include the removal of all or part of a load-bearing wall an RSJ (rolled steel joist) must be inserted to prevent the possible collapse of the walls and/or floor above – a job strictly for the professional.

Non-load-bearing walls may be stud partitions: wooden-framed walls covered with wallboard (the modern equivalent of lath and plaster) which can be timber, plasterboard, insulation board etc. They usually have a plaster 'skim' and can be decorated as any plastered wall.

Floors. A ground floor can be either solid or suspended. *Solid* floors have a hardcore base topped with concrete, then a fine concrete screed to d.p.c. level giving a surface for laying tiles or other floorcoverings. *Suspended* floors consist of timber joists laid on low support walls covered with bituminous felt, and then finished with floor boards or flooring grade chipboard. Flooring above ground level is usually suspended – laid on joists which span the entire construction. If you plan to lay heavy flooring above ground level e.g. thick ceramic tiles, or want to install a large, heavy bath, the joists should be checked for sufficient strength to take the weight. Ceilings are finished in various ways – more often than not, with a plaster skim, although in some modern houses plasterboard is used for economy, and finished with a special textured paint or ceiling tiles.

Roofs can be pitched (sloping) or flat. A sloping roof is usually a timber-frame construction, which can be clad externally with roof tiles (these come in various types, designs and colours), slate, wood (called 'roof shingles'), asphalt or even thatch. Sloping roofs can be gabled or hipped. Flat roofs may be covered with a liquid bitumen which is poured on, roofing felts (usually a bitumen felt) or asphalt, and in some older properties can be finished with cement in part.

Rainwater goods. Rainwater from the roof flows away via gutters and downpipes, usually called 'rainwater goods'.

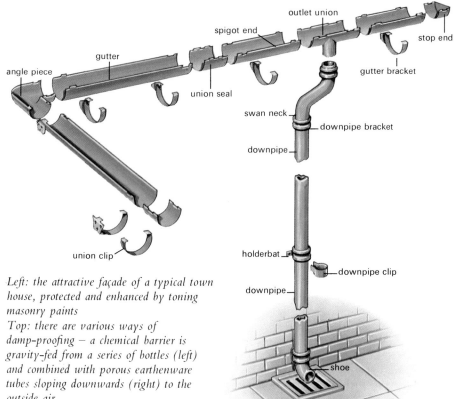

Left: the attractive façade of a typical town house, protected and enhanced by toning masonry paints
Top: there are various ways of damp-proofing – a chemical barrier is gravity-fed from a series of bottles (left) and combined with porous earthenware tubes sloping downwards (right) to the outside air
Above: the component parts of rainwater guttering and downpipes

Old gutters and pipes were made of either cast iron or bituminized asbestos, but modern pipes and gutters are nearly all made of plastic, which is easy to cut, lightweight, does not rust and can be installed by a competent amateur. Plastic piping can be left unpainted, in its (usual) grey form, which blends with most exterior materials, or you can paint it to blend with existing 'rainwater goods'.

ESSENTIAL SERVICES

Water, electricity and gas mains services are normally connected to a house, but in some remote country areas none, or only one, of these services may be available. Main drainage is another service not available everywhere. Most houses in towns and villages are connected to the sewerage system but again, in remote areas, it may be necessary to have a septic tank or cesspit, in which case contact the local council to find out what arrangements are made for emptying/cleaning it.

When you take over a property it is absolutely vital that you know where the stopcocks (taps controlling the inflow) are located so they can be turned off immediately in emergencies such as an overflow. If there is more than one stopcock make sure you know which one turns off what. Similarly, find out where the electricity and gas main controls are so they can be switched off when necessary.

It is also sensible to know and understand the internal runs of gas and water pipes and electrical wiring, so you can avoid damaging them during building or decorating work.

PLUMBING AND WATER SYSTEMS

Water comes into the house via the 'rising main', connected to the local water authorities' main which runs under the pavement. Your responsibility for the pipe begins at the outside stopcock, normally situated in the pavement or at the entrance to driveway or path. Usually this can be turned on and off only by the local authority but, in an emergency, you can always turn off at your own stopcock on the rising main – this is often sited under the sink, although it can be hidden away in a cupboard, under basement steps, beside the front door and so on. Unlike gas and electricity, water is not metered. It is paid for as the water rate direct to the local water authority, which is part of the local council.

Basically, domestic plumbing and water systems are simple, but if you have an older property, which has had various improvements made over the years, you could find that two types of systems are involved. Try to understand your own system as quickly as possible – if necessary going through the house with a qualified plumber.

Cold water system. Most rising mains have a branch pipe 'teed off' from them, a few feet above floor level. This usually supplies the cold water tap to the kitchen sink. This is fresh water and the one that should be used for drinking and cooking purposes. Water that has been stored in a tank should not be used for drinking unless it is first boiled. If there are branch pipes from the main to garden or garage, these are usually fitted with their own stopcocks so they can be switched off independently during the winter.

In some houses the cold water to bath, basin and lavatory is also teed off from the rising main and this is called the 'direct' system. But in most properties the water supply to the bathroom, lavatory and so on are fed from a main storage tank (cistern) located in the roof to ensure that there is no possible risk of contamination to the drinking water supply. This is referred to as the 'indirect' or 'gravity' system, and a pipe from the rising main is taken up into the roof (usually via an internal wall) to supply the cistern, the water being controlled by a ball or float valve. This floats on top of the tank, automatically closing off the flow of water into the cistern when it is full. As water is used, the float sinks, opening the valve to allow water to refill the tank. An overflow pipe, which takes water outside, should prevent it from cascading down the outside of the property if anything goes wrong with the inflow/outflow.

Water rises to the tank by means of *pressure*, but runs into the taps, downhill, by *gravity*. The higher the cold storage tank is above the outlet, the greater the pressure. This is important if you want to install a shower, as there must be sufficient 'head of water' – difference in height between tank and outlet – for it to work properly. This is another good reason for installing a shower downstairs, separately from the bathroom (see *Planning*).

The cold water cistern also supplies the wcs, which work in a similar way to the cold storage tank – a ball valve floats inside and when the chain or handle is pulled, water flushes the lavatory, emptying the cistern; the ball or float sinks, opens the valve and the cistern refills. There is also an overflow pipe, which should go through the outside wall and project some inches; when an overflow pipe gushes out water the cistern in the roof or at the wc needs attention.

In some modern properties, the plumbing pipes, outflows etc. in the bathroom and wc are all concealed behind 'trunking' or panels. Always check where the overflow pipe goes so that you can cope in an emergency.

Hot water system. In order to get hot water, water must be fed from the cold water storage tank to the place where it is to be heated. Usually there is a hot water cylinder, which in most houses is situated in the bathroom or in a linen cupboard on the landing. This supplies the hot water taps throughout the house by means of gravity feed, and as water is drained off via a tap, the cylinder refills from the cold water tank in the roof.

Very often the water is heated via a boiler or back boiler (which can be powered by various fuels), but an electric immersion heater is also built into the hot water tank to provide hot water during the summer so the boiler can be switched off. Sometimes hot water is provided solely by an immersion heater, in which case it is a good idea to have a 'split-level' system – this is when there are two immersion heaters in the tank, one providing a more economical *top-up service*.

Very often the boiler also provides hot water for central heating radiators. Because hot water rises and cold water falls, the boiler must be placed *below* the hot water cylinder. This is why most boilers are in the kitchen, with the hot water tank on the first floor and the cold water tank in the roof. In flats, bungalows and properties with little space for complicated plumbing, it may be necessary to stack the cold and hot water tanks on top of each other. In this case a form of instantaneous water heating may have to be provided at some of the outflow points.

Right: a typical plumbing layout in an average house. This shows the main water and drainage system and how these connect up to the local authority's service pipe and the main sewer respectively

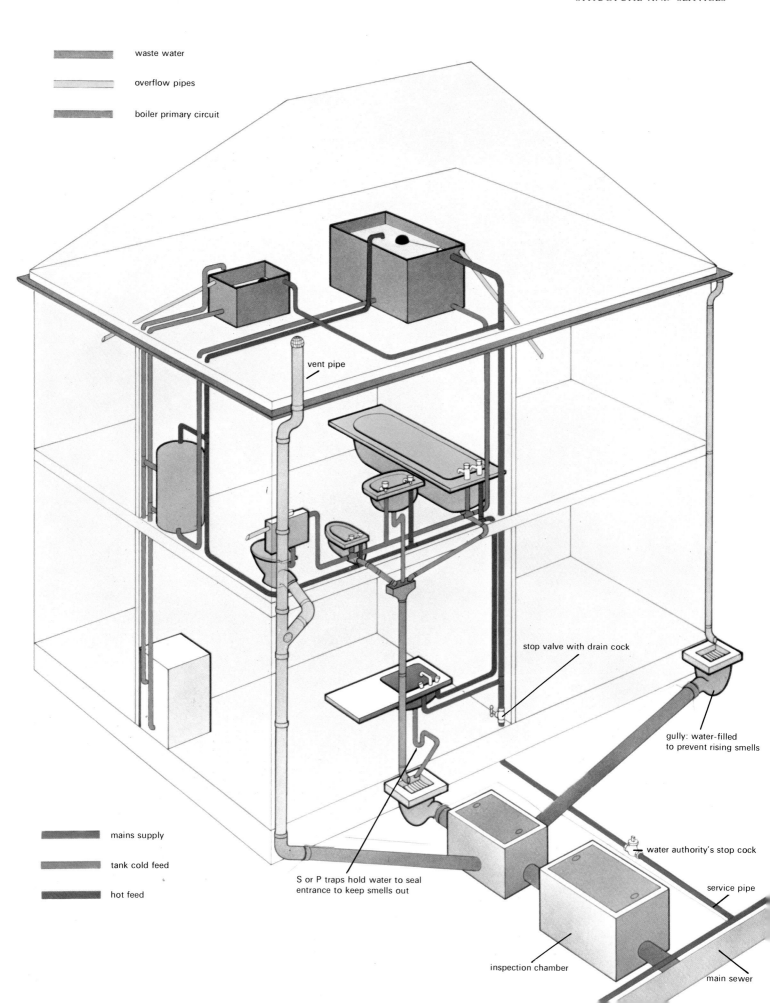

waste water

overflow pipes

boiler primary circuit

vent pipe

stop valve with drain cock

gully: water-filled
to prevent rising smells

mains supply

tank cold feed

hot feed

S or P traps hold water to seal
entrance to keep smells out

water authority's stop cock

service pipe

inspection chamber

main sewer

As water heats in the boiler it rises to the top of the hot water tank (this is why the top always feels hottest), forcing colder water down to the bottom of the tank where it is then reheated by the boiler, passes up to the top and so on. In order for this cycle to work efficiently the pipe taking heated water to the cylinder must be near its top, and the one for the cooler water near the bottom – these two pipes are known as the 'flow' and 'return'.

Most boilers are thermostatically controlled, so that the water does not get excessively hot – the thermostat automatically switches the boiler's heating mechanism off (not solid fuel) if the tank is hot enough and no water is drawn off. However, there is a 'safety valve' built into most systems in case of overheating – a pipe rises from the hot cylinder to the cold storage tank, so that hot water can be harmlessly discharged. If you hear the water in the tank boiling, run off some of the excess – but don't waste it, use it for a bath, shower, washing or washing up.

NOTE: heating water by any fuel is expensive, so hot water cylinders should be lagged or fitted with a 'jacket' to prevent heat loss.

There are *instantaneous* ways of heating water, powered by gas or electricity. These can take the form of small individual heaters or geysers, placed over basin, sink or bath; some have flexible taps which can be used to fill the bath and then pushed round to serve an adjacent basin.

There is also a *multipoint* gas and electric system, whereby one instantaneous multipoint heater connected direct to the water main provides hot water to several points. The development of the gas 'balanced flue' means the heater can be sited anywhere in the house, so long as it is against an outside wall. As you open the tap to run the water, it automatically switches on the gas or electricity supply at the heater, to reheat cold water flowing through the multipoint.

A *storage heater* operates rather like the bathroom or linen cupboard hot water cylinder. It contains its own internal heater (like an immersion heater), is usually powered by electricity and placed near a main draw-off point – like the kitchen sink – but can supply the bathroom as well. When bathroom and kitchen are far apart it may be best to have two separate heaters. This system should not be confused with the 'night storage' system of central heating, which runs off cheap electricity available only at certain times of the day/night. However, electricity to heat the various water systems described here can be supplied at a cheaper rate during off-peak hours, if connected to a special meter.

DRAINAGE

In many older properties there is a two-pipe drainage system, which diverts waste flushed from the wc down a separate soil pipe from that for the waste from sinks, baths and basins. In newer properties a 'single-stack' drainage system discharges all wastes into a single main waste stack, contained within the perimeter of the house. This is visible from outside only as a small, capped pipe extending about 45 cm (18 inch) from the roof. An older house, converted or extended since a change in the Building Regulations during the 1960s allowed this type of drainage to be introduced, may combine both types.

The outlets have a 'trap' to prevent smells from the drains coming into the house – the water in the traps acts as a barrier. The simplest form is a U-bend in the pipe which retains water after the appliance is used, forming the barrier; 'P' traps have horizontal outlets and 'S' traps have vertical outlets, and all traps must have some means of access so they can be unblocked if necessary.

Health factors. It is very important that drainage systems should avoid 'siphonage' from one trap to another and the possible rush of contamination. Water pipes from wash basin, bath etc. must be as short as possible, have minimal fall, and be connected to the main stack in such a way as to prevent the possibility of their outlets being fouled or blocked by discharge when the lavatory is flushed.

Rainwater, too, has to be disposed of. This is collected in gutters along the roof, normally discharged into vertical drain pipes and from those into a drain. The underground drains connect up with the main sewerage system (usually under the road). There is usually an inspection chamber (normally covered by a manhole cover) for the drains within the boundary of the property; this will have a trap at the outlet to prevent sewer gases from coming up the pipe into the house. Inspect drains regularly and clean them out when necessary, as well as keeping exterior gutters/drain pipes clean and clear of blockages.

GAS

Gas is mainly used for cooking, heating and hot water, although there are gas powered fridges and other appliances available. There are also portable cylinders to power appliances such as free-standing convector heaters and cookers – invaluable in remote country areas where there are limited main services, and for caravans, boats etc.

Supply route. Gas usually comes into the house via a main pipe (which is the responsibility of the local Gas Board),

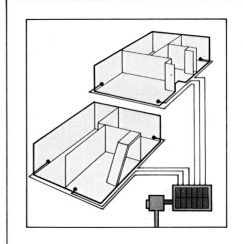

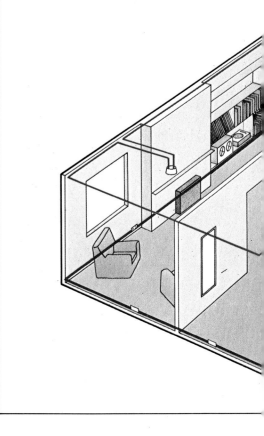

Below left: the old type radial system of wiring. This can still be found in some older properties.
Below: the modern circuit system by which outlet sockets are connected to a continuous loop or ring of cable – one for upstairs, one for down. Cooker, waterheating and lighting all have separate fuses and circuits

connected to a meter which records the amount of gas used. This is read quarterly and the householder charged accordingly. Some houses have a pay-as-you-use meter, which is also the property of the local Gas Board (unless it is the responsibility of the landlord). This is a more expensive way of buying gas.

Gas is piped from the meter to the fixed appliance, and if gas is your choice for heating and cooking, when contemplating buying or renting a property, it is wise to check that a piped supply is available. Many houses have cooker, boiler and water heater gas points in kitchen and bathroom, and points for gas fires/pokers in living rooms and bedrooms, and even if they have been plugged because they are disused they can be unplugged by the gas fitter when he comes to connect your appliance. But if there is not a gas supply from the meter to the place where you plan to fit an appliance, you could face a large extra bill for the cost of running a gas pipe from the meter. Just because there is a gas appliance in your kitchen already, it does not mean you can run several appliances from it – you cannot 'branch off' gas pipes in the same way as for water. If a boiler or cooker is on a time clock mechanism for example, it must have separate pipe runs, because when a sudden surge of gas fills the pipe as the appliance is automatically turned on, there could be 'blow back' which might extinguish the pilot light on another appliance using the same pipe to supply gas. Gas pipes can be laid under floorboards (suspended floors), or neatly run parallel to skirtings (solid floors).

Safety factors. Gas *must* be treated with respect, so call in the local Gas Board to advise you on any problems, and if your plumber/builder/kitchen specialist is involved in the installation of a gas appliance, have the Board round to check that all is well, and their approved gas fitter to connect the appliance to the supply.
NOTE: if you use gas for central heating or hot water it is worth having a contract arrangement with the local Gas Board for servicing and emergencies. Always have gas appliances serviced annually.

ELECTRICITY

Electricity comes into the house via a service cable, terminating in a sealed box which contains a fuse for the positive 'phases' and a terminal block for the neutral. This service unit is mounted on a board alongside the electricity meter which monitors the amount of electric current used. The meter is read quarterly and the householder billed accordingly (as for gas, the bill can be spread over 12 monthly agreed payments if preferred). Adjacent to the meter are the main switch and fuses (called a 'fuse box') and/or a circuit-breaker. If you want to take advantage of off-peak electricity for storage

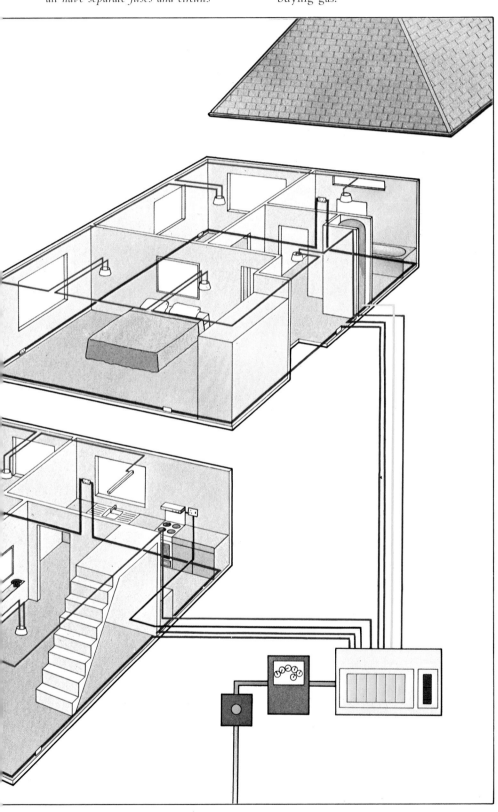

and water heating the Electricity Board will install a special meter with a time clock which automatically switches on the supply during the off-peak period.

A network of wires and cables takes the electricity to various parts of the house – these are called *circuits*, and have different current ratings and colour codings according to the job they are to do: 5 amp (white); 15 amp (blue); 20 amp (yellow); 30 amp (red) and 45 amp (green). These are used for domestic lighting, heating, water heating etc; the 45 amp is used for large electric cookers.

The whole installation is protected by the Board's service fuse, and each circuit is individually protected by a rewirable or replaceable fuse at the fuse box or, with a modern installation, at the circuit-breaker. These fuses protect the system, but modern electric plugs are also fused. If an appliance is faulty, a plug or circuit is overloaded, or there is a sudden surge of current, the fuse may 'blow', either at the plug in the point, at the fuse box or circuit breaker, cutting off the electrical supply to the appliance (if the plug fuses) or to the circuit (if the box or circuit breaker fuses). These fuses can be mended, replaced or reset, *after* the fault has been traced and corrected. Older fuses have to be rewired with fuse wire of the correct amperage, modern ones with a new cartridge fuse. It is possible to place fuses in a circuit-breaker in any order, but preferably the fuse of the highest current rating should be next to the main switch, with the remainder in descending order. At least one spare fuse unit should be included when installing or rewiring a system, to allow for further additions/extensions to the system.

Ring main circuits. Most modern homes are wired for power on a 'ring main'. The main cable runs from the consumer fuse board, circles the house supplying electricity to the various socket outlets and points, and returns to the fuse from which it started. Individual appliances should be fused according to their output (always ensure the plug on an appliance is correctly fused with the right amperage) so that a 'blow' does not harm the cable. For heavy output appliances, like a cooker, separate radial circuits are used and these require specific fuses – a cooker may have a 30 or 45 amp fuse, and must have a proper cooker box with switched socket near the appliance.

Safety factors. Electricity is a clean and instant form of energy, but must be treated with respect. If handled wrongly it can cause an accident or injury – even death. Never try to do any major electrical work yourself, such as rewiring a house, and if you do minor jobs, have them checked by a qualified electrician or the Electricity Board before switching on the current.

CENTRAL HEATING

This can be expensive, and the system selected should suit your requirements and be combined with adequate insulation to give maximum benefit. Whichever system you prefer, it is wise not to put all your eggs into one basket: oil and solid fuel deliveries can be problematical sometimes; power breakdowns and energy shortages may mean that electricity is cut off or gas power reduced. Also, if solid fuel, oil or gas fired central heating systems are small bore (and most are) and powered by an electric pump, water does not circulate if there is a power cut or failure, so the radiators go cold!

Nevertheless, central heating is much the most efficient and comfortable form of heating so long as the house is properly insulated, and an efficient central heating system is much cheaper than having individual room heaters.

The most usual form of central heating is the 'wet' system: water is heated by a boiler and distributed through pipes to radiators and/or skirting heaters. Also, you can connect to this type of system special heaters which are fed with the hot water like a radiator, but fan assisted to pump out the heat when necessary.

Warm air is another popular system, whereby air instead of water is heated and 'ducted' throughout the house, usually there are vents at skirting level.

There are also heated 'structures' to let out warmth: underfloor heating, storage radiators or oil-filled radiators.

The first decision to make is: which fuel to use. Nowadays there is relatively little cost difference between the three major fuels – gas, oil and solid fuel – but there are other aspects to consider.

Gas is the most popular because it is readily available 'on tap' and does not require storage space. It is relatively clean and safe, but as all systems can go wrong at some time or other do enter into a service agreement with the local Gas Board. Some gas systems do not need a boiler – the 'master' radiator will also act as a boiler.

Oil needs a storage tank, which should be sited far enough away from the house so that it is not a fire risk, but readily accessible for fuel delivery (made by tanker).

Oil may be a little more expensive than the other two fuels, and its future uncertain, but it is clean and easy, although some people with sensitive noses say that oil boilers smell!

Solid fuel may be slightly cheaper than gas, but requires storage space. Ideally solid fuel should be stored outside, but close by so that bringing in the fuel is not too laborious a chore. Some older town properties have a convenient cellar with delivery chute from the pavement, so that fuel can be delivered by hopper instead of in sacks. Solid fuel boilers can be fed by hopper too, which means they only need filling/ashes emptying once in 24 hours, but they are dirtier than other types of boiler and humping fuel (even the lighter smokeless type) can become difficult as you get older. Some solid fuel systems can be fed from a back boiler which means you get the advantage of a glowing fire combined with radiator and hot water supply. They are usually suitable only for small properties since the number of radiators which can be supplied from a back boiler is limited. A disadvantage is that you cannot switch off the source of heat instantly – if you need to switch off suddenly, the boiler must be damped down, or the glowing fuel be removed. Some wood burning or multi-fuel stoves can also heat water and provide cooking facilities.

Electricity is clean, compares favourably in price, and such heating systems are not usually connected to a boiler. The night storage system, where special heaters filled with insulated blocks take in cheaper power during off-peak time, provides

Right: a typical hot water central heating system, where hot water is forced through small bore pipes into the radiators by means of a pump situated near the boiler. One or more radiators may also be filled by the gravity feed method on this system. The pump is controlled by thermostat, and cuts out once the house is adequately warm. The whole system is usually operated on a time clock at the boiler

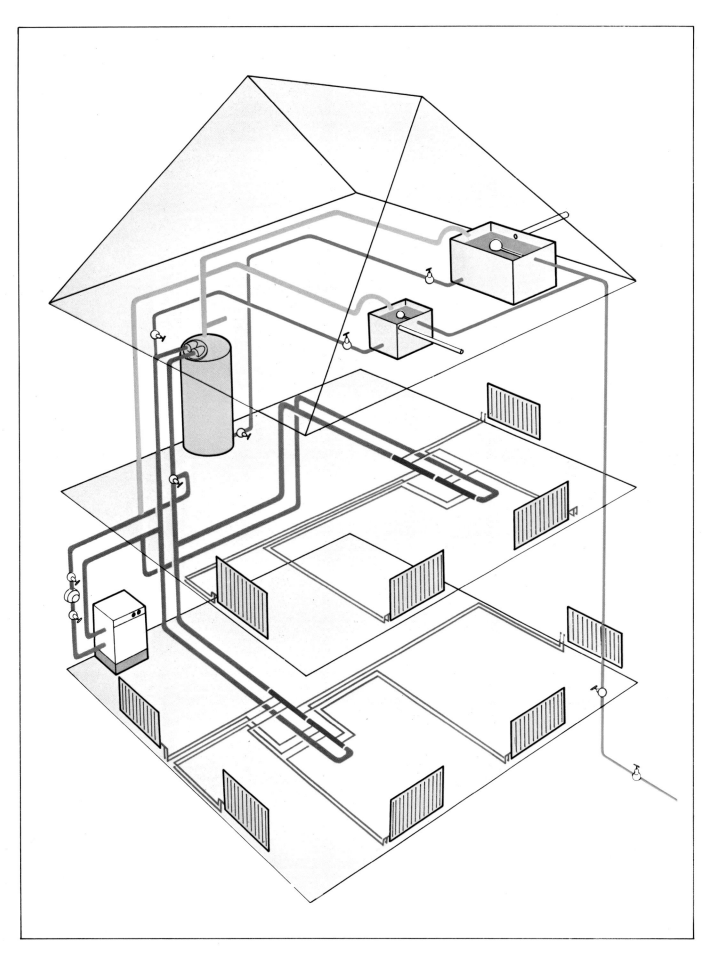

continuous warmth; heaters can also be fan assisted to heat a room quickly. The other form is underfloor or overhead heating: cables are embedded into the structure of floor or ceiling and connected to the main electricity supply. As hot air rises, the warmed floor method is better than the ceiling type; on the other hand, should the system go wrong, it is easier to take down a ceiling than dig up a floor.

Right for your lifestyle? Apart from fuel costs, the advantages and disadvantages of storage, ease of control and regular maintenance and cleanliness, also think about your lifestyle. Something which can be switched on and off or controlled by a time clock is most practical for a family who are out all day; if there is somebody at home all the time, the solid fuel back boiler combined with a fire in the living room may be ideal (remember that night storage heaters tend to cool down in the afternoon before their next intake of energy, so these are not always a practical choice).

Before reaching a decision, contact the producers of the various fuels (the local Gas and Electricity Boards, the Solid Fuel Advisory Council, the oil suppliers), read their literature and listen to their 'sales pitch' – they will also supply you with a list of heating engineers/contractors. Contact several of these and ask them to call to discuss suitable systems and installation costs. Always obtain several estimates before making up your mind and ask about the extent of domestic upheaval necessary during installation.

When discussing installation, make sure you will get just what *you* want. Radiators, skirting heaters or other heaters need *not* be placed under windows or where you plan to place a favourite piece of furniture. Try to think long term, and if you have not already planned your furniture positions (see *Planning on Paper*), try to do this before deciding where to position radiators.

All modern central heating systems are thermostatically controlled and most boilers are operated by time clock, so you don't have to have them running all the time. Ideally the main temperature thermostat should be placed in the coldest part of the house (usually in the hall near front door draughts); don't ever have it positioned in the main living room, especially if you plan a supplementary form of heating there.

OTHER FORMS OF HEATING

Even if you have an adequate system of central heating, it is wise to have some

supplementary forms of heating, in case of power or fuel failure, or to switch on during cool spring, summer and autumn evenings when you may not want to activate the central heating system (but run the central heating occasionally, just to make sure all is well).

It makes sense to have a few portable heaters, such as electric fan heaters and convectors, and an oil-filled electrically-operated radiator (very economical to run) to act as a heated towel rail during the summer. They all heat up quickly and can be used in different rooms. Gas portable convector heaters and oil heaters are also practical, so long as they are safely positioned and adequately guarded. They can be used for supplementary heating in winter too, and to keep the chill off garage, shed and so on.

If you don't have an airing cupboard, there is a tubular electric heater which can be put at the bottom of a cupboard to warm it for the purpose of airing linen. Wall-mounted infra red electric heaters provide a safe means of heating bathrooms, nurseries and playrooms.

For main living rooms there is a wide choice – you can have an open fire to use as well as/instead of central heating, a slow-

burning combustion stove or a wood-burning stove (buy the 'convertible' sort which burns not only solid fuel but also rubbish and peat). There are gas fires, some complete with log-burning effects, and electric fires similarly designed to look like a 'real fire'. The choice is up to you, but it does also depend on the various points already discussed under central heating fuels, and the ease of installation. So think the project through thoroughly first, and get as much advice as possible before making up your mind. It may even pay you to shiver through one winter in a new property *before* reaching a final decision!

SAVING HEAT: INSULATION

If your home is properly insulated, the saving in terms of energy *and* money will be considerable – you can cut your bills by as much as 50 per cent. Also, you may be eligible for a grant to help with insulation, so find out about this first (see *Getting a Grant*).

The roof. As hot air rises, start with the *roof*, and work down. The recommended minimum thickness for roof insulation is 7.5 cm (3 inch), but 10 cm (4 inch) is even better, and triple loft insulation of 15 cm (5 inch) better still. You can use two main materials: glass fibre, supplied in rolls which are unwrapped and laid between the joists, and loose-fill – granules of purpose-made polystyrene or vermiculite which are poured between the joists.

Insulating a loft can be done by most do-it-yourselfers, but if the joists are not boarded over remember not to step off a joist into the gap, or your foot will go through the ceiling below! If you insulate between the ceiling and joists and *then* lay a floor, you will have even better insulation; flooring grade chipboard, hardboard, plywood or boards are all suitable. If you use glass fibre, wear protective clothing, gloves and a mask – a man's fine cotton handkerchief will do. Loose-fill granules are easy to use and good for packing into awkward corners, but can move around in draughty conditions, so fill the eave area to more than the required depth.

Alternatively you can opt for professionally applied loft insulation – spun mineral fibre or a foam similar to that used for cavity wall insulation 'hosed' into place by a contractor.

Do *not* insulate the floor area under the cold water tank as the rising hot air will keep it from freezing up. Always make sure there is *some* ventilation in the loft to prevent condensation.

Cold water tank. This should be protected with a wrapping made from glass fibre or other insulating material such as old underfelt or carpet, but *do not* use anything *under* the tank (see above).

Cold water pipes should be lagged to prevent them from freezing, and subsequently 'bursting' (this is caused by the cold water expanding as it freezes, cracking the pipe so that when the thaw comes water gushes out from the pipe), and *hot water pipes* should be lagged to prevent heat loss. Use either special do-it-yourself plastic foam 'sleeves', glass fibre wrapping, felt wrapping, spare offcuts of underfelt from carpet laying (secure with twine) or even old bits of carpet if the pipes are in an out-of-sight location.

Hot water cylinder. This should also be lagged to prevent heat loss and fuel wastage – there are several types of thermal 'jacket'. Buy one which is at least 7.5 cm (3 inch) thick and conforms to the British Standard BS5615. If the tank heats the linen cupboard, you can buy jackets which tie at the top with a drawstring and can be loosened slightly when you want a specially warm linen cupboard. Most jackets do allow sufficient heat to air garments that are already fairly dry.

Insulation Association and make sure that the materials used have a certificate of approval.

There are several ways of insulating *solid* walls. You can fix insulating board, wall board, wood cladding etc. to the inside of the wall using battens, which immediately creates a cavity between the solid wall and the back of the board or wood which can be filled with various insulating materials. You can also fix fabric to the wall by means of battens or a special track method. This looks extremely decorative, is practical as the fabric can be removed for cleaning, and at the same time you can slip a special 'quilt' of glass fibre or insulating material behind it (one fabric track manufacturer makes a special insulated fabric to be used with his track). You can also cover the exterior walls with weatherboarding or tiles fixed on battens and, again, cavity wall insulation material can be used in conjunction with this treatment.

Floors can be very draughty, particularly when there are wide gaps between the boards, and solid and suspended ground floors can both contribute to heat loss. Thick carpet with a good underlay helps, and this can be laid on top of a 'lining' of newspapers or special felt. When the floorboards are really bad, gaps should be plugged, using filler, papier mâché or fillets of wood. If there are great gaps round the skirtings and the surface is uneven, cover the entire floor with flooring grade chipboard, hardboard – rough side uppermost – or plywood. Take care not to pierce water, or other pipes, with nail or screw. If there are just gaps at the skirting, cover them by tacking on strips of wooden coving or beading.

Solid floors can be hard and cold, but you can put in a wooden floor, using the batten method on horizontal surfaces in the same manner as for vertical ones. This 'floating' floor will be warmer because of the layer of air trapped between and can be surfaced as you wish. *Do not* put insulation material between the layers as this could cause a condensation or damp problem.

Doors and windows can be just as draughty – large single-glazed windows, or those with ill-fitting leaded lights are the worst. Installing double-glazing is the best answer, but if you can't afford this at the moment, use self-adhesive foam draught-proofing strip. Gaps round windows can also be plugged with mastic and there are special kits which will seal leaded lights. Heat loss through windows can be remedied by combining blinds with heavy

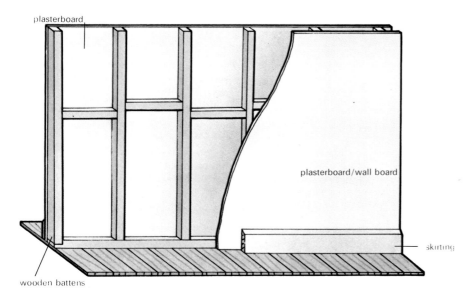

plasterboard

plasterboard/wall board

skirting

wooden battens

Above left: lagging the hot and cold water tanks is essential if heat is not to be wasted, or the water freeze
Above: insulation can help to cut out noise as well as conserve heat. A typical timber/plasterboard wall is flimsy and far from soundproof, but it can be improved by creating a cavity wall as described, with insulation material placed behind the new surface

Walls. The exterior *walls* of a house allow 35 units of heat to escape so wall insulation is the next priority. If you have cavity walls (see *Walls*) the cavity can be filled with foam, polystyrene beads or mineral wool, but this is a job for the professional, as it is vitally important that the damp proof course (d.p.c.) is not affected. Engage a reputable contractor, preferably one who is a member of the National Cavity

lined and interlined curtains, or use insulating lining. You can also buy special insulated pleated blinds which cut heat loss, particularly when combined with curtains.

Ill-fitting doors can have a special strip fitted to the bottom on the inside with bristles or a flange which clear the carpet as the door is opened and sink back firmly, keeping out the wind, when the door is closed. A foam or kapok-filled 'sausage' is another good draught stopper. And so are old-fashioned door curtains, suspended on a portière rod, which rises as the door opens.

Fireplaces can be draughty, too. If disused they can be boarded up with a sheet of chipboard, hardboard, ply or laminate, but should be adequately ventilated to prevent damp seeping through the chimney into the breast. A more permanently sealed fireplace should have a cowl or cap put on the chimney (if this is left on the roof) and again should be ventilated.

Don't become so draught-proofed that you leave *no* air circulating, as this can lead to condensation problems. *Never* block a ventilation outlet for a gas appliance; and never permanently close air bricks, wall or window ventilators.

SAVING HEAT: DOUBLE-GLAZING

The best way of cutting heat loss through windows is by double (or even triple) glazing. When having a new window installed it is well worth spending the extra money and having it double-glazed. This should be a proper sealed unit – the two sheets of glass hermetically factory-sealed and sealed into the frame. Various types are available, some more sophisticated (and consequently more costly) than others. For example, venetian blinds can be built into the gap between the two sheets of glass and controlled from inside the room – ideal for large picture windows, patio doors and sloping roof 'lights'.

Double-glazing cuts out noise too, so if you live near an airport or motorway, or in a busy street, double-glaze as many windows as possible, particularly the bedroom ones, but bear in mind that the space between the two panes of glass must be at least 10 cm (4 inch) to cut out noise effectively. Old windows can be removed and replaced by a sealed unit, often referred to as a 'replacement window' rather than double-glazing. The frames can be of wood, metal or special plastic extrusion, and there are companies who will carry out this work for you. Most are *bona fide* and reliable, but beware – there are some

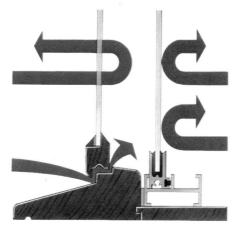
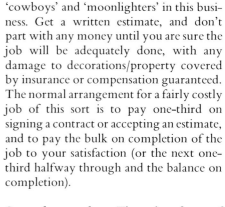

Double glazing prevents heat loss and cuts out noise. Illustrated is the inner window system, where a second window is fitted behind the existing one, trapping an insulating cushion of air. This method is particularly effective in cutting out noise

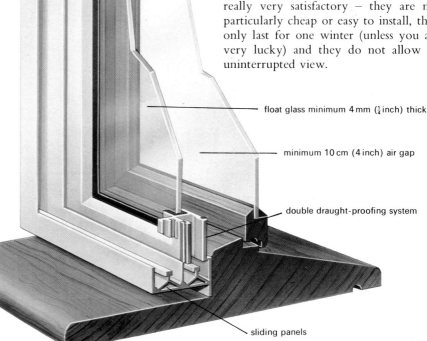

aluminium frame

float glass minimum 4 mm (¼ inch) thick

minimum 10 cm (4 inch) air gap

double draught-proofing system

sliding panels

'cowboys' and 'moonlighters' in this business. Get a written estimate, and don't part with any money until you are sure the job will be adequately done, with any damage to decorations/property covered by insurance or compensation guaranteed. The normal arrangement for a fairly costly job of this sort is to pay one-third on signing a contract or accepting an estimate, and to pay the bulk on completion of the job to your satisfaction (or the next one-third halfway through and the balance on completion).

Secondary sashes. The other form of double-glazing is by 'secondary sash' – this means putting a second window complete with frame inside the existing window surround, or it may even be attached to the existing window frame. It allows the original window to remain unchanged (important in an architecturally interesting old house) but gives the advantage of double-glazing. The inside secondary window can be opened, and may be hinged, sliding or even fixed if you don't want to be able to open either window (a good idea where the window is a security hazard). This type of double-glazing is not as efficient as the pre-sealed type, so ensure the inner frame or window can be removed for cleaning/decorating, wiping up condensation etc. Also make sure you are not left without any form of ventilation because of a completely sealed inner unit. Again, beware of 'cowboys'.

NOTE: some cheap polythene or plastic 'secondary sash' systems are sold as do-it-yourself double-glazing, but these are not really very satisfactory – they are not particularly cheap or easy to install, they only last for one winter (unless you are very lucky) and they do not allow an uninterrupted view.

HOME SECURITY

All too often, home security is not thought about until a burglar breaks in and makes off with the family silver or other precious possessions, yet in many cases this could have been prevented by a little forethought. So it makes sense to think about security along with all the other 'essentials' when planning your home.

BASIC PRECAUTIONS

Have adequate locks on all doors and windows – an average 7-roomed house can be made reasonably secure with standard mortice locks on front and back door, two door chains, internal door bolts for the downstairs doors (on the hall side) and window and fanlight bolts or locks. If you have a door with a glass panel, or there is a window near it, or the door itself is flimsy, fit a 'deadlock' (which has to be operated by a key) or a mortice locking latch which conforms to BSI 3621. If a downstairs window or fanlight is shielded from the view of passers-by (at the side or back of the house and access is easy, or in the basement area) fit bars or grilles to the inside. Louvred glass windows are particularly vulnerable because, although most types lock, it is very easy to cut out one louvre, unlock the window and take out the rest.

Always close the windows and lock up when you leave the house, even if you are only going out for a few minutes – many domestic break-ins take place in a few seconds in the afternoon when children are being collected from school and there is a convenient unlocked door or window.

If you go away for a few days, cancel the milk and papers, and try to have a friend or neighbour to go in and pick up the post, put on lights, draw curtains etc. Alternatively, fix some of your lights, or a radio/television set to a time switch, so they automatically switch on and off. Take any valuables such as jewellery with you or deposit them in the bank; hide other precious things in as safe a place as possible. Anything which makes a quick grab and getaway difficult will deter a thief, and save your belongings.

Never leave the front door key on a string inside the letterbox, or under the mat, flower pot or a stone – make sure all the members of the family who need a key

have one, and don't tie a label with the address on it to a key, just in case it gets lost. Don't leave notes pinned to doors or popped into milk bottles saying you are out or away (try to see the milkman to cancel the milk).

Don't leave spare money lying about, or in a tin or jar on the mantlepiece. If you must have substantial amounts of money in the house, fit a safe.

After dark do be on your guard –

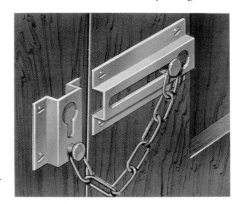

'Think through' your house, imagining you are a burglar! Then protect all vulnerable points of entry with the appropriate locks, bolts and window catches

particularly if you live alone. Put a chain on the door and don't open it to anybody you don't know. Better still, fit a spyhole in the front door so you can view would-be callers. And when you sit down to watch television in the evening, remember to lock back doors and close easy-to-climb-in windows – many a break-in occurs while the family are settled down to an evening's viewing. If you are a do-it-yourselfer, and have long (and short) ladders stored in shed or garage, make sure they are padlocked at all times when not in use. Also lock bicycles with a chain and padlock or security lock, and train children to do likewise. Bicycles should always be locked away in shed or garage (or brought inside) at night.

ALARM SYSTEMS

If you want to make it really difficult, then you can fit an alarm system. This can be professionally installed by a security firm (if you want to know more about these write to the Secretary, British Security Industry Association, 21 Whitefriars Street, London EC4Y 5AL), or there are several very good do-it-yourself systems on the market. However, it is wise to have a professional view on how to protect your home with an alarm system, even if you intend to install it yourself. Contact the crime prevention officer at your local police station, who will gladly come and give you advice. You will also find that your Insurance company is happy to give advice – the British Insurance Association issue literature on security as well.

If you have a system, make sure the alarm bell can be seen by any would-be burglars – with luck this will deter them from trying to break in and they will go elsewhere! And don't forget to turn the system on when you go out – even if you are popping down the road. Most insurance companies won't pay up on goods stolen if you have an alarm system and it was not switched on when the burglar broke in.

NOTE: apart from various BSI standards for locks and bolts, the Design Centre have approved safety and security devices (including do-it-yourself alarm systems) and fire extinguishers on file at their Design Index in London, Cardiff and Glasgow.

PLANNING THE HOME

Successful, happy homes don't just happen, they must be carefully planned to suit the present needs of those who live in them and flexible enough to adapt to the changing lifestyle. Many people start out in a small flat or house just right for one or two, and use it as a stepping-stone to somewhere larger once the family begins to grow. Nobody wants the constant upheaval of moving, but it might make sense to move several times – from first home to family-size (always think ahead and look for a property which will allow for extension), and back to a smaller, easy-to-run property in later years.

TAILORING TO FIT

Ideally, a home should be based on as flexible a design as possible, but this tailoring process is entirely a personal matter; only you know exactly what you require, and what is practical in terms of the space and funds available. It helps to sit down with paper and pencil and work out what you need, then aim for as ideal an arrangement as possible. This often means forgetting conventional ideas about using the space available in many typical three and four bedroomed houses. In an average three bedroomed 'semi' for example, the parents may start off sleeping in the largest bedroom, using the smallest bedroom as a nursery for the first baby, and the second bedroom as guestroom and study. The two downstairs reception rooms may be separate dining and sitting rooms. Later it might make sense to knock them into one large living area (think very carefully about this, see *Conversions*) and extend the kitchen out into the garden to provide a kitchen-dining room with 'utility' area. At the same time, a second bathroom might be built over the new extension, and made *en-suite* with the second bedroom.

The parents could then use this large bathroom as a dressing room and move into the second bedroom, giving their growing family the largest bedroom as a playroom/bedroom, and turning the smallest bedroom into a study/den. The extension might also provide a downstairs lavatory – or extend an existing one to include a separate shower.

Later, when teenagers need a place to do their own thing, the small bedroom might suit one child, the second bedroom become a bedsitting room for another, and the parents could move back into the largest bedroom, making it a dual-purpose bed and adults' sitting room.

Many other permutations can be worked out, depending on the property.

Furnishing to allow such flexibility is not difficult – have as much built-in storage as possible, including adjustable shelving which is fairly easy to move from room to room. Keep most of the furniture basically simple and adaptable, chosen from ranges which can be added to, or will complement other ranges. Two chests with a link top, for example, used in a nursery for clothes and as baby's changing table, can next become a play surface, then a desk for homework and finally a dressing table. Sturdy bunk beds can be taken apart to make two adult-sized twin beds and can be moved round as necessary.

Function and space. Don't be afraid to re-think your home and the way various rooms are used. Just because conventionally we usually sleep upstairs and live downstairs, this may not be the most sensible way for your family to use the available space. Look at each room critically. How much more use could you get out of it? Apart from planning dual-purpose rooms such as nursery/playroom or study/bedroom (see *Making Space*), it may make sense to use one of the larger bedrooms as an upstairs sitting room and to make one of the downstairs rooms – preferably with access to the garden – into a playroom/bedroom for the children. The other downstairs room could then be a family living area.

The hall is often wasted space which could double as a dining area or incorporate a study corner – it is surprising how much room there is *under* the stairs, if this area is not already used as a cupboard. And a downstairs cloakroom/wc will often convert into a small second bathroom, shower room or even a utility area with space for washing and drying machines.

A large bathroom can be used as a utility room too, but appliances such as a washing machine or dryer must be safely, *professionally* installed and any power points sited outside the room.

MAKING SPACE

This may be achieved simply by making some rooms dual-purpose, refurnishing to include lots of storage, or changing the use of some of the rooms as described previously.

The way you use mirrors, combine patterned and plain surfaces or plan colour schemes, can create an illusion of space. If you have a very small house, flat or bungalow, this can best be achieved by continuity of colours throughout. This does not mean that all rooms have to be decorated in the same way or in the same colour scheme, but it helps if you have complementary schemes. It is also sensible to have the same colour, though not necessarily the same material, for all floorings throughout the ground floor and on stairs and landing.

Structural alterations. If your problem is really one of the 'shrinking' house, you may have to contemplate structural alterations, possible extending the property (see *Extending and Converting*).

Knocking the downstairs rooms into one 'through' living room is one of the most common structural alterations made to create space, although this is not always the most practical solution. Apart from the fact that removing load-bearing walls will necessitate strengthening the opening with an RSJ (rolled steel joist) to support the area above, having to tidy up the family clutter before visitors arrive, or sitting in full view of the washing up is not always a comfortable way of living.

It *may* be more practical to enlarge one downstairs room by taking down part of a wall, removing the staircase, and putting a new staircase into an extension hall, or replacing the existing staircase with a spiral or open-tread one, which rises from the newly enlarged room. Either treatment would still leave two separate downstairs rooms. Or it may be possible to make the hall and 'front room' all one open-plan area, with the stairs closed off. If you do this, try to leave a bit of hall as a vestibule or to build a porch on the front of the house to prevent draughts (and so that casual callers cannot see directly into the room). If you can't get permission to build onto the front of your property, screen the front door by hanging a thick curtain on the back of it, or curtain right across the door wall if this is practical.

Sometimes it is possible to take down the wall between two smallish upstairs rooms, to make a bedroom/dressing room/bathroom combined. Floor-to-ceiling wardrobe cupboards can divide the two areas, with the necessary gap closed by curtains or vertical venetian blinds.

Split level. Rooms with very high ceilings can be used for split-level living. A sleeping platform can be built on top of storage cupboards, or it may be possible to have a gallery, half to one-third the height of the room to take the bed, leaving space underneath for a desk or dressing table and storage – or seating accommodation if it is a bed-sitting room. This arrangement is ideal for one room living or for teenage rooms. If the room is not very tall, you can still have a bed platform, supported on low storage units. Adapt inexpensive white-wood ones, or use faced-chipboard ones from furniture warehouses – or support the mattress on a specially constructed frame, with ready-made louvred doors forming the sides, and concealing pull-out storage underneath such as wire racks or boxes on castors. Often there is possible storage space *over* the bed – the type of cupboards used to fill the gap between a wardrobe cupboard and the ceiling can be ceiling-mounted (fixed to the joists) to form a canopy over the bed. If it suits the decorative style of the room, they could have curtain track fixed to them, so the bed can be draped four-poster fashion.

EXTENDING AND CONVERTING

There are many people ready and willing to help you extend, convert and improve your home, but beware of firms who use high-pressure methods of selling, and 'cowboys' who do a poor job or disappear with the money, leaving the work incomplete.

First think through the project thoroughly to be sure that any improvement will be really practical, and give the greatest possible value for money. Often, a little extra spent now will give you twice the amenities for far less than twice the price, whereas if you want to add a little extra at a later stage it could be prohibitively expensive. Also, when you are coping with the upheaval and mess of structural work, you might as well get it all over and done with in one session.

NOTE: once a house has been improved,

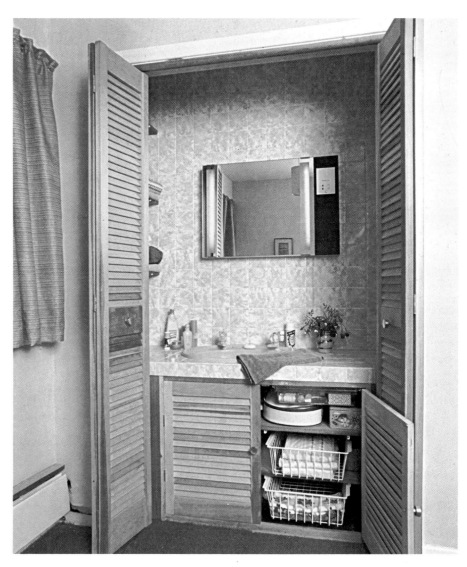

the rates may be increased, so take this into consideration.

Don't over-improve. 'Improving' can mean anything from installing a fireplace or refitting the kitchen to building on a major extension or making a large house into several separate units. Most such improvements add value to your property, making it more attractive to a would-be purchaser (if you have to sell) and a more enjoyable place in which to live.

If you have a small property, decorating attractively, installing a bathroom and central heating, and refitting the kitchen may be sensible, but don't fall into the trap of spending so much on improving that you would not see the return on your investment should you be forced to sell.

If you are redesigning the kitchen, for example, you should not spend more than one-tenth of the value of the property on this improvement, and on the bathroom about one-twentieth of this amount

Planning properly means working out everything down to the last little practical detail. Above we show a large, walk-in cupboard can provide combined washing and storage facilities, hidden behind neat louvred doors – ideal in bathroom, bedroom or possibly on a landing or under-stair area

(unless putting one in from scratch). Other 'sensible' expenditure will depend on what you plan to do, and the amount of increased space and facilities it will provide. If in doubt, ask a surveyor to give you a valuation now, and to say what the house will be worth after the various improvements have been made.

Also beware of spoiling the character of the house – 'bijou' residences, which look out of keeping with their surroundings and over-fussy, do not fetch the substantial price expected if they have to be sold. Always try to retain any interesting architectural details (attractive cornices, fireplaces and ceiling mouldings) and to emphasize and enhance the character of the house. You will find that many extensions and roof-raising alterations have to be in keeping with other properties in the area and the building materials used may have to be the same as those of the original structure, particularly if you live in a conservation area.

Start right. If planning structural alterations you may need planning permission. The rules about this change fairly frequently, and vary in some parts of the United Kingdom. Many extensions and improvements come under 'permitted development' but you will have to obtain the necessary approvals under the Building Regulations – and it is essential to do this *before* you start work, otherwise you could be forced to undo it all. You may have to deposit plans with your local authority for building control approval (or with the District Surveyor in the G.L.C. area). Generally speaking, these regulations

apply to all works involving the erection of new buildings, extensions to existing buildings, structural alterations and the installation of various sanitary fittings and heating appliances. So, if you are installing a bathroom you may have to conform to the Building Regulations but it is unlikely if you are refitting the kitchen – unless you are extending it at the same time. The regulations also apply where there is to be a major change of use (from shop to house or vice versa) or where the property is to be divided to provide more than one dwelling.

As a starting point, visit your local council Building Inspector or District Surveyor, explain what you have in mind (it will help to take your own plans, however roughly drawn) and ask their advice. They may also point you in the direction of a good local builder, architect or surveyor.

Other ways to find a reliable builder are to ask friends locally or, if you notice an attractive extension/improvement nearby, knock on the door and ask who did the building work. Some builders advertise in local papers, others are listed in the Yellow Pages Directory, but this is no guide to their size or competence.

If you do have to submit professionally drawn plans and details of construction you will need the services of a surveyor, architect, draughtsman or competent builder (you will find that some home improvements/conversion companies who offer package deals will also perform this service). The detail necessary will vary, according to the size and complexity of the work, but if you don't give enough information the plans could be rejected.

Above: a modern side extension sensitively planned to be in keeping with the original structure and complement the existing architectural style – windows in particular should be as similar as possible. The striking colour scheme adds to the overall good looks, and cleverly disguises any difference in the colour of the old and new brickwork
Left: when planning furniture for a limited space, don't forget to look above your head! Many rooms, like this bedroom, can accommodate wall-mounted units. There is often so much wasted space above (and sometimes below) a bed

plans, and brief them fully about what you want them to do. You may want them to cope with everything, but if cash is short you could undertake some site clearing/excavation work and some of the finishing yourself. Ask when they could start, and how long they will take – get these facts in writing along with the estimate, and the terms of payment.

Once you have obtained several estimates, wait for the local council's go-ahead before accepting the most suitable one in writing. Work can then commence, but do plan ahead.

Contingency plans. Discuss with your builder what upheaval is likely to be involved, and if water, light and heating are likely to be shut off for any length of time, try to send the family away for those critical days. Similarly, if the work involves the removal of the staircase and some ladder-climbing, young children and pets would be safer elsewhere.

Protect the part of the house not affected by the work. Cover furniture and floor-coverings with dust or plastic decorating sheets and seal doors with masking tape to keep out dust and dirt.
NOTE: if you do decamp while major building work is going on, deposit all valuables in the bank or take them with you. Put all fragile items in a really safe place or, again, take them with you. Even if the work is being supervised by an architect or surveyor who has undertaken to visit the site daily, go as often as you can yourself to see that work is progressing according to schedule. If *you* are controlling the work, visit the property daily – if you can – and try to vary the times of your visits.

GETTING A GRANT

Some house improvements, repairs and insulation work required to bring your house up to modern standards are covered by a home improvement grant, which could pay up to 90 per cent of the cost. These are given by local councils and there are several different types available, so again the starting point should be a visit to your local council office to see the Home Improvements Officer. You can also get several helpful free leaflets from the local council, Housing Aid Centres or Citizens' Advice Bureaux.

To be eligible for a grant you must be either a home owner or a tenant with a certain number of years to run on your lease, and intend to go on living in the property for at least another 5 years. You can get a grant to improve a property

Most authorities want the plans in duplicate, and you should keep a spare copy in case of loss. They may also want a location plan showing where your house is, and the size and shape of the extension in relation to the existing property. This can be shown on a copy of the local ordnance survey map (the 130 cm [50 inch] to the mile scale).

The usual waiting time for approval of the plans is about six weeks, although it can be longer. It is also wise to allow for possible rejection and replanning. Once approved, you will find the work has to be inspected at various stages, according to the job (completion of foundations, laying of damp-proof course, etc.).

Inform the council's Building Control Office several days in advance when it will be ready for inspection, so that work is not held up. If the job is in excess of £1,000 you may have to pay an inspection fee as

well as a deposit when the plans are submitted.
NOTE: builders/contractors usually expect payment in instalments, and this will normally be agreed when you accept the estimate. If you are getting financial help with the work e.g. an increased mortgage, these payments, too, are usually made in stages and the building society may send somebody to inspect progress.

Bring in the builder. Once you have lodged plans with the council, find a builder. If the work is extensive and you are employing an architect or chartered surveyor, he will 'put the work out to tender'; that is, he will contact several builders and get them to estimate for the work (not only in money but in time). If the job is smaller, do the same thing yourself – get at least three estimates. Show the builders the specifications and

Above: open plan areas must be carefully co-ordinated so that colours and patterns do not jar. When they do blend well they create an effect of even greater spaciousness Right, above: planning on paper with a scale floor plan, and cut out furniture shapes in the same scale, makes positioning easy, without the need to hump heavy pieces of furniture round the room

which you intend to let, (but *not* for a holiday or second home) and the rent may subsequently be council controlled. Most grants are not paid on properties over a certain rateable value; at the time of writing this is £225, or £400 in Greater London. Grants fall into three main categories:

1. Full Improvement Grants given to improve homes to a good standard (not to extend or install luxuries). They can help

towards the cost of converting a property into several separate dwellings, or improving a property so a disabled person can live there. These grants are awarded entirely at the discretion of the council. You are unlikely to get more than a percentage of the cost of the work – up to 75 per cent (or up to 90 per cent in cases of hardship), but up to 50 per cent or 65 per cent grant is more likely.

2. Repair Grants, for structural repairs to

homes built before 1919, can include installing a damp proof course, or major repairs to the roof, foundations or walls, but does not cover maintenance work (such as rewiring) – at the time of writing expense limits for this type of grant are £5,500 in Greater London and £4,000 elsewhere in the United Kingdom. Again these are discretionary.

3. Intermediate Grants are mandatory and given towards the cost of installing certain standard amenities, such as a fixed bath or shower, sink (and a hot and cold water supply to these), and an inside wc in a property which does not have one (*not* to replace old ones).

You do not have to carry out all the work at once, and there are no rateable value limits, but there *are* certain expenditure limits – up to a total of £3,500 in Greater London and £2,500 elsewhere. You will have to put the whole property into reasonable repair if you accept the total grant.

You must not start the work until the grant has been approved, in writing; otherwise you may have to meet the total cost yourself. And your rates are likely to be increased when the work is finished, because of the improved amenities and standard of the property.

Several other grants are available – an *Insulation grant* is given towards the cost of insulating the loft, so long as it has no insulation, and normally covers two-thirds of the cost, up to a maximum (at the time of writing) of £65, but pensioners who receive rate rebates or supplementary pensions are eligible for more. Get the leaflet *Save Money on Loft Insulation* from the sources previously mentioned. Sound-proofing and double-glazing against noise is another expense for which you may be eligible for a grant, if you live within a certain distance from an airport or motor-way. Grants have been discontinued in the Heathrow/Gatwick Airport areas, but may be awarded for people living near to the third London airport or some new provincial airports. Enquire at your local council office.

Finally, if your home is one of architectural or historic interest, there are *Historic Building Grants* – to help towards the cost of restoration work in the main. For more details contact the Department of the Environment, 2 Marsham Street, London SW1P 3EB.

PLANNING ON PAPER

Whether you intend to extend, enlarge and improve your home, or merely to redecorate and rearrange your furniture, it

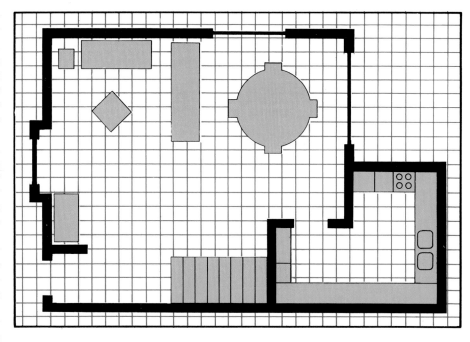

helps if you get your ideas down on paper. This way you can see whether they will actually work. Make sure you have sufficient lighting and power points handy to plug in various gadgets in the kitchen and workroom, as well as facilities for lighting a dining table, desk or worktop. See whether your furniture will fit its proposed new location, or if intended new purchases are a practical size and shape. The 'measure-and-draw' method is invaluable when you are moving home (particularly from a larger to a smaller one, as you can see just how much you may need to dispose of), and essential if you are refitting a kitchen or replumbing a bathroom.

Measuring up. Use a steel rule, or yardstick (dressmakers' tape measures tend to stretch in use) and measure the main dimensions of the room; include the length and height of structural features such as alcoves and protruding chimney-breasts. As corners are rarely completely square, measure the diagonals as well – particularly important in a room which is to have fitted furniture or important plumbing changes, or is an unusual shape. Draw a plan and include these measurements.

Note which way doors (and built-in cupboards) open – measure the width of the door, the jamb (frame round the door) and the distance between this and the corner of the room. Plot the position of existing light/power points and switches, plumbing pipes and radiators. Think 'three dimensionally', and measure the depth of skirting boards, the height of any picture rail from the skirting (and the

floor), depth of any frieze (area between picture rail and ceiling or coving), depth of any cornice or coving, and so on. Take accurate, detailed measurements of the windows: inside frame, outside frame or window reveal, depth of the reveal, depth of the sill, and the height of sill from the skirting and the floor.

Once you have jotted down all these measurements transfer them to a proper workable, scale plan.

Making a floor plan. The easiest way to do this is to use squared graph paper, transferring your first rough sketch and measurements, in scale. Indicate fireplaces, doors, windows etc. and show which way the doors open. Plot the positions of radiators, points, switches and pipes accurately. See if your furniture will fit by measuring it, drawing the shapes to the same scale as your plan on another piece of squared paper – cut out, colour with a felt pen to make them easier to see – and moving them about on the scale plan. If you are buying new furniture, the catalogue should give accurate measurements – but take a rule with you when you visit the shop just in case.

When planning to install cupboards and units allow for the opening of doors and drawers – similarly drawers and doors of freestanding furniture. In a sitting area, allow space to get round furniture and to stretch your legs out in front of settee or easy chair. In the dining room allow for chairs to be pulled back from the table to enable people to sit down. In the bedroom, allow sufficient room for the beds to be pulled out for making.

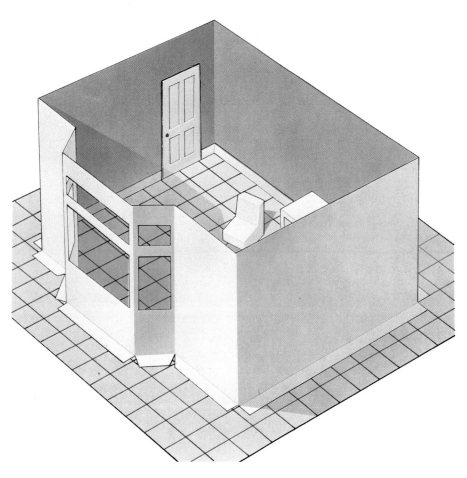

Making an elevation. If you want to work out a special treatment for an awkward wall, or want to see whether furniture will fit three-dimensionally, make an elevation of the walls of a room using the same method. Work in the same scale as for the floor plan; measure first, and transfer the measurements to a scale outline on the squared paper, again marking positions of fixed items. Draw in accurate shapes of doors, windows, fireplaces, fitted furniture and so on.

Making a model. This is the best way to visualize structural, and other, alterations, or work out ways of improving the proportions of rooms (see *Creating an Illusion*). Make a floor plan and elevations of all the walls, to scale. Stick these to stiff card, cut out, and fit together with sticky tape to form a three-dimensional model. Make models of your furniture from card, or cut out of blocks of polystyrene, and fix these to the floor of the model where they will actually be positioned.

PLANNING THE BATHROOM

Apply the same basic principles of selecting and planning, as for the kitchen. Make your list of priorities, make a scale plan and plot the plumbing before 'shopping around'. Visit builders' merchants, home improvement centres, bathroom specialists and department stores, and collect manufacturers' literature. One major difference is that if you don't already have a bathroom or inside wc, you may be eligible for a grant towards the cost.

You will also need a reliable plumber (one who is a member of the Institute of Plumbers), and you will find the Council of British Ceramic Sanitaryware Manufacturers' literature helpful.

Above: sometimes – perhaps because you are considering a very small, or otherwise problematical room – floor plans may not be enough! You can however, use the measure-and-draw technique for an elevation, to see what will fit where. This technique is described in detail in the text
Below: bathroom planning involves allowing enough space for people to move around comfortably as well as positioning equipment and accessories for maximum convenience and efficiency in use

A 'second opinion'. Once you have some idea of what you want, call in a plumber to get an estimate for the work (again make sure you know just what is involved and estimated for). He can also give practical advice about water pressure, whether the hot water tank is likely to be large enough to fill the new bath and so on. But remember, *you* are going to use the bathroom, not the plumber, so be prepared to question and argue if necessary. Obtain two or three estimates – these are usually provided free, even from bathroom specialists who may provide a complete 'package' including supplying sanitaryware, tiles, flooring, all decorating items and carrying out the work. Plumbers, unless they are part of a building team or firm, usually only install the items and

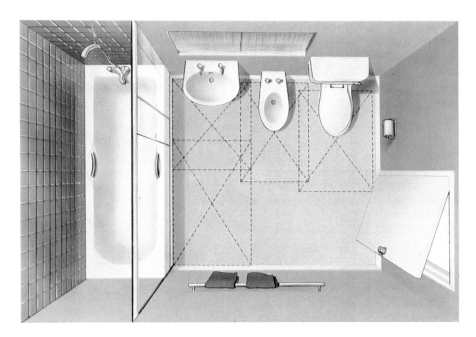

plumb them, leaving you to do the decorating.

Space considerations. There are certain minimum measurements to be considered when planning the bathroom since people need to be able to use the various items comfortably. There should be sufficient space at the side of the bath to allow you to step in and out easily, to dry yourself and, if possible, kneel and bath, dry and dress a child. The basin must have enough space for a person to stand in front of it, allow elbow room on both sides, and be large enough for hair-washing. The optimum recommended height from floor to rim is 80 cm (2 ft 7 inch). Choose a basin which is large enough and easy to clean, and don't site shelves or cupboards too low above it, where heads could be knocked when hair washing.

The shower cabinet should be at least 90 cm (3 ft) square, with a space in front of it for drying yourself at least 70 cm (2 ft 3 inch) square. The wc and bidet need space of 80 cm (2 ft 7 inch) wide, to allow for knees, but if sited side-by-side the overall width can be reduced because they are not likely to be in use at the same time. But there are special regulations for installing bidets – check with your plumber.

If the room is very small, and you can't fit in all the equipment you want, ships' baths are available (contact a ships' chandlers/boat builders' outfitter); these have a seat in them, take up about half the space of a conventional bath, and can be combined with a shower above. If you want a separate shower in your bathroom and there isn't enough space, consider installing one in a downstairs cloakroom or understairs cupboard. Or you may be able to install an instantaneous shower, complete with its own cubicle, in a bedroom, landing cupboard or other walk-in cupboard.

PLANNING THE KITCHEN

Installing a new kitchen is a major investment in terms of time, labour and money, so it is wise to have professional help.

Start by collecting relevant leaflets, and cuttings from magazines of ranges/layouts you like, then 'shop around'. Go to Home Improvement Centres, kitchen specialists and department stores to see the ranges and displays. They may offer to plan your kitchen for you, and so will many of the kitchen unit manufacturers. Most charge a fee (usually about £25), which is refundable if you buy from them, so if you can afford the luxury of two separate plans, you could then choose the one you like

better. Even if this means losing about £25 it could save you from making an expensive mistake.

Choose appliances in the same way – collect leaflets and advertisements, then 'shop around'. Local Gas Board and Electricity Board showrooms have trained home economists who can give you free advice on choosing and using cookers, freezers and other domestic equipment. Visit local electrical goods shops and department stores, too. Many kitchen and home improvement specialists can recommend, supply and install all the necessary 'machinery' at competitive prices.

Take your time. First make your own workable scale plan, marking in fixed items like plumbing/inlets and outlets, cooker points, boiler position, power points, etc. Measure and make in-scale shapes of any appliances to be retained like cooker, fridge, washing machine, etc., and move these about on your plan to see where they can be practically sited. This will give you an idea of what else you can accommodate in the way of units, tables and other appliances. Think 'vertically' too, if necessary making elevated plans of the walls, so that you can see whether units will fit under window sills, or whether wall cupboards will be practical above a table, appliance or work surface.

Make a list of priorities – decide exactly what you must have in the kitchen, but also think ahead and try to include items you would like to add later when the budget allows. Decide on the style of kitchen you want – strictly functional and labour-saving, or more of a country-farmhouse kitchen. Think seriously about the way you use the kitchen. If you are an enthusiastic cook, you may want a pantry as well as a fridge, and possibly a deep freeze, and a large cooker (perhaps with double oven). If food is not so important to you, facilities for cooking and food storage can be simpler, but you may want a micro-wave oven as well as the cooker. If you entertain a lot, a dishwasher will probably top your list of priorities, with a washing machine/dryer well down on the list, but if you have babies, small children or teenagers these last two appliances will be all-important!

If you do call in a kitchen planning expert, kitchen supply specialist or manufacturer to install the new kitchen, brief them thoroughly; explain your list of priorities, and if you don't like their plan, don't be afraid to say so – get them to revise it. And check on the interior fittings available with the units – some have a

range of integral wire racks, revolving shelf units, etc., included automatically in the price, whereas with other manufacturers these are extras.

When they quote for the job be sure that you understand exactly what the estimate includes; ideally, it should cover the removal of old equipment and making good, before the new is installed. Some specialists completely redecorate, others leave this to you – in which case it makes sense to have the old kitchen taken out, then prepare all the surfaces for decorating, and undercoat the woodwork and decorate the ceiling. You can then complete the decorations once the units are installed. Ask how long the job is likely to take – and allow for it to run over time.

The 'work triangle'. If you draw lines between the three main areas in a kitchen – the food storage and preparation area, the cooker and the food serving, and the washing up area – you get a 'work triangle'. Ideally the distance between these points should be kept to under 5m (15 ft) and each area should accommodate all the materials and utensils used there, to save time and the cook's legs!

The sink usually forms one corner of the triangle and is often sited under a window because of ease of plumbing the outflow pipe.

The items needed to wash, drain, dry, chop and prepare food should be kept as near to the *sink* as possible; waste bins, rubbish bags, tea towels, etc. will also need to be near at hand. If you have, or plan to have a dishwasher, this should be positioned next to the sink, under (or on top of) a work surface.

The *cooker* (whether a single unit or split-level with wall-mounted oven and separate hob) should be close by the sink, but never placed opposite the sink, unless this is absolutely unavoidable – there could be an accident with hot pans. The cooker *must* have an adequate heat-proof surface on one side of it, to stand hot pans on when taken from the hob or oven; ideally, there should be a heat-proof surface on both sides. Sometimes one (or both) will double as a food preparation area. Keep seasoning, herbs, stirring spoons, spatulas, oven gloves, etc. as near to hand as possible. The most used pots, pans and accessories should be stored next to, or possibly below (with split-level) the cooker.

The food *preparation* area completes the work triangle and should include storage space for frequently-used ingredients. The refrigerator might be positioned under a worktop which is used for preparation,

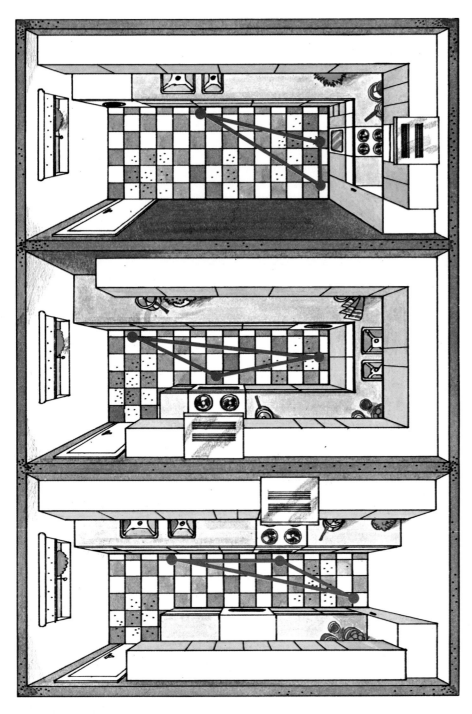

Above: kitchen planning must take into consideration the work triangle (marked in red) allowing for the most convenient food preparation, cooking, serving and washing up. This triangle should be planned to minimise the amount of walking to and fro necessary between the three work areas, depending on the shape of the room. Illustrated are three basic layouts: the L-shape; the U-shape and the galley

and dry goods can all be stored in a wall-mounted cupboard above. You will also need to have preparation tools handy – mixer, scales, can opener, food processor, bowls, baking tins, and so on.

Ideally, there should be a *food serving* area as well, including space for trays, china, glasses, cutlery, mats and all the items needed for serving and eating a meal. In some large kitchens, an island unit can be installed to divide cooking from eating area, and this also provides an ideal serving top. In other kitchens, serving-up can be done on a surface under the hatch to dining or living room, but in very small

kitchens the cooking and preparation surface would suffice, while items for the dining table could be stored in the dining area.

Basically there are six possible layouts for a work triangle – the single line layout; the galley or parallel layout; the L-shape; the U-shape; the F-shape (for larger kitchens which incorporate a dining area), and the island layout.

Think vertically. You also need to think about vertical layouts; plan these to reduce bending and stretching to the minimum. Check which walls are strong enough to take the weight of wall-mounted cupboards *full* of china or tins (some internal walls are made of plasterboard, which could buckle under such a load). You could stack equipment like washing-machine and dryer, or a fridge-freezer combination and/or a broom cupboard against this wall.

Any wall cupboards or open shelves should be mounted at least 40 to 45 cm (16 to 18 inches) above worksurfaces so they don't obscure the back of the worktop, but they must not be sited so high that you cannot reach them easily (a strong 'step-stool' or pair of kitchen steps may be necessary to reach the very back of the topmost shelf). Wall-mounted cupboards can have concealed lighting under them to light the work surface below (see *Planning the Lighting*).

Don't place wall cupboards on an area of wall where there is nothing underneath, as people could walk into them. And cupboards should not be mounted above (or too close to) a cooker hob because of the fire risk – to maintain visual continuity you can line up a cooker hood with the wall cupboards.

SELECTING SURFACES

Before you choose colours and decide on design you will need to think about surface treatments. And this involves some practical planning.

THE FLOOR

As most schemes are likely to start with the floor (see *Colour and Design*), consider the 'traffic' and wear and tear the flooring is likely to get. In a busy family home, for example, it would be impractical to lay off-white shaggy pile carpet throughout, although this might be an ideal floor treatment in a bachelor pad. A tough floorcovering which will not show marks is appropriate and hardwearing carpet with a patterned or textured surface might be a sensible choice.

If money is short, halls, dining areas, childrens' and family room floors can be covered with lino, lino tiles, vinyl tiles, cushioned vinyl, or properly sealed cork – all of which can be softened with (washable) rugs if you wish.

Ceramic, quarry and terrazzo tiles are other possibilities. Although more expensive, they are easy to clean, come in a wide range of colours, textured plains and patterns, and are likely to last a lifetime, but tend to be a little hard on the feet if you are standing for a long time. They look most effective and are practical for halls, stairs, dining areas, sun rooms/extensions, conservatories and utility rooms, bathrooms and shower rooms. But if you plan to install them upstairs, make sure that the joists are strong enough to take the considerable weight.

Wood floors, if in a good state of repair, can be sanded smooth, sealed and polished; partly covered with rugs, they look very elegant. Old floor boards can be repaired, and very bad ones replaced and gaps filled, before sanding (sanding machines can be hired from Decorating Hire Shops). Wood floors can also be painted, colour-stained or stencilled in a variety of ways. Various woodblock floorings are available which may be professionally laid *or* tackled by the do-it-yourselfer.

Cork tiles must be properly sealed, and in bathrooms, kitchens and utility rooms it is wise to lay the pre-sealed type. In other rooms, you can use the sort which are sealed after they have been laid – these can be coloured with wood dyes.

Linoleums and lino tiles are not so popular as they used to be, but some lovely colours and marbled effects are available. Lino is sturdy, and can be inlaid to make individual patterns (really a job for the professional), although tiles are easy to cut to shape and lay.

Cushioned and sheet vinyl come in many widths, patterns, grades and types, as well as in sheet and tile form (some are self-adhesive). Some types have to be professionally laid and stuck down; others – such as most of the tiles – can be tackled by the amateur. There are also 'lay-flat' types which only need to be fixed at doorways.

All these resilient floorings are hard-wearing, although some of the less expensive ranges of sheet vinyl are not so long lasting – rather like a carpet, you get what you pay for.

Carpets. There are so many types of carpeting available, the choice can be confusing. The golden rule is to choose the best quality you can possibly afford for heavy traffic areas such as hallway, stairs,

---

KEY

LD = Light Domestic
MD = Medium Domestic
HD = Heavy Domestic
✓ = Yes
X = No
NR = Not Recommended
* = Cork tiles must be properly sealed in all situations. The pre-sealed type *must* be used in kitchens and bathrooms.
** = Sanded and sealed or painted.

FLOORING CHART

So much confusion exists over the suitability of various floorcoverings to specific domestic situations, so follow our Domestic Floorcoverings Chart when making your choice.

FLOOR COVERINGS / LOCATIONS	Cushioned vinyl sheet and tiles		Solid vinyl sheet and tiles		Linoleum sheet and tiles		*Cork Tiles	Carpet body and tiles		**Strip Wood and parquet		Ceramic tiles mosaics and quarrys		Stone	Artificial grass	Comments
Hall	✓	✓	✓	✓	✓	✓	✓	MD/HD		✓	✓	✓	✓	✓	×	
Stairs	×	×	N/R	N/R	N/R	N/R	✓	MD/HD ✓	✓	N/R	N/R	N/R	N/R	×	×	If smooth flooring used, nosing must be fitted to treads.
Living-room	✓	✓	✓	✓	✓	✓	✓	MD/HD ✓		✓	✓	✓	✓	N/R	×	
Dining-room	✓	✓	✓	✓	✓	✓	✓	MD/LD ✓		✓	✓	✓	✓	N/R	×	
Kitchen	✓	✓	✓	✓	✓	✓	✓	N/R	N/R	If sealed ✓	✓	✓	✓	✓	×	Cork *must* be properly sealed. Carpet not recommended unless specific kitchen type.
Conservatory	✓	N/R	✓	N/R	✓	N/R	✓	N/R	N/R	N/R	N/R	✓	✓	✓	✓	Suitable flooring depends on temperature and humidity reached in conservatory.
Patio	×	×	×	×	×	×	×	×	×	×	×	✓	✓	✓	✓	Ceramic tiles, etc, must be frost-proofed.
Bedroom	✓	✓	✓	✓	✓	✓	✓	✓L/D ✓		✓	✓	N/R	N/R	N/R	×	
Bath, shower	✓	N/R	✓	✓	✓	✓	✓	✓L/D ✓		N/R	N/R	✓	✓	×	×	Floor surface must be non-slip. *Do not* use cork in a shower. Tiles must be closely butted.
Playroom	✓	✓	✓	✓	✓	✓	✓	N/R	N/R	N/R	N/R	×	×	×	×	Suitability depends on age of children.
Sauna	×	×	✓	×	N/R	N/R	×	×	×	✓	N/R	✓	✓	✓	×	Floor must be non-slip and resilient to high temperatures.

landing and main living rooms, and to use the lighter weight, cheaper grades for rooms which get less wear, like bedrooms. The carpet industry has produced a labelling system to help you – see chart. The traditional types of carpet are woven. These are:

Axminster, usually patterned and with an extensive choice of colours within the design. The pile yarn is seen on the surface and the backing is jute or hessian, sometimes strengthened by polypropylene. Different fibres and blends of fibres are used, but frequently Axminsters are made in an 80 per cent wool/20 per cent nylon mixture, and from acrylic fibres.

Many different widths are available, including broadloom up to 5m (16 ft 5 inch) wide. Axminsters are also sold as carpet 'squares' with bound edges, rather like large rugs, the advantage being that they can be turned round to even out the wear.

Wilton is usually plain, though there are some patterned Wiltons, with a restricted number of colour combinations. The carpet is close-textured with a velvet, close-looped or mixed cut-and-loop 'sculptured' pile. Any yarn not used on the face of the carpet is woven into the backing, to add thickness and strength. The backing used is the same as for Axminster.

Different fibres and blends of fibres can be used, but usually Wiltons are made in 100 per cent wool or an 80 per cent wool/ 20 per cent nylon mixture.

Wilton carpet is woven in narrow widths from 68 cm to 2m (27 inch to 6ft) wide, and widths are seamed to fit when fully fitted carpet is required. Widths up to 3.6 m (12 ft) are also available and can be bound to form a carpet 'square'.

Tufted. This is by far the most widely available and comes in many different effects, textures and fibres. Tufted carpets can be patterned or plain and widths can be from 1m to 5m (3 ft to 16 ft 5 inch). The tufts are needled into an already-woven backing and anchored with an adhesive. Backings can be of hessian, Latex or foam – a high-quality, foam-backed, tufted carpet can be laid without an underlay.

Bonded. These are made face-to-face (just like a sandwich), the 'filling' being the carpet pile, held between two specially treated woven backings. The carpet is then sliced through the middle to make two carpets. All the pile is on the surface, and can be in a wide range of lengths and textures from a shaggy effect to a close-cropped velour. The fibres can be traditional, synthetic, or a mixture, and the

carpets are usually plain. Broadloom widths (as with Axminster) are normally available.

Needlefelt or Needlepunch. A fibrous mass is machine-needled into a strong backing, creating a looped 'corduroy' or a dense felt pile. They can be plain, mottled or printed, with a resin-coated or foam backing. The fibres may be natural, synthetic or a blend, but usually this type of carpet is made from synthetic fibres, and broadloom widths are the norm.

Style of carpet. Many distinctive *styles* of carpet are available, creating different surface effects:

Velvet or Velour is a close-cut velvety surface, normally used for plain or two tone carpets, which are made in several different ways, and come in a range of fibres and fibre blends.

Twist or Hardtwist is curly and crush-resistant. The kink is put into the yarn before it is made into a carpet. They are made in several different ways – frequently, high-quality Wilton is woven this way, in different fibres or blends of fibre.

Loop pile is made by a continuous run of loops, which can be used to create different textures. This group includes *Cords*, which have tight loops and look ribbed and are made from a range of different fibres, and *Berbers* which have a larger loop and look more homespun. Originally these were made from an un-dyed, rather coarse wool, but now come in synthetic yarns as well (called Berber-style). *Haircord* is a very hardwearing cord carpet woven from natural animal hair – it is expensive and not seen very frequently these days. The wearing quality of ordinary cord should not be confused with haircord.

Shag-pile or Long-pile carpet has a richly textured surface. Pile lengths can vary from 1 cm to 3 cm ($\frac{1}{2}$ inch to 1$\frac{1}{2}$ inch), or even longer, with a variety of strand thicknesses. The pile can be looped, twisted, 'kinked' or stranded, and a range of fibres and fibre blends are used. This group also includes a fairly new style – *Saxony* – a shaggy pile carpet which has a lustrous look, usually made from shiny synthetic fibre.

Sculptured pile, sometimes called 'cut-and-loop', is made from yarns of different heights, or a combination of looped and velvet pile to create a patterned or 'carved' effect. Sometimes two or three tones of the same colour are used to enhance the patterned effect; two or three different colours can also be used. Fibres can be natural or synthetic, or a mixture.

Printed carpets are made in a number of different ways, including a computer-controlled dye injection system. The overall effect is the same as a patterned woven carpet, but on closer examination the pattern is seen to be only on the front of the pile. Carpet made this way can be multi-coloured or have a two and tri-tone effect, and fibres are usually synthetic.

Shadow style has contrasting colour on the pile – the darker tone is on the base, lightening towards the tip. The pile is usually lustrous, made from a synthetic fibre, and when the carpet is walked on the dark tones show through, creating a shadowed effect. The pile can be velvet or sculptured, and sometimes several different toning colours are used to enhance the iridescent effect.

Types of fibres. Wool and other natural fibres were originally the only ones used in carpet construction, but now the choice is wide, and each type gives its own particular characteristics to the finished carpet.

Acrylics have good resistance to flattening, but do not have quite such long-lasting qualities as wool and show the dirt more. Always try to select one which has been treated to resist staining and to be anti-static.

Blended fibres give, in proportion, the advantages of all the fibres used in the blend. For example, 80/20 per cent wool/nylon blend combines the soil resistance and resilience of wool with the hard-wearing characteristics of nylon. Many different fibres can be blended in carpet construction.

Cotton has the advantage of being cheap and it washes easily, but it also flattens quickly and soils easily.

Nylon. The hardest wearing fibre yet developed for carpets and it can give a lustrous and luxurious look, but on its own it soils easily and can look scuffed and bedraggled very quickly. When nylon is added to other fibres, it increases the strength of the carpet.

Polyester. A soft fibre, usually used in mini-shag and fluffy carpets, it has only moderate wear and appearance retention.

Polypropylene. Often found in cord carpets, it provides moderate wear and appearance retention, is impervious to water and much used for backings.

Viscose rayon. Inexpensive but does not wear well, and soils and flattens as badly as cotton.

Wool. No complete substitute for wool has yet been found. A blend of the right kinds of wool will provide hard-wearing, resilient carpet which shows soiling less than other fibres, but this is expensive. If you want wool, you will have to pay for it. A wool and nylon mixture in 80/20 per cent blend gives the best performance.

Carpet squares and tiles. Carpets are available as 'squares' (not necessarily square) and as tiles. Either type can be manufactured in the ways described, from any of the fibres (or blends of fibres) discussed, and in several different styles.

Carpet squares are like large rugs, are easy to lay, do not necessarily need an underlay and can be turned round to equalize wear.

Carpet tiles come in various sizes and qualities and are usually loose-laid, so they can be taken up when you move or for cleaning. Buy a few extra so you can replace a tile if it becomes damaged. They are easy to lay, and particularly practical in bathrooms where there is a lot of 'cutting-in' round basin, pedestals and so on.

THE WALLS AND WOODWORK

These are the next most important surfaces – woodwork is usually painted with oil-based gloss paint, as this protects it and makes it easy to clean and redecorate, but some people prefer a satin or lustre finish (see *The Right Paint for the Job*) – this is not so practical in areas which get a lot of condensation, or are prone to sticky finger marks. Wood can also be stained, or left completely natural, and sealed.

Walls can be decorated in a number of ways (see *Wall treatments*) including paint, paper and a multitude of different wall-coverings from fabric to wood cladding. Again, the task of selecting a suitable surface is largely one of common sense.

FURNITURE

Upholstered furniture comes in many shapes, styles, sizes and price ranges. If you have children, choose something hard-wearing and robust – this means looking in the medium-price range. Covers should be easy-to-clean or, for more flexibility, choose attractive tweedy or leather textured upholstery and have a set of washable (or dry-cleanable) loose covers as well. In an 'adults only' household, more fragile fabrics can be used, but the choice still depends on the style of the decorations and the likely wear and tear.

Cabinet furniture. The choice is enormous: wood, veneered chipboard, moulded plastic, laminated plastics, metal, glass and Perspex, rush and cane. When choosing furniture, price, function, lifestyle etc. all need to be taken into consideration.

Beautiful inlaid antique tables and fragile furniture are fine in a home without children and pets (or confined to rooms they do not use), but more robust finishes should be selected for family rooms. In children's own rooms, painted furniture from a range which can be added to as the children grow is a practical choice. 'Junk shop finds' can often be painted to match and supplement it.

Kitchen units should be easy-to-clean, inside and out, and as good a quality as you can afford. Remember, you are likely to live with them for a long time, so stick to colours you really like and around which you can plan several different schemes. Avoid over-bright or jazzy patterned worktops.

NOTE: the same comments apply to selecting colours for bathroom sanitary-ware, ceramic wall and floor tiles, and any other surfaces which are difficult to change.

PLANNING THE LIGHTING

Once you have worked out the likely furniture positions for each room you will be able to see just where you need direct light, and make any necessary arrangements for rewiring and fixing new points.

Think about this at planning stage, so that any channelling out of walls or lifting of floorboards can be done before you start decorating.

Direct lighting. All main rooms will need direct lighting to enable various activities to go on, and background lighting to provide a soft glow.

In the living area you will need indirect lighting behind or to the side of the television set when viewing: lamps positioned behind (or to the side of) chairs and settees to give adequate lighting for reading, sewing etc; lamps to light surfaces so you can see what you are doing when pouring drinks, putting on records or tapes. A study corner or desk should be lit by concealed lighting from the front and above the writing surface, with an adjustable lamp if a typewriter is used.

In the dining area, the table needs illuminating, without direct light shining in the eyes of the diners, and this is best lit from above with a lamp on a rise-and-fall fitting with a wide shade – if the table is a long one you may need two lights. Units or storage cupboards need adequate lighting from lamps or concealed lighting under shelves.

In the bedroom, lighting should be thought about in relation to the function of the room. The main bedroom should have lamps each side of the bed, for reading – high enough to throw light onto the page when the reader is sitting up in bed, but not to shine into the eyes of the partner who may want to sleep. Dressing tables should be lit so the light shines on the face, not into the eyes. In bed-sitting rooms, a desk lamp may be needed, and any play surface in a child's room should be adequately lit. A nursery should have soft indirect lighting, which can be left on (perhaps on a dimmer control) if a child is afraid of the dark, as well as *safe* direct lighting for nappy-changing etc. Illuminate cupboards from inside, with a switch mounted on the door frame which comes on when the door opens.

In the hall, lighting must be safe, light the edge of stair treads well, and be dual-switched for control from both landing and hall. Treat any understairs or linen

A 'rise and fall' ceiling light and angled reading lamp allow the users to adjust lighting to their requirements

cupboards as bedroom ones, and have a lamp on any hall tables, plus a porch or front door light controlled from inside.

In the kitchen, lighting must be really adequate. Have lighting above the sink, so you can see what you are doing at night (often forgotten when the sink is placed under the window) – this can be pelmet lighting, strip lighting or spots. The stove should be lit from above (some cookers have a built-in light) so both the hob and oven can be seen clearly. Work surfaces should be well lit – concealed lighting under wall-mounted cupboards, which shines onto the surface is best. The insides of deep cupboards should also be lit. Treat a table or breakfast bar as for the dining table. Small kitchens can have strategically placed ceiling-mounted track with several movable spots.

In the bathroom, the mirror should be well lit for shaving, make up etc; illuminate from the side, not above. Linen cupboards should have interior lighting, and the bath should be well enough lit for reading in the bath as well as seeing to wash oneself – again spotlights, mounted on track, can be a practical possibility.

Background lighting. Background or diffused lighting can be used to create a mood – or very dark corners may need some form of lighting during the daytime. Wall lights are one solution but they must be carefully sited – not too high – and are most useful if dimmer-controlled.

Pelmet lighting can provide soft background illumination, but if you have curtain poles and pleated headings the curtains can still be softly lit from strategically placed spots to emphasize lovely fabric. In old houses, spots can be concealed behind beams. Illuminated alcoves or shelves, lit from above with concealed lights, also provide good background lighting.

Pools of light can be provided by lamps (table and standard) and house plants or flower arrangements look really dramatic if illuminated from below (stand them on a glass table) by uplighters.

Always plan for much more lighting than you think you will need, so you can change the mood and atmosphere of a room at will, and won't have to rewire when you change the scheme or decide to move the furniture round.

Kitchen and dining room lighting has to be functional, but it can be decorative too. In the kitchen, work surfaces and cooker should be adequately lit. Here, recessed downlighters in the ceiling provide plenty of light, without glare. The adjoining dining area is multi-purpose and can be used as a study, so the lighting is softly diffused with lamps added when needed

HOME DESIGN

If you are creative or artistic, you will derive great satisfaction from the pre-planning stages of home-making: the colour scheming, pattern mixing and matching, and choosing suitable textures for the various surfaces. But some people find the prospect rather daunting – partly because so much mystique surrounds the subject. In reality, it is a fairly simple one. There are a few rules you can follow – and these are set out in this section – but breaking all the rules and 'doing your own thing' can produce some very exciting, dramatic and original schemes.

ELEMENTS OF DESIGN

COLOUR THEORY

Colour is basically explained in two ways: in terms of the effect of light of varying wavelengths on the human eye, and in terms of pigments and dyes – which provide the colour used in interior decoration.

All colour comes originally from the three *primary* colours of red, yellow and blue. If you look at the colour wheel you will see when these are mixed they form the *secondary* colours: red + yellow = orange; yellow + blue = green; blue + red = violet. These subdivide again to form the *tertiary* colours of red-orange; yellow-orange; yellow-green; blue-green, blue-violet and red-violet.

The colour wheel can be divided down the centre and on one side you will find the warm colours of yellow, yellow-orange, orange, red-orange, red, red-violet – and their various tints, tones and shades (defined below). On the opposite side of the wheel, the colours are cold – yellow-green (which often appears as greeny-gold or olive), green, blue-green, blue, blue-violet and violet. Again, different values of these colours are still cool.

The hot, warm and strong colours seem visually to *advance* towards you, and the cool, pale colours *recede*; some very pale, cool colours almost fade into insignificance. So, if you use lots of bright, warm colours in a room, the eye jumps from one to another – highly stimulating and ideal for a child's playroom or a cold bathroom, but quite unsuitable for a room where you want to relax. To create an atmosphere of calm spaciousness decorate with pale, cool tints.

Neutral colours do not appear on the wheel. Most people think of beiges, creams, off-whites and tones of grey as being neutral but the only true neutrals are black and white, and a combination of black and white which forms pure grey. All the other so-called 'neutrals' are versions of one of the colours on the wheel, and they can be cold, or warm, just like their original hue – blue-grey or greeny-grey look cold, for example, while a pinky-beige or yellowish cream are warm.

Neutrals, being subtle and pale toned (in the main) usually create a quiet, relaxed atmosphere but they can be very hard to colour-match.

The colour vocabulary contains several other words worth understanding before you start colour scheming:-

Hue is used to describe a pure colour, and indicates the name of the colour (blue, green, yellow, violet, red, orange).

Shade. If you take a pure *hue* and mix it with black the result is a *shade*.

Tint. If you take a pure *hue* and mix it with white, the result is a *tint*.

Tone. If you mix a *shade* with white or a *tint* with black the result is called a *tone*. If you mix black and white together the result is a pure grey which can vary in *value* depending on the proportions used. If you mix a pure *hue* with grey the result is again called a *tone*.

Value refers to the lightness or darkness of a colour, depending on how much white or black is added – this is usually quoted as ranging from 0 (black) to 10 (white). Maroon is a dark *value* of red, pink is a light *value* of red.

Chroma or colour intensity, describes the strength of a colour and its brightness or dullness.

Monochromatic means literally *mono* 'one' and *chroma* 'intensity of colour', so 'one-colour'. Different values of one colour can be used to produce a monochromatic or

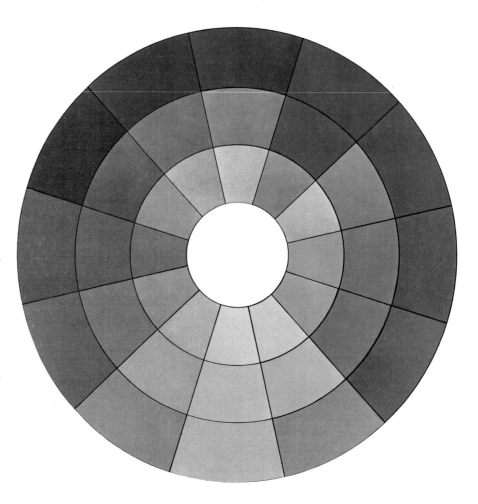

tone-on-tone effect in a room. For this type of scheme to work well there must be enough contrast of tone, from light to dark, and the colours must all stem from the same basic colour.

Greyness is a new way of measuring colour. The *greyness scale* shows any hue graduated from clear down through shades containing increasing amounts of grey – for example from bright clear yellow to dull gold.

Weight is used to distinguish the apparent lightness of the colours of any *hue* or *greyness*.

Pastel colour. The term used to describe a pale colour which has a large proportion of white in it.

Muted colour is either a *shade* or *tone* which has a fair proportion of black or grey added.

Colour theory in use. Look at your room critically, and think about size and aspect. If it is a very small third bedroom, you will probably want to make it look larger *or* cosy and intimate. On the other hand you may want a large, cold and uninviting area to be made to appear warm and welcoming, without losing the sense of space.

A cold, north-east, north or east-facing room can be brightened with a colour scheme chosen mainly from the warm half of the wheel. If it is a warm south, south-west or west-facing room, you can choose mainly from the cooler colours for your scheme.

But remember that a room decorated mainly in cold or cool colours can strike a positive chill, and one in warm colours may look a little too hot. Create a balance – or give a scheme extra impact – by introducing contrast from the opposite half of the wheel. Try soft shades of apricot in a blue and green room, a brilliant flash of Siamese pink in a room decorated mainly in tones of cool green, or a touch of jade green to 'lift' a brown, beige and terracotta colour scheme.

The neutral colours benefit from this treatment too, a few bright splashes of colour prevent a 'neutral' room from looking boring – brilliant scarlet accessories in a black, white and grey room, for example, or strong coral and turquoise contrasted with off-whites, beiges and creams.

Characteristics of colour. Colours have definite characteristics of their own and can create a particular atmosphere.

Red is a bright, exciting and dramatic 'advancing' colour, but pure red must be used with discretion because it can be overpowering. Don't use too much red if you want a restful room.

If used as the major or dominant colour, it must be relieved by neutrals such as brilliant white, beige, cream or wood tones. It can be used in large rooms successfully, but very sparingly in small rooms.

It can make you feel physically warm, so it is good for a north-east exposure or a room that does not receive much sunlight. Take care when using red in a room that gets plenty of sunlight.

Greyed shades of red – such as plummy and rose tones, have a depth of warmth and interest when used in large rooms and create a cosy atmosphere.

Pink is a pale version of red, but much more restful, has a high reflective quality, and brings a light, airy look to a room which lacks sunshine. Adds warmth to a scheme. When pink becomes lilac-pink, blue has been added, so it begins to look colder.

Orange is very similar to red and can be used in the same way. It advances, is dominant and creates a warm atmosphere. When orange becomes greyed it appears as terracotta or tan, even brownish, but remember these are warm tones. It often needs contrasting, or livening up with neutrals, particularly sparkling whites or clear creamy beige, or contrasting sharply with a cold colour.

When orange becomes less intense it becomes apricot or peach and can be used like pink.

Tans (and beiges) are extremely versatile due to their subtle warmth and natural association with all other colours.

Yellow creates a feeling of a sunny day, and has a high reflective value. Pale tones are ideal for rooms that receive little or no light, and to make small rooms appear larger. Also helps to make a cool room seem warmer.

Bright yellows *advance* and are excellent used as a focal point in small amounts. Should have a neutral background when used prominently.

Muted yellows – such as gold and mustard – appear rich, have subdued warmth and can be used in large rooms where you want to create a cosy feeling.

Yellows mixed with green become lime (in the lighter range) and olive (in the greyed range). They can become cold as they go towards green; use as greens.

Green is rich and refreshing – the colour associated with nature and spring – but at the same time it can be restful, quiet and easy-on-the-eye.

As it is a cool colour it can be used to tone down sunny rooms.

Pale greens suggest coolness and are best used in a room with plenty of sunlight. They produce a spacious, restful feeling.

Deeper greens help to create an out-of-doors atmosphere. Olive can look very dark – almost grey at night. Illuminate with particular care because the colour absorbs light.

Most greens need the addition of warm or neutral 'accents'.

Blue is one of the coolest colours and can visually change a room's atmosphere from warm to cool, especially the deeper shades of blue; becomes warmer when mixed with red to produce violet and purple tones. It is good in rooms that receive lots of sunlight, because it is low in reflectance and helps to diffuse and soften bright sunlight.

Blues are good in rooms with southern exposure, but not in northern rooms.

Excellent for small rooms, the pastel tints of blue associated with expanse of sky seem to push back the walls, giving an illusion of space.

Dark blues need contrasting with sparkling white. Icy and navy blues need a warm contrast.

Violet or Purple. The colour of royalty and pageantry. Vibrant and demanding, the richer values should be used with care. When nearer to red, it looks warm, so use as red; when closer to blue, it becomes cold, so treat as blue. The paler version of this colour, lilac, has high reflectance value, so creates an impression of space and light. Lilac can be blue-lilac and cold, or pink-lilac and warm.

Neutrals. In the main, these 'non-colours' tend to make a room seem spacious and restful, but need touches of bright colour for contrast.

The warm or cold atmosphere will come from the original source of the neutral.

Black and white used in almost equal quantities create a highly stimulating atmosphere.

COLOUR HARMONY

One of the 'problems' in interior decoration is deciding what goes with what. Basically, all pure colours or *hues* will harmonize with white or black (and in many cases pure grey); *shades* of all kinds will harmonize with black; *tints* of all kinds will harmonize with white and *tones* of all kinds will harmonize with grey.

Many attractive decorating schemes can be achieved by using one of the accepted five 'colour harmonies' and this means going back to the colour wheel. For example, a *triadic colour harmony* is the use of three colours that are an equal distance apart on the wheel such as red, yellow and blue (the primary colours), yellow-green, red-orange and blue-violet. (A scheme involving a fourth colour is called a *tetrad*.)

Adjacent colours involve the use of colours which lie next to each other on the wheel, and which are 'good neighbours'. Any portion of the wheel can be chosen, but some colour combinations are more attractive than others, for example, yellow harmonizes with yellow-orange and yellow-green.

Complementary colour harmony means using colours directly opposite each

other on the wheel, for example, red and green or blue-green and red-orange. In this harmony the selection does not have to be too strict, since red and blue can look as good together as red and green, and blue-violet can harmonise with red-orange.

A split-complementary colour harmony occurs when a basic hue is combined with two that lie adjacent on the opposite side of the circle: for example, red with blue and green (a combination frequently found in nature), or orange combined with blue-violet and blue-green.

Monochromatic colour harmony is when only one basic colour is used in varying values and intensity; this needs to be combined with a neutral – usually black or white, off-white or cream – and should have a few sharp 'accents' introduced in accessories, to prevent the scheme from being boring.

COLOUR BALANCE

It is important to use colour in the correct proportion. You can apply the 'rule of three' – 60 per cent of the room's surface in one basic colour (walls and floor); 30 per cent in a second colour (curtains and upholstery) and 10 per cent in a third or possible third and fourth colour (accents

and accessories), with a linking neutral used for woodwork and ceiling.

If you decide on a monochromatic scheme, you will need to achieve balance with the different weights of colour you use, by using a neutral effectively, and adding bright 'accents'. A green monochromatic scheme for example, might have an olive green carpet; paler grey-green walls; an even paler ceiling; with all these tones of green used for the curtain fabric. Sparkling white woodwork would bring in a neutral, and the upholstery could then include three items in different tones of green and one in brilliant scarlet. This contrast colour could also be used for some other accessories.

If you want to base a scheme on two main colours, use these in exact proportions, separated by a neutral. For example, in a kitchen with 50 per cent of the surfaces (the units) in dark brown, the walls could be orange; the ceiling apricot; the floor brown *and* orange in equal quantities; the work-tops a neutral beige. Jade green or strong turquoise could provide 'accents'.

If you want to play safe, base a room on different values of a neutral colour, creating basically a monochromatic scheme, but bringing the 'accent' colours in fairly

Above, left: a basically neutral colour scheme creates a restful atmosphere. The addition of a sharp contrast in the green chair and foliage, brings the scheme to life Right: a cool blue and white scheme is ideal for sophisticated city living, and makes a small room seem much more spacious. Cool schemes need warm accents, here provided by the sharp pink and terracotta

strongly. You might have a beige carpet, soft cream walls and ceiling, brown upholstery and creamy-white woodwork. The curtains could be in browns and beige on an off-white ground, but with coral flowers. Use coral and green for the accessories – lampshades, scatter cushions, pictures and house plants.

BASIC COLOUR SCHEMING RULES

Consider the characteristics of the various colours, and make them work for you to create atmosphere.

In a cold room, use warm colours, with contrasting (cold) colours to emphasize or accentuate them.

In a warm or sunny room, use cool colours, with warm colours for contrast.

As a link or contrast, use neutral colours. Introduce strong 'accents' into a mainly neutral scheme.

To bring a monochromatic (tone-on-tone) scheme to life, use a bold, contrasting colour.

In large rooms, use strong *advancing* colours. In small rooms, or to create a feeling of space, use pale *receding* ones.

For a relaxed atmosphere choose from the pale tones and cooler colours, and don't mix too many in the one scheme.

To stimulate, use vibrant tones. Two colours facing each other on the wheel, used in equal quantities, make the most stimulating scheme of all.

If you want objects to merge into the background, use closely blended colours to conceal them.

If you want something to stand out, use contrasting colours for emphasis.

COLOUR MATCHING

Start with an idea of the atmosphere you want to create and the colours you want to use, then do what most professional decorators do – choose the flooring first. This is often the largest, uncluttered area of a room since most walls are 'broken up' with doors and windows, or have furniture standing against them, and ceilings are not frequently looked up to!

When deciding the type, quality, colour and design of floorcovering, you may well find two or three 'possibles'. Ask for samples of all of them, and if the shop can't supply them, write to the manufacturers for adequate samples. You can then take these with you when you select the wallcovering or paint; paint for the woodwork; upholstery and curtain fabric, etc.

NOTE: if you are a first-time colour schemer, or find colour-matching very difficult, start off with a patterned item which incorporates several colours. This can be a floorcovering, wallpaper, or curtain or upholstery fabric. Then use one of the colours in the design for your flooring; another for your upholstered furniture; another for walls and woodwork, and a fourth for 'accents' and accessories etc. – depending on the item selected for the starting-off point.

The importance of 'sampling'. Nobody can 'carry' colour accurately in their eye, and there is nothing worse than a mismatch, so get samples of all the items you intend to use *before* spending any money.

Some people try to play safe with a neutral scheme, but neutrals can be the hardest colours of all to match. Off-white furniture, for example, comes in many different tones of creamy white, so you could put an off-white carpet with it only to find this makes the furniture look dirty – or vice versa. Just as much care has to be taken with colour-matching for neutrals as it does with the strong primary colours.

When shopping, always try to see as large a piece as possible. Fabric should be

unrolled, and seen as a 'drop'; rolls of wallpaper unwrapped (if possible, two placed side-by-side if it has a bold pattern). The same applies to flooring – in the case of tiles, look at these forming a square of at least 1 m (3 ft) – or in a mirrored box, which creates the impression of a much larger area. Items should be looked at on the correct plane – flooring horizontally *and* at ground level; wallcoverings vertically, both opposite and next to the light; curtain fabric vertically, and *against* the light; kitchen unit colours vertically and their worktops horizontally, and so on.

Making a colour board. This does not have to be a complicated production – use a piece of stiff card or an offcut of hardboard and a bulldog clip. Clip your scale room plan and room measurements (see *Planning on Paper*) to the board, plus a note of the various quantities you will require (see *Calculating Quantities*). Add any catalogues, samples of existing items, or other colour guides, and clip your new samples to the board as you get them.

If you find it difficult to reach a decision, and have several different options open to you, make several colour boards for the same room. When your board(s) is (are) complete, take it (them) home and look at the samples in the room where you will use them and on the actual plane they will be used (see above). Look at them in daylight and the artificial light under which they will be seen. Leave the board (or boards) in the room for a few days until you, and the family, are sure which scheme is the one you all like.

Light and colour. Colour-matching in different lights is important because colours can look quite different according to the type of light, and can also seem to change depending on the surface on which they are used.

Quite often, the same-coloured floor-covering used throughout the ground floor of a house appears to be a slightly different shade in each room. One wall – often the one opposite the window – can seem to be several tones lighter than the other three, even though the same paint or wallpaper has been chosen. This is because the light bounces off the surface in a different way.

The texture of a surface can absorb light differently too, and this makes colour look different. Smooth surfaces, which reflect light, make colours seem lighter, brighter and more intense. Rough surfaces, which absorb light, make colours appear darker and reduced in intensity. Consequently, a

shiny gloss paint will look brighter or lighter than the same colour in a matt emulsion; the colour of a tweedy-textured fabric may seem more subtle than a brocade or a *moiré* taffeta, even though the same dye has been used; a 'velvet' pile Wilton carpet will look quite different from a cushioned vinyl in the same colour. So it is important to collect actual samples when colour-matching and judge the effects of light on the different surfaces. Daylight, domestic and shop lighting are all likely to affect colour in different ways. You may choose something in a shop under fluorescent lighting and find it looks totally different at home in your own domestic lighting. This is particularly true of some shades of grey, green and gold, which look fairly clear and bright in daylight or under shop lighting, but look very drab and dull at night when the curtains are drawn and the lamps are lit.

Blending old and new. Usually, when you are redecorating and planning a colour scheme you will have to incorporate existing items into the new scheme. Whether they be carpet (or other floor-covering), upholstery, curtains or possibly lovely accessories (like a collection of glass or a dinner service), this old friend will become the starting point for your new scheme, and you will need colour samples clipped to your colour board when you shop around for the rest of the scheme.

If you don't have a spare piece of carpet, cushion or button from the upholstery, or extra wall tiles, etc., colour match to wool, cotton, paper, embroidery silks – even a paint manufacturer's colour chart. If the existing item is patterned, try to take samples of all the colours – also, half-close your eyes to get the overall impression of colour and take a sample of this, too.

PATTERN AND PLAIN

Pattern and texture must be chosen as carefully as colours and blended together with equal skill. Colour creates the atmosphere, but it is the pattern which sets the style. Certain traditional designs are necessary if you want to decorate in a specific period style. Some pattern should be introduced into a scheme to give contrast and an extra visual dimension.

Even 'plain' colour will not look absolutely plain because the surface may well have texture interest and look different in different lights (see *Light and Colour*). Plain items can also be mixed together to create a patterned surface – tiles laid chequerboard, dog's tooth or herringbone fashion, for example, or a group of pictures or

prints arranged together on a plain wall.

Where to find pattern. Pattern can be printed on papers, wallcoverings and fabrics; stencilled, or painted on walls; added with friezes and borders; woven into carpets; printed on other floorcoverings; sealed into ceramic tiles; laminated on to work surfaces and so on. Pattern can also be provided by light filtering through shutters or a blind; the silhouette of a carved chair-back; the basketweave texture on cane furniture, or the grouping together of a collection of objects.

A sense of proportion. Big bold patterns or very busy ones are dominant, just like the strong *advancing* colours, so they create a lively, stimulating atmosphere. They can be just right for a large forbidding hall, a chilly bathroom or a child's playroom; they can also make a room look very small and claustrophobic, so avoid them if you want to create a feeling of space.

Small patterns can add interest to a scheme without spoiling a restful mood. You can use them to create a spacious atmosphere because, seen from a distance, they look like an interesting surface rather than a definite design, so they act rather like a pale, cool *receding* colour.

Simple stripes and checks can give patterns interest too, without looking too hectic – like neutral colours they can provide a link between patterns of a different size or type, or between patterned and plain surfaces.

Scale is important too. Very small patterns look lost on large areas of wall, floor or fabric. Big, bold designs look silly on small surfaces, particularly if the pattern repeat is not fully shown or it has to be cut at an unfortunate place.

Right: colour-matching should not be a hit-and-miss affair! Making a colour board is the way to tackle the problem. Use a stiff board or piece of card, a stout clip, add your room plan and any samples or colour swatches for existing items, and add extra samples as you build up your room scheme

improved with a breath of 'country air' provided by a floral pattern.

Mixing of scale is easier with geometrics than with florals – a small squared pattern on the floorcovering can be echoed in a large squared design on the wallpaper, but geometrics must be similar in type if they are to settle happily in the same room. Some can have a distinctly traditional look, although most geometric designs nearly always look modern, and are better used in a fairly sophisticated setting in a modern home. They also tend to create a rather stark atmosphere and to be highly stimulating, so do not use them for a room where you want a restful or cosy atmosphere.

Visualizing. Translating the effect of a small sample on to a large area can be difficult. So try to see as large a sample as possible, or a picture of the pattern used in a room setting, or two pieces of wallcovering or widths of fabric side-by-side.

As rich and strong colours and patterns *advance*, they will look much bolder and will tend to dominate a room when used over a large area. Pale colours and small patterns *recede* and so they can fade into insignificance when used over a large area.

A sense of balance. In a well-balanced scheme, probably two or, at the most, three surfaces should be patterned, unless specifically co-ordinated designs are used, when more are acceptable. If you mix together too many patterns, particularly of different types, the result could be a mess.

Pattern can be practical. Choose a hard-wearing patterned floorcovering for areas used by all the family, or in heavy traffic areas such as the hall, kitchen, family living rooms and childrens' playrooms. Where walls take a lot of punishment from sticky fingers, a washable patterned surface is practical. Similarly, upholstery in a family living room should not be perfectly plain. Some compromise will be necessary, however, since all these surfaces cannot be too busily patterned.

Avoid using very strong, dominant pattern on surfaces which are difficult to change. Kitchen worktops, for example, are better with simple, textured effects in fairly quiet colours; bathroom tiles can be simply veined with colour, or have a stippled effect, and have a few patterned tiles let in.

It is sensible to use the bolder patterns in a room on the surface which is easiest to change – the walls, for instance, which can be re-papered or painted. Use simpler patterns and textured effects for floor-coverings and upholstery, except in areas

like kitchens and bathrooms, where a good design can offset the often heavy look of plain units and bathroom equipment.

Pattern types. Pattern breaks down roughly into three types – florals, geometrics and the more 'neutral' stripes, checks and abstracts. Florals can be used together successfully, so can geometrics, but the two types of design do not mix together very well, though the more 'neutral' stripes, diamond trellis and checks can be used with either, to help create a balance.

There are also specifically traditional patterns which can be used to create a period scheme, such as Regency stripes, Tudor tapestry, classical Greek-key and so on, and certain distinctly 'foreign' influences such as Oriental and ethnic.

Romantic or Impressionistic, slightly misty floral designs can create a soft, pretty, feminine room. In a small room, or an attic with sloping ceilings a tiny mini-print floral looks effective; the definite flowing florals in the *art nouveau* style are particularly right in a Victorian or Edwardian house, just as the more modern abstract, geometric, or stylized floral treatments suit a modern house or flat.

Try fresh looking florals in a kitchen, conservatory or sunroom. Small town houses, dark basement rooms, rather dreary or characterless flats can often be

Top left: bold-patterned flooring adds visual interest to a richly coloured bathroom
Top right: a room with mainly plain surfaces is given an ethnic look by clever use of brightly patterned rugs and cushions
Above: pattern can unify a bitty or cluttered room, and make ugly shapes seem less prominent. In a small area like this kitchen, restrict the scheme to a main colour with a neutral, such as white

Texture types. Basically, texture divides into the same three groups as colour – cool, warm and natural (as opposed to neutral).

The cool ones feel cool to the touch, and are often shiny. This group includes ceramic tiles, laminates, chrome and glass, gloss paint, mirrors and metal.

Warm textures feel warm to the touch and are frequently matt, such as flock wallcoverings, tweed, fur, dense-piled carpet and velvet.

Natural textures are normally rougher and 'honest' – cane, cork, brick, slate, wood, hessian, Berber-style looped pile carpet and so on.

Balancing textures. Texture is both visual *and* sensual – you have to 'feel' your way towards using it skilfully. Getting the correct balance of textures in a room is as important as mixing the right colours, or patterned and plain surfaces. A room composed of all shiny materials, for example – foil wallcovering, mirror tiles, chrome, glass and laminated furniture, satin drapes and a silky nylon carpet could be as disturbing to the eye as a room decorated with unrelieved bold patterns. At the other extreme, a room entirely decorated with matt surfaces can look dull and lifeless. So combine warm, matt surfaces with cool, shiny ones, and introduce natural textures for contrast, or as a link. This is particularly important if you are building up a *monochromatic* scheme (see *Colour scheming*) – there should be enough texture contrast to make the scheme interesting.

If you have created a scheme where the balance of textures is too weighted in one direction, you can save it by introducing the contrast in 'accents' and accessories, just as you can enliven a boring colour scheme by bringing in sharp splashes of colour, or tone down an over-busy room by painting at least one wall with matt emulsion, and adding plain, natural-textured accessories.

Atmosphere and style. Textures create atmosphere too, and help to set the style of a room. Ceramic tiles, gloss paint, plastics and laminates are cool and efficient; shaggy-pile carpets, woven wool fabrics, leather upholstery and velvet are cosy; silks, brocades and satins are luxurious and elegant; lace and open-weave sheer fabrics are fragile and feminine.

Texture, like certain patterns, can also help to create a definite style or a period flavour. Exposed brick, slate and stone, wood *cladding*, chrome and glass are all distinctly modern in feeling, while wood

Large, bold designs can make a surface look smaller and can create an oppressive atmosphere in a medium-sized or small room; some of the smaller patterns and lighter looking designs can make a room seem more spacious and bright.

Co-ordinates. If you want to use several patterns, but are a little unsure how to combine them successfully, use one of the co-ordinated ranges available at all prices.

'Co-ordinates' as applied to home decoration can mean a matching design printed on wallcovering and fabric – although they rarely completely match because they are printed on different base materials; co-ordinated designs within a separate fabric or wallcovering range, or a combination of both.

The same pattern can be used in different scales; one can be the positive and the other the negative of the same design; or one can be the mirror image of the other. Sometimes a fabric or wallcovering is printed with a fairly bold design and the co-ordinate has a repeat of part of the design – perhaps as a background, or a single motif repeated on a plain ground, or part of the design printed as a border down the edge of a plain fabric or wallcovering, or printed as a separate border or frieze on paper. Linens, curtains and bathroom accessories can be similarly co-ordinated. All

these ranges are easier to work with than trying to co-ordinate two or more individual designs.

Remember, co-ordinated designs create a spacious effect, so carrying pattern through from one area to another can make a small house or flat look much larger. 'Through' living rooms, or separate sitting and dining rooms with a dividing door or wall between should be decorated harmoniously, but often co-ordinated designs are more successful than using exactly the same scheme throughout. Main bedrooms with a bathroom *en suite* and kitchen/dining rooms also respond well to this treatment.

TEXTURE

Texture applies to the surface character of a material – how it feels to the touch and how it reflects or absorbs light, sometimes making identical colours look quite different when they are used on two separate surfaces.

Some colours appear dull and lifeless on a flat surface while on an interestingly textured surface they can look positively vibrant. Smooth surfaces reflect light and consequently show up any faults, so gloss paint or foil wallcoverings are not a good idea for poorly plastered walls. Dull, warmer textures absorb light and so help to disguise a bad surface.

panelling, brass, wrought iron, velvet and lace are more traditional. Some, like the moiré stripes, and brocade fabrics and wallcoverings are almost synonymous with the Regency style of decorating, while flock wallpaper, plush and chenille fabrics and brass oil lamps are all 'Victorian'.

DESIGNING EYE

Colour, pattern and texture are all used to transform a room – to give it a certain atmosphere, to make it practical and functional perhaps, or to suggest a period flavour. But it is also important to relate colour, pattern and texture to the architectural style of the house. If you have a very modern home with large picture windows, vast areas of exposed brick, stone or slate and very little wall surface that needs decorating, it makes sense to use bold pattern or interesting texture on the curtain fabric, with plain colours and subtle textures on the walls to enhance the brick, slate or stone – and to furnish mainly in modern style. Flock wallcovering, Regency-striped brocade and Dralon velvet upholstery would look out of place.

On the other hand, if you have a fairly modern 'box' with square rooms you can add character by decorating in either modern or traditional style – or a mixture of both. But beware of over-powering

pattern or texture on small areas. And if you have a modern pseudo-Georgian home or a property built in the 1930s, you do not have to stick slavishly to the style of the times, although it is worth considering taking the best of design from the period, and combining it with modern materials, textures and colours.

If you have a genuine old house, never be tempted to over-modernize it. By all means add up-to-date plumbing and central heating (see *Planning the home*) but if it has beautiful architectural features, decorate to emphasize these, and choose colours, patterns and textures to create the correct style. If you live in a thatched cottage, with exposed beams, cross-beaming on the walls and small lattice-paned windows, paint the wall area between the beams in a plain colour to show them off to advantage, or use small mini-print floral wallpapers in the bedrooms and choose small traditional patterned fabric for curtains.

If, however, your house is a vast Victorian vicarage you can use bold design and strong colour as dramatically as you like – again search out the right type of pattern – one which might well have been used by the Victorians, but possibly with new, more acceptable colouring. Look for large items of furniture of the period, and make them individual by stripping or

painting and re-upholstering. That is the essence of interior design – putting together various materials to create a scheme which will dramatize or enhance a room – give it atmosphere and style, while not losing sight of the fact that homes are for living in.

Search for inspiration. If you don't have a natural flair for colour scheming and pattern mixing and matching, don't despair. Look at books on the subject, and read the specialist home-making magazines. Collect a file of pictures and schemes which attract you, cut from magazines, newspapers, etc. and try to analyze why they are successful. Look at the 'sets' for television dramas, stage productions and films with a 'designing eye'. Professional set designers always plan with a person (or family) and a certain lifestyle in view and have thought about the architectural style of the set. Occasionally the end result is purposely a mistake or a mess but, particularly with period drama, the greatest possible attention is paid to accuracy and authenticity, so period sets are most helpful if you want to recreate the same era and flavour in your own home.

Visits to museums which have specific displays of furniture, rooms, wallcoverings and fabrics are also helpful, and local art galleries and craft shops can be a rich source of ideas. A lovely painting can provide a good starting-off point for a colour scheme, or a hand-crafted item can become a focal point for a room design.

Creating an illusion. For most of us, the home of our dreams is likely to be on a small scale, and with rooms which are far from perfect; but with clever use of colour, pattern and texture you can emphasize good features, tone down bad ones and play all sorts of eye-deceiving tricks.

If a room is very small, you can decorate in pale *receding* colours, use mostly plain or muted patterns on the main surfaces and choose some shiny 'reflective' textures. A monochromatic scheme, with the ceiling, walls and woodwork all decorated in the same pale tone will create an illusion of space. It also helps to increase the apparent size of the floor, by choosing a plain, light-coloured flooring and painting the skirting boards in the same colour – or by having floor or carpet tiles in two different colours laid diagonally, so the eye is drawn from corner to corner (the largest dimension), or chequerboard-fashion.

Mirrors can increase the size of a room visually and, strategically placed, give reflected light as well as a mirror-image of

creating a cosy corner. The furniture arrangement can also help. A settee, facing the sitting end, might be placed at right-angles to the long wall and backed by a sideboard or units facing the dining area. Split-level treatments also help.

To make a room look longer and narrower, use a strong vertical pattern on the side walls and a plain treatment on the end ones. You can also lay a floorcovering with a definite linear pattern to run the length of the room (lay it across the width for the opposite result).

The height of ceilings is another frequent problem – they are either too tall or too low. Many Victorian and Edwardian houses have high ceilings which looked right at that time because of the large, heavy furniture, and the ornate fireplaces and overmantels. Once this type of room is modernized (always think more than twice before ripping out a genuine period fireplace) and furnished with smaller pieces, the room can look top-heavy.

surrounding wall area to contrast. This is also a good way to treat a large character-less area of wall, and used on one wall only of a long narrow room can make it look more square.

If the ceiling still seems disproportionately high, don't resort to false ceilings. Add some tall pieces of furniture or mount a wall of book shelves, from floor to ceiling. Put back a correct style fireplace, if the original one was removed (if you don't want open fires you can put in a false fireplace), fill the opening with a sheet of slate, marble or laminate and stand an electric fire on the hearth.

In some conversions, where one room has been divided to create two or three (often to make kitchens or bathrooms in flat conversions), you can make a visually decorative false ceiling. Pin white-painted garden trellis to battens suspended across the room at picture-rail height, after painting the area above the trellis with a strong or rich colour. Slatted wood or a special

the room. In a small bedroom, a wall of units with mirror-faced doors are practical and decorative.

If the room is *box-like* as well as small, this can be corrected by treating one wall differently. Use either a slightly different colour, texture or pattern on it (or the mirror treatment previously described), or even paint a mural simulating a vista. If this seems too ambitious, 'pattern' one wall with pictures and prints grouped round a mirror. You can also make it look more interesting by putting up coving, painting the ceiling a tone or two lighter than the walls and picking out the coving in a neutral colour.

If a room is long and narrow, as often happens when two rooms are made into one, you will need to make the two smaller end walls appear closer to one another. If there are windows at both ends, you can achieve this by having boldly patterned curtains, from floor to ceiling and wall to wall. If there are windows at one end only, use a co-ordinated range of wallcoverings and fabrics, so you can still use the same design at both ends, or use strong, plain colour in interesting textures for the wall and window treatment. Another alternative is to treat just the chimney-breast on one long wall differently – and boldly, so it draws the eye towards it – or treat the recesses each side of the breast dramatically. You can also make a break in the floorcovering, so that the sitting area is more clearly defined. Use the same flooring throughout, then place a large rug or carpet square at the sitting end of the room,

The solution is to make the walls look less tall by colour-matching the ceiling and floor and picking out cornices, covings or ceiling mouldings in a contrasting neutral, such as white. Any other horizontal line – such as a picture rail or frieze – picked out in the same neutral will also help, and so will a definite horizontal pattern on the walls and at the windows. Wood cladding, fixed horizontally, is another good decorative treatment. You can also make wall panels by pinning up simple picture-frame beading – have a bold pattern or strong colour inside the panel and paint the

Far left: pretty floral wallpaper sets the traditional style of this bathroom. The chequerboard tiled floor helps to create an illusion of space
Top left: a strong ceiling treatment with the horizontal lines of picture rail, cornice and frieze picked out in a contrasting colour help break the height of a tall room
Above: bold vertical stripes on all walls will make a low ceiling look much higher. The light ceiling, dark floor and long, low seating units help the illusion

system of slats like venetian blinds can be similarly used to make an attractive false ceiling, without being too oppressive.

When ceilings are *too low*, try the reverse treatment – strong vertical patterns on the walls or at the windows, wood cladding fixed vertically, or ceiling and walls all painted in the same pale neutral with toning vertical venetian blinds forming a wall of window. Remove any horizontal lines such as picture rails, and take the decorations up to the ceiling. Use a contrasting floor colour and furnish with low, very simple designs. Don't forget that ceilings can be mirrored effectively.

If the *ceiling slopes*, as in some attic rooms, conversions and extensions, decorate the walls and ceiling as one, using a plain colour or small overall floral pattern – avoid stripes, geometrics or very strong colours. Wood cladding on the sloping ceiling and walls of attics can be an effective treatment too, and provides extra insulation.

Ugly features can be hidden or disguised. If there are old, large radiators, for example, or a wall is festooned with pipes, paint these in the same colour as the wall so they merge into the background. An even better treatment for runs of pipes is to

decorate the wall with a patterned paper and paint the pipes to match the predominant colour in the paper. If a fireplace is ugly, paint this the same colour as the chimney-breast or wall.

If you want to draw attention to a decorative feature, paint it to contrast with the surrounding area, or paper it boldly and keep the other surfaces plain (or vice versa).

If you are a little nervous about the various decorative treatments suggested, first make an elevated plan of the room, and then add overlays on tracing paper or acetate sheets, or make a model (see *Planning on Paper*).

ACCENTS AND ACCESSORIES

The importance of the right finishing touches is often under-estimated. But, in fact, the addition of pictures, lampshades, cushions, ornaments, plants and flowers can unify a bitty scheme, save a dull one or tone down a too stimulating atmosphere.

A group of objects always looks more interesting than a few things placed sparsely round the room. Think of unusual ways to display a collection and it will more than double its effectiveness. Glass, for example, always looks better with the light shining through it, so if you have

blank windows which are not overlooked, fix narrow glass shelves across the reveal (screw up the window and remove handles etc. first) and display a collection of coloured glass there. This is also a good treatment for 'porthole' type windows and small recessed ones each side of a chimney-breast.

Small, colourful objects look even more effective arranged on a piece of mirror glass – and this treatment works well with flowers and houseplants, reflected from behind or below. Houseplants also look marvellous if they are grouped on a glass-topped table, and illuminated from below.

Always choose accessories in a variety of shapes and textures. Scatter cushions, for example, can be made from a mixture of pattern and plain fabrics, or embroidered, patchworked, crocheted, knitted – and in several different sizes as well as shapes.

One nice way of displaying small pictures, and other objects, is to hang an empty frame on the wall (you can make one from picture-frame beading) and group the objects interestingly within it.

Don't underestimate the use of bathroom jars, cosmetics, etc. in the bath-room and bedroom; the addition of storage jars and attractive cooking implements in the kitchen; table linen, china and glass in the dining room.

Accents and accessories add interest to a dull scheme or 'tone down' an over-busy one. Use of an accent colour (centre left) to contrast can enliven a simple scheme

HOME DECORATING

Once you have planned your home, decided on the various surface treatments and chosen the colour schemes, it only remains for you to get down to the 'chore' of decorating! It can be a very enjoyable and rewarding chore, so long as you 'start simple' and work up to the more difficult jobs. Do not try to do anything in too much of a rush – always allow plenty of time, buy the best tools you can afford, and hire those you do not want to buy. Remember, too, that new decorations must be applied to properly prepared surfaces; the time and labour involved will seem well worth while when you step back to admire the result.

DECORATING TOOLS AND EQUIPMENT

The starting-off point for any decorating is an adequate supply of basic tools. This you can add to as and when you can afford it, or as your expertise grows and you are ready to tackle more complicated jobs. Always buy the best quality you can afford; save on decorating materials rather than tools if you have to economize.

If you are working to a very tight budget or storage space is a problem, you can hire most decorating tools from neighbourhood decorating hire shops; these are also useful if you don't know your capabilities as a do-it-yourselfer, and want to 'test the water' before investing in your own tools.

PAINTING – INDOORS

Most tools for painting are best bought outright rather than hired. You will need:

Paint brushes. Assorted sizes, 12 mm, 25 mm, 50 mm, 75 mm ($\frac{1}{2}$, 1, 2, 3 inch) brushes for woodwork; a 100–150 mm (6 inch) brush for painting large areas of walls and ceilings. Buy the best quality you can afford – top quality brushes have bristles of varying lengths which taper to a helpful wedge when loaded with paint. The best bristles are hog – others are made from a mixture of natural and synthetic fibres or just from synthetics.

Paint rollers are made from plastic foam, lambswool and mohair, and some have removable 'sleeves' so that you can replace or change them when they become worn or you need to use a different type. They are much faster in use than a brush and therefore most convenient if you have large areas to cover.

Roller trays. The roller is used in conjunction with a tray, which is sloped so that you can load the roller then remove the excess paint by working it up and down the slope. Plastic trays are easier to clean and do not rust, but metal trays usually have flaps underneath which means they can be hooked securely to the stepladder while you work.

Paint pads come in various shapes and sizes and have a felted fibre surface backed with foam attached to a handle. They are dipped in paint, and the loaded pad is then drawn across the surface to be painted. They are useful for getting into awkward corners, and really come into their own if you want to stencil a pattern onto a wall.

Paint sprayers cut down decorating time and they are ideal for use outside if you have large areas to cover, but the surfaces all round the area being painted have to be masked. Sprayers are not often used indoors because they release a fine spray into the atmosphere; for this reason it is wise always to wear a mask if working inside with a paint sprayer. You can hire paint spraying machines, and this is the most

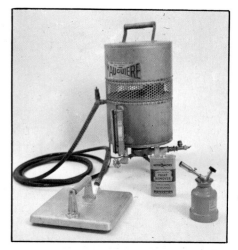

practical thing to do if you want to try out the technique, or want to cover a large area very quickly. Aerosols do the same job and are a sensible buy if you want to spray a small area such as a radiator, or a piece of fitted furniture, but they work out prohibitively expensive for large expanses of wall or woodwork.

Paint kettle. This is an optional item but important if you are using emulsion paint. Paint is transferred to the kettle from the can and stirred well (unless it is a non-stir paint). Paint kettles have a wider top than a can, so they are practical if you are using a large brush, and they have a handle which hooks conveniently onto a stepladder.

Cutting-in tool or **paint shield.** Another optional item, this 'masking' tool prevents paint getting onto glass and other surfaces adjacent to the area being painted.

Stepladder. Most decorating jobs involve

climbing up and down, so a stable stepladder is essential. Buy the folding type with a platform at the top. When using ladders, *safety* must not be overlooked. If you buy a secondhand ladder or hire one, make sure that it is in a good state of repair, with firm treads. The same safety check is important if you have not used your ladder for some time and it has possibly been stored in a damp place. To check the treads, particularly of long ladders (not the step type), lay the ladder on the ground and walk along the treads.

Apart from these basic essential tools for painting woodwork, metalwork and walls, further equipment may be needed if you are painting a ceiling or large wall area (see *How to Wallpaper*). You will also need the following tools for the all important preparation work:

Scrapers, strippers, shavehooks for scraping walls or woodwork to remove old, perished or flaking paint.

The tools of the trade vary according to the job to be done. Top left are stripping tools for preparation work. Below are preparatory and painting tools. Buy the best you can afford and look after them well, cleaning paint brushes after every decorating session and protecting the bristles as shown. Scrapers should be lightly greased before being stored in a dry place

Blow lamp/torch may be needed if you are going to burn off a lot of old paint-work, but this is a tool which can be hired.

Sanding block and abrasive paper for rubbing down paintwork, to give a smooth surface for repainting. The abrasive paper is wrapped round the block and held firmly in place by strong clips to make the job easier and avoid sore hands and broken nails. You can, of course, improvise with a small offcut of wood in place of a block but those clips are very helpful.

Filling knife for filling small holes and cracks or for renewing and trimming putty.

Sponge for wiping up small spills and removing paint from window panes and so on.

Sundries. Strong rubber gloves, old newspapers, heavy cotton or plastic dustsheets (you could use old sheets for this purpose) and a supply of old cloths will also be useful, unless the painting job is a very minor one. You will also need paint thinners, removers, strippers, brush cleaners (for some oil-based paints) and proprietary cleaner for washing down old paintwork and/or walls.

'Paintmate'. This latest innovation in painting equipment is a completely self-contained, portable powered painting system which makes painting blissfully simple and clean. The specially formulated paint (available as a wood primer, plus Vinyl matt, silk and gloss), comes in its own plastic container with a plugged lid. You just shake the paint, place it – container and all – in the Paintmate drum and close the lid. Then you insert a transparent 'delivery tube' into the plug hole, fit a specially designed roller, pad or brush onto the control handle, fit a soda syphon bulb into the carrier, press a button and the head is primed with paint via the 'delivery tube'. Heads are interchangeable and pads/roller sleeves can be thrown away if you don't like cleaning, although the paint will wash out under the tap. A roller, three paint pads and two brush heads are available with the kit, or can be bought separately. There is a clip so that the machine can be attached to belt or stepladder, and a handle so that it can be carried over your arm.

    This ingenious system can be used for painting walls, ceiling, metal and wood-work, inside and out.

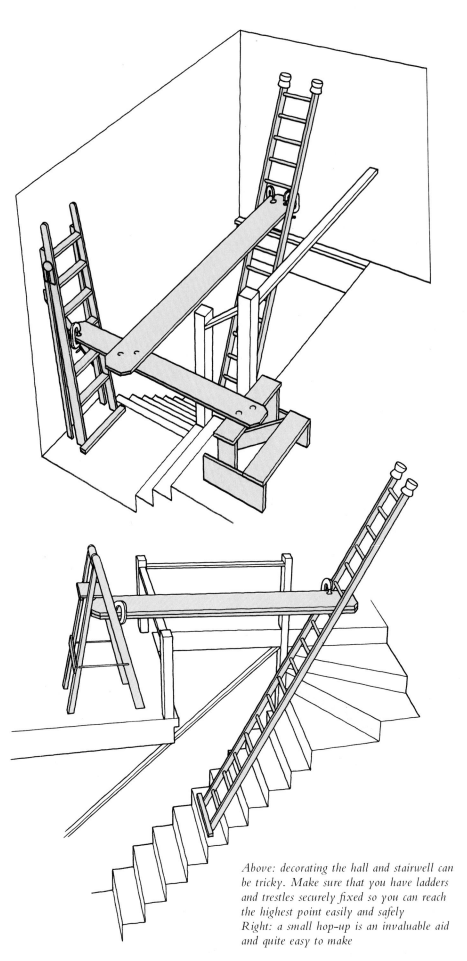

Above: decorating the hall and stairwell can be tricky. Make sure that you have ladders and trestles securely fixed so you can reach the highest point easily and safely
Right: a small hop-up is an invaluable aid and quite easy to make

CLEANING TOOLS

When decorating it is essential to clean up as you go along, and to keep your tools clean and in good working order. Paint brushes need not be cleaned every evening, if you are painting again the next day – instead, store them upright in a jar of water, just up to the shank.

When the job is finished, wipe excess paint off brushes or rollers onto old newspaper. If you have been using *emulsion* paint, simply wash the brushes or rollers under the tap, carefully squeeze out excess moisture and shake dry. If you used *oil-based paint with easy-brush-care properties*, work the brush up and down in a solution of water and detergent, repeat with fresh solution, rinse out in warm water and shake dry. Rollers can be cleaned by working vigorously on the corrugations of the tray, filled with a detergent/water solution. Rinse and shake dry. If you use *traditional oil-based paint*, clean the brushes with turps, turpentine substitute, white spirit or proprietary paint brush cleaner, then wash them thoroughly, rinse and shake dry. Leave in an airy place to dry (don't put brushes or rollers on boilers, radiators or similar hot places), then wrap brushes individually in newspaper, greaseproof, oiled paper or polythene, and store flat to avoid crushing the bristles – to preserve the pile on rollers, they are best stored hanging up.

PAINTING – OUTSIDE

Many of the tools listed under *Painting – indoors* can also be used for exterior decorating, but you will need some additional items.

Ladders. You will probably need a set of long, extending ladders. It is more practical to hire these unless you are likely to use them frequently. Sometimes neighbours club together to buy a set, which they can all use.

Ensure that ladders (bought or hired) are at least 60 to 90 cm (2 to 3 ft) taller than the highest point to be reached, after allowing for at least a 3-rung overlap once the ladder is extended. Make sure that they are safely positioned before you start climbing – slant about 30 cm (1 ft) away from the wall to every 1.22 m (4 ft) of ladder height, and wedge the base firmly. Always store long ladders in a locked garage or shed when not in use, padlocking them to a shelf, bracket or other fixed item so that burglars cannot make 'climb-and-entry' use of them. Don't be tempted to stretch too far from the top of a ladder – it is safer

to get down and move the ladder; otherwise you may arrive at the bottom in a sorry, crumpled heap.

Scaffolding or tower platform. If the exterior painting job is extensive (decorating outside walls for example), a simple scaffolding or tower platform is much more sensible than a ladder – you can get these with 'jacking feet' which ensure a level base on which to construct the platform. It is nearly always better to hire, than buy this type of equipment. Get quotes from several hire companies, since they can vary. At the same time, check whether they will arrange delivery and collection of the hired equipment if it is large, heavy – or both! If you don't know how it works, ask for instructions.

Wire brushes for removing rust, corrosion and loose material from metal and walls.

Extra paint brushes – these may well be needed, especially a large, strong-bristled wall brush or bannister brush if you plan to paint the walls with masonry paint.

S-Hook for hanging the paint kettle or can from the ladder.

Trowels for repair to rendering, filling large holes and repointing brickwork.

WALLPAPERING

Again some of the tools will already be in your basic tool kit, but you may well need these extra items.

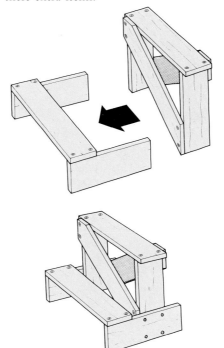

Ladders. When papering ceilings and walls, it is frequently necessary to have two ladders with a *Scaffold board* positioned between them, so that you can balance on this while working at ceiling height. These can be hired.

Paper holders. These are optional, but helpful if you are papering a ceiling for the first time, and do not have a helper. The paper is folded up, concertina fashion, and placed on the flat tray at the top of the holder.

Special platforms. If you are decorating the stairway and hall (don't make this the first decorating job you tackle) and the ceiling is very high, you may need a special platform to reach. Some can be balanced on the stair at one end and scaffold tubing at the other. It is best to hire this type of equipment.

Hop-up. Also optional, this is a wide two-step mini platform ideal for reaching awkward corners, like the area above and over the bath. A reasonably handy person can make one, but they can be bought or hired.

Scrapers and strippers. These are necessary for removing old wallpaper.

Steaming machine (sometimes called a *Stripping machine*). You may need one of these if the paper has been overpainted (particularly with gloss paint), or is a varnished washable one, or layers of paper have been built up over the years. These machines are powered by cylinders of bottled gas with a tube-like attachment (rather like the upholstery fitting on a vacuum cleaner) and a flat rectangular plate which has small holes on its sole. The plate, or iron, is pressed against the paper, and steam released through the sole peels the paper (scoring it first will speed the process and is in fact essential if the paper has been varnished over). You will need to work hard to strip off the old paper, and these machines make rather a lot of noise. They can be hired from most decoration hire specialists.

Wallpaper pasting table. These usually fold up and are light and easy to carry round. You can use a kitchen table instead, so long as its surface is large enough, but it is not sensible to cut and paste wallpaper on a good dining table – even if you do protect the surface – as accidents can happen. If you are using a ready-pasted wallcovering it is still useful to have a table

Paperhanging tools include a trestle table (which can be hired), scissors, brushes, a plumb line, seam roller and trimming knife

for measuring and cutting the lengths, but not essential. Pasting tables can be hired, but they are fairly cheap to buy and are a worthwhile investment if you plan to do a lot of decorating. Alternatively, you can improvise by using a flush door, taken off the hinges and laid over a table or across two chairs.

Wallpaper scissors and trimming knife. Buy the best you can afford, and get proper paper hangers' scissors as these have long blades which make cutting much easier. If you are using a hand-printed paper or specialist imported wallcovering you may need a *Wallpaper trimmer*, to remove the 'selvedge' edges, although scissors can be used. If you have never decorated before, try to persuade your supplier to trim the paper for you if you buy this type. Most ordinary wallcoverings are sold pre-trimmed.

Rule or measure. This should be made of wood or metal as fabric tapes stretch in use.

Pencil to mark wall and/or paper.

Plumb line or plumb-bob and piece of string to ensure that the paper hangs vertically.

Paste bucket and paste brush. The bucket can be metal or plastic, but must be wide enough to allow you to dip the paste brush in easily. Tie a piece of string across the top of the bucket to wipe excess paste off the brush. Always use a proper pasting brush (not an old paint brush) for paste. If you are using one of the wallcoverings where you paste the wall (this applies to some hessians and other fabrics, and poly-ethylene wallcoverings) you may prefer to use a *roller* to paste the wall, preferably a foam plastic one. Buy a new one, or a new 'sleeve' and keep this specially for pasting; the paste can be poured into a roller tray if your bucket is not large enough to take the roller, or you find it difficult to control the amount of paste collected.

Seam roller. A small, firm roller used to smooth the join when two pieces of wallcovering have been hung edge-to-edge. *Do not* use a seam roller on an embossed or textured wallcovering as it flattens the surface and the joins become obvious.
NOTE: you can buy firm, slightly wider, heavier 'smoothing' rollers for use with contoured vinyl wallcoverings. The roller smoothes over the entire strip of material once hung.

Paperhangers' brush. A special wide, short-bristle brush with a hand grip rather than a handle; this is used to brush out the strips of wallcovering after hanging to ensure they adhere smoothly to the wall without air bubbles.

Sponge for wiping paste off the front of the wallcovering and woodwork.

Water tray/trough. If you are hanging a ready-pasted wallcovering you will need this to immerse the cut lengths (to activate the paste backing). These trays are usually supplied free with the ready-pasted pro-duct, but if not, they can be bought cheaply from do-it-yourself and decorat-ing shops. You may still need a little paste and small brush in case the edges of the wallcovering don't stick firmly, and you have to apply extra paste. If you prefer to paste the wallcovering rather than im-mersing it in water, you can – just apply paste in the same manner as you would for normal paper.

Sundries. You will need a cleaning agent to wash down previously painted walls and glasspaper to 'key' the surface i.e. make the wall slightly rough so the paper adheres to it more readily. You may need size, to seal previously undecorated wall surfaces (use a diluted solution of wall-paper paste if you prefer). You may also like to brush on a coat of wallcovering release agent, before you paper, as this makes subsequent stripping easier; it is especially helpful if you are papering over plasterboard.

Then, of course, you will need wall-paper paste. There are several kinds available, so make sure you buy the right one for the wallcovering you want to hang. Most manufacturers recommend the appropriate paste on the hanging in-structions included with each roll, or your supplier will advise. Most ordinary wall-papers simply need a conventional wall-paper paste of the type you mix with water, although some come ready-mixed. Heavier wallpapers need a heavy-duty paste which is usually ready-mixed. For washable and vinyl wallcoverings the paste must contain a fungicide, since this type of wallcovering does not 'breathe' and otherwise mould could grow on the wall behind the covering. Some speciality wallcoverings, such as hessians and grasscloths, must be hung with special pastes which will not spoil the surface if they seep through the wallcovering — follow the manufacturers' instructions to the letter.

DECORATING TREATMENTS AND MATERIALS

WALL TREATMENTS (INTERNAL)

There are many ways of decorating internal walls, but when you drew up your basic plan (see *Planning on paper*) you will have thought about suitable surface treatments, depending on the wear and tear the rooms will get, and your lifestyle. These practical aspects must be considered *before* you choose wall materials.

Brick. Natural brick walls can be cleaned and left natural, sealed, or painted with emulsion or gloss paint. Some plastered brick walls can be exposed by hacking off the plaster and treating as above.

To create a brick effect you can use wafer-thin facing bricks, fixed like tiles, or a special paste which is spread onto the wall over a grid which acts as a kind of masking tape. When this is removed the paste left behind looks like pointing between bricks. Imitation brick wallcoverings and laminates are also available.

Carpet. To create a luxurious look, carpet can be stuck, tacked or stapled to walls. In a modern setting it is quite usual to continue the floor carpet onto part of the wall area, and it is a practical way of using up excess carpet. Other floorcoverings, such as sheet vinyl, can be used this way also. Sheet vinyl makes excellent co-ordinating splash-backs in bathrooms and kitchens, and can be used to make a waterproof shower area, so long as the joins are butted together closely and impact adhesive is used.

Cork comes in two forms – as tiles and panels and as very thin slivers mounted on a paper backing. The former can have a rather coarse texture, and is ideal for pin boards etc. or may be sealed, for use in bathrooms and kitchens.

Fabric and felt can be used as wallcoverings. Paper-backed varieties (see *Hessian* and *Natural textures*) can be hung as paper, although they are quite difficult to handle because of their weight. Fabric and felt can also be stuck directly onto a good wall surface (paste the wall), but they are difficult to remove and impossible to clean

satisfactorily. A more practical method is to use battens, or a special track which is fastened to the outer edges of the wall; the fabric is tucked between two flanges in the track, using a special tool shaped like a shoehorn. Either method enables you to take down the fabric for cleaning, and it can have insulating material placed behind it for extra warmth or sound-proofing.

Laminates come in a variety of colours, patterns and textures, and frequently simulate natural textures such as wood, marble and brick. They can be used to clad walls, particularly if the original surface is poor, or if you want to cover up old tiles or similar wall treatments. The laminate has to be stuck to a backing such as chipboard (it can be bought in this form) to create proper panels. These can be stuck to the wall, but a more usual method of fixing is by means of battens, screwed to the wall. Because of their tough, waterproof qualities, laminates are popular for bathroom and kitchen use.

Mirror is available in sheet form and as tiles – usually self-adhesive. Small mosaic-mirror-tiles – similar to mosaic ceramic tiles – are also available, but should only be fitted to an absolutely flat wall surface; otherwise you get a distorted image.

Aluminium foil, which looks like panels of mirror glass, but is much lighter and easier to hang, is particularly suitable for areas where there is a condensation problem.

Paint. If the wall surface is good, paint can be applied directly to the plaster. A matt,

satin or silky finish emulsion paint is the most usual type for walls. Others such as eggshell and gloss oil-based paints can be used if preferred, but remember – a high gloss will show up any imperfections in the wall surface. A heavier textured emulsion paint is also available for walls, and this is used in a similar way to the *textured finishes* described below.

Some of the silicone polyurethane (sometimes called *Silthane*) *multi-surface* paints, specially formulated for use on walls, ceilings, metal and woodwork, are practical for first-time decorators. The same paint can be used on the main surfaces of a room without fear of smudging, and rollers and brushes can be washed out under the tap or in hot water and detergent.

If the wall surface is poor even after filling and sanding down, but you want painted walls, a *lining paper* can be hung

Top left: a decorative surface can be created using wafer-thin facing bricks
Above: mirror and other glossy, shiny surfaces will increase the brightness of a room and magnify the apparent size

be applied to walls, giving a velvety or felt finish; this is mixed to a paste and spread thickly on the wall, rather like rough-icing a cake.

Tiles. Ceramic wall tiles used to be a job for the expert tiler, but now there are ranges specially designed for amateur installation. These have spacer 'lugs' to make aligning easier, and glazed edges so that separate 'nosings' (edging tiles) are unnecessary, and you get a neat watertight edging to the tiled area.

Mosaic tiles, which come in panels on a net-fabric backing, are also easy to handle, particularly in a situation where cutting conventional tiles to fit round projections could be complicated.

WALLCOVERINGS

These come in various types and textures. One important thing to remember when buying wallcoverings is that they should all come from the same batch to ensure uniform colour and printing. Before you leave the shop check the batch numbers printed on the rolls or on the labels to make sure they are all the same. Ordinary wallpaper is printed by machine, and can have an embossed or textured surface. It is sometimes possible to sponge this but generally it is difficult to clean. Some ordinary wallpapers have a plasticized or varnished surface, which makes them 'washable' – but they won't stand up to rough cleaning or scrubbing. Some wallpapers are pre-pasted.

Embossed wallcoverings. These are heavily textured papers, sometimes called 'whites', which are overpainted.

Flock wallcoverings have a velvety texture and usually come in traditional patterns and stripes. The base material can be a

before painting. This gives a reasonably smooth finish, and consequently tends to show up any dents and bumps in poor plasterwork. Lining paper is sometimes hung horizontally under other wallcoverings: this is called 'cross-lining'.

For walls which resemble a contoured map, the best answer is to hang a relief wallcovering such as Anaglypta, embossed or woodchip paper, sometimes called 'whites' (see *Wallcoverings*). These camouflage the bad surface, and can be overpainted. Emulsion is normally used, but other paints – gloss or eggshell oil-based paints for example – are frequently used when this type of wallcovering has been hung to form a dado on the lower part of a wall. But do bear in mind that this type of overpainting can make it difficult to remove the textured surface when you want to redecorate.

There are many exciting ways of decorating with paint apart from the conventional slap-it-on-with-brush-or-roller method. Murals, stencils and painted *trompe l'oeil* effects can all add an extra dimension to a room, and are usually added after the wall has been prepared, lined if necessary, and pre-painted.

For those who prefer a traditional look, there are techniques such as dragged paint-work, marbling and graining. These used to be professionally done by craftsmen, using scumble glazes 'combed' over a painted surface. But now it is possible to achieve the same effect yourself with modern paints and very simple tools.

Self-adhesive wallcoverings have peel-off backings and can be applied to any smooth, dry surface. They often have a 'feature design' such as a mural, forest view or seascape, or they simulate ceramic tiles, wood cladding and other natural textures. They tend to be rather expensive (sold by the metre) and so are not really practical for a whole room. If you *do* want to cover a large expanse with them, you will need help, as once they come in contact with the wall surface they stick firmly, so there is no room to manoeuvre!

Textured finishes are like rather thick paint, and are available ready-mixed in tubs or as powder for mixing yourself. They are applied directly to the plaster – old wallcoverings must be stripped off – and are textured by various methods: stippled with a brush, raked with a comb, swirled with sponge or fluffed-up with a plastic bag.

There is also a fibrous texture which can

Above: the beautiful natural texture of a stone wall or chimneybreast is in keeping with this cottage-style property
Right: a selection of wallcoverings to create different effects: 1. Patterned, ready-pasted narrow border 2. Hessian 3. Suede 4. Relief 5. Wide border 6. Ready-pasted 'gold' vinyl 7. Silk 8. Wood effect 9. Tweed 10. Woodchip 11. Marble effect 12. Hand-printed foil 13. Grass cloth 14. Flock 15. Acrylic-coated washable paper 16. Cork 17. Hand-printed paper 18. Trimmed, screen-printed 19. Untrimmed, screen-printed with self-border 20. Untrimmed, moiré effect Nos. 1 to 18: Arthur Sanderson & Company Limited 19 and 20: Colefax and Fowler Designs Limited

WALLCOVERING SYMBOLS

The range of wallcoverings is now so sophisticated, that a series of international performance symbols has been worked out, and these now appear on the backs of the samples in wallcovering pattern books and on product labels for your guidance.

Symbol	Description	Symbol	Description
～	spongeable	▐🖌	paste-the-wall
≈	washable	→|°	free match
≋	super-washable	→|←	straight match
▭	scrubbable	→|↓←	offset match
☼	sufficient light fastness	50 cm / 25	design repeat distance offset
☀	good light fastness	▐	duplex
▌	strippable	▩	co-ordinated fabric available
▌	peelable	↑	direction of hanging
⊔	ready pasted	↕	reverse alternate lengths

87

WHAT GOES OVER WHAT CHART: PAINT

New paint must always be applied over a properly prepared surface. If necessary, scrape burn or strip off all perished or blistered paint before priming (or patch-priming). Wash down good paintwork with water and detergent, sugar soap or a proprietary cleaner, rinse and let dry thoroughly. 'Key' the surface (rub down) with sand/glasspaper.

If painting over wallcoverings, make sure that they are adhering firmly to the wall (small air bubbles can be slashed and restuck) and no old wallpaper adhesive is sticking to the surface (wash/rub down if necessary). Some papers – particularly those with gold or silver patterns on them – are not always suitable for overpainting. Test for suitability on a spare piece of wallcovering or experiment on a small unobtrusive area of wall.

	OLD SURFACE	PLASTER	PLASTERBOARD	BUILDING BOARD e.g. wallboard, hardboard, insulation board etc.	GLOSS PAINT	EGGSHELL PAINT	MULTIPURPOSE PAINT 'GEL'	
PREPARATION		Make sure new plaster has dried out. Wash/rub down if necessary. Fill cracks	Tape joints and line	Tape joints and line	Clean down, remove any perished paint, rub down, patch prime if necessary. Apply the recommended undercoat			
NEW COAT	GLOSS PAINT	n/r	n/r	n/r	✓	✓	✓	
	EGGSHELL PAINT	✓	✓	✓	✓	✓	✓	
	MULTI-PURPOSE 'GEL' PAINT	✓	✓	✓	✓	✓	✓	
	MATT OR SILK EMULSION PAINT	✓	✓	✓	'Key' with sandpaper first to provide a suitable surface		✓	
	WATER BOUND PAINT e.g. DISTEMPER	n/r	n/r	n/r	×	×	×	

paper or a vinyl, and some are ready-pasted. Take care not to get paste on the flocked surface of paper-backed flocks. Vinyl-flocks can be washed if stained or marked. Both paper- and vinyl-flocks should be brushed lightly with a soft hand-brush from time to time to keep the pile dust-free.

Foil and metallic wallcoverings are made from a metallized plastic film on a paper backing. They are highly reflective and so create an illusion of space and light. Hang with a fungicidal paste, and do not place behind light switches and power points.

Friezes and borders. These bands of decoration come in various widths and can be used with co-ordinating papers, plain textured papers or painted walls. They can be used to great effect, outlining doors, walls, windows, fireplaces and other focal points. And they provide an attractive 'disguise' for an uneven ceiling line in a room that does not have a cornice. Usually they need trimming before pasting and hanging horizontally, vertically, or even diagonally, as you wish.

Foamed polyethylene is a very light wallcovering sold under the brand name of Novamura. Despite its lightness, it is tough and easy to hang, and warm to the touch. It is good for bathrooms and kitchens and can be hung on new plaster as it is porous and allows the wall to 'breathe'. The wall must be pasted and the wallcovering then slid into position. It is easy to strip since no backing is left on the walls.

Hand-printed wallpapers. Very expensive and exclusive, these papers are printed by hand, may not be colourfast and the edges usually have to be trimmed before hanging. They are hung like ordinary wallpapers.

Hessian is a coarsely-woven fabric which looks most attractive on walls as a background to pictures, mirrors and so on. It comes in a paper-backed variety on a roll which is hung like ordinary wallpaper and a fabric bought by the yard/metre. It is usual to paste the wall and slide the hessian fabric into position, but it can be tricky and is not therefore a good choice if this is your first attempt at home decorating.

Hessian comes in natural and a wide range of colours, but some tend to fade in bright sunlight. There are simulated hessian textures available in the vinyl and embossed wallpaper ranges.

Natural textures. Various wallcoverings fit into this category – grasscloth, silk, sisal, slivered cork, wool-weaves and wool-strands, as well as other fabric effects are now available.

The natural fibres are usually stuck on to a paper backing. Some are sold by the yard/metre and others are sold by the roll. Care is needed in hanging, as paste must not get onto the textured surface.

Relief wallcoverings have a heavily textured surface and are used in conjunction with paint, as *Embossed wallcoverings* (see previous page for details).

MATT or SILK EMULSION PAINT	WATER BOUND PAINT e.g. DISTEMPER	RELIEF & EMBOSSED WALL COVERINGS e.g. ANAGLYPTA	WALLPAPERS VINYL WALLCOVERINGS	HESSIAN	SPECIALITY WALLCOVERINGS e.g. grass-cloth
Wash down, 'key' if necessary. 'Size' or use thinned coat of emulsion if necessary OR undercoat if recommended	If non-powdery type, wash down several times with warm, soapy water to remove loose material. Apply one coat stabilizing primer. Undercoat as necessary. If powdery, all old paint must be washed off first. Re-line wall or ceiling	Make sure these are sticking firmly to the wall and no paste has been left on the surface	Make sure covering is sticking firmly and no paste is on the front of paper. If paper has heavy relief or gold/silver pattern, test first. If necessary, remove it and re-line the wall. Some hand-printed papers can also 'bleed' through paint, so test first	Make sure the wallcovering is sticking firmly to the wall and no paste has been left on. Dust down before you start decorating	
✓	n/r	n/r	n/r	n/r	n/r
✓	✓	✓	✓	n/r	n/r
✓	✓	✓	✓	✓	n/r
✓	✓	✓	✓	✓	n/r
× ×	✓	n/r	n/r	n/r	n/r

Suede wallcoverings. Velvety-textured wallcovering made from thin suede (leather) bonded to a paper backing, which can be hung like paper, but care must be taken not to get paste on the front. Many imitation suedes are also available, and these combine the qualities of suede texture with the easy-hang, easy-care properties of vinyls. Suede finish also appears as crushed suede with a slightly more crinkled texture.

Vinyl wallcoverings come in many disguises, looking like paper, foil, flock, hessian and so on. Basically they are a vinyl layer, which incorporates the pattern, backed with paper – although fabric backing may be used. They are tough, durable, frequently scrubbable, and certainly washable. When you want to strip the walls to redecorate, the vinyl surface usually peels away, leaving a paper backing on the wall which provides an ideal surface for redecorating.

About 50 per cent of vinyls have a ready-pasted backing. Lengths of wallcovering are cut to size, immersed in a water trough until the paste is activated, then hung in the normal way.

Thicker 'contoured' vinyl wallcoverings, which often simulate ceramic tiles, wood cladding and other natural textures, are also available. These need a heavy-duty wallpaper paste containing fungicide, and the wall can be pasted rather than the backing, if preferred. These are ideal for kitchens and bathrooms and where there is a condensation problem.

Wood cladding or panelling. Wood gives an attractive 'country' look to a room, and again can be used to cover a poor surface without much preparation. Various types of wood cladding are available, both as panels and as planks. These are frequently made to interlock (tongue-and-groove boarding, for example) and are fixed to the wall by means of battens and a technique called 'secret nailing'. Some are designed to overlap, and others to fit flush. Some wood panels can be stuck to the wall with a contact adhesive.

Once fixed in place, the wood can be stained and sealed, treated with linseed oil or varnished with matt, semi-matt or shiny polyurethane varnish, or even painted – apply primer and undercoat first.

THE RIGHT PAINT FOR THE JOB

With so many types of paint to choose from, it is important to select the right one for the particular decorating job. Basically there are *oil-based* and *water-based* paints. The former may be called gloss, lustre or eggshell and include primers and undercoats. Water-based paints used to be available as distemper or water paint, and were supplied in powder form, to be mixed with water and applied to newly-plastered walls and ceilings. These are now almost obsolete and have been replaced by *emulsion* paints. However, some surfaces in old houses are still covered with distemper, and this cannot be covered by any other form of paint – it will blister and flake if you try! It must be washed off completely, or the wall relined (see *Preparation and What-Goes-Over-What-Chart*, before you redecorate).

But there is a new type of paint, sold under many brand names, that can best be described as a *multi-purpose* paint. Oil-based, it is suitable for indoor woodwork such as doors, skirtings and window frames, and can also be used on metal, ceilings and walls. Because it washes out of brushes and rollers with hot water and detergent, it is sometimes described as 'easy-brush-care' paint, but it is also called 'silk', 'lustre', 'eggshell', and so on. The ingredients used in its manufacture include silicone and polyurethane, hence the word 'silthane' which is often synonymous with this type of paint.

Emulsion paints are highly versatile and can be used for ceilings and internal walls; an exterior quality emulsion can be used on brickwork and other outside wall surfaces.

These paints usually come in a matt (velvety) and a silk or satin (slight sheen) finish, dry very quickly and can be re-coated within two or three hours. There are also 'textured' emulsion paints for walls and ceilings. These can be applied thickly and moulded to form a textured surface either simply as a decorative finish, or as a very effective disguise for an uneven wall, or a ceiling which has cracks but is not in a sufficiently bad condition to warrant extensive repairs or complete replastering (see *Wall Treatments*).

Gloss paints are normally oil-based which makes them tougher and more able to stand up to hard wear. Ideal for protecting metal and woodwork both indoors and out, they are available under many brand names and most contain additional strengtheners to provide a tough quick-drying surface. Gloss paints are available in creamy, flowing form and a non-drip (thixotropic) quality, which brushes out easily when used but – because of its jelly-like consistency – should not drip unless you load the brush or roller too full. Because it is easy to handle, with less risk of runs and sags on the finished surface, non-drip paint is a practical choice for beginners. More experienced decorators may prefer to use the freer flowing gloss finish. NOTE: thixotropic paints must not be stirred or they lose their consistency. If you inadvertently do this, leave the can to stand and the paint will 're-set'.

Undercoats, primers and sealers. Gloss paints, and other oil-based paints such as lustre or eggshell finish (*not* the multi-purpose type) need to be applied over an oil-based undercoat. Most paint manufacturers recommend a suitable undercoat for their gloss paint (it will be printed on the tin), sometimes stipulating a particular colour if the topcoat is a strong shade. Follow the suggestions, using a topcoat and undercoat both made by the same

CHECKLIST FOR PRIMERS

Primers are used to seal exposed metal, wood, plaster, etc. before painting; it is important to use the appropriate primer for a particular surface – and always allow sufficient time for complete drying-out before you proceed to the next stage.

Unpainted softwood (new or stripped), man-made boards	Ordinary wood primers, all-surface primers or primer/undercoat
Resinous softwood and hardwood	Aluminium wood primer
Insulation board	Stabilizing primer
Plastic-faced boards	All-surface primer
New plastering, plasterboard, rendering or brickwork	All-surface primer under resin-based paints, no primer needed under emulsion
Porous or powdery plaster, rendering or masonry	Stabilizing primer
Washable distemper	All-surface primer or stabilizing primer
Old wallpaper	Treat metallic inks with knotting
Relief wallcoverings and lining paper	Apply a coat of emulsion paint first if using resin-based paint
New iron and steel	Calcium plumbate primer outdoors, zinc chromate primer indoors
Bitumen-coated metal	Aluminium spirit-based sealer
Galvanized iron and steel	Calcium plumbate primer
Aluminium	Zinc chromate or zinc phosphate primer (*not* lead-based primers)
Copper and brass	No priming necessary
Lead	Allow to weather before painting; no priming necessary
Asbestos sheet	Stabilizing primer if porous, all-surface primer otherwise
Ceramic tiles	All-surface primer or zinc chromate metal primer
Plastic, glass fibre	All-surface primer

manufacturer. Do not use oil-based lustre or eggshell finish paints for exterior metal or woodwork.

Multi-purpose and emulsion paints can be applied directly to a clean, smooth, dry, prepared wall or ceiling surface without a primer and undercoat. Emulsion can be thinned with water (being water-based) to form a 'size' or undercoat, but plaster may need a primer/sealer if the surface is very powdery, chalky or porous. If the multi-purpose paint is being used on wood or metal, priming may be necessary, but it acts as its own undercoat.

New wood, some stripped wood and metal may need a primer or sealer. A universal primer does most priming jobs, but galvanized iron and aluminium need a special metal primer; chromate and bitumen-coated surfaces need an aluminium sealer.

Masonry paints are tough emulsion paints, specially formulated to protect as well as decorate outside walls. Most contain a mould and algae inhibitor. They can

be either smooth-textured so that atmospheric dirt particles are not trapped easily and the surface remains clean longer, or rough-textured – containing sand or granite chips for added strength and covering power. The smooth ones are kinder to paint brushes and rollers!

CALCULATING QUANTITIES

If you've never decorated before, this may seem a formidable task, but if you take careful measurements as outlined below, then consult the relevant chart included in this section, you should get it right.

Ceilings. Simply measure the length and width of the room at ground level, multiply the two measurements to get the area in square metres or feet, then use the *Paint Coverage Chart* to calculate how much emulsion paint to buy. Multiply by two or three, as necessary, according to the number of coats required. If the room needs papering first, use the *Wallpaper Quantities Chart* to work out the number of rolls required.

Walls. For *paper*, measure round the room as above, then measure the height, and use the *Wallpaper Quantities Chart* to work out how many rolls to buy. Include the doors and windows (unless one wall is all window), as this extra will allow for any errors. Also allow for pattern matching if you have chosen a bold design; it is better to buy an extra roll or two, which the shop may take back if it is still wrapped – check whether this is an acceptable arrangement when buying – than to run short before the job is finished. This is particularly important because if you do go back to the shop you may find the pattern is out-of-stock, or the same batch number is no longer available. This number, printed on the rolls of paper, or on the leaflet wrapped in with each roll, shows which printing they

come from. The only way you can ensure that all your rolls will colour-match is by buying them all from the same batch.

If you plan to *paint* the walls, use the same technique as for ceilings, then deduct the area taken up by doors and windows from the total. Check the quantities on the chart and then, before buying, double-check the coverage printed on the can (always double-check in this way). Again, allow for the appropriate number of coats.

Calculating the area of exterior walls is more difficult. Measure the length at ground level. Then estimate height by measuring 1.83 m (6 ft) up the side of the outside wall and estimating how many such measurements there are in the total height of the building. Multiply these two

PAINT COVERAGE PER LITRE

Paint type	Coverage area
Matt emulsion (liquid)*	15m²
Matt emulsion (non-drip)*	12m²
Silk emulsion*	14m²
Gloss emulsion	14m²
Wood primer*	9–15m²
Aluminium primer	16m²
Stabilizing primer*	6m²
Metal primer	10m²
Primer/undercoat*	11m²
Undercoat	11m²
Liquid gloss	17m²
Non-drip gloss	13m²
Satin gloss (eggshell)	12m²
Polyurethane varnish*	16–24m²
Exterior wall paints*.	5–10m²

*Coverage will depend on the roughness and porosity of the surface; if you have to apply a second, or even a third coat, allow sufficient drying time between each one. Guidance is usually given on the container.

measurements together to get the overall area, then deduct the area of windows and doors. If you are using a masonry paint, and the wall surface is poor, or heavily textured (for example, rough cast or pebble dash), allow an extra one-third to twice as much paint as quoted.

Woodwork and metalwork. Paint quantities are calculated as follows:
Windows. Measure the height and width of the window opening and multiply. This should give enough paint to include frames and sills.
Doors. Measure the height and width including the frame. If the door is a heavy moulded one add an extra 10 per cent to the measurement area.
Skirtings, picture rails and cornices. Measure the total length all round the room at floor level and multiply by the depth or 'girth'.
Drain and down (fall) pipes. Measure 'girth', estimate height as described for exterior walls and multiply.
Gutters, facia boards and eaves. Measure the overall length at ground level, estimate the width or 'girth' (you can usually do this fairly accurately from an upstairs window) and multiply.
NOTE: once you have decorated a room, or the exterior of your home, keep a note of the quantities for future reference.

WALLCOVERING QUANTITIES CHART

Standard wallpapers come in rolls approximately 10.05 metres (11 yards) long by 530 mm (21 inches) wide. Many speciality wallcoverings are sold by the metre or yard, and are usually wider than the standard roll of paper, but widths vary according to type. Some hand-printed and imported wallpapers are different widths/lengths, so always check with the supplier before ordering.

The chart below will help you to work out the average quantity required if you are using the *standard size* roll, but remember to allow for pattern matching. If the paper has a large design you will need to buy extra rolls. Ask the retailer's advice, and it may be possible to have one or two extra rolls on 'sale or return'.

CEILINGS To calculate the number of rolls required, work out the square area in metres and divide by five

Figures show you number of rolls required									
WALLS Height from skirting	**Distance around the room (doors and windows included)**								
	30' 9m	34' 10m	38' 12m	42' 13m	46' 14m	50' 15m	54' 16m	58' 17m	62' 18m
7'–7' 6" 2.15–2.30 m	4	5	5	6	6	7	7	8	8
7' 6"–8' 2.30–2.45 m	5	5	6	6	7	7	8	8	9
8'–8' 6" 2.45–2.60 m	5	5	6	7	7	8	9	9	10
8' 6"–9' 2.60–2.75 m	5	5	6	7	7	8	9	9	10
9'–9' 6" 2.75–2.90 m	6	6	7	7	8	9	9	10	10
9' 6"–10' 2.90–3.05 m	6	6	7	8	8	9	10	10	11
10'–10' 6" 3.05–3.20 m	6	7	8	8	9	10	10	11	12
	66' 19m	70' 21m	74' 22m	78' 23m	82' 24m	86' 26m	90' 27m	94' 28m	98' 30m
7'–7' 6" 2.15–2.30 m	9	9	10	10	11	12	12	13	13
7' 6"–8' 2.30–2.45 m	9	10	10	11	11	12	13	13	14
8'–8' 6" 2.45–2.60 m	10	11	12	12	13	14	14	15	15
8' 6"–9' 2.60–2.75 m	10	11	12	12	13	14	14	15	15
9'–9' 6" 2.75–2.90 m	11	12	12	13	14	14	15	15	16
9' 6"–10' 2.90–3.05 m	12	12	13	14	14	15	16	16	17
10'–10' 6" 3.05–3.20 m	13	13	14	15	16	16	17	18	19

PREPARATION

Proper preparation of surfaces (both indoors and out) is a tedious and time-consuming job, but must not be skimped, otherwise old materials will 'break through' the new and spoil the redecorations. Also, if you prepare thoroughly the end result looks better, and redecorating the second time round will be much easier.

Assemble the relevant tools, plus plenty of old lint-free cloths, at least 1 bucket, a sponge, detergent (or washing soda), sugar soap, a soft brush for dusting down, a broom, dustpan and brush, the vacuum cleaner if it has an attachment for sucking up dust, and lots of old newspapers. You may also need household (abrasive) cleaner, a scrubbing brush, white spirit, wire wool, several grades of glasspaper and 'wet-and-dry' – a silicone-carbide paper used both wet and dry – for rubbing down certain surfaces.

SURFACES INSIDE

Complete the pre-preparation described in *Order of work*, including any structural work such as removing a fireplace or wall. Even if you have removed the floorcoverings, exposing the floorboards, cover them completely with old newspapers, dust sheets or plastic sheeting; if you get decorating dirt and dust between the floorboards, this can show up later as ridges on a light-coloured carpet, and any lumps of paint sticking to the floorboards can quickly 'work through' a new floorcovering.

New walls and ceilings. If you are decorating a new house or a new extension make sure that the plaster is completely dry. Use a wide-bladed scraper to scrape off any 'nibs' of plaster, efflorescence (powdery substance) or mortar. Fill cracks or holes with proprietary filler, leave to harden, then use glasspaper to rub down the surface until smooth. If the surface is porous, seal with a coat of stabilizing primer.

It is usual to paint newly-plastered walls with emulsion paint so they can 'breathe' – enabling a thorough drying out process to take place (this usually takes about 12 months). If further efflorescence shows itself you can scrape it off – never wash it off. It also enables you to fill any settlement cracks before applying a new decorative wall treatment. The polyethylene (polythene) type of wallcovering can be hung on new plaster as it is porous, but you cannot cope so easily with settlement cracks if you cover the wall.

New plasterboard or wallboard should be treated as new plaster; coat any nail or screw heads with metal primer. Seal the board with a plasterboard sealer or emulsion paint before wallpapering.

New woodwork. Rub down, working along the direction of the grain. Use a medium-grade abrasive paper (glasspaper) dry, and finish with a fine-grade. Dust off. Apply one or two coats of patent knotting to any knots in the wood to seal the resin and prevent it 'bleeding through' the new paint. Fill any cracks, holes or open joints with cellulose filler if you plan to paint the wood, or wood stopper if you plan to use varnish. Leave to harden, rub down and dust off.

Prime the wood with an all-purpose primer if it is a softwood – use an aluminium primer on hard or resinous wood. Let the primer dry thoroughly, then apply the recommended undercoat. If you plan to varnish the wood, do not prime it, just wipe it over with a cloth dipped in white spirit.

Joinery such as window-frames may come already primed (usually a reddish pink colour). Wash, if necessary, with detergent and water. Rub down with fine grade 'wet-and-dry'. Patch-prime if there are any knocks or chips, then apply undercoat.

New metal. Make sure the surface is free from grease and oil – clean with wire wool dipped in white spirit if necessary. Prime with an all-purpose primer, or one appropriate for the metal you are dealing with. If the metal is already primed (new radiators usually are, for example), patch-prime if it has become chipped. If the metal already shows signs of rusting rub down with emery cloth, fine abrasive paper or 'wet-and-dry' to remove all traces of rust before priming.
NOTE: do not leave metalwork exposed for long, as rust quickly forms. Apply recommended undercoat without delay.

Previously painted walls and ceilings. If the surface is flaky, first remove all loose material with a scraper, sand the bare areas and paint the patch so it is the same level as the rest of the wall or 'feather off' with proprietary filler.

If the paint used previously was *emulsion*, this normally only needs washing down with detergent and water. Always wash from the bottom of a wall, working upwards. If you start at the top you may get streaks down the wall which will show through new paint. Use household cleaning powder to remove any stubborn greasy marks. Wash with clean water and leave to dry. Then treat as for newly plastered walls.

If the surface was *gloss-painted*, treat as for emulsion but then remove the glossy surface by sanding down with medium-grade glasspaper or 'wet-and-dry'.

If the surface was previously *distempered* (found on ceilings and walls in older houses) test by wetting with a damp cloth: if a powdery substance comes away on the cloth you will have to remove all the old paint. Scrub, if necessary, with warm water and prime with stabilizing primer. If it is impossible to get all the old distemper off, you can cover the surface with lining paper before repainting or cross line (see *How to wallpaper*) before papering.
NOTE: some *water-based* paints look like distemper, and were used on walls and ceilings in many older houses, but they don't show on the cloth as a powdery substance and can be treated as emulsion paint.

Previously papered walls and ceilings. Sometimes paper has been hung (frequently the embossed type) and then over-painted. This is much harder to remove than ordinary paper. If you want to repaint it rather than strip it off, you can do so providing it is in good repair and firmly adhering to the wall. You can also paint over some existing wallcoverings (see *What-Goes-Over-What* chart), but again, only if they firmly adhere to the wall and are in good condition; do not overpaint if they have a gold, silver, or other metallic pattern as this usually 'bleeds' through new paint. Test a small area first to see if it can be over-painted,

Above: when painting a ceiling, do a small strip round the edge first with a narrow brush, before painting the larger area with a wider brush, or roller
Right: some of the tools and materials needed for filling cracks in walls, ceilings and woodwork. From top, left to right: plaster and trowel, plasterer's hawk, plasterer's float, filling knives, ready-mixed and powder filler. If preparation is properly done, decorating will be very much easier the second time around

and if not, it will all have to come off!

To strip *ordinary wallpaper*, first lightly score the surface then soak thoroughly with warm water to which a little washing-up liquid can be added – sponge or brush this on to the paper, or use one of those garden hand-held sprayers. Then leave for a few minutes, before you start scraping with the scraper, taking care not to damage the wall plaster under the paper. Re-soak the paper as you work if it does not come off easily. Put the old paper straight into a plastic sack or cardboard carton as you work, since it will be sticky and get onto feet, hands etc. Go over the area a second time, to make sure that you have removed all traces of paper and old size or adhesive. Then wash the wall down thoroughly with clean water.

Fill any hairline cracks as for newly plastered walls, but if the surface is bad you may have to do a much more complicated filling job. Cracked or broken plaster will have to be 'raked out' carefully and cut back to a firm edge, after which the hole

can be filled and the area replastered. If the hole is large, this may have to be done in stages, allowing drying-out time between each one. Always dampen the wall immediately round the part to be filled or plastered, otherwise the wall can draw all the dampness out of the filler which then quickly becomes loose.

When the holes and cracks are filled and the area has dried out, rub down to a smooth surface with glasspaper and dust off. If you plan to paint the wall, continue as for *new surfaces*, but if you plan to re-paper, treat the wall with a coat of size or thinned-down wallpaper paste.

Washable wallpaper and *over-painted paper* can be more difficult to remove. Score the surface with a wire brush or serrated scraper (take care not to damage the plaster underneath) and give it a thorough soaking. There is a new proprietary wallpaper stripper specially formulated to 'eat' through painted or varnished surfaces, so you could use this if you prefer, following the instructions on the

tub. It is quicker and easier to use, but more expensive.

If the paper proves to be very stubborn you may have to score the surface and use a steam stripper (see *Tools and Equipment*). These can be hired and come complete with instructions, but take care not to scald yourself while working. When the walls are completely stripped continue as above, depending on the type of new surface you plan to use.

Vinyl wallcoverings are easy to strip – simply peel off the top, patterned layer of vinyl and it should leave a soft backing paper on the wall. Re-stick or patch any peeling areas and, if you plan to repaper or use some other wallcovering, there is no need to remove the backing – use it as a lining. If you plan to paint the wall strip off the old backing as for ordinary wallpaper. NOTE: if polyethylene (polythene) light wallcovering has been used, the paste will have been applied to the wall. The wall-covering will come away easily, but you will probably have to scrape or rub off the old wallpaper paste before washing down and preparing the wall.

Previously tiled walls and ceilings. If *ceramic tiles* are firmly stuck to the wall, you may be able to retile or redecorate over them (see *Wall treatments* and *What-Goes-Over-What* chart), since removing them can be a very messy job. Otherwise, they will have to be chipped off using a cold chisel or brick bolster and hammer. If the tiles are Victorian or Edwardian patterned ones, they are probably worth preserving, so work very carefully. You will have to re-plaster the wall (call in the expert; this is a difficult do-it-yourself job) unless you plan to use woodcladding, laminate, wall-boarding or other covering which is battened-on to the wall.

Cork tiles can be difficult to remove as they will have been stuck on with impact adhesive, which means lumps of tile will remain firmly stuck to the wall and will have to be chipped off as above. If possible, don't remove them; use a new surface which can be battened-on, or recolour the tiles with wood stain or cross-line with lining paper (see *How to wallpaper*) and hang the new wallcovering on top. You may find that you have to size the cork several times before lining as it can be highly porous.

Polystyrene tiles are frequently found on ceilings and should not be painted, since this makes them a fire hazard. If the ceiling is in a good condition, just wash down. If the tiles are dirty or damaged, you will have to remove them – prise them off with

a small cold chisel and hammer if necessary. Scrape off the old adhesive and treat as for newly plastered ceilings.

Acoustic tiles (the type with little perforations) can be painted. Wash them down, then prime with a stabilizing primer before painting. If they have been painted already, treat as for previously painted surfaces.

Previously painted woodwork and metal. Wash down with sugar soap and water, household soda, or detergent and water, taking care to remove all grease or old polish from areas which are frequently handled, such as doors. Rub down with fine grade glasspaper or 'wet-and-dry', dust down or wash off, using clean warm water. Make good any cracks and continue as for new wood and metal. You may have to patch-prime before undercoating.

If the paint surface is poor, completely strip off the old perished paint. Remove all loose or flaking material with a scraper,

and use a shavehook for difficult-to-reach corners (also remove any defective putty). Then strip off any remaining paint with a proprietary stripper or blowtorch – use this carefully, to make sure that you do not singe the surrounding surface or crack any window glass. Scrape the paint as it blisters, and clean up perished paint as you go along to avoid treading it all through the house. If you use a liquid chemical stripper, follow the instructions carefully, wear rubber gloves and protective clothing. Make sure that the room is well ventilated and work on small areas at a time, taking care not to spill the stripper on other surfaces. A new chemical stripper which looks like thick paste and comes in a tub is very good for coping with carved and other intricate areas, but is a bit expensive to use for all paint stripping.

For safety's sake work without the 'help' – or hindrance – of children.

Clean the surface with white spirit to remove all trace of the stripper (if you use

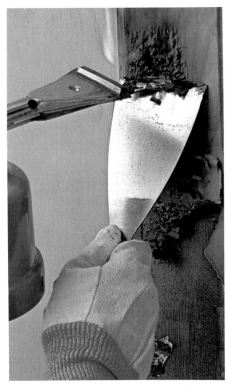

Above left: old perished paint must be removed using paint stripper, blowlamp, sander, abrasive papers and scrapers
Above: work carefully with blowlamp and scraper – the perished paint can be scraped off mouldings with a shavehook

the paste type, *washing* down is recommended), sand down, dust off, and continue as for new wood and metal – use a rust-preventer under the primer and undercoat on metal radiators and pipes, particularly in areas of high condensation.

Previously varnished woodwork. Basically you can treat a varnished surface as a painted one – wash down, sand and rinse. If the varnish is pitted or badly discoloured, or you plan to paint the wood, completely remove the old surface. Scrape, if necessary, then use a chemical stripper as for painted woodwork. Treat as new wood.

SURFACES OUTSIDE

If the building is a new one, or part of it is a new extension, the wood and metal may be ready-primed. If so, treat as interior primed woodwork and metal. Otherwise prepare as follows, remembering to prime bare metal as soon as possible to avoid rust forming.

New, unpainted metal. Make sure it is free from oil and grease, and wipe over with white spirit.

Iron and steel. Remove any rust and loose scale by scraping and wire-brushing; for less severe rust, use an emery cloth. Prime at once with a universal primer.

Galvanized iron is best left to weather and lose its shine, then prime with universal primer. If you cannot wait, rub down with medium grade glasspaper, wipe over with white spirit, wipe clean and prime with chromate metal primer.

Aluminium should be rubbed down with fine grade glasspaper and white spirit. Wipe down and prime as galvanized iron.

Bitumen-coated metal should not be painted until the coating is hard and well weathered. Then it can be rubbed down (as above) and primed with aluminium sealer, following by wood primer. Then apply an undercoat suitable for the gloss finishing coats you have selected.
NOTE: some garage doors, particularly the up-and-over type come already primed, and these only need treating as pre-primed indoor metal before undercoating. Others have a factory applied finish and, if possible, this type should *not* be painted, or they will need constant re-painting.

New plastic. Many new gutters, fall pipes, soil pipes and so on are made of plastic. This does not need painting, and the universal grey colour blends with most bricks and colour schemes. Many experts say do not paint plastic – partly because the joints can be clogged with paint and subsequently difficult to remove if you want to do any repairs. But if you want to paint plastic to blend with the house or existing ironwork, remove any grease with white spirit, then undercoat and topcoat with a suitable paint.

Previously painted metal. The chances are most metal work (old gutters, pipes and so on) will have some rust. If pipes and gutters are very bad, it is better to replace them. You will find the plastic do-it-yourself type much easier to handle, but you may have difficulties with sizes – new piping does not have the same circumference as some very old iron work, so you may have to replace the whole run of piping (save any good pieces to repair other areas of old piping). Treat new metal work or plastic piping as previously described. Rust, loose scaling and dirt should be treated by brushing with a wire brush, scraping where necessary, or rubbing with emery cloth. Rub down with medium grade glasspaper, prime any bare parts and undercoat. Any type of guttering can be painted *inside* with bituminous paint to protect it.

Metal windows need special care – remove old perished paint, rust and so on and replace defective putty with metal glazing putty. Prime and undercoat as necessary. If the paint is in poor condition, burn or strip off (as for metal and woodwork inside) then prime and undercoat as for new metal.

New, unpainted woodwork. Treat as for unpainted woodwork indoors, prime and undercoat. If you intend to seal or varnish exterior woodwork: decorative wood panels, doors, frames and so on, treat as for indoor woodwork, but apply extra coats of sealer or varnish, lightly rubbing down between coats. Varnished woodwork in a sunny, very exposed or coastal position needs fairly frequent rubbing down and re-varnishing, so painting might be a better treatment. The word 'varnish' always suggests a high gloss, but many of the new wood sealers and varnishes have a matt or semi-matt finish.

Timber claddings look best left natural but treated with a solvent preservative or sealed and varnished. Creosote is *not* a wise choice for wood cladding as it darkens the wood and usually hides the natural grain. If creosote has been used, let it weather, then rub the surface down and varnish. You can paint it if you first apply an aluminium wood primer (see *Checklist for primers*).

Previously painted woodwork. Treat much the same as for interior woodwork, by scraping and cleaning down if the surface is fairly good, but any old blistering and perished paint must be burnt or stripped off, the surface rubbed down, bare areas patch-primed, or the entire surface newly primed, before the undercoat is applied.

Wooden window frames are often the worse for wear, and any defective putty must be replaced, and defective wood cut out and replaced. Small holes can be filled with proprietary wood filler. Sometimes on older houses the sills of wooden windows are painted stone or concrete. Perished paint must be completely removed, the sill scraped clean and smooth (you may have to use a metal file) and cracks or holes filled. Fill small ones with exterior quality proprietary filler: larger areas with a cement/sand mix. Leave to dry, sand smooth, prime with masonry sealer and undercoat.

Most wood and metal surfaces inside and out are best rubbed down or sanded by hand. Sanding woodwork with an electric sander can, in fact, do more harm than good, resulting in a very uneven surface if you become too 'tool happy'. But if there is a lot of smoothing down to do on exterior window sills, or other flat surfaces, a mechanical tool can be used, with *great care*. Remember, if you use electric tools outside they must be fitted with a heavy-duty exterior cable. Always make sure you work with the cable in a position where you cannot possibly damage it with the tool (e.g. over your shoulder).

Walls. Exterior walls do not always need painting – in fact, it is a pity to paint an attractive-coloured brick and sacrilege to paint a mellow stone wall. However, you can waterproof the walls without spoiling their 'natural' appearance.

New walls should be in a good state of repair, but may need a gentle scraping to remove spare bits of mortar. Never use a wire brush, and do not use the scraper too heavily on soft surfaces such as brick and stone. Apply two (or more) coats of masonry sealer to seal the surface and make it waterproof. Some sealers contain a fungicide, which can make the wall look darker or bright red, but this will fade. If

A word about ASBESTOS. This material is sometimes used in building – for wall panels on garages and extensions, as part of the eaves, lining a porch, carport or side way. Some pipes and gutters are also made of asbestos. Great care must be taken with this product. *Never* sand asbestos dry, since you could inhale dangerous asbestos dust. Wet it before sanding down – if you have to strip off old paint, use a water-based proprietary paint stripper *not* a chemical based one, wash thoroughly and paint with exterior-quality emulsion or other water-based masonry paint. Asbestos gutters can also be treated inside with bitumen to seal and waterproof them.

you want to colour new walls, they can be painted without further preparation – use a water-based masonry paint.

If *old* walls are to be sealed or painted, inspect the pointing (mortar between the bricks) and, if necessary, re-point. If damage is extensive it would be wise to engage a builder to do the re-pointing.

Previously painted walls. Brush down with a stiff brush (bristle not wire) to remove loose and flaking materials. Rake out large cracks and fill with a sand/cement mix (1 part cement to 4–6 parts of clean sharp sand). Fill small cracks with exterior quality proprietary filler. Allow to dry, sand down edges and dust off.

If the walls are stained (from leaky gutters and pipes), repair the fault first and leave the wall to dry out. Scrape or brush off any mould or algae, then sterilize with bleach solution. If necessary, prime with alkali-resisting primer before painting with masonry paint.

If the wall is *pebbledashed*, and the condition is poor, remove any loose or broken pieces to expose the smoother rendering underneath and treat the exposed part with stabilizing solution. Then mix masonry paint with sand binder, extra sand and water to a thick creamy consistency and use this to fill the gaps before stippling the surface to match the texture of the surrounding wall – 'feather' the edges into the existing pebbledash, so that the filler is not too obvious. Leave to harden before painting.

Tools and materials needed for filling cracks in exterior walls and woodwork

DECORATING TECHNIQUES

HOW TO PAINT

Once you have decided which paint to use and have prepared the surfaces properly, you will be ready for the transformation act – putting brush (or roller) to paint, and changing a drab wall or door into a pristine, colourful surface.

Don't rush at it! First check your measurements, the can or cans, and the *Paint Coverage Chart* (see *The right paint for the job*), to make sure you have enough paint. If you run out halfway through the job, the new colour could be slightly different. If this does happen, use the new paint on a different wall or at an edge – never use paint from a new batch on a partly-painted surface, where the change in colour could be obvious.

Always read the instructions on the can first, to find out whether the paint needs to be stirred – a traditional *oil-based gloss* needs very thorough stirring, but a *thixotropic* (jelly or non-drip) paint should not be stirred. If, when you open the can, there is liquid on top – like curds and whey, this means the binder has separated out, and you will have to stir this in and leave the paint to re-set into its jelly-like consistency.

If painting with oil-based paint, strain it into a paint kettle through a piece of nylon cut from an old pair of tights. It is wise to do this even if the paint is brand new. Then charge the brush by dipping about one-third of the depth of the bristles into the paint. Lift out and squeeze out any excess paint by pressing the bristles against the side of the kettle or can. With non-drip paint there is no need to do this so long as you have not overloaded the brush.

Work with a flexible wrist, holding the paint brush firmly, but not too tightly (see illustration). Flex the bristles against the surface, so that the paint flows towards the tip of the brush, allowing you to control the spread of the paint.

Apply the paint in parallel strips, a brush-width apart, working along the direction of the grain. Do not reload the brush, but cover the unpainted area between the strips by drawing the bristles across the grain. Now 'brush out' by brushing the paint film lightly along the direction of the grain.

Thixotropic paints should not be brushed out too much, so load the brush to about half the depth of the bristles, and apply the paint fairly thickly along the direction of the grain, without leaving the bare-strip – do not 'brush out' across the grain.

To paint a door. This should be painted in sequence, and the paint should be drawn out towards the edge so that you don't get a build up. The easiest way to paint a door is to take it off its hinges and lay it flat

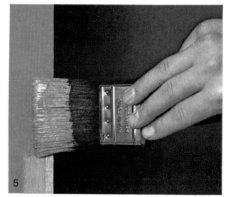

across a work bench or table, or suspended between two chairs, but unhinging it may seem a drastic treatment if you are a first-time decorator. If you leave the door *in situ*, remember to leave a spindle or stick of wood in the handle hole when you have removed the handles and door furniture, or you could shut yourself inside the room.

Flush doors are fairly easy: divide them into 3 or 4 horizontal sections in your mind, start at the top and work down. 'Lay on' the paint by making two or three separate down strokes and fill in by cross

How to paint, step-by-step.
1. Remove excess paint from the brush by pressing the bristles against the side of tin or paint kettle
2. Paint two parallel strips working along the direction of the grain
3. Draw the brush across the surface to cover the bare patch
4. Brush the paint film lightly along the direction of the grain for a smooth finish
5. Draw the brush out towards the edge of the surface to avoid a build-up of paint

brushing, drawing the paint out towards the edge so you avoid getting a build up. Join up each section with very light, vertical, upward strokes.

If the door is painted both sides, the general rule is to paint the edge with the hinges to match the closing face of the door, and the edge nearest the handle to match the opening face of the door.

Panelled doors are harder to cope with, but if you paint them in the correct sequence it should not be too difficult. Paint any mouldings first (1); then paint the recessed panels (2); next paint the centre uprights (3); the horizontals, working from top to bottom (4a, 4b, 4c); side verticals (5); side edges (6). Some people prefer to paint the frames (door jambs) first, while painting the skirtings, etc. – others prefer to paint them at the same time as the door. If you decide to do this, paint the frames last.

Glazed doors: paint the glazing bars first, using a small brush. Then paint the top and bottom rails and lastly the verticals and edges.

To paint a window. As with doors, if you follow the correct sequence you should manage. One of the worst problems with windows is getting paint onto the glass. The paint film should extend about 2 mm ($\frac{1}{8}$ inch) onto the glass in a smooth straight edge, to prevent condensation from seeping into the putty. You can use a cutting-in tool (see *Tools*), cut a template from card, or use a paint shield, but the paint often gets onto these and still ends up on the glass. Much the easiest way is to use masking tape. It takes time to stick this in place, but is compensated for by the speed with which you can then paint the window, and by the nice neat edges. Stick the masking tape to the face of the glass, parallel to the glazing bars and at least 2 mm ($\frac{1}{8}$ inch) away from the putty (outside) or glazing bead (indoors). Make sure the tape joins at right-angles to form nice neat corners. Paint the window, and leave until the surface is perfectly dry before removing the tape (about 3–4 days, depending on atmospheric conditions), but do not leave it on any longer or it may become difficult to remove.

If paint does get splashed onto the glass, the best way to remove it is to rub with the edge of a copper coin. You can also use a razor blade, if it is in a protective holder.

Fixed windows (those which do not open) should be painted as for glazed doors. Paint the glazing bars first, then the horizontal parts, then the verticals. Paint the frame last.

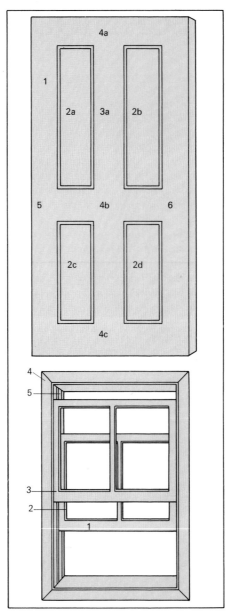

Casement windows: first paint the glazing bars (rebates) (1); next paint the cross bars (2); then the cross rails (3); side verticals and edges (4), and finally the frame (5).

Sash windows are usually found in older properties. If the sash cord breaks while you are working it could be dangerous, and if it breaks after the window is painted, you will spoil the new decorations to get at the sash cords, so check the cords for fraying before starting to decorate and, if necessary, repair them. Push the bottom sash up and pull the top sash down. Paint the bottom meeting rail and vertical sections of the top sash as far as you can (1). Push the window back into the normal position. Paint the rest of the top sash (2); paint the rest of the bottom sash (3); paint the frame (4). When the window is dry, paint the runners (5) taking care not to paint the sash cords.

Cutting in. Painting up to an angle or a straight line, as when painting windows, is known as 'cutting in' and can be difficult. Use a small easy-to-handle brush, possibly one with slightly worn bristles. Dip in the paint, press the bristles on to the surface at an angle, a few millimetres away from the edge, press a little harder and draw the brush down, parallel to the edge. The bristles will spread out, and if you have a steady hand you will obtain a straight line with the paint spread evenly along. Recharge the brush and repeat until the cutting in is complete.

The principles are the same for painting inside and out, and garage and front doors are painted as internal doors.

Painting walls and ceilings. You will almost certainly be using a water-based paint such as emulsion for this job. If you are using one of the multi-purpose paints you can use the same painting technique as for water-based paints. As walls and ceilings are usually much larger areas to cope with than woodwork or metal you will be using a wider brush, but not too wide, a roller or paint pads (see *Tools*). There is no need to strain emulsion paint, but it must be stirred – unless it is the non-drip type which is a wise choice for ceilings – and transferred to a paint kettle if you are using a brush or pads or a special tray if you are using a roller.

Ceilings first! Make sure that you can reach the ceiling comfortably (see *Papering ceilings*). Start painting at a corner nearest to the window and work away from the light. Whether you are going to use a roller, pads or a wide brush, first paint a strip about 5 cm (2 inch) wide all round the edge of the ceiling, since rollers, big brushes and pads won't get right into the corners.

Do not overload the roller, or paint will drip down onto your head as you work – wear a protective head covering anyway! To load the roller, push it backwards and forwards in the paint in the tray until it is well covered, then run it up to the top of the tray slope to remove excess paint. Work with criss-cross strokes, pushing the roller forwards and backwards across the surface – do not take the roller off the surface suddenly or it will splash. When you recharge the roller, apply it first to an unpainted part, working towards the previous wet edge with criss-cross strokes.

If you are using a brush, work in sections about 5 to 7 cm (2 to 3 inch) square, or in long strips, joining up the wet edges as quickly as possible, and 'feathering' if necessary so that the two areas blend. The same technique applies to paint pads, except that these are drawn smoothly across the surface – use a small pad for the edges and a larger one for the bulk of the ceiling.

Painting inside walls. The tools, materials and techniques will be similar to those for painting ceilings. If you are right-handed start at the top right-hand corner of the wall (preferably the window wall). If you are left-handed start at the top left-hand corner and work as previously described. If you are painting over wallpaper or relief wallcovering you may find the paper 'bubbles up' a little; do not be too concerned as this should dry back flat to the wall.

Painting outside walls. Basically, painting exterior walls is the same as for painting walls inside, except that you are working on a larger scale, and can use slightly larger tools. You may even decide to hire a paint sprayer if you plan to decorate all the outside walls. If you do this, remember to mask all windows and doors. The most important thing is to make sure your ladders or other access equipment (see *Tools*) are safe. If you are right-handed, start at the top, on the right-hand side of the house, working across in sections, or on the left-hand side if you are left-handed.

Apply *masonry paint* generously by means of brush, bannister brush, heavy-duty roller or spray.

Stone paint is another type of masonry paint containing 'fillers' to give the surface a rough texture. This has to be applied with a brush or roller, which it tends to wear out! You can use spray equipment, but the filler particles tend to clog up the nozzle even though the spray gun must be fitted with a special one.

Emulsion paint – exterior quality can also be used on external walls, using any of the methods previously described.

Whether you are painting inside or out, or papering the inside walls, you should never try to do too much in one session. If you become tired and irritable, and are half-way through painting a wall, it will seem like weeks before that wall is finished – but it is not wise to stop work half-way through an area like this.

Always clean up after each job, and when you have finished one stage of decorating, clean all tools thoroughly and put them away before starting on the next stage.

HOW TO WALLPAPER

If you have decided to paper your walls (or hang some other form of wallcovering), measure up, work out quantities and choose your wallcovering, not forgetting a suitable paste with which to hang it. Prepare the wall surface as previously described (see *Preparation*) and assemble the necessary tools and pasting table.

If the wall surface is poor, the wall was previously distempered, you have some other 'difficult' surface to contend with – or possibly you have bought a very special wallcovering which you want to hang with very special care – you will need to cross-line the walls first with a fairly thick lining paper.

To line the walls. Start hanging from the top corner at one end of the room, working parallel to the ceiling. Cut the lengths of paper to the width of the wall, allowing about 12 mm ($\frac{1}{2}$ inch) extra to continue round the corner onto the next wall. Butt each length of paper on each wall right into the corner. Cut, paste and hang as for ordinary paper – except working horizontally (see below). Leave the lining paper to dry out for at least 24 hours.

Papering ceilings. Fortunately, it is not usually necessary to re-paper ceilings every time you decorate – but if you *are* planning complete redecoration, paper the ceiling before the walls. Make sure you can reach it adequately by using two ladders and a scaffold board if necessary (see *Tools*). Work away from the window. Traditionally, paper is hung parallel to the window wall, but you can hang the paper at right-angles to this wall, if it will be easier and mean that you are handling a shorter length of paper.

Mark a chalk line just less than the width of the paper across the ceiling (use string dipped in chalk and 'snap' a chalk line. See *hanging wallpapers* below). Cut the lengths of paper, paste – folding the paper into a series of 'S' or concertina folds as you go – then allow the paper to become supple (you can paste 2 or 3 before you start hanging, so long as you hang first the one which was pasted first). Use the same pasting technique as for pasting wallpaper. Part of an unpasted roll, or a proper paper holder or broomhead can be used to support the bulk of the paper.

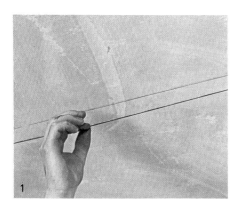

Far left: follow the numbers printed on our door and window for a perfect, no-trouble finish

Above: step-by-step to papering a ceiling
1. Make a chalk guide-line by snapping a chalky string across the ceiling, just narrower than a width of paper
2. Support the folded paper, and position along the chalk line, starting in a corner
3. Brush firmly into position, tapping into the angle between wall and ceiling, leaving an edge for trimming

Open the first fold from the corner and, keeping the paper butting to the guide line, open and brush the paper into position against the ceiling as you walk along the scaffold board – take care when you are doing this. Brush the paper firmly into the angle between wall and ceiling and leave the slight overlap on cornice/wall edge for trimming. When the first length of paper is up, trim the overlap from the long side then the short ends, using scissors or a knife. Hang the next piece of paper to butt up to, and parallel to, the first piece, and continue in this manner until the ceiling is completely papered.

Hanging ordinary wallpapers and wall-coverings. First unwrap (but do not unroll) the rolls of paper. If you have bought extra, don't unwrap the ones you might not need. You will have checked that they all come from the same batch number when buying (see *Wallcoverings*); now check them for 'shading' i.e. make sure they are all the same colour. Sometimes rolls of paper have been exposed to sunlight and may have faded or, even if they come from the same batch number, the printing machine may have printed the ink too thickly and the fault may not have been noted at inspection stage. Once you are satisfied that all is well, you can start!

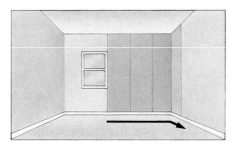

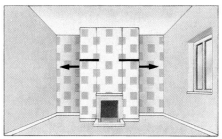

If the paper is quite plain or has a small pattern, start papering beside a window and work towards the door. Try to finish in the darkest corner, so that if there are any slight mistakes in pattern matching they won't be too obvious. If the paper has a large design, centre this on the focal point of the room. This is usually the fireplace, in which case make sure that the central motif comes dead centre of the chimney-breast.

Cutting the lengths – having worked out where the first piece will be positioned, and measured the wall from ceiling to skirting board, trim the end of the roll before cutting the first length so that the pattern will start at the top of the wall after allowing a spare 5 cm (2 inches) for final trimming. This is particularly important with a large or bold design; there is nothing worse than a bold motif, or a bird, flower or animal with its head chopped off at the ceiling. It may mean wasting a few feet of paper from each roll cut, but you should allow for this when estimating the quantity required (see *Calculating quantities*).

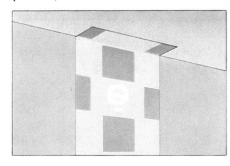

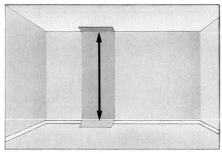

Cut the required length from the roll, allowing that extra 5 cm (2 inch) top and bottom for trimming. Measure the next length, and line up with the first one before cutting to make quite sure the pattern matches. Continue in this way for the rest of the paper, but check and measure the wall at intervals to allow for any slight change in ceiling height – no room is ever truly square.

Match the pattern each time, wasting a strip of paper if necessary; number each piece on the back as you cut it and indicate which is the top, with an arrow, so you don't accidentally reverse the lengths (unless it is a special wallcovering with instructions that alternate lengths should be reversed when hanging).

Pasting. When you have cut sufficient lengths, prepare the paste according to the manufacturer's instructions, using the recommended adhesive for your wall-covering. Lay the first length of paper face down on the pasting table and, using the

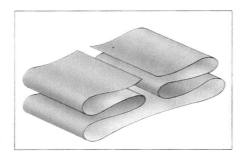

paste brush, apply the paste down the centre back, working out towards the edge herringbone-fashion. Make sure that the paste evenly covers the back of the paper and goes right to the edges but does not mark the front. Keep a damp cloth ready for wiping over the surface of the pasting board after each length is pasted, to avoid marking the next one. Fold the paper, pasted surfaces together, with a large fold at the top and smaller one at the bottom. For long lengths, fold concertina fashion. Allow the paste to soak in for a few minutes until the paper is supple. With thick paper you can paste 2 or 3 lengths before hanging, so long as you remember which was pasted first. Ensure all lengths soak for approximately the same amount of time.

Hanging. As few walls are perfectly vertical, mark a vertical line on the wall using a plumb line and chalk. Coat the line with chalk, pin it to the top of the wall and allow it to hang plumb. At the skirting, hold the plumb bob with one hand, so the string is taut, pluck the string with the other and let it 'twang' back against the

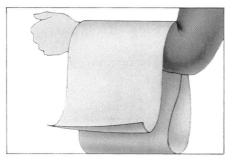

wall. This should leave a perfectly vertical chalk mark on the wall. Hang the first length against this line: fold the prepared paper over your arm, take it to the wall and – starting at the top of the wall – unfold the top end of paper and position the top edge at the top of the wall, allowing that spare 5 cm (2 inches) at the ceiling line for trimming. Slide the paper into position so that the edge butts exactly to the vertical line.

Using the paper-hanging brush, smooth down the centre of the paper and work

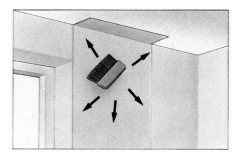

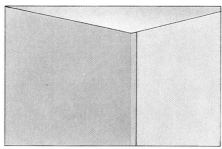

with herringbone strokes outwards and downwards, unfolding the bottom half as you go. Make sure the brush strokes are firm enough to remove any wrinkles or air bubbles. Then, at the ceiling 'knock' the paper into the angle, using the cut edge of the bristles. Mark the cutting line by drawing the back of the scissors across the paper at ceiling height. Trim off with the scissors following the creased line, which may mean you have to peel the paper back a little from the top of the wall. Make sure that you brush it back firmly once you have trimmed the top – if necessary apply a little more paste before doing so. Run the scissors along the bottom of the paper at skirting level and repeat the trimming process. Give the paper a final brush over. Then, with a damp sponge, remove any paste sticking to the front of the paper. Repeat with the next strip of paper – butt it up to the first strip, keeping it vertical and aligning the pattern.

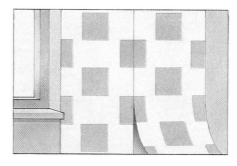

Should wrinkles or air bubbles appear, carefully peel the paper back from the wall and rebrush into position. The paper remains perfectly pliable for quite a long time, so don't be afraid to peel it back more than once if necessary. Small wrinkles and air bubbles should disappear on drying. When paper is over-painted, these bubbles reappear, but again should lie flat on drying. If the paper is *not* embossed or textured, use a seam roller to gently flatten the joins – do *not* roll embossed or textured ones.

Continue papering in this manner until you get near a corner. You should never try to hang a full width of paper round a corner because it only results in creasing, so

measure the distance from the edge of the last piece of paper into the corner at several points down the wall, to find the greatest width. Add 1 cm ($\frac{1}{2}$ inch) to the widest measurement and cut the length of paper to this width, carefully reserving the off-cut. Paste, hang and firmly smooth the paper into the corner, tapping the cut edge of the bristles into the angle. Trim so that a uniform 1 cm ($\frac{1}{2}$ inch) overlap occurs all down the wall.

Mark a vertical line the same distance from the corner as the width of the paper off-cut (use the plumb line and chalk again). Paste the strip and hang it with the

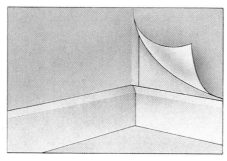

right edge to this line, so that the left-hand edge fits into the corner, slightly covering the overlap from the previous piece. Continue hanging strips of paper as before. NOTE: if you have an *external* corner (the sides of a chimney breast for example) a full width of paper can be taken round this, so long as the corner is plumb, but again, it quite often is not. If not, cut a 5 cm (2 inch) overlap and take this round the corner. Hang the next piece to overlap this, as plumb as possible to the edge. You cannot overlap vinyl wallcoverings in this way.

Coping with obstacles – no room is composed entirely of flat walls – you will have to cope with obstacles such as doors, windows, light switches, electric sockets and so on.

If you come to a *door* and there is only a narrow strip between the last length and the frame, it is best to treat it like a corner, measuring, cutting and starting again with the off-cut over the top of the door. If the distance between the last length and the door frame is just short of a roll width, it

will be more convenient to hang the length and to brush it into the side of the door frame, then mark the outline of the door frame with a pencil, and cut away the surplus paper down the side and at the top of the door.

At the *window*, paper the sides and overhead first, using the corner technique to paper recesses.

Light switches and *power points* are not difficult to cope with, but always switch off the electricity at the mains first, then unscrew the switch cover, tuck the paper down behind, making a small hole for the switch, and screw the cover back.
NOTE: never put a foil wallcovering behind, or too close to a switch plate as it could conduct the electricity.

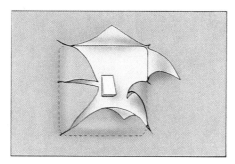

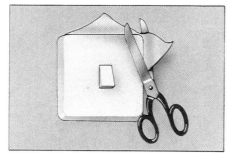

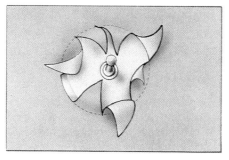

When switches and points are fixed, you will have to cope differently. Brush the paper down as far as you can and press it against the fitting. Pierce the paper at the centre of the fitting and make four diagonal cuts from the centre to the corners, so that the fitting juts out through the centre of the cuts in the paper. Brush the paper round the fitting, mark the outline in pencil and trim away the surplus. For a round switch, make a series of star-shaped cuts. This technique can also be used for ceiling roses.

Ready-pasted papers don't need pasting. Simply measure, match and cut the lengths as for ordinary paper. Roll up each length loosely from the bottom, with the pattern on the *inside*.

Place the water trough at the base of the wall and immerse the cut length in the water for the recommended time. Slowly pull the top end of the length of paper up the wall, letting it unwind in the water so that surplus water runs back into the trough.

Position the length on the wall, slide into place, and brush out using the paper hangers' brush. Mark and trim as previously described. Continue, using the same techniques as for hanging ordinary papers and wallcoverings, to go round obstacles, cope with corners and so on.

Paste-the-wall products. If this method is appropriate for your wallcovering, use the recommended adhesive to paste the wall, using a roller or brush, and covering an area a little wider than the width of the wallcovering. Work from the bottom to the top of the wall and make sure the paste is evenly spread.

With the light polyethylene (polythene) type of wallcovering you can work straight from the roll, without pre-cutting the lengths. With a heavier wallcovering (hessian for example) you will have to cut the lengths first. Start at the top of the wall, position the first width as previously described and slide into place over the paste. Unroll, or unfold, smoothing into position as previously described. Trim top and bottom with a sharp knife or scissors, and continue with the next width, matching the pattern, and brushing out the wrinkles and air bubbles. Use a seam roller if necessary.

Hanging other wallcoverings. Some other specialist wallcoverings may need a different technique, including reversing lengths, although the basic principles are still the same. You will normally find full instructions supplied with the product. With the heavier 'contoured' vinyls for example, you can paste the back (use a special paste) or some people prefer to paste the wall. You will need to use a heavy-duty roller to smooth it back flat to the wall.

HOW TO TILE

Probably you will already have some of the necessary tools for this work in your tool kit and others can be hired from do-it-yourself hire shops, or bought if you prefer.

1. A scriber. This is a type of knife, used for cutting the tile across the glazed surface. (This is done by scoring along the glazed side against a straight edge and breaking over a small slate or piece of tile.)
2. Tile 'nippers', which are rather like pincers and are used to 'nibble away' at unnecessary edges to make a tile fit.
3. Notched adhesive spreader.
4. Spreader with rubber blade, for applying grout to the tiled area once the tiles are stuck in position.
5. Ordinary decorators' sponge, to clean off excess grouting.
6. Spirit level.
7. Try-square or set-square to check right-angles.
8. Plumb line and bob.

Ceramic tiles. It is essential to prepare the surface properly first; make sure the wall is even and free from dirt. If the wall is brick or concrete, scrub to remove loose material and screed if necessary. New plaster or plasterboard must be allowed to dry out *thoroughly* before you add tiling. It is wise also to give the wall a coat of all-purpose primer so that it does not absorb the adhesive. If the wall is old plaster, and very uneven, it may have to be sanded down. Rake out any loose plaster and fill cracks and holes just as you would before re-papering a wall.

Previously painted or papered walls should be washed down, and the paint 'keyed' with sandpaper if it is a gloss finish. Any flaking paint should be scraped or burnt off, and if necessary, apply a coat of stabilizing primer to prevent further flaking under the tiles, otherwise this could 'break through' the adhesive, causing the new tiles to become loose. Always strip off old wallpaper, and prepare the surface as previously described. Tiling over old tiles is possible, if you use the new thin do-it-yourself tiles but, ideally, it is better to remove old tiles and repair the plaster. If you do decide to tile over existing ones, first wash down thoroughly with detergent and repair any cracks or stick back any loose tiles.

Work out how many tiles you need following the Tile Quantities Chart.

To tile a wall using ceramic tiles. Start at the bottom and work up. Place the first tile in position on top of the skirting and mark the top edge, then draw a horizontal line along the wall at this height, checking with straightedge/spirit level to ensure that the line is absolutely level, then tack a batten (which can be easily removed) into place along the line. Centre a tile on the batten – making sure it is at right-angles with a plumb line, and mark widths of tiles outwards, from end to end. Then mark a vertical line on the wall. Try the first line of tiles 'dry' (no adhesive) to check they are going to fit. Then, using the notched spreader, apply tile adhesive or cement (the tiling instructions in the pack or your supplier will advise you which type to use) to an area about 1 m (3 ft) square – press the tiles securely into position on this

HOW MANY TILES?

Measure the height and width of the area to be tiled and use the chart to calculate how many tiles you will need.

	Approximate Number of 15 cm×15 cm (approx 6″×6″) Tiles Required											
9′	36	72	108	144	180	216	252	288	324	360	396	432
8′	32	64	96	128	160	192	224	256	288	320	352	384
7′	28	56	84	112	140	168	196	224	252	280	308	336
6′	24	48	72	96	120	144	168	192	216	240	264	288
5′	20	40	60	80	100	120	140	160	180	200	220	240
4′	16	32	48	64	80	96	112	128	144	160	176	192
3′	12	24	36	48	60	72	84	96	108	120	132	144
2′	8	16	24	32	40	48	56	64	72	80	88	96
1′	4	8	12	16	20	24	28	32	36	40	44	48
	1′	2′	3′	4′	5′	6′	7′	8′	9′	10′	11′	12′

Room Height

Step-by-step to ceramic tiling
1. Fix a batten horizontally to the wall, parallel with the skirting
2. Mark a vertical line on the wall at right-angles, down the centre
3. Press first tile in place. Start at lowest row, on centre line and work out
4. Mark tile to fit gap when batten is removed
5. Break by scoring and snapping over a straight edge, another tile or matchstick
6. 'Nibble' away an area of tile to fit awkward angles or corner

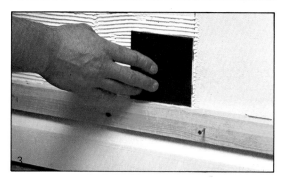

adhesive, in the angle of the flat batten and vertical line. Check each row with a spirit level.

If you have to cut tiles to fit at the ends of each row, cut the tiles as described previously. Use pincers to 'nibble' any tiles where necessary. Mix the grouting according to instructions and spread across the tiles with the special spreader, or a sponge. Wipe off excess grouting with a damp sponge before it dries. Before grouting 'sets', smooth joints with a rounded stick.

NOTE: if you are tiling round a corner (for example, a window sill which joins a tiled wall at right-angles) make sure that the edging (which must be glazed) aligns with the edge of the adjacent tile.

Mirror tiles. These are very popular because they are easy to fix, mostly being self-adhesive (little sticky pads on the back), and do not need grouting. They also increase the apparent size of a room because of their reflective quality. However, they do need to go onto a perfectly flat surface, or they can present a distorted image. Also, this type of tile is not always perfectly right-angled, so butting the tiles up together can present problems. Most of these comments are also applicable to metallic tiles.

To tile a wall using mirror tiles. First test the tiles for square corners – lay them out on a perfectly flat surface, and move them round until you get the best arrangement. Number each tile with a felt-tip pen when you get as good a match as possible.

If the wall is not perfectly flat, cover it with chipboard or insulation board, fixed to the wall by means of battens. Give this a coat of emulsion paint, so that the adhesive pads on the back of the mirror tiles will adhere firmly.

'Square-up' the area with a plumb line, straightedge or T-square and pencil or chalk, drawing a central vertical line, and crossing a central horizontal line. Fix the tiles one by one, following the pack instructions and using the adhesive pads, starting with the central 4 tiles, and working outwards towards the edges. Follow the numbers you previously marked on the tiles. Press each tile firmly into position, making sure it is accurately aligned with its neighbours.

Cut any tiles to fit the gaps round the edges, using a glass cutter to score the surface of the tile and snapping over a matchstick (as with ceramic tiles) for a clean break. Fix in position. Extra self-adhesive pads can be used if necessary – buy these at do-it-yourself shops.

Cork tiles. Most cork tiles, or cork panels, are fixed to the wall by means of a contact adhesive (use the one recommended by the manufacturer), so they are likely to be with you for a long time once they are in position! If you think you are likely to tire of them, it might be better to fix them on panels of hardboard or chipboard (as recommended for mirror tiles), fixed to the wall on battens, so you can remove the whole panel if you want a change of scene.

As with mirror tiles, it is best to start at a central point and work outwards towards the edges, so any small in-fill pieces come at the edge of the wall area.

Mark the wall surface using a plumb line etc. as previously described for mirror tiles. Spread the contact adhesive on the back of the first 4 tiles (to be centrally placed) and on the wall area, or panel of board. Leave for the recommended time, usually until the adhesive is touch-dry.

Align one edge of the first tile with the central mark on the wall, taking care not to let the two adhesive-covered surfaces touch until you are sure the tile is correctly positioned, then press into place. You will find it is firmly fixed to the wall at once, and cannot be moved, so it is important to be sure that it is correctly positioned *before* pressing home. Repeat with the remaining 3 central tiles, aligning and butting them up as closely as possible to their neighbours. Complete cork-tiling the wall this way, cutting tiles as necessary to fit round the edges.

If the tiles are to be sealed, leave for about 24 hours, to let the adhesive dry completely, then dust the surface of the tiles and apply two coats of clear polyurethane varnish. If you want to colour cork tiles you can use one of the coloured wood sealers/stainers.

DEALING WITH DIFFICULT AREAS

Decorating a square (or almost square) room should not present too many problems for a first-time decorator, if you prepare the surfaces properly. Then decorate following the instructions and illustrations, and using the right tools, paint and wallcoverings for the job. Just take it easy and work through the task step-by-step.

However, some areas *are* difficult to cope with and it is wise to wait until you have gained experience and confidence before you tackle them.

The stairs and hallway, even in small modern homes can be surprisingly large, and the wall of the stairwell very tall and

difficult to cope with. You *must* have a safe working platform (see *Decorating tools and equipment*), and the right arrangement will depend on the style of your house and the way the stairs rise. You can hire special scaffolding and platforms for decorating steep stairs. Whenever possible, the angle of the ladder should *oppose* the angle of the stairs, but if this is not possible, fix the longer ladder securely by nailing a stout batten across the uncovered stair tread, and resting the foot of the ladder firmly against this. Where there is a half-landing, you will need to fix scaffold boards in an 'L' shape to reach the ceiling and top of the walls. This can be done by angling a tall ladder in the hallway, using a small step-ladder on the half-landing, and a stout box or 'hop-up' on the main landing. Always make sure that everything is sound and firm before starting to decorate – scaffold boards should be clamped together securely or fixed with a bolt through holes drilled in the boards.

The decorating sequence is the same as for any other room, but if you try to paper a long drop by yourself you will find that the paper will tear with the weight. A join in the wallcovering would be bound to show however, so get some help with the papering. A 'mate' can take the weight and unfold the paper for you as you work down the wall, brushing out with the paperhangers' brush. Hang the longest piece of paper first and work outwards from there.

Above the bath can be a difficult area to reach, and it is not wise to stand in the bath or on the edge. Improvise a platform (see illustration) so that you can reach the ceiling and wall safely; put a plastic dust sheet over or in the bath to catch any

trimmings or paint splashes. Paint and paper as described earlier in this section.

Round kitchen cupboards, particularly wall-mounted ones, can make decorating difficult. If you are decorating the wall from ceiling to counter top (or skirting) use the same technique as for papering round a door (see *How to wallpaper*). One way round the problem is to make a 'midway' panel between the counter top and the bottom of the cupboard, which can double as a splash-back. You will only need to cope with a small amount of material if you do this. The panel can be of tiles; laminate; self-adhesive plastic material; or offcuts from your vinyl floor covering can be stuck to the wall with an impact adhesive, which gives the room a nice co-ordinated look at the same time. Alternatively, take the cupboards off the wall and rehang after decorating.

Papering behind radiators is another tricky job. Ideally the heating system should be switched off, the valves closed and the radiator emptied, then lifted off the brackets (un-screw the inlet pipes), so that you can paper the wall down to the skirting and then re-hang the radiator. If you cannot do this, treat the radiator as though it was not there, cutting paper to skirting length. Let it drop in front of the radiator, while you 'brush out' the paper from the top to about half-way down the wall. Then carefully slide the lower half of the paper down behind the radiator – you can buy a special radiator brush or simply use a wire coat-hanger covered with cloth and firmly fastened to a cane handle. Always remove any excess wallpaper paste from the front of the radiator immediately; otherwise it can cause the paint to perish.

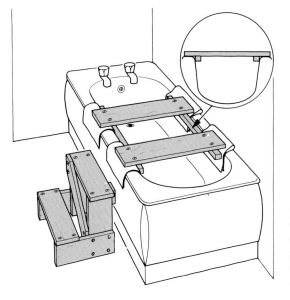

Never stand on the edge of the bath to reach behind or above. Use a hop-up and make a rough timber platform to fit the bath; protect the edge with old underfelt or piece of thick fabric

CARING FOR YOUR HOME

However much time, thought and money you expend on decorating and furnishing your home, you will also need a working knowledge of cleaning materials and techniques to preserve its good-looks and comfort – and that is what the following pages are all about. Fortunately, modern technology has made home-care much less arduous than it once was, but knowledge and skill are still required if it is to be carried out satisfactorily. Here, you will find all that you need to know to keep your home looking its best.

CLEANING AROUND THE HOME

BASIC EQUIPMENT

As with any job, you can clean better, faster and more easily if you have the right tools and materials, so it pays to invest a little time and money in getting yourself well equipped.

Brooms and brushes. A broom is an old-fashioned cleaning basic which is as useful today as ever. Remember that in general brooms and brushes with soft bristles are for smooth, hard floors, and those with hard bristles are for soft floors, such as carpeting. You will need at least one long-handled broom with soft bristles for sweeping hard floors such as vinyl, wood or cork. To complement this, you will need a hand brush with soft bristles and a

dust pan. Dust pan and brush sets designed to hang up as one unit are very convenient. An additional small brush with stiff bristles is useful for small carpet-cleaning jobs such as brushing up dried mud or spilt sugar. A second long-handled broom with stiff bristles is useful for sweeping drives, paths and yards.

The bristles in broom and brush heads can be made of either natural materials such as cocoa fibre or horsehair, or synthetics such as nylon, polypropylene, pvc or polyethylene. Often, two or even more fibres will be mixed together to provide the right brush for the job. Try to buy from a quality range that offers a wide choice. One specialist manufacturer offers horsehair for 'really long-lasting indoor sweeping of hard floors', crimped poly-

propylene for 'carpet sweeping, particularly around edges of fitted carpets', and red polypropylene for 'heavy-duty outdoor work'.

Broom handles are attached to their heads by various methods. It is important that the head fits securely – you cannot sweep properly with a loose-fitting broom head which may well come off completely just when you are at your busiest. Some handles simply fit into a hole in the broom head, although you may first have to shape the handle a little with a file or sandpaper so that it fits. Put a little wood adhesive into the hole in the head before banging the head onto the handle with the broom upside down. You may find there is a hole in the broom head through which you can drive a small, thin screw; use a gimlet or

bradawl to make a starting hole in the handle to avoid splitting the wood. Many modern ranges of brooms have their own patented 'connectors' – strong and easy-to-fit ways of joining broom head to handle.

Try to keep brooms and brushes as clean as possible. Remove fluff from the tufts with a wide-toothed comb. Periodically, wash the heads in a bowl of warm water to which has been added a squeeze of washing-up liquid. Then rinse well, giving bristle brushes a final rinse in cold salty water to stiffen them up again. Suspend brushes to dry heads *down* but clear of the ground; this prevents water soaking into the heads and distortion of the bristles.

Specially designed brooms and brushes are available for some tasks. For example, you can buy a cobweb brush with a soft head – particularly useful if you have high ceilings; look for one with an extending handle. A radiator 'mop' is invaluable for cleaning down behind radiators. A bottle brush will get inside not only bottles but also vacuum flasks, vases, decanters and so on, and there is even a tiny brush designed for cleaning teapot spouts! An old tooth-brush comes in handy for many fiddly jobs such as cleaning around taps and cooker knobs. Every wc should have its own lavatory brush.

Mops. Most homes have some areas of smooth, hard flooring – vinyl sheet or tiles, cork, wood, stone and so on, and for these a mop is an essential. You can still buy the old-fashioned type with a stranded cotton head, but if you do you will also need the old design of metal mop bucket in order to press the water out properly. This can be rather bulky to store, and most people nowadays use sponge mops on a long

Left: various shapes and sizes of bowls and buckets are available. A plastic bowl placed in your sink protects china from knocks and chips; if you fit the tap with a rubber splashguard, you can rinse plates etc. alongside, even in a single sink. Square buckets are best for use with squeezie mops. A long-handled broom with a soft head is essential for sweeping smooth floors, and you will also need a soft handbrush for transferring sweepings to the dustpan. A sink 'tidy' guards against blocked drains; sterilize frequently in a weak solution of household bleach. Washing-up brushes should also be sterilized from time to time Above: special brushes to make household tasks easier include a vegetable brush, pastry brush, bottle brush and a brush for teapot spouts. You will also need scouring pads

handle, with a built-in squeezer for pressing out the water. The heads are usually made of cellulose and should always be rinsed very well after use, otherwise remains of dirt or food will literally eat away the mop head. For the same reason, never cover the mop head during storage; leave it to dry naturally. Make sure that before use the mop is completely immersed in water so that it becomes wet and soft, otherwise the squeezing motion will crack it. You will also need a bucket large enough to take the mop head.

Dishcloths and floorcloths. You will need dishcloths for general cleaning and mopping up in the kitchen and bathroom, and floorcloths as heavy duty versions for mopping up spills on hard floors. Absorbent cotton dishcloths are best, but they must be kept scrupulously clean. Sterilize them by soaking overnight in 5 litres (1 gallon) of cold water, adding $\frac{1}{4}$ eggcup of household (chlorine) bleach. Rinse thoroughly. Alternatively, you can boil up dishcloths on the stove with a little washing powder added to the water. They will smell sweeter if they are hung to dry in between use (over a small rail, perhaps) rather than being left in a crumpled heap. You will also need *scouring pads* and *steel*

wool for very dirty pans, but use with caution (see notes on cleaning different surfaces, which follow).

Dusters. You can easily make your own dusters from cut-up clothes. Cotton tee shirts and men's cotton vests make the best ones; synthetics are not suitable because they are non-absorbent and some are scratchy. In addition to dusters, it is useful to keep a 'rag-bag' of material for really messy cleaning-up jobs. Keep your dusters clean, washing them regularly, rinsing them well and drying them thoroughly. If you buy the traditional yellow dusters, wash them separately from your clothes because the dyes are not fast.

Cleaners and polishes. *Washing-up liquid* is useful for all kinds of cleaning jobs – use just a brief squirt of this in a bucket of warm water, for example, to wash vinyl floors or clean paintwork. But do not use it for small stains on carpets as you will simply re-attract dirt; instead, buy a small bottle of *carpet shampoo*, of the type that dries to a dry foam and is then brushed off.

Harsh cleaning powders and liquids are really only necessary for very dirty surfaces: indeed they are not recommended by many flooring manufacturers. Liquid

A good selection of cleaners and polishes will help keep your home clean and bright. Store them tidily in a safe place, away from children: most are poisonous

SAFETY NOTE. Most products used for household cleaning are poisonous; many are flammable; many will irritate the skin or eyes. Pay careful attention to warnings printed by law on packs. Always read carefully any directions for use, diluting solutions strictly in accordance with instructions on the pack. Store all bottles upright (clearly labelled) with caps tightly fastened. Never sniff or taste old chemicals. Do not transfer cleaners or chemicals into other containers; in particular do not use containers which have held food or drink. Keep all cleaning products in a securely closed cupboard out of the reach of young children – you may not have young children yourself, but they may come to visit you. When using any of these products, work in well ventilated rooms, away from naked flames.

floor cleaners are available which can be diluted for damp-mopping or used neat on very dirty areas. A little *ammonia* (do not inhale the fumes or let them near your eyes) added to detergent solution will cut through grease (4 tablespoons to $4\frac{1}{2}$ litres [1 gallon] of water); do not use for vinyl floors or paintwork. *Washing soda* is useful for keeping drains free from grease; once a week, pour down the sink a solution of 225 g ($\frac{1}{2}$ lb) soda to 7 litres ($1\frac{1}{2}$ gallons) of boiling water. *Scouring powder*, sold in tall cannisters with perforated tops, should be used with caution as it can scratch stainless steel, plastic or enamel surfaces. Use only for tackling very dirty saucepans or baking pans and rinse well afterwards. *Scouring creams* are preferable for most surfaces, but do remember that even these are abrasive, although less so than the powders. Always apply them on a damp pad, do not squeeze them directly on to the surface to be cleaned.

Household bleach is an essential since it is useful for a wide range of cleaning and sterilizing jobs. But always dilute as recommended on the bottle as strength varies a little from brand to brand. Some bleaches are now thickened so that they

cling to surfaces to provide a longer-lasting effect, and some have a 'directional cap' so that you can aim them under, for example, the rim of a wc bowl. *White spirit* is useful for removing marks from paint-work etc., and as a general solvent for greasy marks. Caution: it is flammable. It is also useful to keep a liquid and an aerosol branded solvent stain-remover (sometimes called a dry cleaner). Other solvents such as methylated spirits (flammable) and acetone (very flammable) are useful for shifting particular stains, as suggested in the *Stain removal chart. Lavatory cleaner* will shift lime scale in wcs which household bleach will not: but never use bleach and lavatory cleaners together as, when combined, they give off a dangerous, possibly even fatal, gas. *Household disinfectant* is useful for washing out pedal bins, dustbins and so on (although you can also use a dilute solution of bleach for this).

There are all kinds of special cleaners and polishes available for different surfaces, and you will find more notes on these under the relevant subject headings which follow later. But a can of general purpose aerosol *cleaner-polisher* is handy.

Vacuum cleaners. Make sure you buy the type best suited to your needs. If possible, try out the cleaner in the shop, to test for weight and manoeuvrability. If you cannot afford a new cleaner, you may be able to buy a 're-conditioned' one; these can be perfectly satisfactory, provided you buy from a reputable well-established dealer.

Upright cleaners have 'beater bars' (revolving brushes) which are particularly good for pile carpets. Some models now available will get right to the edges of fitted carpets and there are attachments specially designed to cope with smooth floorings, upholstery and curtains. But uprights should not be used on shag or long piles with pile tufts longer than about 30 mm ($1\frac{1}{4}$ inch), because the pile can become entangled in the beater bars. Use a cylinder cleaner instead (see below), then fluff up with a 'shag rake' – like a plastic garden rake.

Many people find *cylinder cleaners* more convenient in use though generally they do not have the power of uprights. Cylinders can usually be taken from carpets onto smooth flooring without the need to change to another tool, and they are often lighter and easier to carry round.

Push vacuum cleaners slowly over carpets, doing a section the width of the cleaner at a time. Make at least three strokes: once forwards, once backwards, and then forwards again and on to the next section, if possible leaving pile sloping in right direction. The correct direction for

plain carpet pile is the direction which looks and feels the smoothest. Carpet pile has a natural 'fall' or 'slope' like a cat's fur: you can tell the right direction when you stroke it – and it is obvious if you are actually looking at a carpet. If correctly laid, velvet pile carpets will have their pile laid slanting away from the light. For notes on looking after your cleaners, see *Care of household appliances*.

There is one golden rule however: empty dust bags regularly, before they become more than half full. A vacuum cleaner cannot work efficiently with a full dust bag, which can block the passage of air through the cleaner. This can strain the motor, necessitating early, costly repairs.

Carpet sweepers are less expensive than vacuum cleaners and are not as quick or thorough, but they are very useful for a quick clean-up when you do not want the trouble of getting out the vacuum cleaner. They also make a useful stand-by against the possibility of your vacuum cleaner breaking down. They are light and easy to carry up and down stairs. And they do not make a noise; useful if someone is trying to watch television, study, or is ill in bed while you are doing the cleaning.

STORAGE FOR CLEANING EQUIPMENT

Keep your cleaning equipment all together in one place (remember many of the cleaners and polishes may be poisonous, see preceding safety note). Long-handled brooms and mops should be hung up with their heads clear of the floor, so that the bristles or sponge do not get crushed. You can make a slotted rack to hold broom heads, or use large spring clips, sometimes

Above: a carpet sweeper provides a useful back-up to your vacuum cleaner, being light, quiet and easy to handle. On this model, special brushes reach right to carpet edges and the brush height can be adjusted to cope with different heights of pile
Right: a well-organised cleaning cupboard can save a lot of time and temper!

called 'terry clips'. Or, from hardware stores, you can buy rings that fit onto the end of the handles so that you can hang them from a hook or nail. Alternatively, insert a screw eye into the handle, and hang the broom up by a piece of string. Keep small, often-used cleaning equipment in an easy-to-carry container with a handle so that you can take it easily from room to room; you can buy plastic 'cleaning caddies' from chain stores for this, or you could use a small plastic pail.

Use bags or boxes to keep your cleaning cupboard or drawer tidy – plastic carrier bags or shoe boxes are ideal. If you have a cupboard with a sturdy door, you could line its inner side with shallow, 'lipped' shelves to take bottles and cannisters, or buy wire racks from hardware stores. These can be suspended from two screws inside the cupboard door. If you keep your cleaning things under the stairs, do have a

light fitted so that you can see to get things out easily and safely. One idea is to store cleaning equipment on a trolley that stows away under the stairs; this can be wheeled out when needed, and even wheeled around the house with you, provided you do not have too many steps up and down. You could buy an old trolley very cheaply from a junk shop, and give it a coat of bright gloss paint.

Of course, the cleaning materials and methods you use will vary according to the surfaces to be cleaned.

CLEANING ROUTINES

These days, few people can afford the luxury of doing their cleaning on regular weekday mornings. Many of us have to do household chores in the evenings or at weekends, or fit them in as best as we can around the demands of small children (who often seem to undo everything as

soon as it is finished anyway). Everybody finds their own best ways of coping and a set cleaning routine is definitely not necessary. However, there are a few general hints which might prove useful.

Try to wear suitable clothes for the job. You cannot clean properly if you are worrying about keeping your clothes smart, so take the time to change, or at least put on an apron or an old shirt as a cover-up. Change into comfortable flat shoes, if you have them.

Before you start, take a few moments to plan what you are going to do. Be realistic, it is often better to do one job thoroughly than to skimp quickly through two or three. If you are short of time with visitors imminent, concentrate on a thorough tidying-up: it works wonders. Have plenty of storage available such as bins or baskets for toys, racks or trolleys for newspapers and magazines, baskets for sewing projects and so on. If you have 'a place for everything' things can all the more easily and quickly be returned to their places when the heat is on.

Always take time to clear surfaces completely before cleaning. When in a hurry there is a great temptation to try and clean around things and it is never satisfactory. For example, before you do the floor you must pick up all toys, magazines and so on, and move out light chairs or put them up onto other furniture. Shelves must be cleared before dusting: use a tray or a plastic washing-up bowl to hold items such as ornaments or framed photographs.

Cleaning floors used to make a lot of dust, and the advice then given was to clean the floors first and then go on to the dusting. With modern vacuum cleaners, it is not important in which order you clean a room, but dirt on the floor or carpet does seem to be more conspicuous than dust on a shelf.

As your children get older, do try to train them to help you with the cleaning. If you are very busy and frequently tired, training possibly unwilling teenagers can seem more arduous than simply doing it oneself. But making the effort does pay off. Even quite small children can be taught to clean baths and basins and dust furniture. Older children can become expert at vacuum cleaning and keeping their own rooms tidy.

Walls and ceilings. A cobweb brush with an extending handle is invaluable for removing those grimy threads of dirt which suddenly and horrifying appear when the sun shines brightly (they were

However beautifully you furnish your home, it will soon begin to look shabby unless you establish a regular cleaning routine, with due consideration for the number of different surfaces and materials involved. In this living room alone there are carpets, upholstery, paintwork, windows, curtains, china, silver, furniture, pictures, books and ornaments, all needing different kinds of attention at different times – see text

there all the time, of course, but we didn't notice them!). A vacuum cleaner attachment with soft brush is useful for occasionally brushing down walls, or you can use a broom with a soft duster tied over the head. Remove light fittings, pictures or mirrors before you start, to avoid breakages.

Painted walls can be washed down when they get dirty. First take down any pictures. Move furniture into the middle of the room, get help with this if moving heavy items. Cover the furniture with an old sheet, blanket, or newspapers taped together with sticky tape. Turn back floor coverings if possible. Brush down walls, or use a vacuum cleaner attachment to remove as much loose dust as you can. Take two buckets, and fill one with warm water plus a squeeze of washing-up liquid; fill the other with cool clear water. Do not use soap powders sold for washing clothes; they usually contain 'fluorescers' which may brighten up your washing, but can change the colours of some paints. Before starting to wash walls all over, treat any very dirty or greasy patches with a little neat washing-up liquid squeezed onto a clean damp cloth. Wring out a sponge or cloth in the detergent solution and, working from the skirting upwards, wash the walls in strips of about 1 m (3 ft) at a time. Alternatively, you can use a sponge floor mop. (The reason for working from bottom upwards is that if you start at the top water running down into dirty areas can 'set' the dirt and make it almost impossible to remove). When you have washed a complete 1 m (3 ft) strip from bottom to top, take a second cloth or sponge, wring it out in the clean water, and wipe down the washed area, this time from top to bottom. Now move on to a fresh section, and repeat the routine. But do try to complete one wall in one session, or you could get a line where the cleaning stopped. Before you clean around power points or light switches, it is safest to turn off your electricity at the mains.

This routine can be adapted for *painted ceilings*: but if your ceilings have the old-fashioned *distemper* they cannot be washed, or even be repainted until every scrap of removeable distemper has been scrubbed away. When you have removed as much as you can (using warm water, a sponge and a scrubbing brush or even a scraper for very thick coatings) give the ceiling a coat of primer sealer from a builder's merchant or decorating shop, and allow to dry, according to the directions on the can. This should prevent blistering or flaking of the new paint when it is applied.

Polystyrene ceiling tiles can be dusted very gently (remember, they are soft) with a cobweb brush or with a duster tied around a broom head. Or use a vacuum cleaner attachment. Wash the tiles gently with a solution of warm water and washing-up liquid, then rinse with clear water. But never use solvents of any kind, e.g. white spirit, as the tiles will simply dissolve. After washing the tiles and allowing them to dry, freshen them up with a coat of emulsion paint; but never use oil-based paints as these are a fire risk.

Washable wallpaper should not be taken at face value. You cannot actually wash it, but you can sponge it. First dust down the walls. Then take a bucket of warm water with a squeeze of washing-up liquid, and after wringing out your cloth or sponge thoroughly so that it is barely damp, gently sponge the wall, working from the bottom upwards. Be very careful not to overwet and do not rub the wallpaper. Do not use white spirit or solvent dry-cleaner stain-removers, as they could damage the paper's finish.

Non-washable papers. An old-fashioned but effective method for erasing dirty marks is to rub them gently with a piece of bread. Or you can try a soft, clean pencil rubber. A dry-cleaning stain-remover may remove some marks, but always test in an out of sight place first. Sometimes you can lift grease by covering the damaged area with blotting paper and applying a warm iron.

Vinyls are much easier to clean. After dusting well, wash them down using a cloth, sponge or even a soft scrubbing brush, and a bucket of warm water containing a squeeze of washing-up liquid. Work on a small area at a time, and wipe off as you go with a clean cloth well wrung out in a second bucket of clean water. Work upwards from the skirting board, and avoid rubbing across the joints. Try treating stains with a very small dab of white spirit on a clean cloth, or rub very lightly with scouring powder. But these treatments are *not* suitable for vinyls with metallic colourings. If the joins are coming unstuck (very common on overlaps) you will find that vinyl will not stick to itself with ordinary wallcovering adhesive. You can buy a special adhesive for resticking vinyl overlaps, from decorating stores, or use a latex white liquid craft adhesive.

Speciality wallcoverings now include paper-backed hessians, silks, grasscloths and so on. The supplier should be able to advise you about suitable cleaning techniques. In general this type of wallcovering can only be dry dusted, using if possible the attachment brush to a vacuum cleaner (but make sure the brush is scrupulously clean before you start). It may be possible to treat marks and stains with a solvent dry-cleaner stain-remover but do test this out first on an area that doesn't show: for example behind a piece of furniture. Unfortunately, if wetted with water – or even if cleaned with a solvent – many of these wallcoverings may shrink back along the joins, or lose their colour.

Ceramic wall tiles are very easy to clean. A wipe-over with a clean cloth well wrung out in a bucket of warm water to which a squeeze of washing-up liquid has been added should usually be all that is needed. Add a few drops of disinfectant if cleaning tiled areas around the wc. Rinse the tiles with clean water, and polish them dry with a soft cloth. You may be able to whiten old discoloured grouting by applying a solution of household (chlorine) bleach on an old toothbrush. But often the only satisfactory solution is to rake out the old grouting and to replace it with new grouting.

Paintwork on skirtings, doors etc. should be dusted regularly. A damp cloth with a little washing-up liquid should remove most marks, but you can also use a cream cleaner or an aerosol general purpose cleaner/polisher. A little white spirit will usually remove black heel marks. When very dirty, wash down, adapting the methods described for painted walls, above.

Floorings. Always use the cleaning products and procedures recommended by your flooring manufacturer. If you have new flooring or carpets, find out what these methods are. Write to the manufacturer, if necessary.

Clean floors as often as you can: embedded dirt is difficult to remove and can cause permanent damage.

Wipe up all spills at once: they can stain, they can be dangerous, and they can cause permanent damage.

Make sure you have door mats front and back.

The basic floor cleaning techniques which are suitable for many different smooth floorings, are:

Sweeping. See notes on brooms and brushes at beginning of chapter. Always clear a floor before you sweep, and sweep towards the middle of the floor. Always empty your dust pan immediately after use.

Vacuum cleaning. See notes on vacuum cleaners. Suitable for carpets and smooth floorings.

Damp-mopping. See previous notes on floor mops. In general, use a little washing-up liquid in a bucketful of warm water; if necessary, damp-mop with clear water to rinse. Work towards an exit, and try to choose a time when your floor will have a chance to dry undisturbed.

Polishing. This is often not necessary for today's floors – for example, many vinyls have a shiny clear 'wear layer'. Some floors – bare wood and cork, stone, slate, brick and unglazed ceramic tiles such as quarries – cannot be satisfactorily polished unless first sealed; see note on sealers, below.

There are two main types of floor polishes, so always read directions and recommendations on packs very carefully. *Water-based emulsion polishes* contain acrylics and/or wax and are suitable for most types of floor. They dry to a soft shine. Before applying polish, damp-mop and rinse off as described above under damp-mopping. Then apply polish with a damp clean cloth or mop: a dry cloth soaks up too much of the polish. The polish will take about half an hour to dry and should be left undisturbed for this time. You can apply a second coat about a day later if you wish.

You will not need to polish again for about six weeks; in between times, simply damp-mop. But after about six applications of polish you will need to strip away the polish build-up, as this can make your floor seem very dingy or even discoloured. Half-fill a bucket with cold water and add a quarter of a cup of floor cleaning powder, and one cup of ammonia (do not breathe in the fumes, and keep the solution away from skin and eyes). Scrub the floor with this solution, using a soft brush, then rinse thoroughly with clean water. Allow to dry, then re-apply polish as above.

Solvent or spirit-based wax polish can be solid or liquid. The liquid types actually clean off traces of old polish and dirt as you put them on, but *do not* use these polishes on vinyl sheet or tiles or on cork tiles with a vinyl coating. And never apply a water-based polish to a floor previously polished with a solvent-based polish or the other way around. Sweep the floor before you apply a solvent based polish, then apply the polish on a clean dry cloth and allow to dry for at least half an hour before buffing up with a second clean dry cloth (which you can tie around the head of a broom). Or you can use an electric polisher if you have one.

Sealing. Many floors are easier to keep clean if they are initially sealed. Indeed it is essential to seal bare new wood (which should be freshly sanded), and bare cork. Use a polyurethane or oleo-resinous seal, carefully following the directions on the pack. Sealers may need renewing periodically, and should always be applied to scrupulously clean floors. Special sealers are sold by flooring specialists for stone, slate, brick, concrete and unglazed ceramics such as quarry tiles, and will make these floors easier to keep clean. But always try out on a small test area first, as some sealers can change the colour of these floors. When sealed, all types of floor can be polished with a water-based emulsion polish or with a solvent wax polish. Do not seal vinyl floors.

TREATMENTS FOR FLOOR SURFACES

Here are some notes on how to treat particular floor surfaces commonly found around the home.

Brick. Sweep. If necessary, scrub over with a solution of warm water plus washing-up liquid, using a cleaning powder if floor seems very badly soiled, but do not over wet. Rinse off, if necessary, then use a dry mop to dry the floor as much as possible. You can buy special sealers for brick and stone floors, which will make subsequent cleaning much easier. Sealed floors can be polished with a liquid solvent wax polish, or an emulsion polish.

Ceramic tiles. For *glazed* tiles, simply sweep, then damp-mop occasionally, but never polish. Always mop up spills promptly as these can make the floor dangerously slippery. *Unglazed* types include *quarry* tiles. Sweep, and damp-mop as for

The average home contains a wide variety of flooring surfaces, all needing different cleaning techniques and products. When you are planning furnishings, try to install the same type of flooring in adjacent rooms to make life easier. Wherever possible, get detailed cleaning instructions from the manufacturers. Write, asking them to recommend specific cleaning products and techniques for your particular flooring. Some carpet makers will also supply guidance on stain removal

brick flooring above. White patches sometimes appear on newly laid tiles. Wash with neat vinegar, leave to dry for about one hour, then rinse. You can seal quarry tiles if you wish, using a mixture of half white spirit and half linseed oil, applied very sparingly, or a special floor sealer. Sealed floors can be polished. Red coloured wax paste polishes are available to restore the colour to old floor tiles.

Cork. You must find out which finish your cork floor has, as this affects the way to treat it. *Unsealed cork* tiles must first be sealed with an oleo-resinous floor seal, or with polyurethane, and they will need at least three coats. Always follow carefully any directions on the can. In general each coat of varnish will take around 8 to 10 hours to dry, and you should aim to apply each coat within 24 hours of the last. When the seal is completely dry, floors can be damp-mopped, and polished if you wish with an emulsion or solvent polish. *Waxed cork* tiles can be swept, then polished with a liquid solvent-based wax polish. A little of this polish can also be used to remove any stubborn marks. *Polyurethane-coated* tiles can be swept and damp-mopped. Polish, if you wish, with a water-based emulsion polish, and a little of this can be used to remove stubborn marks. *Vinyl-coated* tiles should be swept, damp-mopped and then polished (if necessary) with a water-based emulsion polish, but never use a solvent-based polish.

Linoleum. Don't confuse this with modern vinyls (see below) which have largely replaced old-fashioned lino in the shops. Many people still call vinyl 'lino'. New lino may benefit from sealing: follow maker's recommendations. In general, lino floors can be swept, then damp-mopped, but do take care not to overwet the floor. Use either a water-based or solvent-based polish depending on which has been used before (the two types of polish are incompatible). You can use a little polish on a damp cloth to remove stubborn marks, or try rubbing gently with a cloth moistened with a little turps or white spirit.

Marble. Sweep, then damp-mop, with a bucket of warm water plus a squeeze of washing-up liquid. Rinse, and use a dry mop to dry off floor. Always wipe up stains and spills immediately (fats and oils in particular) as these can stain badly if left.

Stone and slate floors. Sweep and damp-mop with a bucket of warm water to which has been added a squeeze of washing-up liquid. You can buy special sealers for stone and slate floors, but always test a small area first, as a sealer could cause discolouration. Sealed floors are easier to clean and can be polished if you wish with an emulsion or a solvent-based liquid wax polish.

Vinyl sheet and tiles. Sweep and damp-mop as necessary. Polish if you wish with a water-based emulsion polish – do not use a solvent-based polish – see notes on *Damp-mopping* and *Polishing*. Sometimes stubborn marks can be removed with a soft clean india rubber or you can use a little polish on a damp cloth. Beware of the following, all of which will harm a vinyl floor surface: paint stripper, nail varnish remover, white spirit and paraffin. Leave small spills to evaporate, otherwise you may simply spread the damage; but mop up large spills immediately and throw away the cloth in the outside dustbin.

Wood. Bare wood must first be sanded smooth and clean, then stained (if required) and sealed either with oleo-

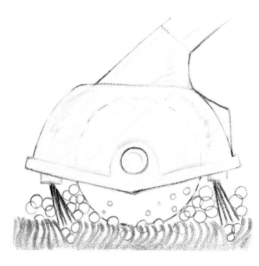

Left: hard-wearing sisal has been chosen for this busy dining area; regular vacuuming will help to retain its tough good looks and prevent a build-up of dirt underneath
Above: if you have large areas of carpet in your home, it is worth while to invest in a carpet shampooer, which forces the shampoo foam deep into the carpet pile. See text for full details on shampooing carpets

resinous floor seal or with polyurethane – apply at least three coats, following the manufacturer's instructions to the letter. Once sealed, wood can be swept and even damp-mopped, but do take care not to get it too wet. As the sealer becomes worn, renew it, or water can penetrate through to wood fibres and make them swell. You can polish sealed floors with a water-based or solvent-based polish as you wish. Waxed wooden floors should be swept, then polished with solvent-based liquid floor polish which will also clean as it polishes (see *Polishing*). A little polish, or white spirit should remove stubborn marks; use very fine steel wool if necessary – working parallel to the grain (you may then have to touch up your sealer).

Carpets. Regular cleaning is essential as embedded dirt and grit will actually harm the carpet pile. Vacuum at least once a week, more often if necessary. First clear the floor as much as is possible but do not drag heavy furniture over the carpet. Shag pile carpets are best cleaned by a cylinder type vacuum cleaner or a carpet sweeper as the long pile can become entangled in upright vacuum cleaners. You can buy a special 'shag-rake' (a plastic rake that looks a bit like a lawn rake) which is very effective for fluffing up the carpet pile.

Wet-cleaning. Once or even twice a year, your carpet may need wet cleaning, to shift stains and remove ground-in dirt. If the carpet is valuable, or is badly soiled, is flattened, has been flooded, or has colours which are likely to run, it is best to call in a professional cleaner, who may use a shampoo system or the newer method of 'steam' cleaning often called 'hot-water extraction'. Your cleaner will advise you on which method is the most suitable for your carpet. New or newly-cleaned carpets can be chemically sprayed to resist subsequent soiling or staining: consult a professional cleaner. Rugs and carpet squares can be taken away for factory cleaning, but fitted carpets must be cleaned 'on site'.

Alternatively, you can tackle wet-cleaning the carpet yourself. It is now possible to hire machines for steam cleaning from many drycleaners and hire equipment shops. Always follow the directions very carefully: do not exceed temperatures recommended and never make the cleaning solution stronger than the instructions specify.

Shampooing, however, is the method familiar to most people. Use a proprietary carpet shampoo of the 'dry foam' type. When these shampoos are dry, they can be vacuumed up with any remaining dirt. Never use a solution of washing-up liquid, as this will simply reattract dirt. Follow the instructions on the shampoo pack.

There are various ways of applying the shampoo. You can use a small sponge or brush, but it is difficult not to over-wet the carpet in the process, or to distribute the shampoo evenly.

You will get better results if you use a carpet shampooer, a special upright appliance with a container for the shampoo solution, and foam rollers at the bottom. As you push the container back and forth, the shampoo comes out of the bottom as a foam. You could buy one of these and share it with friends; it would certainly pay for itself in time if you have large carpeted areas in your home. Or you can hire electrical versions of this machine from many hardware stores and these are even more effective. If you have shaggy long pile carpets, check that the machine you intend to hire is suitable for them – the pile can become entangled in some types of electric machine.

Before shampooing always test for colour fastness. Rub a small patch of the carpet in an out-of-the-way spot with a cloth wetted with the shampoo solution. If the colours of patterned carpets appear to run, transferring themselves onto the cloth, you should call in a professional cleaner. Plain carpets may transfer a little colour onto your cloth, but you should nevertheless still be able to carry out a satisfactory home shampoo, provided that you apply it evenly.

Choose a time for shampooing when the room can be left unused for at least six to eight hours afterwards – or better still, overnight. You will need to remove heavy furniture and you should get help with this. Never drag furniture over the carpet. For pieces that cannot be removed, cut little pieces of aluminium foil to place under their feet. Make up the shampoo solution exactly as directed on the pack. Mix it in a large bowl, jug or bucket before you pour it into your shampooer. If you prefer to mix shampoo in the machine, insert shampoo first, then add the water. Shake gently to mix. Vacuum thoroughly, passing the vacuum cleaner at least five times over each strip of carpet. Treat any spots with 1 tablespoon of white vinegar to 1 litre ($1\frac{3}{4}$ pints) of shampoo solution. Then open any windows and start shampooing opposite the door, working on strips of carpet about 30 cm (1 ft) wide. Push the shampooer back and forth several times, then leave pile sloping in the right direction. As you move to a fresh area, allow a slight overlap. Always take care not to overwet the carpet.

When you have finished, close the door, leaving carpet to dry for at least six to eight hours. Avoid walking on it while it is wet. When it is dry, vacuum all over very thoroughly. This is very important. You will be removing the freed dirt plus the remains of the shampoo, which would simply re-attract dirt if left in the pile. Then get help with moving back the furniture.

Rugs. In general these can be cleaned with a vacuum cleaner or carpet sweeper. Occasionally, turn them over and clean the back as well as the front. However, there are so many different types of rugs now available that it is difficult to give more specific advice. Keep any cleaning instructions that come with the rug. Some types are washable: these may include cotton shag piles, acrylic long piles, and flokati white wool rugs from Greece. Wash by hand in warm water with mild detergent and spin dry if possible. Then dry over two lines, to support the weight. When dry, fluff up the pile with a clean stiff brush. Other rugs, made in the same way as carpets, can be shampooed as described above, but oriental carpets of any value should always be sent away to a specialist cleaner. Many rugs from overseas such as the numdah

embroidered felts and dhurries (flat-weaves in cotton or wool) cannot be washed or shampooed but can be dry cleaned. Fur rugs should not be vacuumed; shake them gently outside from time to time. Some rugs without a backing can be gently shampooed with a sponge and a solution of carpet shampoo, but you must avoid wetting the skin. For fur rugs with a backing try sprinkling with fullers earth (from your chemist). Leave the powder on for a few hours then brush it out.

Mattings e.g. rush. Vacuum thoroughly as often as possible; if you can, lift to sweep up or vacuum dirt that collects underneath. Sponge or scrub dirty matting with

a solution of warm water and washing-up liquid, then sponge over with clean water and allow to dry. Treat greasy marks with warm water into which you have dissolved a little washing soda.

Carpet stain removal: general advice. Treat all stains as quickly as possible to prevent a permanent mark. Don't panic. Blot up liquids with a clean absorbent cloth, or use white tissue or toilet-paper: do not use coloured paper napkins. Do not rub stain in. Specific action for particular stains is listed under the *Stain removal chart*. Remember to test all methods on an unseen part of the carpet before using them on a larger area which shows.

FURNITURE

Tables, and cabinet furniture, such as wooden chests of drawers, wardrobes and cupboards.

Furniture polishes are made from combinations of various waxes, both natural and synthetic. Silicones are usually added to aerosol and liquid polishes to make them easier to apply and to give a more protective finish to the furniture.

Modern furniture. Always check the manufacturer's recommendations. In the absence of instructions on a swing ticket or in a brochure, it is worth writing to the manufacturer to get cleaning advice: you will want to keep your furniture for a long time. In general, dusting with a soft clean cloth along the direction of the grain is all that is necessary for modern furniture. To remove greasy marks, use a few drops of detergent solution on a damp cloth on most modern furniture finishes, including polyurethane, melamine and foil finishes. Alternatively, you can use a general purpose aerosol cleaner/polisher, but apply sparingly. Modern furniture does not need polishing to 'feed the wood', but a good brand of aerosol or liquid wax furniture polish may well revive a tired-looking finish. However, much modern furniture is intended to have a matt finish, and should not be polished to a high shine. Teak in general only needs dusting and should not be polished. However, two or three times a year, you can apply teak oil, very sparingly, on a clean cloth.

Old furniture. If very dirty, wipe over with a solution of one part vinegar to eight parts water, using a clean cloth or a chamois leather. Or use a special furniture cleaner/reviver. Follow with a good paste wax polish. But on well-polished pieces do

Left: furniture with a rich sheen enhances any room. Much modern furniture needs little polishing, but you can use an aerosol or liquid wax polish from time to time to revive a tired-looking finish. Old furniture will benefit from sparing applications of a good paste wax polish, buffed up well with a soft cloth
Right: cane and bamboo furniture can be cleaned with warm water, soapflakes and laundry borax. Sometimes, you can tighten a slightly sagging cane seat by sponging with a washing soda solution, pushing the seat upwards and leaving it to dry in sunlight

not use a liquid or aerosol polish containing silicones which can clean away layers of old polish, destroying the patina and creating a patchy effect. Apply polish sparingly and buff up with a clean soft cloth, working along the direction of the grain. Get professional treatment for marks and stains on valuable old furniture.

Otherwise, on furniture old and new, the following methods can be used with caution: test on an unseen part first.

Scratches and stains. First try rubbing with the finger dipped in wax paste polish; or try rubbing with the cut kernel of a brazil or walnut; or try a little linseed oil on a clean cloth. Sometimes you can disguise a scratch with a little shoe polish or with a wax crayon. Or you can buy scratch removers from hardware stores.

Ring marks. There are special cleaners to remove ring marks caused by heat or alcohol. Alternatively, try rubbing them with metal polish, or with a paste made from salad oil and cigarette ash. Always rub in the direction of the grain.

Cane and bamboo furniture. Use a soft brush, a vacuum cleaner attachment, or a hairdryer on the coolest setting to remove

dirt and dust. If the furniture is unvarnished, sponge with warm water containing sufficient dissolved soap flakes to give a good lather, plus 1 teaspoon of laundry borax. Do not overwet. Then wipe over with warm clean water and leave to dry naturally.

If the furniture has been varnished, a wipe with a damp cloth should be sufficient (add a few drops of washing-up liquid if necessary), or use an all-purpose aerosol cleaner–polisher.

Sometimes you can tighten up a sagging cane seat by sponging on both sides with a handful of washing soda crystals dissolved in warm water. Push the seat upwards, and leave to dry in hot sunlight, or dry off with a hairdryer on the hottest setting.

Plastic furniture. Avoid dusting with a dry cloth, as trapped grit can scratch the soft surface. Wipe with a soft cloth well wrung out in warm water to which has been added a few drops of washing-up liquid. Leave to dry naturally, as rubbing dry increases 'static' which attracts more dust. Or use an aerosol cleaner/polisher – one type is now 'anti-static'. Avoid abrasives of any kind, even cream cleaners. But if furniture is scratched, try rubbing gently with a little metal polish.

Chrome. In general, dust or rub over with a damp cloth well wrung out in warm water to which has been added a few drops of washing-up liquid. A little bicarbonate of soda can be rubbed onto stubborn marks. If chrome has become badly pitted, treat with a special cleaner/restorer available from car accessory shops.

Upholstery. Upholstered furniture is expensive but you can prolong its life with care and correct cleaning. By its very nature, upholstery is more vulnerable to wear and staining than wooden furniture. Always vacuum or brush regularly to prevent dirt becoming ingrained into the fabric covering. But do not use a stiff brush which may damage the fabric. To remove pet hairs, use a barely damp sponge. Special aerosol 'fabric protectors' are available from most department stores for spraying onto new or clean upholstery.

Reversible cushions should be turned regularly. Plump up cushions with loose fillings such as feathers: do not vacuum. Do not have your upholstery close to fires or radiators, and try to keep it out of the sun. Draw blinds or curtains on very sunny days, if possible. Consider having slip covers to protect backs and arms.

Always treat spills immediately; this is very important to prevent the padding underneath the fabric from becoming saturated. Scrape off excess spillage with the blunt edge of a knife or with a spoon. Then *blot up* liquids with a clean white cloth, or paper tissues. For advice on specific stains, see *Stain removal chart*. Never rub, and always test any cleaning method first on an out-of-sight spot. If in any doubt, call a professional upholstery cleaner.

Two or three times a year, as needed, you can clean many types of fabric all over with an upholstery shampoo, using a special sponge applicator, so that you do not overwet. Follow directions carefully, and always shampoo before the upholstery looks very dirty. Shampooing is usually safe for cotton, wool, linen and synthetics such as Dralon velvet and polypropylenes. But if possible check with the manufacturers of the upholstery before shampooing. Professional cleaners should be called for suede, silk, satin, and velvets (other than Dralon). Always vacuum before and after shampooing. Do not overwet in particular Dralon velvets, as the cotton backing could shrink.

Leather-covered furniture. Much leather sold as upholstery is 'treated' with a lacquer, but some is not. Rub a hidden part of the furniture with a damp cloth. If a little colour comes off onto the cloth, then your furniture is untreated.

Treated leather. This can be washed with a solution of water and soap flakes; or you can use a good toilet soap containing glycerine. Do not use washing-up liquid or laundry soap. Do not overwet. Use a soft nail brush for very dirty patches, then sponge over with clean warm water; but again, do not overwet. Feed the leather occasionally with a branded leather food obtainable from specialist suppliers or from department stores.

Untreated leather, however, should *never* be treated with leather food. Simply sponge greasy marks with a little white spirit on a damp cloth. Then use soap and water as above but only barely wet the surface. You can treat oily stains with rubber solution from a cycle repair kit. Squeeze over the mark and allow to dry for 24 hours. When you roll the solution off, you will find it has absorbed most of the oil.

Vinyl-covered upholstery. In general, simply dust, or wipe over with a soft cloth or sponge well wrung out in a solution of warm water and soap flakes. Wipe over with clear water, and dry off with a soft cloth. If it is very soiled, you can buy a special upholstery cleaner from car upholstery shops. Try a little white spirit on obstinate marks; biro marks may respond to rubbing with a little scouring powder on a cloth dampened in detergent solution, or methylated spirits, but always go gently or you may damage the surface. Special paints for vinyl upholstery are available from car accessory shops.

Loose covers. Heavy covers, and those that are not colourfast, should be dry-cleaned. Other covers may be washed, but first mend any small tears. Then brush well outside to remove loose dirt. Or run your vacuum cleaner attachment over the covers before removing them, then shake them. Wash by machine, provided you have care instructions on or with the covers which recommend machine-washing, and a specific programme. Otherwise, wash by hand: the bath makes a suitable large container. Squeeze covers through a solution of warm water plus mild detergent. If covers seem very dirty, give them a second wash. Then rinse three times, and spin for one minute, or wring. Hang to dry, if possible between two lines so that air can get into folds of the fabric. Iron while slightly damp: wrong side for a matt finish, right side for a shiny finish. Iron any pleats and frills before putting the covers back on the furniture; but the sides and backs can be touched up when covers are in place. A light starching improves the appearance of many cotton and linen covers, and makes them last longer. Do not starch crease-resistant or glazed fabrics.

Stretch covers can usually be washed and need no ironing.

BEDS AND BEDDING

Never leave a new mattress in its plastic wrapping: always remove this at once. If left on, a plastic wrapper will make the mattress damp, as moisture condenses inside the wrapper. Also, the human body gives off a lot of moisture during sleep, and it is important that both bedding and mattress should be absorbent for a comfortable night's sleep – apart from which, plastic wrappings are noisy! Turn mattresses at least once every three months (other than foam which should not be turned). Every so often, clean mattresses and upholstered bases with a soft brush or vacuum cleaner attachment to remove dust and fluff. Treat any spills quickly to avoid wetting the upholstery fillings. For large spills, try to stand the mattress on its side, as seepage is slower on an upright surface. Then blot up as much of the spill as you can, using a clean cloth, towel, or white tissues. Simply sponging with cold water will remove many stains. You can add a few drops of washing-up liquid, or upholstery shampoo. But for milky drinks, including tea and coffee, and for fruit drinks such as orange juice, sponge with a solution of 1 teaspoon of laundry borax to 300 ml ($\frac{1}{2}$ pint) warm water; then sponge with clear water. Grease stains can be treated with an aerosol dry-cleaner when the stain is dry. For spills or accidents that smell unpleasant, add a few drops of household antiseptic to your rinsing water. You can dry off large wet areas with a hairdryer, or you can support the mattress safely lengthwise on its edge in front of a fan heater. But **do not** place it near a radiant electric or gas or open coal fire, and be sure to inspect frequently while drying.

Different types of bedding, such as sheets, blankets, pillows and duvets, all need different washing or cleaning techniques to keep them clean and in good condition. Full details are given in the text on this page and overleaf

Duvets (continental quilts). These should always be used with a washable cover which can be removed immediately in the event of spills. For difficult stains, see *Stain removal chart*, washable fabrics.

If the spill has penetrated to the duvet underneath, try to push the filling away from the stained area, then gently sponge with warm water to which you have added a few drops of washing-up liquid.

Quilts filled with feathers, down, or mixtures of the two, should be cleaned professionally. (Domestic washing machines are usually too small to take a quilt though you may be able to find a large capacity machine in a launderette.) But quilts with synthetic fillings (e.g. Dacron) can be washed in the bath, provided covering is washable. Knead gently in warm water to which you have added a mild detergent, rinse well and squeeze lightly before hanging outside to dry, well supported over two lines.

Pillows. Those filled with *down, feathers,* or *mixtures*, should not be washed unless necessary, as this removes the oil from the feathers. Use an inner pillow case to protect your pillows from soiling. But if necessary, badly soiled pillows can be gently squeezed through warm soapy water, and rinsed well with at least three changes of water. Spin dry if possible for two minutes. Hang up by two corners to dry outside, and shake occasionally during drying. Alternatively, take pillows to a professional cleaner.

Polyester-filled pillows can be washed as for continental quilts with synthetic fillings, above, finishing off with a one-minute spin in a spin-drier, if you have one.

Latex pillows can usually be sponged clean, but if badly saturated the whole pillow can be washed. It is best to keep the pillow in its inner case as light can harm latex. Use warm water plus soapflakes, and do not twist or wring. Rinse well. Squeeze out as much of the water as you can into a dry towel, then leave the pillow in a warm place until dry.

Blankets. It is often more convenient to have blankets dry cleaned, but if you use a coin-op machine, be sure to air the blankets thoroughly before you use them, to get rid of any lingering toxic fumes. To wash blankets, follow carefully any maker's instructions which may be stitched onto one corner of the blanket. In general, use the relevant washcode indicated on your washing machine, and check that your machine is big enough before you start. Twin tubs can usually

only handle a single or thin double. Automatics can usually take a double but not king size. Wool blankets take up less room when they are wet, but acrylics do not reduce in bulk. When washing by hand, the bath makes a good container, and you should use warm water and a good lather of soap flakes. Rinse well and then use a fabric conditioner to restore softness. Hang the blanket outside if possible, over two lines about 90 cm (3 ft) apart. While it is still damp, ease the blanket into shape. When dry, shake well and brush up the pile.

WINDOWS

When cleaning the glass, choose a warm dull day if possible. Bright sunlight makes it difficult to see exactly what you are doing and your cleaning water may well dry onto the window before you have time to wipe it off with your squeegee. This will give you dirty smears which are difficult to remove. You can use a liquid or aerosol window cleaner, but these are expensive. It is better to buy a rubber squeegee with a hard edge designed specially for window cleaning. Telescopic versions are available for reaching upper floors. Use your squeegee with a bucket of warm water containing a squeeze of washing-up liquid plus a few drops of ammonia. First wash the window over with a sponge (some squeegees have a sponge side for washing). Then draw the hard rubber edge of the squeegee in strips across the window for a smear-free finish. Alternatively, you can finish off with crumpled newspaper.

Blinds. Usually modern blinds can be wiped down with a damp cloth and detergent solution, but do not use solvents such as white spirit, which could attack the protective finish. Traditional Holland blinds and paper blinds should only be dusted. Split cane blinds can be brushed clean, or gently use the attachment of a vacuum cleaner. Some types can be lightly

From top, left: how to use a squeegee. First wash over the window with warm water to which has been added a few drops of ammonia. Then, starting at the left vertical edge of the window, tilt the squeegee down slightly to force water to the bottom of the window pane and pull across width of window. Return to the left edge, letting squeegee slightly overlap first portion and repeat process. For the final stroke, squeegee across the width of the window with the rubber touching bottom moulding. Turn blade so that the right edge touches the vertical edge and complete the stroke against the bottom of the window sponged. Venetian blinds can be cleaned one slat at a time; wipe them with a soft cloth dampened in a detergent solution. Or you can put on an old pair of cotton gloves, and dampen the fingers to wipe slats clean. Or you can buy special gadgets that clean several slats at a time. Try to clean the blinds before they get very dirty: be very careful around the pull-cords, or you will soil them with your cleaning cloth. If you wish you can take down the whole blind and wash it in the bath, but do not immerse the top section in water as it may rust, and be very careful to avoid scratching the bath enamel.

Curtains. Dirt can destroy fabrics, so clean curtains regularly. Use linings to protect fabrics from sunlight. Large, inter-lined or very heavy curtains are best dry-cleaned, as are curtains with special headings. Some firms will come and take down your curtains for you, clean them, and then re-hang. If curtains are only barely long enough, dry-cleaning is safer than washing, but even then, shrinkage can occur.

To wash curtains, first take out all the hooks, and put them in a safe place (remove loose linings and wash separately). Then unknot the heading cord at the top, and ease out the gathers so that the curtain can lie flat. Shake the curtains outside, or brush them down, to remove as much loose dirt as you can, then soak for about 10 minutes in cold water with a little liquid detergent. Rinse, and remove as much of the water as you can. Squeeze, or use a spin-drier if you think the fabric is strong enough to take it. Now wash the curtain by hand in mild detergent and warm water, or by machine if you think the fabric is strong enough. Remember that fabrics can be weakened by dirt, polluted air and sunlight, and will be even weaker when wet. You can use the bath for larger curtains. Rinse well, then give them a short spin if you think the fabric is strong enough. Otherwise squeeze out as much water as you can, and hang to dry outside, supported over two lines.

Glass-fibre curtains should always be hand washed to avoid cracking the fibres. Wash them in the bath, then hang them to drip-dry without folding.

Net curtains should be washed as often as possible, separately from natural fibres. Soak them first in cold water with a little detergent, and then wash by hand in hand-hot (as hot as your hand can bear) water, or by machine on programme 4. Do not boil. Always be sure to rinse thoroughly, as scum can dull brightness. Do not wring and only spin for a short time. Drip-drying

will cut down creasing, and you can hang nets at the window while still damp so that any creases can fall out, or use a warm iron. You can buy products at hardware stores specially formulated for whitening dis-coloured net curtains: follow the instructions carefully.

LAMPSHADES

First unplug the table lamps from sockets, then remove shades before attempting to clean them (apart from a light dusting). For *pendant lamps or wall brackets*, turn off electricity at the mains before removing the shade. You will probably have to remove the light bulb, and unscrew the bottom part of the lamp-holder in order to remove most types of shade. If *fabric shades* are made from washable fabrics, first remove any trimmings which might run, or be harmed by washing. Then simply swish the whole shade through a bowl of warm soapy water, rinse in clear water and dry away from heat. Sometimes, fabrics can be slipped off the shade frame for washing. But non-washable or delicate fabric shades should be professionally cleaned. Or you can dust them down well with a scrupulously clean soft brush, then clean all over with a cloth moistened in a liquid dry-cleaning stain-remover. For *parchment shades*, make up a solution of 1 teaspoon of soap flakes in a small bowl of warm water, plus 2 teaspoons of methylated spirits (caution: flammable). Wipe the shade with the solution, using a clean soft cloth. Wipe off any lather, and then wipe over again with a cloth moistened in pure methylated spirits. Allow to dry, then polish with a soft dry cloth. A little olive oil rubbed over the shade will restore its soft sheen.

Plastic shades should be washed in a solution of warm water and a little washing-up liquid. Let them drain dry without rubbing as this will help to cut down static electricity.

Paper shades can only be dusted clean, as often as possible, to minimise heavy soiling.

CLEANING IN THE KITCHEN

It is important for your family's health to keep your kitchen as clean as you possibly can.

General kitchen hygiene. Always thoroughly wash your hands before handling any food, and after handling raw meat and poultry. After getting a meal or washing-up, wash down work surfaces, preferably adding 1 tablespoon of washing soda to the water. Line pedal

bins with newspapers or use plastic bin-liners. Strain liquids off refuse, and wrap in newspaper before putting in the bin. After emptying the bin, wash it out with a solution of household disinfectant or bleach. Allow to dry. In hot weather, use a disinfectant powder in your dustbins, which should be kept as clean as possible.

Keep vegetables dry and well-ventilated, and occasionally wash out their container with a weak solution of bicarbonate of soda. Rinse well, and allow to dry. Do not allow stale bread to ac-cumulate, and wash out the bread bin once a week with a weak solution of bicarbonate of soda. Rinse, and allow to dry before putting any bread back. Defrost and clean your fridge regularly, as described under appliances (*General care and maintenance*). Clean out food cupboards regularly, brushing out loose crumbs, then wiping out with a weak solution of bicarbonate of soda, and allowing to dry before putting back the food. Keep your cooker clean, as described under appliances (*General care and maintenance*).

Pour a little neat bleach down the sink every day, and once a week pour a little bleach or household disinfectant down the outside drain. If you cannot leave washing-up to drain dry, use a clean tea towel every day; change your kitchen hand towel regularly. Sterilise dishcloths regularly. Allow them to soak overnight in a weak solution of bleach, then rinse very well. Or boil them for 10 minutes with enough soap powder to give a good lather.

Clean out pet bowls after every meal, washing them separately from the family dishes. Scald them, or sterilise them with a weak solution of a disinfectant recommended as a mouthwash, rinse well and allow to dry.

Plastic laminate work surfaces and cabinet fronts. Wipe up spills as soon as they happen to avoid permanent stains. Blackcurrant juice, hair dyes and paint stripper, in particular, should be removed immediately. For general cleaning, wash down with warm water and a few drops of washing-up liquid. Rinse well. Or use an aerosol cleaner/polisher. These are the only treatments recommended for glossy laminates. On matt laminates, cream cleaners can be used to remove stains, but rub very gently, as even these are abrasive. On cupboard fronts, you can use a general purpose aerosol cleaner/polisher.

On very stubborn stains, try the following. Take half a cup of bicarbonate of soda and fill up with water, mix to a paste and

apply to the stain then cover with a piece of polythene. Leave for a couple of hours, then rinse off. Alternatively, you can use a mild solution of hydrogen peroxide (1 part hydrogen peroxide to 5 parts water). But do not leave on laminate for longer than two minutes and be sure to rinse off very well. To remove spills from textured laminates, use a fine stiff-bristled brush with a solution of warm water and washing-up liquid, then rinse off well.

Sinks. *Enamel sinks* can be cleaned with a cream household cleaner. You can use diluted household bleach on obstinate marks, if necessary allowing the solution to stand in the sink overnight. Special stain removers for sinks and baths are available from hardware stores. Or you can try making up a paste of cream of tartar and hydrogen peroxide. Scrub onto stain, then

rinse off. Clean *stainless steel* sinks with washing-up liquid or with a cream cleaner. Do not use household bleach if possible; if you must, always be sure to rinse it off very thoroughly, as it can corrode your sink. Salt or undissolved detergent powders can cause pitting: rinse them off at once. Beware of silver-dipping solutions which can cause marks which are impossible to remove. If you have a very badly stained old sink, try using a special metal cleaner obtainable from motor car accessory shops.

Saucepans. Cleaning methods vary according to type. New pans should be 'conditioned' according to the instructions supplied by manufacturers – usually this involves a coating of cooking oil. In general, most pans can be cleaned in hot water with washing-up liquid; soaking

will remove hardened or obstinate food deposits. Burnt pans can be boiled up with a tablespoon of vinegar or lemon juice, or you can try soaking the saucepan in a biological detergent.

Non-stick pans. Never use metal utensils, and keep the pans scrupulously clean, as burnt-on food particles will destroy the finish. Soak off food deposits, and only scour if absolutely necessary, rubbing gently with a nylon pad, not metal scourers.

Badly discoloured pans can be one-third filled with water plus half a cup of laundry detergent and boiled-up. Wash well afterwards, rinse thoroughly and then re-oil.

Aluminium pans can be scoured with wire wool. Do not use copper scouring pads, and do not soak in washing soda solutions: both of these can set up harmful reactions. Although aluminium discolours fairly easily, the discolouration is not harmful. To brighten up the insides of pans, simmer a solution of vinegar, or an acid fruit such as rhubarb. Try to avoid leaving food in these pans, as to do so can cause pitting of the metal. Scour *stainless steel pans* with nylon pads, but avoid using metal scourers. Soak burnt deposits for as little time as possible as the metal may become pitted. Rub the pans with vinegar to remove the blue marks caused by overheating; polish up the outsides with a stainless steel cleaner.

Cast-iron pans should always be dried at once, as they can rust, unless they have a protective coating. If uncoated, rub them over with a little cooking oil, or grease with a butter paper, to prevent rusting during storage.

Copper pans need careful looking-after. Most are lined, usually with tin. Avoid overheating which can damage the lining, and for the same reason, scour as little and as gently as possible. On the out-side, you can use a copper cleaner, or rub with a cut lemon dipped in salt. But some copper preserving pans are unlined, as are copper mixing bowls. Before you use them, scrub them very thoroughly with salt and cut lemons until all traces of discoloration have vanished. Then wash in hot water, and dry before using.

Enamel pans need gentle treatment to avoid chipping or scratching the enamel coating. Always soak off any stubborn or burnt deposits, and use a nylon scourer, not a metal one. Use a solution of biological washing powder to remove stains. The same treatment can be applied to *ceramic glass* cookware.

Left, above: it is important to keep your kitchen clean, not only to maintain its attractive appearance, but also for reasons of hygiene. Advice on how to treat the various surfaces involved is detailed on these pages. See also the preceding section on floors
Right, above: basic cooking equipment is available in a wide variety of materials, all of which need different treatments to keep them fresh and new looking

Tinware usually has a base of mild steel which will rust if the tin coating is scrat-ched, so always soak off burnt deposits and avoid scourers and abrasive cleaners. Very badly discoloured items can be boiled up in a washing-soda solution. Dry well before storing.

Woodware. Wooden draining boards should be scrubbed daily with cold salt water. Keep wooden chopping boards scrupulously clean, scrubbing after use with a solution of hot water containing a little dissolved scouring powder. Rinse well and stand on edge to dry.

TABLEWARE

Woodware such as salad bowls and plat-ters should not be washed unless absolutely necessary; wipe clean with paper towels after use, and oil with olive oil if necessary.

Any marks can usually be removed by rubbing with fine steel wool moistened with a little olive oil. Never leave wood-ware to soak in water.

Cutlery should always be washed as soon as possible as food deposits can cause pitting. Do not wash in a dishwasher unless specifically recommended by the cutlery manufacturer. Polish silver, stainless steel and bronze with appropriate branded cleaners. See also notes on *Cleaning metals*.

Chinaware. You can buy stain removers for stained chinaware from hardware shops. Or try rubbing with a cloth dipped in bicarbonate of soda, or soak overnight in a washing soda solution.

Glassware should be washed separately from other items to minimise chipping.

Always wash by hand fine crystal and cut glass; everyday tumblers can usually go in a dishwasher, but check with the maker's recommendations. Glasses used for milk or for alcohol should be rinsed out in cold water before washing in warm water with detergent. Stained or cloudy glass can be soaked overnight in water to which has been added 2 teaspoons of ammonia; hardwater stains on glass can sometimes be removed by soaking in distilled water (or rainwater). Impregnated silver wadding will also shift some stains. Stained decanters can be half-filled with vinegar, plus 1 tablespoon of cooking salt. Add raw rice grains, and swill mixture round vigorously. Rinse out well.

CLEANING IN THE BATHROOM

As with the kitchen, it is important for health reasons to keep your bathroom and lavatory as clean as possible. It also makes them more attractive and pleasant to use.

Baths should be cleaned regularly, preferably after each use, while still warm. Try to train your family to do their own cleaning.

Enamelled baths in general should be cleaned with a cream cleaner (avoid scouring powders which may scratch and dull the surface). Special stain removers are available from hardware stores, but always follow directions to the letter, and try them out on a corner of the bath first. Some stains can be removed with a paste made of cream of tartar and hydrogen peroxide. Rub brown iron and green copper stains with a cut lemon dipped in salt. Rinse off.

Plastic baths should only be cleaned with a squeeze of washing-up liquid on a soft cloth, but in hard water areas you can use a little cream cleaner from time to time. Metal polish may be effective for removing small scratches; apply when the surface is dry, and be sure to rinse well.

Lavatories should be cleaned every day with a brush and a weak solution of household bleach: also use a bleach or disinfectant solution to wash the seat, cover, cistern and handle, and any tiled areas adjacent to the lavatory. Rinse out brushes well after use. Once a week, clean bowl with lavatory cleaner to dissolve lime scale. Or leave neat bleach in the bowl overnight. *But never mix bleach and lavatory cleaner together*: the resulting fumes are very poisonous. You can shift very bad stains in old lavatory pans with spirits of salts, an acid which can be purchased from hardware stores. But be very careful as this is very poisonous and corrosive. Pour a little into the pan and stand well clear of any fumes. As soon as stains vanish, flush several times, and then get rid of any remaining acid by pouring a little at a time down the wc and flushing repeatedly.

Washbasins can be cleaned in the same way as baths, see above. Clean out overflows, using an old toothbrush or a pipe-cleaner dipped in diluted bleach, or disinfectant.

Taps. An old toothbrush is useful for cleaning the crevices around taps. *Chromium plated* taps should simply be wiped with a cloth wrung out in detergent solution, but if they are very dirty, you can use a little cream cleaner (sparingly, because it is abrasive). *Gold plated* taps should be cleaned with a barely damp cloth, rubbing as little as possible, as the gold plating is very thin.

The bathroom is another room where hygiene is particularly important. On this page you will find notes on cleaning the various surfaces

CLEANING METALS

Aluminium can be wiped clean with a damp cloth, and then polished off with a soft dry cloth. See also saucepans, above.

Brass. After a time unlacquered brass will tarnish, then corrode. You can clean brass with a cut lemon rubbed in salt, or with salt and vinegar. Or use a good metal polish. Acetone will remove old lacquer finishes.

Bronze. Usually, dry dusting is all that is needed, as some ageing of the metal is considered desirable, but very dirty articles can be washed in a hot detergent solution and then rubbed with turpentine to restore the sheen. You can buy multi-purpose polishes which can be used on a number of different metals, including bronze. Use one of these polishes on bronze cutlery, which should not be placed in a dishwasher.

Chrome usually only requires wiping with a damp cloth plus a little detergent. Avoid abrasives. Use a cloth which has been dipped in a little bicarbonate of soda to treat grimy or greasy areas. For badly pitted chrome use a rust remover, if necessary, or a chrome cleaner from a motor car accessory shop.

Copper can be rubbed with a cut lemon dipped in salt. Copper cleaners are also available from hardware or department stores. See also saucepans, above.

Gold should only be washed if necessary in a warm soapy solution. Dry gently with a soft cloth.

Iron and steel will rust if left unprotected and exposed to the air (except for stainless steel which does not rust). To remove rust, use emery paper or a wire brush, plus a rust

remover (from hardware stores or motor shops) following directions very carefully, as some contain dangerous chemicals.

When the metal is clean and bright, protect immediately with a coating of grease. Or prime with special paint primer, followed by undercoat and gloss (do not use emulsions on metal). You can buy special matt black paints for black ironwork, and the finish can then be revived from time to time with a black lead-like polish sold in a small tube, available from hardware stores.

Pewter can be washed in warm water with a few drops of washing-up liquid, and dried with a soft cloth. Then rub over with methylated spirits. Beware of using metal polishes which will scratch mirror finishes.

Silver is tarnished by sulphur and moisture in the air. Gradually, the tarnish turns silver black and finally will corrode the metal. The following will all stain silverware and should be removed as soon as possible, in particular from cutlery: eggs, fish, green vegetables, fruit juices, sugar, mustard, salt and vinegar. Use a good proprietary cleaner for silver, polishing

with a chamois (chammy) leather; polishes are now available which actually retard future tarnishing. In between polishing, use an impregnated cloth to keep silver bright. For intricately patterned pieces, silver foams are available which can be rinsed off under the tap. Cutlery can be soaked in silver-dipping solutions, which will clean but not polish. Remove cutlery as soon as stains disappear. Avoid soaking the join between the handle and knife blade. After use always rinse well in cold then hot water, and dry with a clean cloth.

Keep your silver in a box or drawer with a soft lining to avoid scratching. If it is not being used frequently, wrap it in acid-free tissue paper, from a jeweller. Never wrap in newspaper, because printer's ink contains sulphur, and never secure wrappings with rubber bands which can corrode through several layers of paper.

Stainless steel. Never leave to soak longer than necessary. Beware of neat bleach, undissolved detergent powders and salt, all of which can cause pitting. Use a special stainless steel cleaner.

Stone and brick. Dust down regularly, if possible using the appropriate vacuum attachment, or a soft brush. Wash over with plain warm water, adding a few drops of washing-up liquid if necessary. Do not use scouring powders or soaps. You can use a wire brush dipped in water for soot stains on fireplaces. For other bad stains, buy a special cleaner from a builder's merchant, and follow directions very carefully. Use of a special sealer sold for semi-porous natural materials will make stone and brick easier to keep free from dust and dirt.

Slate can be cleaned as above. Use a mixture of white spirit and linseed oil to restore the sheen after cleaning.

Marble. Always mop up spills immediately to avoid stains. In general wash white marble with warm water plus a few drops of washing-up liquid. You can add a few drops of ammonia if soiling is heavy. But always test a small area of coloured marble first. Rinse off with clean water and polish with a soft dry cloth. You can apply a wax furniture polish if you wish. Use a rust remover for metal stains. For other stains, try diluted hydrogen peroxide plus a few drops of ammonia. Leave this solution on the stain for a few minutes, then repeat again as necessary. Alternatively, on greasy stains, try a branded stain-removal aerosol solvent.

LAUNDERING

WASHCODE SYMBOLS

Modern machines and wash-day products have undoubtedly taken the hard labour out of washing and ironing. Nevertheless, the variety of colours, fabrics, fibres and finishes you will find heaped in your linen basket is enormous. To get good results, you will need a certain amount of knowledge and you will need to take a certain amount of care. It is no good packing everything into the machine and hoping for the best.

The golden rule of successful washing is to *look for the label*. This sounds so simple, but research has shown that labels are often ignored or misunderstood. If you cannot find a label at the back of the neck or the waist band of a garment, try the side seams. Some furnishing fabrics have care symbols printed on the selvedge. Some garments and furnishings come with swing tickets giving special care instructions: keep these labels all together in one safe place, writing on each one the name of the article and when it was bought.

Most laundry care labels present information in the form of symbols established by the International Textile Care Labelling Code (I.T.C.L.C.) and pioneered in this country by the Home Laundry Consultative Council (H.L.C.C.).

You will find it very useful if you can memorise the main washcode symbols. You do not have to remember all the details for the symbols are fully set out on virtually every washing powder packet, and in every machine handbook. But you can use the symbols better if you understand the reasoning behind them. Most British labels provide the washing instructions in words as well as symbols, but continental labels often have symbols only.

There are 5 main symbols to remember:

The **washtub** tells you how to wash by machine and/or by hand

The **triangle** tells you about bleaching

The **iron** tells you about ironing

The **circle** tells you about dry-cleaning

The **square** tells you about drying

Each of these symbols contains extra information to help you further:

The washtub usually contains a temperature expressed in degrees Centigrade: this is the maximum recommended temperature for that particular machine washing. The washtub may also contain a number: this is the washcode number, which will correspond to the programme numbers on most British machines. But machine programme numbers and washcode numbers do not always match up, particularly on foreign machines, so **always** refer to the machine hand book, which will usually have a chart explaining how the washcodes match the machine programmes for that particular model.

A full explanation of which washtub code numbers to use for various fibres follows later in this section.

If the washtub contains the symbol of a hand, this means 'hand-wash only: do not machine-wash'. It does *not* mean 'wash in hand-hot water', as many people think. Many machine programmes feature hand-hot water, which as you will see from the chart, is water as hot as the hand can bear. Hints for hand-washing with special sections for woollens and silks, follow later in this section.

The triangle means that you can use household chlorine bleach on the fabric if you wish. Sometimes the triangle contains the letters CI. Bleach must always be diluted in accordance with the manufacturer's instructions, and must be thoroughly rinsed out. In this country, bleaching is not usually necessary because our washing powders contain bleach. This symbol is usually of more importance to continental housewives.

The iron symbol contains one, two or three dots, according to the recommended temperature for the fabric. Most modern iron dials have dots which match the symbol. One dot is cool: for acrylic, acetate, nylon, polyester and triacetate. Two dots is warm: for polyester mixtures, and wool, and wool/nylon mixtures. Three dots is hot: for cotton, linen, viscose or modified viscose.

The circle contains a letter indicating which dry-cleaning fluid may be used. If the circle contains the letters A or P you

can, in practice, use any drycleaner or coin-op drycleaning machine. But if the circle is underlined, special precautions are necessary, so do not use a coin-op machine. And if the circle contains an F, the cleaner must use a special drycleaning fluid. Not all cleaning firms have this fluid, so draw your cleaner's attention to the symbol. Do not use a coin-op.

The square drying symbol with a circle inside means that the article can be tumble-dried. This is now the only drying symbol in common use. However, previously there were symbols as follows:

drip-dry   dry flat   tumble   line dry

You may have these older symbols on some of your clothes. Hints on drying clothes appear later in this section.

If one or more symbol is crossed out, this means emphatically 'do not . . .'. Thus the washtub crossed through means: do not wash, either by hand or by machine. The triangle crossed through means: do not bleach. The iron crossed through means: do not iron. The circle crossed through means: do not dry-clean, and the square crossed through means: do not tumble dry. These are important signs to recognize as they could avert a laundry disaster: with washing and ironing, what you do *not* do is as important as what you do do!

There are three main ways in which methods for washing clothes can be varied:

1. The water temperature can be altered.

2. The amount of agitation or rubbing can be varied.

3. Different methods can be used for getting the water out of the clothes, e.g. short or long spin, drip-drying and so on. You can see how the washcode chart establishes the best combinations of water temperature, agitation and water extraction for every possible fibre.

PRODUCTS FOR WASHING FABRICS

Soap products are available as heavy-duty powders or as light-weight easy-to-dissolve flakes. You may prefer to avoid

SUMMARY OF WASHING SYMBOLS

| Symbol | Washing Temperature | | Agitation | Rinse | Spinning/ Wringing | Fabric | Benefits |
	Machine	Hand					
1 / 95	very hot 95°C to boil	hand-hot 50°C or boil	maximum	normal	normal	White cotton and linen articles without special finishes	Ensures whiteness and stain removal
2 / 60	hot 60°C	hand-hot 50°C	maximum	normal	normal	Cotton, linen or viscose articles without special finishes where colours are fast at 60°C	Maintains colours
3 / 60	hot 60°C	hand-hot 50°C	medium	cold	short spin or drip dry	White nylon; white polyester/cotton mixtures	prolongs whiteness – minimises creasing
4 / 50	hand-hot 50°C	hand-hot 50°C	medium	cold	short spin or drip dry	Coloured nylon; polyester; cotton and viscose articles with special finishes; acrylic/cotton mixtures; coloured polyester/cotton mixtures	Safeguards colour & finish – minimises creasing
5 / 40	warm 40°C	warm 40°C	maximum	normal	normal	Cotton, linen or viscose articles where colours are fast at 40°C, but not at 60°C	Safeguards the colour fastness
6 / 40	warm 40°C	warm 40°C	minimum	cold	short spin	Acrylics; acetate and triacetate, including mixtures with wool; polyester/wool blends	Preserves colour & shape – minimises creasing
7 / 40	warm 40°C	warm 40°C	minimum do not rub	normal	normal spin do not hand wring	Wool, including blankets, and wool mixtures with cotton or viscose; silk	Keeps colour, size and handle
8 / 30	cool 30°C	cool 30°C	minimum	cold	short spin do not hand wring	Silk and printed acetate fabrics with colours not fast at 40°C	Prevents colour loss
9 / 95	very hot 95°C to boil	hand-hot 50°C to boil	medium	cold	drip dry	Cotton articles with special finishes capable of being boiled but requiring drip drying	Prolongs whiteness, retains special crease resistant finish

 DO NOT MACHINE WASH

 DO NOT WASH

WASHING TEMPERATURES

100°C	Boil	Self-explanatory.
95°C	Very Hot	Water heated to near boiling temperature.
60°C	Hot	Hotter than the hand can bear. The temperature of water coming from many domestic hot taps.
50°C	Hand-hot	As hot as the hand can bear.
40°C	Warm	Pleasantly warm to the hand.
30°C	Cool	Feels cool to the touch

DRYING

The vast majority of textile articles can safely be tumble dried. Care labels may be used to indicate either that tumble drying is the optimum drying method for a particular article, or that tumble drying should not be used if the article is likely to be harmed by this treatment.

 Tumble drying beneficial.

 Do not tumble dry.

In cases where the tumble drying prohibition symbol is used, any special positive instructions, such as 'dry flat' for heavier weight knitwear, should be given in words.

BLEACHING

 This symbol indicates that household (chlorine) bleach could be used. Care must be taken to follow the manufacturer's instructions.

 When this symbol appears on a label household bleach must *not* be used.

IRONING

The number of dots in the ironing symbol indicates the temperature setting – the fewer the dots the cooler the iron.

 cool   warm

 hot   do not iron

DRY-CLEANING

 Goods normal for dry-cleaning in all solvents.

 Do not dry-clean.

 Goods normal for dry-cleaning in perchloroethylene, white spirit, Solvent 113 and Solvent 11.

 Goods normal for dry-cleaning in white spirit or Solvent 113.

soap products in hard water areas, because of the problem of rinsing away the scum: detergents will lather more easily. Do not use soap products on fabrics with flame-resistant finishes.

Soapless or synthetic detergents are available as heavy-duty powders, light-duty liquids and light-duty powders. 'Solvent' detergents are intended for particularly greasy clothes. Do not use detergents on proofed rainwear.

Low-sudsing powders are made especially for automatic washing machines; in fact, they are essential for machines of this type. Front-loading automatic machines have a particularly vigorous washing action, and therefore do not need the 'slippery' soap suds that are necessary when washing by hand, or by twin tub. Indeed the clothes cannot move around properly if there are a lot of suds and may suffer from 'suds-lock'.

Biological powders contain enzymes which break down protein stains such as blood, sweat, egg and gravy and make them soluble in water so that they will wash away. You can get heavy-duty powders with enzymes, or low-sudsing powders with enzymes for use in automatic washing machines. Clothes must be allowed to soak, but see notes on soaking below. These powders will not work at temperatures above 60°C, (because the enzymes are killed) and the colder the water, the longer the soak required. Clothes must soak overnight if the water is very cold.

Strange though it may seem, water used on its own is not very effective for making fabrics wet! This is because of 'surface tension', which prevents the water from penetrating fibres and getting to the dirt. All washing products, therefore, contain wetting agents together with ingredients for loosening soil.

Most heavy-duty powders sold for machine washing contain sodium perborate bleach which works quickest at high temperatures (from 80 to 100°C, washcode 1) to remove stains such as wine, coffee, tea and fruit juice. Of course there are many fabrics (synthetics in particular, fabrics which are not colourfast and those with special finishes) that must be washed at lower temperatures (see H.L.C.C. chart in this section). But at lower temperatures the bleach does not have such a strong effect, so the colours of clothes are not altered. In general there is no need to add more bleach to your washing, although

Simple laundry equipment is essential for coping with washday. Train your family to place dirty clothing in a central linen basket. While pegging out washing, support the clothes basket on a chair to avoid backache. Make sure that the line is well secured and keep both line and clothes pegs clean

you may want to use diluted bleach occasionally for stain removal as detailed in the section on *Stain-removing methods*. Today's powders also contain 'optical whiteners' or 'brighteners' which have replaced the traditional 'blues'.

Washing products may also contain dirt suspending agents to help prevent the dirt from settling back into the fabric, so that you can rinse it away. Metal protectors may be included to protect your washing machine. There may also be colouring to improve the look of the product without affecting your wash, and even perfume to give – in the maker's opinion at least – a fresh clean fragrance.

Light-duty washing products (whether flakes, powders or liquids). Do not use these products to cope with the main bulk of the family wash. They are only intended for more delicate items washed by hand and do not contain the same bleaches and special cleansing agents as heavy-duty products.

MAKING LIGHT WORK OF LAUNDRY

Whatever product you choose, always read the pack instructions carefully. Keep to the quantities specified: don't use more or less. Always make sure that washing products are completely dissolved before you add your clothes. Never add powders to a basin or machine which already holds clothes. Concentrated undissolved powders can cause streaks or spots or even irremovable patches of bright colour.

For this reason, never use grains of undissolved powders to treat dirty areas at, for example, collars and cuffs. Instead rub with a bar of household soap, or use an aerosol pre-wash spray.

Soaking can be effective for shifting heavy dirt and/or stains, particularly if you use a biological powder (one brand is sold in small packets especially for soaking). Using biological powder and cold water soak overnight, but if using warm water

(40°C) soak for three to four hours. Using hot water (60°C) soak for half an hour, but do not use water any hotter than this, or you will set stains, and destroy the enzyme action of the powder.

You should approach soaking with caution. First make sure that there is no label in the clothes which says 'do not soak'. Items must be colourfast: articles with washcodes 1, 2 or 3 are usually suitable for soaking. But do not soak a mixed batch of washing of which some items are not colourfast. The classic example is stockings or tights left to soak with white underwear. Stockings are not colourfast, and the underwear becomes permanently dingy. Always thoroughly dissolve the powder before you add the clothes, and choose a large enough container for them to move about freely.

Soaking may damage the surface of enamelled sinks or baths, so use a plastic washing-up bowl instead.

Above all, *do not soak* (in addition to items which are not colourfast) woollens,

silk, flame-resistant or rubberised fabrics, or garments with metal fasteners or trimmings.

Fabric conditioners added to the final rinse when washing by hand or machine make fabrics feel softer and fluffier, make ironing easier and reduce static electricity in man-made fibres. A fabric conditioner will also stop a nylon slip from clinging round your legs, and help to reduce dirt attraction in synthetics generally.

Starches may seem old-fashioned, but they can be useful for putting body back into cotton and linen fabrics. Starch actually strengthens weak fibres, and helps fabric to resist soiling. *Traditional starch* is mixed with boiling water to burst the starch grains, but *cold water varieties* are also available. Follow pack directions very carefully, choosing between a crisp, medium or light dressing. Starch is also available in aerosol form, for greater convenience. Starch is best used for natural

fibres; for synthetics, try an *aerosol fabric finish* that you spray on just before ironing.

Washing by machine. Always use the type and quantity of washing powder recommended in your machine instruction booklet. Keep the booklet handy and re-read it from time to time. Sort your clothes into groups according to the wash-codes on their labels. Probably, you will want to make up mixed loads. You can group fabric codes 1 and 2 together and wash as 2. Code 3 fabrics must be washed on their own: white nylons and white polyester/cottons will pick up colours from the rest of the wash and retain them permanently. You should wash code 4 fabrics on their own, as they need not only a water temperature of 50°C but also a cold rinse and short spin to minimise creasing. Code 5 fabrics must be washed on their own because they are not fast above 40°C: indeed some deep dyes may not be fast even at 40°C, and are best washed individually. Consider hand-washing for code 5 fabrics, particularly if you have a spin drier. Fabrics from codes 6 and 7 can be washed together on 6, but take out of the machine immediately after washing cycle is completed. Caution: as some washing machines do not conform to these codes, **always** refer to the handbook.

Before machine washing, mend any small tears, and empty pockets. Brush off loose dirt, and close zips and fasteners. Tie tapes, apron strings etc. in a loose bow, and button long sleeves to the front of shirts and blouses. Treat heavily soiled areas with a bar of household soap.

Washing by hand. Garments with the hand-wash only symbol *must* be washed by hand. These are likely to include wool and silk, and any fabrics which are not colourfast. Washing hints for wool and silk are also given later in this section.

However, if you do not have the use of a machine, you may need to wash by hand cottons and linens which are white or colourfast. Use the hottest water you can bear (rubber gloves help) and make sure correct amounts of powders are dissolved completely before adding the clothes. Boiling can help shift stains, on nappies and teatowels for example. To boil, use as large a container as possible (an old tin bath is ideal). Use enough of a heavy-duty washing product to give a 5 cm (2 inch) lather and boil for not longer than ten minutes; after that, you start to re-deposit soil onto the clothes.

Rinse all fabrics thoroughly after hand-washing: at least three times. Synthetics

will benefit from a cold rinse and a short spin (15 seconds maximum but check appliance instructions). Many easy-care synthetics can be drip-dried; check the label, and see notes on *Drying*. But in general do not drip-dry heavy knitted garments whether in synthetic fibres such as acrylics or natural fibres such as wool or cotton. Dry flat to avoid stretching.

Garments which are not colourfast should be washed individually by hand in warm suds as quickly as possible. Rinse very thoroughly, and spin or roll in towel.

Drying. Have a length of strongly secured plastic clothes line outside if possible, well away from dirty fences or prickly hedges. Or you could invest in a more expensive rotary fold-down clothes line. Always wipe an outdoor line with a clean cloth before pegging out clothes. A line or rack inside is also useful, as are clip-on racks for radiators.

Drip-dry garments should be hung from a hanger as wet as possible. Give pleated garments a hand-hot rinse, and other garments a cold rinse. Make sure your hangers will not mark the wet clothes. Wire hangers from the dry cleaners are usually suitable, as are plastic or painted wood hangers. But natural wood hangers may mark wet clothes, unless enclosed within a plastic bag.

Many heavy knitted garments should be dried flat after only a short spin (15 seconds maximum, but consult appliance booklet), to avoid stretching them. These include knitted woollens, acrylics and some heavy cotton garments. Spread a towel out on the floor, or place a piece of hardboard with a towel on top over the bath for these garments. Alternatively, support the weight of the drying garment over the back of a chair, first covering the chair back with a clean towel.

Many fabrics may be tumble dried – look for the label. Garments must first be spun or wrung. Do not fill drier more than two thirds full. Tumble synthetics at lowest possible heat, but consult appliance booklet for recommended times and temperatures for various fabrics. A period of tumbling with the heat off helps reduce creasing: when machine stops, take out clothes as soon as possible.

IRONING

Again, look for the label. See earlier explanation of ironing symbols (older irons may have numbers as follows: 1 for cool, 2 for warm, 3 for medium hot, 4 for hot and 5 for very hot).

If there is no care label, look for the fibre content label and work out the heat setting from this. If you can't find either label, first use a cool setting, and if creases do not

come out, only try a higher setting with great care – first testing the iron on the facing or seam of the garment.

Always allow your iron a good 5 to 7 minutes to heat up and settle down before starting to iron: consult your appliance booklet for exact times. Many irons may overshoot the marked temperature in the first instance.

Take a little time to organise your work. Have the ironing board at the correct height so that you do not have to stoop if standing up; or fix the board at a lower height for sitting down. Place a chair or small table on one side to hold the basket of damp washing, and have a rack and plenty of hangers ready to take the freshly ironed clothes.

Always iron garments which need the coolest setting first: then you will not risk spoiling fabrics with an iron that has not sufficiently cooled.

Always iron fabrics until they are dry as garments which are still damp can easily be creased.

Where possible, iron on single layers of fabric to avoid creasing under layers. First iron thick parts such as facings, collars and cuffs on both sides, wrong side first. Do not iron over buttons or fastenings such as nylon zips – use the tip of the button groove (if your iron has one) to iron around buttons. Never iron over seams or hems, as they will leave a mark. Use the point of the iron for gathers and frills.

Fabrics best ironed when damp. These include cotton, linen, cultivated silks, viscose, modal, acetate, and triacetate. Wool should be slightly damp. Where possible, iron garments before they get too dry. Otherwise you can use a steam iron on fabrics which will take a warm or hot iron (cotton, linen, viscose, modal). Alternatively, you can sprinkle or spray colourfast cottons or linens with water and roll up tightly a little while before ironing. Do not use this method for garments which are not colourfast. Some fabrics will waterspot and must therefore *never* be sprinkled with water. These include viscose, acetate and triacetate and silk. If these fabrics get too dry immerse them totally in water and then allow to dry until sufficiently damp for ironing. Or try rolling the garment in a damp towel (you can use a steam iron for viscose).

Fabrics to iron when dry. These include wild, slubbed silks (see extra notes on caring for silks, below), and acrylics, which should be ironed from the back. In particular do not use a steam iron on

knitted acrylics, or iron them while damp, as they develop an unattractive glazed effect which it is impossible to remove. Some very delicate fabrics such as chiffon and georgette are often best ironed dry.

Some smooth heavy fabrics easily develop a shine: these include woven wools, viscose rayon and some polyester/wools. Use a damp cotton pressing cloth and press them from the front. Or use a thin cloth, and a steam iron.

Fabrics to iron on the wrong side. In general iron on the right side for shiny fabrics, such as glazed cottons, taffetas, satins, and on the wrong side for matt fabrics, such as crêpes, or heavier cottons and linens in dark colours. Iron piqués and embossed fabrics on wrong side over a thick pressing cloth to avoid flattening the raised pattern. Also use this technique for fabrics with raised embroidery, to avoid flattening.

Fabrics that need no ironing. Do not iron candlewick, but when it is dry, shake well to fluff up pile. Iron corduroy as little as possible. Give it a short spin, or drip dry. As fabric dries, smooth pile with soft cloth in right direction, and shake from time to time. If you need to iron, gently press from wrong side over thick cloth. Generally, if you iron velvet you will crush the pile. But for pressing velvet with a raised surface you can buy a special cloth which protects the pile as you iron from the back. You can run velvet ribbons quickly along the bottom of an iron stood on its heel. Sometimes, it is possible to remove small creases from velvets by using the steam from a kettle. Do not touch the fabric while still damp, or it will mark.

Other fabrics which require extra care are woollens and silks, as detailed below.

Care of woollens. Some woollens can now be machine-washed. Look for the label. Garments marked 'Super-wash Wool' can be machine-washed on code 5; garments marked 'machine-washable wool' can be washed on code 7. However,

Left: on rainy washdays extra lines and racks inside provide welcome alternative drying space. Some racks can be clipped onto a radiator, as here, but do not dry wet woollens close to radiator heat
Right: ironing skills are worth acquiring, to give freshly-washed clothes a crisp finish. Having the right equipment is a great help. A steam iron saves the need for damping down clothes and a sleeve board is essential for fine blouses, dresses and shirts

many knitted garments should still be washed by hand, hand-knits in particular.

Always use a gentle washing product: liquid flakes or powder, sold specifically for hand-washing. Products made especially for use with cold or lukewarm water are ideal for wool. Carefully measure as directed, using lukewarm (35°C) or cold water. Wash each garment separately. Shake to get rid of any excess dirt, button up garment if appropriate, and turn inside out. Gently squeeze through the washing solution. Do not rub, twist or wring. If the water is too hot, and if you rub, the wool will 'felt', and once this happens, it cannot be corrected. Rinse three times with water as nearly as possible the same temperature as the washing water.

Take care as you lift out garments always to support the weight. Do not

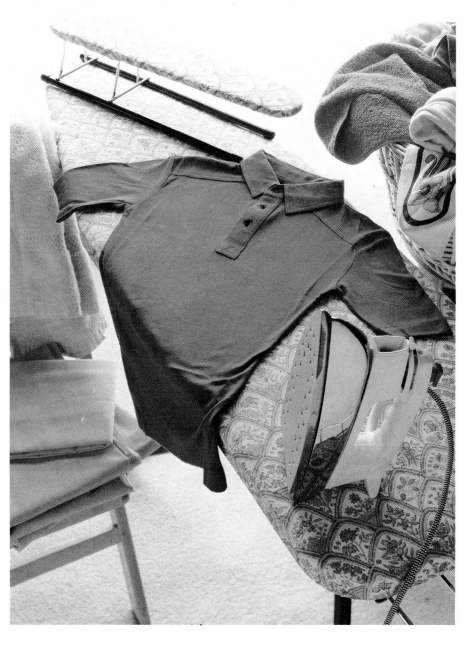

wring. Roll in a clean towel to absorb excess water, or spin-dry for 30 seconds wrapped in a towel. Dry on a flat surface (see notes on drying, below), at normal room temperature, out of sunlight and away from any direct heat. Make sure that you arrange the garment as nearly as possible in its correct shape, and take particular care not to stretch the rib.

Correctly washed woollens require little ironing, but you can press while slightly damp with a warm iron (two dots) or when dry with warm iron and damp cloth, or with a steam iron. Use an up and down action: do not push iron backwards and forwards, and do not press the rib.

Do not press cashmere, which can be washed as above but should never be rubbed in any way.

Take special care with mohair and

angora, reshaping them carefully while drying flat. Take the measurements of the dry garment if its shape is very important or cut out its shape in brown paper to act as a pattern to which you can shape the wet garment for drying. Do not press. When dry, brush up the pile of mohair and angora using a soft clean brush. Alternatively, most woollens can be dry-cleaned: look for the label.

Care of silks. First, you *must* test for colourfastness. Dip a small corner of the article into warm water and iron between two white cloths, with iron set to warm (two dots). If traces of colour are transferred, then the garment must be dry-cleaned. Dry-cleaning is also recommended for badly stained garments (always tell the cleaners what the stain is if you know).

Certain other types of silk should also always be dry-cleaned. These are taffetas, chiffons, brocades, many multi-coloured prints, dressing gown fabrics, ties and scarves. Cultivated (spun) silk, crêpe de chine and wild silks such as Tussore and Shantung are usually washable. Do not soak silk and do not use chlorine bleach. Always wash by hand, using luke-warm water and a mild washing product, carefully measured and well dissolved. Squeeze garment gently through suds but do not twist, scrub or rub. Rinse twice in clean warm water, and then give a final rinse in cold water, to stiffen the fibres and clear the colour.

Do not wring. Roll in towel to absorb excess moisture, then hang carefully to dry away from direct sunlight or heat to avoid 'yellowing'.

Iron all cultivated smooth silks when slightly and evenly damp, on wrong side with a moderately warm iron. Press crêpes and wild (tussore) silks (including slubbed silks such as shantung and pongee) when dry, using a pressing cloth for slubbed silks to avoid making the fabric fluffy. Finish off lightly on the right side. Do not redamp in part or sprinkle or spray with water, as this may cause water spotting. Do not use a steam iron. If cultivated spun silks have become too dry for ironing, dip in warm water for about three minutes, allow to dry and then iron while slightly damp.

STAIN REMOVAL

Stain removal at home is always a risky business. It is very difficult to give specific advice because of the number of variables involved: type of stain, type of fabric or furnishings and fibre, colour of fabric, age of stain and so on, but speed is essential.

The hints on the following chart are intended only for guidance: *always test methods first on an unseen or inconspicuous part of the article, before going on to tackle the stain.*

It is useful to keep together in one place your own personal stain-removal kit. Store chemicals and so on in original containers out of the reach of children because most items are poisonous. Do not decant into containers which have held food or drink. Many items are also very flammable, and may give off harmful fumes, so always carry out stain removal in a well ventilated room and avoid breathing any fumes. Do not work near a naked flame (this includes open coal fires, fires with gas or electric exposed radiants, and gas pilot lights.) And do not smoke, or light a match.

STAIN-REMOVAL KIT AND CHEMICALS

You will find the following items useful to keep in your kit.

Clean white absorbent cloths (well-washed old nappies, white towels or tea-cloths are ideal); or use white tissues.

Spoon or blunt knife for scraping off excess matter, or *wooden spatula*.

Glycerine (from a chemist) to lubricate old stains. Dilute with 1 part glycerine to 2 parts water. Apply and leave for about one hour, then soak in cool suds before washing according to fibre.

Laundry borax, which is safe for most fibres. Make up a solution of 1 tablespoon borax to 500 ml (18 fl oz) warm water for sponging or soaking washables, methods 2 and 3, below. You can also use the boiling water method, method 5 below, for white fabrics.

Methylated spirit (preferably white: from a chemist or hardware store) Use solvent method 1, below. Do not use on acetates. Flammable and poisonous.

White vinegar (acetic acid) from a grocer. Use for soaking or sponging (methods 2 and 3). Use 1 teaspoon vinegar to 250 ml water. Do not use on acetates and keep away from skin.

Ammonia. Dilute 1 part ammonia to 3 parts water. Use for sponging or soaking, methods 2 and 3 below. Keep away from eyes and skin. Do not breathe fumes.

Acetone or amyl acetate (from a chemist). Use solvent method 1, below.

Highly flammable: buy only in very small quantities and if possible store outside the house. Nail-varnish remover makes a reasonable substitute, but most types now sold contain oil which may itself stain. Do not use acetone, amyl acetate or nail varnish remover on acetates: substitute white spirit for these fabrics.

Branded stain-removal solvent. Always read carefully directions on pack. A bottle of liquid is useful: use solvent method 1, see below. In addition, buy an aerosol type which is particularly handy for delicate fabrics which may ring mark if you use liquids. Spray on, allow to dry and then brush off. In general, do not use branded solvents on rubberised or waterproofed fabrics, or on plastics, leather or silks. Take care: solvents are flammable.

White spirit, turpentine and lighter fuel are other useful solvents, apply by solvent method 1, below. Poisonous and highly flammable: store outside the house.

Petrol can also be used for very heavy grease stains but this is highly flammable and volatile, and *must* be stored outside the home. Use solvent method 1. A safer alternative can nearly always be found.

Bleaches. *Heavy duty washing powders* contain *sodium perborate bleach* which is most active at high washing temperatures, above 80°C. Thus washing white cottons and linens at a high temperature in a heavy-duty washing product will shift many stains but first always soak protein stains such as blood, gravy and perspiration in cool, biological washing powder suds as immediate hot water will set the stain, making it impossible to remove.

Household (chlorine) bleach is inexpensive and easy to obtain but should only be used on white cotton and linens (without special finishes e.g. drip-dry or flame-resistant finish.) Always dilute according to the instructions on the bottle but in general use 1 teaspoon to 300 ml ($\frac{1}{2}$ pint) of water. Use method 6, rinsing well. Poisonous. Store upright away from children.

Hydrogen peroxide bleach is more expensive. Buy it from the chemist, and ask for '20 vol' which denotes the strength. Use 1 part 20 vol to 6 parts cold water. You can use it on all fibres, but take care with coloureds as it may fade them a little. Rinse well. See method 6. Poisonous. Store in dark place, away from children.

STAIN REMOVAL METHODS

Numbers are used in the chart which follows.

N.B. Always try any stain removal method on an unseen part of the article first. Only proceed to the stain when you are sure method itself will not harm the fabric.

In all cases, first scrape off any solids with blunt knife, spoon or wooden spatula; gently blot up excess liquids with clean tissues or white cloth. *Always treat stains quickly: they may 'set' if left.*

Method 1: Solvents. For washable fabrics and, with caution, for non-washables. Place an absorbent pad of clean white fabric against the stain on the right side of the fabric. Take another pad of the same fabric, moisten as sparingly as you can with solvent and apply to the stain on the wrong side of the fabric, so that you are pushing the stain out the way that it went in. Work from the outside of the stain inwards to avoid making a 'ring'. Keep turning the pads around to present clean surfaces, and continue until no further staining matter is being transferred to the clean dry pad. Then take a clean pad just moistened with solvent and lightly 'feather-out' from the centre of the stain outwards. Then wash in usual fashion according to the fabric (look for the label).

Method 2: Sponging. For washable and non-washable fabrics. Sometimes, if you act quickly, you may be able to avert a permanent stain simply by sponging. Use cold water to which you have added just a drop of washing-up liquid. Place a pad of clean cloth under the stain and with a clean barely-moistened white cloth or sponge lightly stroke the right side of the fabric. Do not use coloured paper napkins which will stain.

Method 3: Soaking. For washable fabrics only. **Do not** soak wool, silk, non-fast colours, flame-resistant or rubberised fabrics, or articles with metal fasteners. Many stains respond to soaking, but never use hot water which will simply set the stain. Sometimes it helps first to 'lubricate' the stain by rubbing in a little glycerine solution or neat washing-up liquid. A soak in detergent solution is frequently beneficial; or you can use an enzyme 'biological' washing powder designed especially for soaking. These are particularly effective for protein and water-based stains which include gravy, blood, egg, tea and coffee. The colder the water the longer you must leave the fabric to soak. Soak overnight in cold water or for 3 to 4 hours in warm water (40°C). Then wash in usual fashion according to the fabric: look for the label.

Method 4: Washing. For washable fabrics only, of course. Look for the label. Many stains will simply wash out in good rich suds, providing you treat them quickly. Use as hot water as the fabric can stand, but some stains must be soaked first in cold water, see chart. If possible soak the stain (or at least sponge it) until you can wash the article. A pre-wash aerosol stain-removal spray can be helpful. Stains that will usually wash out, if you act quickly, are: beetroot, fruit juices, blood, chocolate, cocoa, coffee, cream, egg, gravy, iced lollies, jam, meat juice, milk, mud, pickles, sauces, soft drinks, soups, stews, syrup, tea, tomato ketchup, washable ink, and wines and spirits. But see additional notes for some of these stains on chart, which recommends any special treatments necessary.

Method 5: Boiling water. This method is only for white linens and cottons. Sprinkle stain with laundry borax and stretch article over a basin, then pour boiling water through from about 30 cm (1 ft) above. Wear rubber gloves and take care not to scald yourself.

Method 6: Bleaching. For washable, colourfast and white fabrics only. See notes on different bleaches under *Stain-removal kit and chemicals.* Soak only the stained part of article in the bleach solution, and first twist the fabric around the stain to prevent the solution from spreading to the rest of the fabric. Always use bleaches with great caution and rinse thoroughly.

Method 7: Absorbent powders. Mainly used for greasy stains on non-washable fabrics. Dampen stain slightly and sprinkle with an absorbent powder such as French chalk or talcum powder. If the fabric is likely to mark with water (e.g. satin, silk, acetates) simply hold it in front of a kettle spout. When the powder is dry, brush off. Alternatively use an aerosol stain-removal solvent.

Method 8: Sponging for carpets and upholstery. Obviously here you cannot work from the back. Act as quickly as you can. Scrape off any solids and blot up excess liquids with white tissues or clean white cloth. Do not rub. Sponge with solutions as recommended in the chart; but test first on unseen part (e.g. under furniture for carpets or under a cushion for upholstery). Work from the edge of stain inwards and use solutions as sparingly as possible. Always finish by repeatedly sponging with cold water to 'rinse' and blotting to dry. Do not overwet. Leave carpet piles to dry with the pile sloping in correct direction. For bad old stains, call in a professional cleaner.

Dilute solutions as follows. Carpet and upholstery shampoos as directed on packs; never use stronger solutions. Laundry detergent: 1 teaspoon to 300 ml ($\frac{1}{2}$ pint) of warm water, dissolve thoroughly. If colours do not appear fast when testing, add 1 teaspoon of white vinegar to the detergent solution. Ammonia (for synthetics only, do not use on wool): 1 tablespoon of household ammonia to one cup of warm water. NOTE: Branded solvents for stain removal may harm some carpets with foam backs.

STAIN REMOVAL CHART
Before using this chart it is essential to read preceeding notes on Stain-removal kit and chemicals and Stain-removal methods

WASHABLE FABRICS	NON-WASHABLE FABRICS	CARPETS AND UPHOLSTERY
	N.B. When taking to dry cleaner, outline stain with coloured tacking thread and attach note describing its cause, if possible.	In general use method 8, although method 7 may be effective on some greasy stains.
Adhesives *Clear adhesive* Acetone, method 1. Except for acetates: try white spirit, method 1. *Contact adhesive* As above. *Epoxy resins* Meths or white spirit, method 1, if not set. Impossible to remove once set. *Latex adhesive* Damp cloth, until set. If set, try paint-brush cleaner, method 1, or write to manufacturer for special solvent. *Polystyrene (model-making) adhesive* Use special solvent available from model shops, method 1.	Fresh stains may be lightly sponged with solvents suggested for washable fabrics; otherwise take to dry cleaners.	Apply methods for washable fabrics with caution; or call professional cleaner.
Alcohol *Beer* Fresh stains: soak briefly in luke-warm water, method 3. Then wash, method 4. Dried stains: white fabrics, hydrogen peroxide solution, method 6. Coloured fabrics: vinegar solution, method 3. But use borax solution for acetates. Then wash, method 4. Or try biological detergent solution and methods 3 and 4.	Cool water, method 2. If stain persists take to dry cleaners.	Treat all alcohol stains even if apparently colourless: they can yellow with age. Squirt with soda syphon and blot dry. If necessary apply carpet-shampoo solution, then when dry branded stain-removal solvent. Try meths, with caution, on old stains.
Spirits (gin, whisky etc.) Sponge with clear, warm water, method 2. Then wash, method 4.	Cool water, method 2. If stain persists take to dry cleaners.	Sprinkle with absorbent powder, e.g. talc, to stop stain spreading. Then blot off with clean cloth. Follow with squirt from soda syphon, or sponge with clear warm water. Then apply carpet-shampoo solution. Follow with laundry detergent solution if necessary, and use meths on any stubborn stains.
Wine Most fresh stains will wash out, method 4. Old stains: hydrogen peroxide bleach solution, method 3.	Cool water, method 2. If stain persists take to dry cleaners.	Sprinkle with absorbent powder to stop stain from spreading. Blot off with clean cloth or tissues. Sponge with clean warm water, then apply laundry detergent solution.
Ballpoint As for Inks.		
Beer As for Alcohol.		
Biro As for Inks.		
Blood Soak in *cold* water and salt or in biological detergent, method 3. Then wash, method 4. Stubborn stains may be lubricated with glycerine then treated with diluted hydrogen peroxide plus few drops of ammonia, method 6.	Take to dry cleaners as soon as possible.	Sponge with cold water, then with laundry detergent solution. Use an ammonia solution for synthetics.
Butter As for Fat, grease, oil.		
Candlewax Scrape off excess; or harden with ice-cube. Place stained area between blotting paper and use warm iron to melt out wax. Then use branded stain-removal solvent, method 1.	As for washable fabrics, or take to dry cleaners.	Pick off excess. Cover stain with blotting paper, and apply tip of warm iron to melt wax, but do not let iron touch any unprotected part. Then apply branded stain-removal solvent.
Car and cycle oil Carefully scrape off deposits, so as not to spread stain. Rub with a little neat washing-up liquid, or spray with pre-laundry aerosol, then wash at as high a temperature as fabric can stand, method 4. But if fabric cannot take a high temperature use liquid branded stain-removal solvent.	Carefully scrape off excess and take to cleaners as quickly as possible. A solvent, method 1; or aerosol, method 7, may be effective with light stains on some fabrics.	Apply branded stain-removal solvent; then carpet-shampoo solution.
Carbon paper Dab with methylated spirits; but use white spirit for acetates.	Try dabbing cautiously with a little meths or white spirit; or take to dry cleaners.	Apply methylated spirits, followed by upholstery shampoo.

WASHABLE FABRICS	NON-WASHABLE FABRICS	CARPETS AND UPHOLSTERY
Chalks and crayons Brush off as much as possible; then sponge with warm detergent solution, method 2 and wash. Treat any remaining traces of colour with meths.	Brush off excess and take to dry cleaners.	Brush off excess; apply methylated spirits, followed by carpet-shampoo solution.
Chewing-gum Harden deposits with ice-cubes, or for small items place in fridge inside plastic bag. Crack and pick off excess with fingernail. Then apply liquid branded stain-removal solvent, method 1. Finally wash, method 4.	Treat with ice-cubes and pick away or take to dry cleaners before stain can spread.	'Freeze' with an ice-cube; pick off as much as you can with finger nail. Then apply methylated spirits or branded stain-remover solvent, and rinse.
Chocolate Scrape off deposits and proceed as for cocoa, below.	Remove excess; you may be able to sponge light stains, method 2; otherwise take to dry cleaners.	Remove excess; apply carpet-shampoo solution followed when dry by branded stain-removal solvent if necessary.
Cocoa Blot up excess with clean cloth; soak in warm suds, method 3, then wash, method 4, preferably in biological detergent. Any difficult stains can be treated with hydrogen peroxide solution, method 6.	Blot up excess; sponge, method 2; or take to dry cleaners as quickly as possible.	Blot up excess; apply carpet-shampoo solution; when dry apply branded stain-removal solvent if necessary.
Coffee As for Cocoa, above.		
Cooking fat/oil As for Fat, grease, oil.		
Cosmetics Carefully blot up excess; try not to rub in. Apply branded stain-removal solvent, followed by methylated spirits for any remaining traces of colour, method 1. Then wash, method 4.	Blot up excess; use branded stain-removal solvent cautiously, depending on fabric, or take to dry cleaners.	Apply branded stain-removal solvent, followed by carpet-shampoo solution. Use methylated spirits on any remaining traces of colour.
Creosote, tar Carefully scrape off excess so as not to spread the stain. Soften stain with neat washing-up liquid or by rubbing in a little butter. Wash in as high temperature as fabric will stand, method 4.	Scrape off excess very gently and take to dry cleaners as quickly as possible.	Scrape off excess deposits. Apply branded stain-removal solvent; obstinate stains can be softened first with a little eucalyptus oil (from a chemist).
Egg As for Food.		
Face/foundation creams As for Cosmetics.		
Fat, grease, oil Scrape and blot off excess gently. Apply a little neat washing-up liquid, or pre-wash laundry stain-removing spray, or for delicate fabrics use eucalyptus oil, then wash, method 4, in as hot water as fabric can stand (look for the label). Finally when dry use branded stain-removal solvent if necessary.	Light staining can sometimes be treated with branded stain-removal solvent, method 1 (use aerosol/powder type for delicate fabrics, method 7). But take heavy stains to dry cleaners.	Scrape off and blot up excess. Apply branded stain-removal solvent, then carpet-shampoo solution. If stain reappears later, re-treat (fat stains etc. may work their way up from base of carpet pile).
Felt-tip pens As for Inks.		
Food Scrape off excess gently; soak fresh or dried stains in cold biological detergent solution (method 3). Or apply pre-wash aerosol stain spray. Then wash, method 4. Any remaining grease stain can be treated with branded stain-removal solvent. Treat stains from any colouring matter with hydrogen peroxide solution.	Scrape off excess gently; sponge cautiously with warm water and a few drops of washing-up liquid, method 2, or apply liquid branded stain-removal solvent method 1 or try method 7; or take to dry cleaners.	Scrape off excess, blot with cold water. Apply carpet-shampoo solution. Allow to dry and if necessary apply branded stain-removal solution. For traces of colouring matter, apply methylated spirits.
Fruit juice Rinse under cold tap. Soak and wash in biological detergent, methods 3 and 4. For white cotton and linen, try laundry borax, method 5. For stubborn stains, try hydrogen peroxide solution, method 6.	Sponge with a little cold water, method 2. Blot dry. Or take to dry cleaners.	Sponge with clear warm water, then apply carpet-shampoo solution. If stain persists try laundry detergent solution, or ammonia solution on synthetics. Any last traces of colour can be treated with methylated spirits.
Grass Apply methylated spirits, method 1, and soak and wash in biological detergent solution, methods 3 and 4.	You may be able to treat small stains with methylated spirits, method 1; otherwise take to dry cleaners.	Dab with methylated spirits and then apply carpet-shampoo solution. Repeat if necessary.
Gravy As for Food.		
Grease As for Fat, grease, oil.		
Hair Oil As for Fats.		
Hair spray As for Nail varnish.		

WASHABLE FABRICS	NON-WASHABLE FABRICS	CARPETS AND UPHOLSTERY
Handcream As for Fats.		
Ice-cream As for Food.		
Inks Treat as quickly as possible. Blot up excess. *Washable ink* Rinse under running cold tap. Wash in heavy-duty detergent. Treat any remaining stains as for iron mould.	Take to dry cleaners.	Blot up as much as possible; apply methylated spirits followed by carpet-shampoo solution. For bad stains, call professional cleaner.
Permanent ink Write to manufacturers for special advice. Or apply methylated spirits, method 1. Or try sprinkling with salt and dampening with lemon juice and leave for an hour. Rinse, then wash, method 4.	Take to dry cleaners.	As above.
Ballpoint Do not wet. Apply methylated spirits, method 1, then wash, method 4. Take bad stains to cleaners.	Small marks may respond to methylated spirits, method 1; or take to dry cleaners.	Apply methylated spirits, then sponge with carpet-shampoo solution.
Felt-tip pens If water-based, lubricate with a little washing-up liquid and wash method 4. Otherwise apply methylated spirits, method 1, then wash, method 4.	Try methylated spirits on small stains, method 1; otherwise take to dry cleaners.	Apply methylated spirits, then carpet-shampoo solution.
Iron mould (rust) Apply a little lemon juice and leave for about 15 mins; rinse and repeat if necessary. For white cottons and linens, buy proprietary rust remover. Stains on wool and silk should be treated professionally.	Take to dry cleaners.	Try branded stain-removal solvent followed by carpet-shampoo solution. Or try sponging with lemon juice, followed by carpet-shampoo solution, or call professional carpet cleaner.
Jam As for Food.		
Ketchup, chutney, pickles As for food.		
Lipstick Carefully remove any excess so as not to spread stain. Apply methylated spirits; then lubricate with a little neat washing-up liquid and wash, method 4.	Take to dry cleaners.	Apply branded stain-removal solvent followed by carpet-shampoo solution; treat any traces of colour with methylated spirits.
Marmalade As for Food.		
Mascara As for Lipstick.		
Mayonnaise As for Food.		
Meat juice As for Blood.		
Medicines Soak in cold water, method 3 and wash, method 4. Traces of colour can be treated with methylated spirits, and any persistent greasy stains with branded stain-removal solvent, method 1.	You may be able to sponge small stains, method 2. Otherwise take to dry cleaners immediately.	Sponge with warm water and apply carpet-shampoo solution. When dry, apply branded stain-removal solvent. Any traces of colour can be treated with methylated spirits.
Mildew Avoid if possible: never leave damp clothes crumpled in ironing basket or in a heap on the floor, or in cupboard. Washing several times, method 4, will remove light marks. Otherwise use chlorine bleach on white cottons and linens or hydrogen peroxide solution on other fabrics, method 6.	Take to dry cleaners.	Try carpet-shampoo solution followed by laundry detergent solution. Bad stains will require professional treatment. Cure cause of damp to prevent re-occurrence of stain and preferably treat with proprietary fungicide.
Mould As for Mildew.		
Nail varnish Carefully scrape and blot up excess; do not spread. Apply acetone but not on acetates, method 1. You can use nail-varnish remover but most types contain oils which may themselves stain. Finally wash, method 4.	Use acetone with caution, and never on acetates, method 1. Preferably take to dry cleaners.	Apply acetone then branded stain-removal solvent.

WASHABLE FABRICS	NON-WASHABLE FABRICS	CARPETS AND UPHOLSTERY
Oil As for Fats.		
Paint Act immediately. Take bad stains to the cleaners. Some dried marks cannot be shifted. Water-based emulsion paints, e.g. 'vinyls': scrape off excess but do not spread. And then sponge at once with clear cold water (rinse under running tap if possible). Wash, method 4. You can try methylated spirits on dried stains. Oil-based 'gloss' paints: scrape off excess without spreading. But do not wash. Apply generous amounts of white spirit, method 1. Then sponge with cold clear water before washing, method 4.	Water-based emulsion: sponge off small fresh marks with damp cloth. Take large stains to dry cleaners. Oil-based paints: treat small stains with white spirit, method 1. Take larger stains to dry cleaners.	Many dried stains are impossible to treat yourself: call a professional cleaner. Water-based emulsion paints: sponge with cold water and then with carpet-shampoo solution. For dried stains, try paint-brush cleaner or methylated spirits, followed by branded stain-removal solvent, then carpet-shampoo solution. For oil-based gloss paints, apply white spirit or turpentine followed by branded stain-removal solvent, then carpet-shampoo solution.
Perfume If possible rinse immediately. Lubricate dried stains with glycerine before washing, method 4.	With caution, try rubbing with glycerine solution, followed by sponging with cloth dampened in warm water; but take bad stains and delicate fabrics to dry cleaners.	Lubricate with a little glycerine solution then sponge with warm water and blot.
Perspiration Fresh stains: dampen and hold over open bottle or small saucer of ammonia but do not breathe fumes yourself. Then wash, if possible in biological detergent, method 4. Old stains: Sponge with vinegar solution, then soak in biological detergent solution, method 3. You can try hydrogen peroxide solution on bad stains, method 6.	Try cautiously sponging with vinegar solution, method 2, or take to dry cleaners.	
Rust As for Iron Mould.		
Sauces As for Food.		
Scorch marks Moisten with water, soften with glycerine and wash, method 4. You can try bleaching heavy marks with hydrogen peroxide solution, method 6, but fibres may be permanently damaged.	Take to dry cleaners.	For slight burns, snip off charred fibres carefully with small scissors. Bad burns will require patching.
Shoe polish Remove excess carefully, then apply branded stain-removal solvent, method 1. Then wash, method 4.	Remove excess and take to dry cleaners.	Apply branded stain-removal solvent then carpet-shampoo solution.
Soft drinks As for Fruit juice.		
Spirits As for Alcohol.		
Tar As for Creosote, Tar.		
Tea As for Cocoa.		
Urine Soak in cold water, method 3, then wash method 4. Treat old stains with hydrogen peroxide solution, method 6.	Take to dry cleaners.	Treat immediately: old stains are difficult to remove and may need a professional cleaner. In an emergency squirt with soda syphon, blot well, and then sponge with carpet-shampoo solution plus few drops of household disinfectant. Then sponge with cold water.
Vomit Remove as much as possible with spoon, blunt knife or spatula. Soak in warm biological detergent solution, with few drops of disinfectant, method 3. Then wash, method 4; if smell lingers, repeat.	Remove excess; sponge with warm water plus few drops of ammonia; or take to dry cleaners.	Scrape off solids, blot up liquids, do not rub. Sponge with carpet-shampoo solution plus few drops of household disinfectant. If necessary, follow with laundry detergent solution. Rinse and blot well. If stains persist, when dry, try branded stain-removal solvent.
Wine See Alcohol.		

CARE OF HOUSEHOLD APPLIANCES

ELECTRICAL APPLIANCES

General safety points. Whenever you can, buy appliances marked with the BEAB (British Electrotechnical Approvals Board) label of approval.

Read your instruction book and keep it handy near to the appliance. Read it again from time to time: it is easy to miss important points. Failure to read instruction books is a prime source of consumer complaints, according to many manufacturers. If you lose your book, write off to the manufacturer for another one, quoting the model name and number.

After using electrical appliances, always turn off at the wall socket and unplug. This

Make sure that you know how to put on a plug correctly and fit the right fuse

particularly applies to television sets. Never leave an appliance such as an iron or deep fat frier unattended while you answer the door or the telephone. Switch them off and unplug. Never take portable electrical appliances into the bathroom.

Fuses. Do make sure that the plug you use for the appliance is fitted with a correctly-rated fuse. Again, an incorrectly-rated fuse is a most common cause of faults. Appliances rated below 700 watts need 3 amp fuses, coloured red. Appliances rated between 700 and 3000 watts need 13 amp fuses, coloured brown. The wattage of an appliance is usually stated on its rating plate, and in the instruction booklet. It is particularly important not to use a 13A fuse for an appliance which should have a 3A fuse, because you will not be getting

proper protection from your fuse. Many plugs are sold with 13A fuses, so you may have to change the fuse yourself, or ask for this to be done in the shop where you buy the plug.

As a general guide, the following appliances need only a 3A fuse (but always check with the instruction booklet): table-lamps, standard lamps, blenders and mixers, towel rails, record players, sewing machines, black and white TVs. Some motor driven appliances require 13 amp fuses because of a high starting current, see instruction booklet.

If an appliance should fail, don't panic. Never examine any electrical appliance without first turning off at the socket and unplugging. Then unscrew the back of the plug. CHECK that the wires in the plug are still firmly connected to the correct

terminals. (See putting on a plug, below). CHECK that the fuse has not blown.

You can check a cartridge fuse by testing it in an appliance of a similar rating which you know is working satisfactorily. Now check the wall socket by plugging into it an appliance you know to be working, eg table lamp.

If the fuse in the plug has not blown, check the fuse in your mains box (consumer unit). Before calling repair service, re-read the instruction booklet: sometimes there is a safety cut-out, for example, which may simply need setting. It may be necessary to wait for an appliance that has over-heated to cool down, or there may be some other point you have overlooked: a safety door lock, perhaps. Electric cookers may need to have timing mechanisms re-set (these can easily be disturbed during cleaning, for example).

Have all electrical appliances serviced regularly by the agents recommended by the manufacturer. Always keep carefully any receipts showing the date of purchase, so that you can prove an appliance is still within its guarantee period. When telephoning the service agents, state clearly the model and serial number – you will find this information on the rating plate and in the instruction booklet. Describe as clearly as you can the nature of the fault, and always enquire about charges at this stage.

Cleaning electrical appliances. First read carefully the points about cleaning listed in the manufacturer's handbook. In general, all appliances should be switched off at the socket and unplugged before you attempt any type of cleaning. Do not immerse electrical appliances in water (apart from mixer and liquidiser jugs/bowls and pans of some table top cookers, specifically described by the manufacturer as able to be immersed in water. Generally, the plastic or metal casings of most electrical appliances can be wiped (when unplugged) with a cloth dampened with warm water and a little washing-up liquid. Use a little washing-up liquid neat on any very dirty marks, or a cream cleaner, or general purpose aerosol cleaner polisher. But do not use abrasive cleaning powders. When cleaning food processors, food mixers, liquidisers and so on, be careful of any sharp blades.

GAS APPLIANCES

General safety points. Always look for the B.S.I. (British Standards Institution) safety mark when buying any gas appliance. The installation of gas appliances and use of gas in the home are governed by the

Always look for the appropriate safety mark or seal when buying household equipment; it pays to play safe

following Gas Safety Regulations, 1972.
1. You are bound by law not to use or let anyone else use an appliance you suspect or know to be dangerous.
2. Only competent people may install or service appliances: such work must not be carried out by anyone who is not qualified.
3. If gas should escape, you must turn off the supply at the mains, and then contact your local gas service centre. You will find this listed under GAS in the telephone directory.
4. You must not turn the supply back on again, or use a suspect appliance until the escape and/or the appliance has been repaired by a competent person.

You can be fined if you do not observe these regulations. Accordingly, you should always use qualified gas fitters for the installation of gas appliances: either a fitter from your regional gas authority (the 'gas board') or a CORGI registered fitter

(CORGI stands for Confederation of Registered Gas Installers).

Read carefully any instruction books supplied with the appliance, and keep them handy so that you can refer to them from time to time. If you lose your instruction book, write to the makers for a replacement.

It is vital to have all gas appliances serviced regularly by a qualified gas engineer. Gas central heating boilers, water heaters and fires should be serviced once every year (the summer is a good time). Other gas appliances should be serviced every two years. A faulty appliance may well be dangerous; it will almost certainly be wasteful, burning gas uneconomically.

Ventilation. Remember that all gas appliances must have air in order to work properly and to be safe in use. You should *never* block ventilators or air bricks in the same or connecting rooms to gas appliances; such ventilation may be in walls, windows or doors. Some gas appliances have flues to carry away harmful waste gases to the fresh air outside the home. Such appliances include boilers and fires. Your service engineer will check the flues as part of the regular servicing. However, it is a good idea yourself to watch for any possible signs of a blocked or faulty flue, such as discoloration or staining on the wall or on the appliance where appliances are fitted to a wall. If you do notice marks of this kind, call your gas service centre at once: don't delay, because it could be dangerous.

Old-fashioned water-heaters need particular care in use, because they have open flues. You must have them serviced once a year, and you must keep the bathroom window open when running hot water. Always keep the bathroom ventilator unblocked. Before you get into the bath, turn off the hot water, and don't run in any more once you are in the bath. Make sure that your family knows about these safety precautions, too. But modern gas water-heaters have balanced flues, so the spent gases are discharged directly to the open air, and the safety precautions outlined above will not be necessary.

Small modern gas instantaneous water-heaters fitted at the kitchen sink should not be allowed to run for more than five minutes at a time. You must not use them to fill washing machines or to fill baths.

Gas appliances should be used only for the purpose for which they were designed. Thus, you should not try to heat a room with a cooker, you should not build a cupboard around a boiler for use as an airing cupboard, and you should not use gas fires for drying clothes.

GENERAL CARE AND MAINTENANCE

Cookers. Here are some general hints on cleaning gas and electric cookers. In every case, first read the manufacturer's instruction book, which will have a special section devoted to cleaning. Note which cleaning products are recommended, which sections can be detached for cleaning, and what you must *not* do as well as what you should do.

Always make sure that an electric cooker is switched off at the main control panel before you start cleaning.

Wipe down hobs after each use. Mop up spills as soon as they happen, before they 'bake on', but be careful not to touch any very hot parts. For stubborn marks use a little cream cleaner of the type recommended by the Vitreous Enamel Development Council and marked with their symbol on the pack (see below). Avoid harsh scouring pads and powders which can scratch enamels and metals.

Where possible lift off removable parts and soak them in the sink in hot water and washing-up liquid, or in hot water and washing soda. You can use cream cleaner and a nylon scouring pad if necessary, then rinse well, dry off and replace. Glass oven doors can usually be removed for cleaning at the sink, but never use steel wool which can scratch the glass, and do not use aerosol oven cleaners on glass doors.

The dirtiest part of your cooker is likely to be the oven: try to clean it while it is still warm, but not hot. Take out shelves and any other removable parts and wash all over with hot water and washing-up liquid solution. If your oven is very dirty, use a branded oven cleaner. This is likely to contain caustic soda, so follow directions on the pack to the letter, protecting your

hands with a pair of rubber gloves, and avoiding breathing in any fumes. Keep the kitchen well-ventilated throughout and do not leave cleaner on for longer than the time specified. Do not use such cleaners on self-clean oven liners; these should only be cleaned in accordance with the manufacturer's instructions.

You can clean the new ceramic hobs with a damp cloth and a little cream cleaner. Special cleaners are also available from your supplier and from Electricity Board shops.

Electric kettles. All B.E.A.B. approved kettles have a safety cut-out which operates if a kettle boils dry; once the safety cut-out has operated you may have to leave the kettle for around ten minutes before refilling.

When using a new kettle for the first time, boil up some water and then empty it away. Always see that the element is covered with water before switching on; do not fill below or above marks for minimum and maximum water levels. Do not fill or pour from the kettle without withdrawing the flex connector. Keep the connector out of reach of children and do not leave flex or connector where they can get wet. Make sure that kettles stand on a level surface and do not stand them on a hot surface as this might damage their small plastic feet. In hard water areas you may find that scale or furring starts to build up in your kettle. To remove this, buy a branded de-scaling product from your hardware store, first checking that the pack says that it is suitable for electric kettles. Follow the directions carefully.

Other small kitchen appliances. Mixers, blenders, slow cookers, deep fat fryers and so on all have some part that comes into contact with food and must therefore be kept scrupulously clean. Many different materials are used in the manufacture of such items, so it is important to follow the directions for your particular model. Some parts (bowls, goblets and jugs) may be able to be removed for washing at the sink. But in general do not immerse in water the part which contains the electrical motor or controls. Metal blades of mincers, mixers and food processors should be handled with extreme care both during use and during cleaning: keep lids securely on during use (many types have safety cut-outs). Wash and dry the blades immediately after use, and store in a dry, safe place. Where possible, use dust covers to protect such appliances when not in use.

Make sure that all small appliances have a fuse of the rating recommended by the makers; most of them are double insulated and will not have an earth connection. However, there is usually an earth connection when the appliance performs some kind of heating function, such as a kettle, toaster or fryer.

Coffee-makers may require descaling periodically as detailed for kettles, above.

Make sure that the leads to these small appliances are short and do not pass over any hot surfaces such as a cooker hob. *Never* attempt to clean or adjust in any way without switching off and unplugging; in particular do not try to dislodge bread from a toaster without first switching it off and unplugging, and take care not to break the fine element wires inside, in the process.

Inspect flexes regularly, particularly at the point where they enter the plug or appliance (do this when the appliance is unplugged). If connections seem worn, or if flex is worn in part, or hard or cracked, get it replaced by a qualified electrician.

Dishwashers. Follow the maker's instructions precisely, using the detergent recommended and loading the machine exactly as suggested. If you have any problems initially, consult the service agents: they can often explain on the telephone what you are doing wrong, without the cost of a service call. Always make sure that your tableware is suited for a dishwasher before you place it in the machine. In general the following should not be washed by machine: antique or hand-painted china; wood; lead crystal and cut glass; and cutlery with special handles of bone or wood. Take care to clean out all filters after each wash, and clean around the door seal with a damp cloth. If you are not using your machine for a little while, leave it clean with the door slightly open. Fill-up 'rinse-aids' and water softeners regularly as directed in your instruction booklet. Never allow silverware to come into contact with other metals inside the machine: always place it in a separate basket, otherwise it may be blackened or even pitted by a process known as 'electrolysis'. It is often sensible to unload the bottom trays before top ones, in case small amounts of water are trapped on top of cups etc.

Washing machines. As always, it is vital that you follow the maker's instructions. Keep them nearby your machine, and re-read them from time to time. You will find a guide to the washcode numbers and

Above: always use distilled water in your steam iron. Or you can use a de-mineraliser as shown here. Top up the crystals in the container with tap water, shake and leave for a few minutes.
Left: the symbol of the Vitreous Enamel Development Council
Right: as with all electrical appliances, fridges and freezers should be used and maintained correctly. Defrost regularly

symbols on most washing powder packets. Always use the type of powder recommended: a common fault is to use a high lather detergent in a front loading automatic machine. The result is that the clothes cannot be washed properly and you may even get water seeping out onto the floor. Do not overload machines: refer to instructions for permitted load sizes. Make sure that supply and outlet hoses are always well-connected; if the machine is not plumbed in, make sure that water can drain away easily. Otherwise check that outlet hoses remain unblocked. Clean the filter regularly if required. Stand the machine on a level surface, otherwise excess vibration could damage the motor and/or turn the machine off. Always check that the water pressure of your home is within the limits given in the instruction book.

Spin driers. Consult instruction booklets for spin times for various fibres/fabrics. If the drier vibrates and makes a noise, it is probably unevenly loaded. Switch off at once and redistribute the load. Knitted garments which may lose their shape should only be given a short spin (maximum 30 seconds) wrapped in a towel. When using the drier, tuck the maker's

rubber retaining mat down over clothes, or tuck them down with an old towel.

New spin-driers have a safety lock which prevents anyone from opening the machine until the drum has stopped spinning, but some old machines may continue to spin for a little while even after the lid is opened – in this case take special care yourself and keep children away. After use wipe the machine dry and leave the lid open.

Tumble-driers. Never place sopping wet clothes in this type of machine: always wring or spin clothes first. Be sure to clean the front filter of your machine after use. Do not fill it more than two-thirds full, and consult instructions for the right heat and drying time for different fibres. In general, synthetics should be tumbled on the lowest possible heat and then, if possible, tumbled for a short while with the heat off to minimise creasing.

Irons. Never use an iron with a worn or damaged flex. Clip a flex guard onto your ironing board to protect the flex at its most vulnerable point: where it enters the iron. Special iron cleaners are available from hardware and chemist stores for cleaning the sole plates of irons that become stained or covered with sticky deposits (often from using too high a setting for synthetics). Use these in preference to scourers which can damage the sole plate.

If you have a *steam iron*, always use distilled water from a chemist, not from a garage. Or you can use one of the newer 'de-mineralisers' sold in the chemists or hardware store. These are crystals which you top up yourself with tap water and are therefore much lighter than distilled water to carry home. Some irons now advertise 'Tap water may be used.' These are exceptions to the above advice. Always turn off a steam iron before you fill it, and empty it after use. Stand it on its heel whenever you stop ironing.

Fridges. Set temperatures according to the manufacturer's instructions. It should not usually be necessary to run a fridge at its coldest setting: if you do, food may start to freeze in the fresh food compartment. Site your fridge away from sources of heat such as boilers or cookers. An electric fridge should have its own earthed electrical point so that you do not turn it off by mistake. Store and wrap food carefully as recommended in the maker's handbook. Do not put hot food into the fridge.

Make sure that there is sufficient air ventilation around the back of the fridge as

recommended by the manufacturer; if fitted under a worktop your fridge should have a little space at top and sides (about 20 mm/$\frac{3}{4}$ inch). Make sure that it is standing level or it may be very noisy; try adjusting the levelling screws, or even simply moving its position slightly. Keep the condenser units at the back of the fridge free of dust: switch off, unplug and then dust.

Defrost fridges regularly, and always when ice has built up to a thickness of around 3 mm ($\frac{1}{8}$ inch). After defrosting, clean out the fridge thoroughly, using a scrupulously clean cloth (e.g. well-washed teatowel) and a bowl of warm water (about 1 litre/2 pints) to which you have added 1 teaspoon of bicarbonate of soda. Do not use washing-up liquid as it can taint plastic interiors. Dry thoroughly, switch on again and put back the food.

Freezers. As with the fridge, your freezer should be connected to its own separate earthed electric point. And, as always, do follow the individual manufacturer's instructions. They are well worth reading, for they usually contain much additional information on the exact methods to use for freezing different kinds of food.

Also follow the maker's guidance on food packaging, which must be done

efficiently to preserve the food. In general, packaging should be air-tight, able to withstand low temperatures and clearly labelled, preferably with a chinagraph pencil. You can see special ranges of freezer packaging at most good hardware and department stores.

Follow carefully the maker's instructions for defrosting, but in general do not allow ice to build up to a thickness of more than $\frac{1}{2}$ cm ($\frac{1}{4}$ inch). You can use wooden or plastic spatulas to scrape away the ice as it melts but never use a sharp metal implement of any kind. When it has been defrosted, wipe out your freezer with a bowl of warm water to which you have added 1 tablespoon of bicarbonate of soda, and then wipe it dry with a clean cloth and leave open to dry before turning on for about an hour. Then put back the food (which can be wrapped in thick layers of newspaper, or put in fridge on coldest setting, meantime).

Vacuum cleaners. There are two main types: *upright cleaners* with rotating beaters, and *cylinder suction only cleaners*. With both kinds, it is essential to empty dust bags regularly.

If the hoses on cylinder cleaners split, you can often make a short-term repair with special wide adhesive tape for mending pipes and hoses sold at hardware shops. But in the end, you will probably have to order a new hose. If the hose becomes blocked, you may be able to clear it by fitting it to the blowing end of your cleaner: follow the directions in your instruction booklet. Or you can sometimes use a long length of wire to dislodge obstructions: a length of springy curtain wire with an eyelet screwed into the end is ideal; keep one handy in your cleaning box. Beware of making a hook in the end of the wire; if this gets caught anywhere inside the hose (and it always does!) it is almost impossible to detach again.

Upright cleaners have little to go wrong; but you may need to replace from time to time the rubber belt which drives the roller brush. Take the old belt with you when you go to buy a replacement as there are different sizes. Follow the directions in the instruction book for this relatively simple task.

Televisions. Always switch off the set and unplug at night, and close the door of your sitting room before going to bed (in fact, closing the door is a fire precaution applicable to all empty rooms). Never try to mend your television, and *on no account* take off its back even when switched off.

Do not put vases of flowers or plants on top of the TV. Keep the screen clean with a general purpose aerosol polisher/cleaner (switch off first).

Electric blankets. Do not buy second-hand blankets. *Overblankets* can be used all night: *underblankets* must be switched off before you get into bed, unless of a special design. Follow maker's directions to the letter. Do not use blankets which are wet: let them dry naturally: do not switch them on to dry. Do not plug blankets into light fittings, or use on an adaptor with another appliance. Make sure that *underblankets* lie flat, held securely in place by their tapes. Do not use a blanket which is creased or folded; do not fold to store. Store blankets flat on a spare bed, or rolled up. Never use an overblanket as an underblanket or vice versa. Check frequently for frayed edges, and loose connections at the plug and controls, but always unplug blanket first. Watch for scorch marks and damage to flex. Have any faults attended to immediately.

Always have your blanket serviced regularly and return it to the makers if you see any sign of any damage.

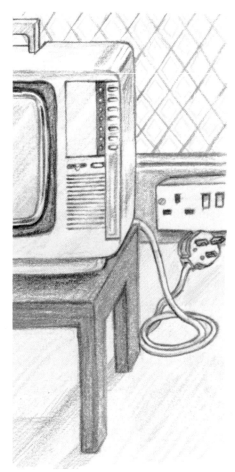

Electric fires (portable). It is most important that these stand in a safe place away from flammable materials such as curtains and bedcovers. *Never* take this type of heater (or, indeed, any portable heater) into the bathroom.

Keep reflector plates of radiant types clean, but always unplug before cleaning, and remember to refit the guard. Do not use time switches or thermostats with this type of heater, and provide an additional guard if children are to play in the same room. Keep fan and convector heaters well dusted (switch off first).

Oil heaters. Do not buy second hand. Follow basic safety precautions, as follows: Do not fill or move heaters when they are alight. Take the tank to the fuel, which should if possible be stored outside, or at any rate in a room separate from the heater. Use the correct grade of paraffin, pouring carefully from a container made for the purpose, and wipe up any splashes.

Have good ventilation in rooms where heaters are burning but do not stand them in a draught. Bolt heaters to the floor or bracket to the wall if possible. Don't use a heater to dry clothes or to cook on; keep it away from all fabrics such as curtains. Always pour old fuel away onto the ground: it is an offence to pour it down a drain.

Immersion heaters. Make sure that your hot water tank is adequately lagged with insulation that is at least 7.5 cm (3 inch) thick. Set your thermostat at 60°C, to provide water hot enough for most domestic purposes. This is important in areas with hard water, because a higher setting will cause build up of hard water scale.

Fit your heater with a time switch to save money: for example it can be set to turn on for an hour or so in the morning and an hour or so at night to meet your own hot water needs. To adjust the thermostat, turn off at the mains, remove the head cover and turn the thermostat adjuster with a screwdriver (refer to maker's directions).

Boilers. Follow carefully the maker's directions for routine maintenance, relighting pilot lights, keeping flues swept and so on. If you have lost these instructions, write off for a new set. Have boilers serviced regularly: at least once a year. Only build cupboards around them which conform meticulously to the maker's recommendations as regards fire-proofing, ventilation etc. and then do not use them for storage of any kind.

HOUSEHOLD REPAIRS AND MAINTENANCE

Buying a house or flat is a major investment and it is obviously in your own best interests to maintain and increase the value and comfort of your home by keeping it in a good state of repair. This may entail exploring many new areas of practical knowledge but, with practice, you will gain in confidence, expertise – and ambition! Read the following advice on basic home maintenance carefully and start applying it without delay. Remember, small repairs made now will save the cost of large ones later.

DAMP, ROT AND CORROSION

DAMP

Damp in the home is not only ugly, unpleasant and unhealthy. It is also potentially costly, possibly leading to the start and spread of rot (see below) which could prove very difficult and expensive to eradicate.

Never, therefore, ignore a damp patch. It may go away in sunny weather, but it will always return with the rain. And its effects could well soon extend far beyond what is immediately visible to the eye.

A damp patch or – worse still – drips or pools of moisture are there for all to see, along with the resulting growth of mould, flaking paint, and peeling paper. But the cause of the damp is usually less obvious. And before you can tackle the problem it is essential that you find out why the damp is there.

Penetrating damp comes into your home via a weakness in the external structure, so check outside for possible defects, including the following: gaps around the doors and windows, porous brick or stonework, leaking gutters or

downpipes, defective flashings or cracked or missing roof tiles or slates.

Rising damp is moisture which is coming up through the walls of the house from the soil foundations. Rising damp occurs when there is no damp proof course (d.p.c.) or if the d.p.c. is faulty. Further details on installing a d.p.c. in older houses, or identifying d.p.c. faults in a newer house also appear later in this chapter.

Plumbing faults may cause damp inside the home. A sudden catastrophe like a burst pipe or cracked cistern is usually immediately obvious and dramatic in its effect. Steady hidden dripping may not be so noticeable; nevertheless, it could be the cause of the damp and then rot over a

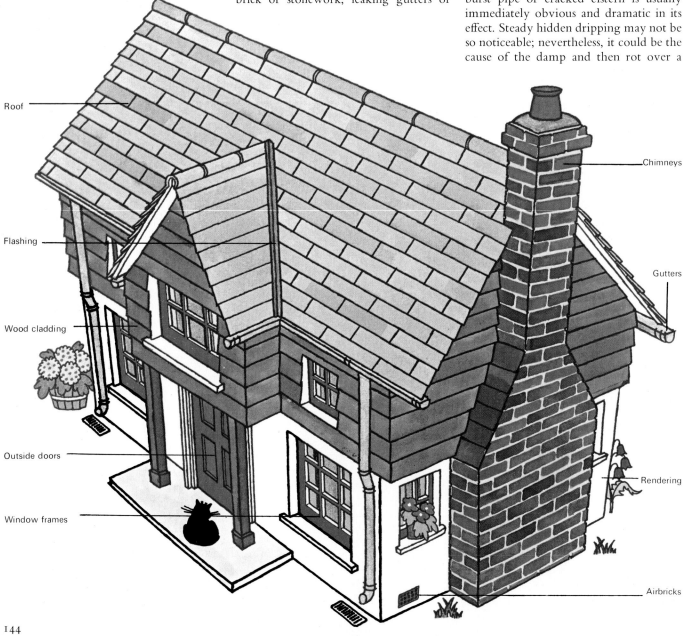

Roof

Flashing

Wood cladding

Outside doors

Window frames

Chimneys

Gutters

Rendering

Airbricks

longish period. Regularly inspect concealed pipework and watch out for seepage from the connection between pipes and waste fittings. Make sure that baths, basins and sinks have the gaps around their edges well filled with a waterproof sealant; the long gap along the edge of the bath is particularly vulnerable.

Condensation should not be confused with either penetrating or rising damp. When you use facilities such as cookers, baths, sinks, etc., they give off large amounts of water vapour which become little drops of water as they hit a cold surface such as a wall or window pane. You can cut down on such condensation by improving ventilation. Consider installing an extractor fan in your kitchen and possibly in your bathroom as well. Less costly and easier to instal are air vents.

Condensation can also be cut back if you improve the insulation of your house, thus eliminating cold surfaces. You could line walls and ceilings with insulating materials such as cork or fire-retardant polystyrene sheet or tiles or, if you have cavity walls, fill them with plastic foam or dry mineral fibre.

Once you have diagnosed and eliminated the cause of damp in your home, you may still be left with mouldy patches. Wash these over with a solution of one part household bleach to one part water, and leave to dry. Then rinse off with clear water and leave to dry again before sealing the stain with an aluminium or multipurpose primer – this, too, should be allowed to dry out thoroughly before decorating. For treating bad crops of mould, you can buy special fungicides at hardware stores or builders' merchants.

Various short-term remedies are available for treating damp inside the home. These include water-repellent liquids and damp barrier linings – available at good builders' merchants. Some can even be applied to walls which are still wet. However, it must be stressed that damp-repellent liquids and linings for the inside of the home are only treating the result of the damp. In the long term it is vital to find and cure the cause of the damp problem.

ROT

Rot unfortunately follows on from damp. Indeed, rot is usually the result of damp that was ignored. Rot attacks the wooden parts of your home. The timber affected may be structural such as roof beams or floor joists, and the resulting damage may therefore be far greater than the simple

Above: dry rot can be devastating; if you detect it, seek expert treatment urgently
Left: exterior maintenance checkpoints

replacement of the timber itself. Or the timbers may be non-structural such as skirting boards or door frames.

It is important to know that there are two kinds of rot (both are forms of fungal decay) which can attack the timbers in your home: 'dry rot' and 'wet rot'. The names are a little confusing for, in fact, both types of rot thrive on damp, poorly ventilated wood. In time, both break down the timber they have attacked and can destroy it completely. The danger signs, which you can see easily, are warping and cracking in the wood such as skirting boards, and window and door frames. If you suspect that wood has become rotten underneath a coating of paint, stab it with a key or knife, which will sink in easily if the wood is rotting.

Dry rot thrives when the moisture content of wood is around 20 per cent, distinguishing it from wet rot, which prefers a moisture content of around 40 per cent (see below). Dry rot is rightly feared because of the insidious way in which it can spread, by means of minute air-borne spores or through white strands of fungal growth which will travel across brickwork to find fresh timber on which to feed. Dry rot breaks down the wood into cube-shaped sections called 'cuboid cracking'. You may notice a musty smell, and you will be able to see the growth of fungus quite clearly. A flat orange-yellow pancake shaped fungus, called a 'fruiting body' gives out tiny rust-coloured spores. These travel through the air, and some settle on damp wood. Here they start to put out thin white strands which will

eventually form themselves into a thick white web of fungus, which in turn will produce a fresh fruiting body, and so on. If you suspect dry rot it is essential to call in a timber specialist immediately. Surveys are usually free and the treatment is guaranteed for 20 or 30 years. Remember that dry rot spreads very quickly once established so act without delay. It is not advisable to attempt treatment yourself.

Wet rot requires wood which is substantially wetter than dry rot: around 40 per cent minimum moisture content. You may well see wet rot, for example, at the bottom of door frames or in window sills. The wood will have a blackened, charred appearance and when it is wet will seem spongy. Wet rot is not nearly so dangerous as dry rot because it does not spread in the same way, but it should be eradicated, First, as always, try to find and cure the cause. Sometimes you can cure wet rot simply by drying out the affected timbers. Otherwise cut away the timber which has been destroyed by the rot and replace with new wood that has first been treated with preservative.

CORROSION

This is another domestic hazard which can cause enormous damage if left unchecked. The most common form of corrosion is *rust* which occurs when iron and steel (ie 'ferrous' metals) are exposed to moisture and air; gradually they change into iron oxide – the powdery red substance we call 'rust'.

Rust is not only ugly but in time will eat through metals and totally destroy them. Like damp and rot, rust does not go away: it always gets worse, so deal promptly with any traces you find around your home on window frames, radiators and so on. Minor outbreaks should be rubbed away with steel wool, emery paper or with a wire brush, until only bright metal remains. This should be treated at once with a metal primer, because rust can start again within a matter of hours, due to the moisture content of air. When the primer is thoroughly dry, paint to match the surrounding surface.

For very bad outbreaks of rust you can buy special liquid products from hardware stores or motor car accessory shops which, when painted on to rust, convert it into a non-rusting substance which can then be painted over. Carefully follow the directions on the pack, including the safety precautions suggested.

Steel and iron tools will rust unless protected during storage – this particularly applies to garden tools left, say, in a damp shed over winter. Before storing tools thoroughly clean the metal, then coat it with grease to prevent rust. If possible store all metal equipment *inside* the house in a dry warm cupboard, drawer or box, ideally wrapped in a rust-inhibiting paper (from your hardware store).

Non-ferrous metals such as zinc, copper and lead will not rust, but will corrode to some extent. However the corrosion causes oxidization in the form of a protective film which then prevents any further wasting away of the metal.

Electrolytic action. Corrosion is commonly found within plumbing systems due to what is known as 'electrolytic action' between two different metals in the same system. The metals involved are usually galvanized steel and copper. For example, you will often find that copper pipes have been connected up to a galvanized (i.e. zinc coated) steel cold water tank.

If you have a metal cold water tank, inspect its underside regularly and watch out for signs of corrosion which appear as brown and white spots. If you see these, call your plumber because you may need a new tank. Modern plastic tanks cannot corrode.

It is possible to drain metal cold water tanks and give them two coats of bitumen paint which will protect the metal against corrosion and will not taint the water when the tank is refilled. But if corrosion has already caused the surface of the tank to flake away, all loose particles of rust should be removed before repainting with a rust inhibiting liquid (see above). Rub the loose rust away with wire wool, emery paper, wire brush or, better still, use a wire cup brush attachment fitted into an electric drill, which will be less hard work. If corrosion/rust is well advanced, the only alternative is to replace the tank completely – a job for your plumber.

Metal water tanks, hot or cold, can be protected from corrosion by installing what is known rather strangely as a 'sacrificial anode'. This is a lump of magnesium connected to the zinc surface of the tank. Electrolytic action then takes place between the anode and the tank. It is not necessary to understand the science behind this ingenious device but it is important to know the result: that it is the anode rather than the tank that gradually wastes away. In other words, the anode sacrifices itself – hence the quaint name. This device will remain effective for around two to three years.

Corrosion builds up in central heating systems because of the electrolytic action between steel radiators and the copper pipes which supply them. The result can be a black iron oxide sludge called 'magnetite'. As this forms, the metal of the radiators is eaten away, and can eventually disappear completely. The iron oxide sludge can also be the cause of the knocking noises which can build up inside a boiler and pipes. The solution here is to add a corrosion inhibitor to the feed-and-expansion cistern which supplies the water to your central heating system.

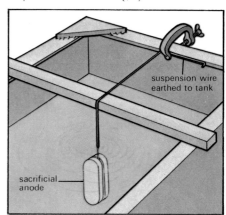

Left: various aids are available to remove rust from iron and steel. You can buy rust removers from hardware stores – always follow the instructions to the letter. You can also scrape off rust with a wire brush or, even better, use a wire brush cup attachment with your electric drill. Abrasive paper is also useful. As soon as you have removed all traces of rust, protect the clean metal with primer or a film of grease
Above: a magnesium 'sacrificial annode' protects metal water tanks from corrosion

TOOLS AND EQUIPMENT

Behind any well-maintained house is not only a conscientious householder but also a good set of tools. It is impossible to carry out even simple maintenance repair jobs inside the house or out without the right tool so start building up a good set right away.

BASIC TOOLS AND AIDS

Even if you do not intend tackling ambitious construction projects, it is useful to have the basic tools and aids for maintenance and small repairs. Always buy the best you can afford: good tools are costly items, but if you look after them properly they will last a lifetime and serve you well.

Adhesives. Keep a selection in your tool kit; make sure you always replace their caps and keep their instructions! Always read carefully any directions for use, and in general make sure that surfaces to be joined are clean and dry. *Clear household adhesive* is useful for quick lightweight jobs. *Epoxy resins* will make a longer lasting repair for china and glass (mix together the two tubes supplied, carefully following the directions). *PVA woodglues* are virtually essential, being the best to use for small woodworking jobs and repairs. *Latex fabric adhesive* is another good stand-by, recommended for repairing carpets, fabrics, and for sticking down overlaps on vinyl wallcoverings. The 'superglues' (*cyanoacrylates*) certainly do give a very strong bond, but they are rather fiddly to use, and must be handled with great care; it is essential to read the warning on the pack. Various other special adhesives are useful for particular jobs: your D.I.Y. shop or builders merchant will advise. Where possible keep any leftovers, along with small quantities of materials used as these come in handy for repairs or touch-up jobs.

Bradawls and gimlets. One of these is essential.

Both tools are used to make starting holes in wood for screws and other fittings with threaded shanks. A bradawl is simply a metal spike set into a wooden handle; you dig the spike into the wood and turn it round. A gimlet has a threaded spike, and goes in more easily.

Drills. A drill is the tool which you use to make holes in wood, walls, metal and so on. The part that actually makes the holes is called the 'bit', which is held in place by the 'chuck'. Bits are changed according to the size of the hole required, and the type of material being drilled. On electric drills, you need a special chuck key to open the chuck or jaws of the drill to insert and take out the appropriate bit. Twist drills are used for making holes in wood and masonry bits for brick and stone.

Hand drills can be used for woodwork and small jobs around the home, but it pays to invest in an electric drill from the start. Power ratings for electric drills may range from around 350 watts to 500 watts; the higher the wattage the more powerful the drill and the longer it will last. Small single-speed drills cope with a limited range of tasks and may not be able to penetrate very hard masonry. With two-speed models, the slow speed is especially for drilling into masonry and for making larger holes in wood. Hammer drills are even better for very hard masonry and concrete: they have a special action to rotate and hammer the bit, chipping the masonry away.

If you do not have a drill, or only a drill of limited power, you can use a small tool called a 'jumper' for making holes in masonry. This you hit with a hammer, turn slightly, and then hit again. It is essential to wear goggles to protect your eyes from flying particles.

Electrical repair kit. This is another essential: it should contain a screwdriver with insulated handle; fuse wire and spare fuses; torch with working batteries (a small metal-cased torch is useful for testing cartridge fuses, but a larger rubber-cased torch is better for actually seeing by); and a sharp knife or, better still, wire strippers.

G-Clamps are essential if you need to hold work steady while cutting, and for holding pieces in place while adhesives set. You can also improvize 'clamps' for adhesives from rubber bands, string, or sticky tape, so keep these in your tool box, too.

Hacksaw. You will need this in addition to a general purpose wood saw. For example, a hacksaw will cut through metal pipes and rods, and plastic piping and gutters. Blades are removable, so always keep a packet of spares, and replace them frequently.

Hammer. From the several weights available choose the one you find most comfortable to handle. Wooden shafts should be fitted securely to the hammer head with tightly-fitting wooden wedges. Hammers with the steel or glass fibre handles are more costly – but much longer lasting. Buy a claw hammer, so that you can use the claw for levering out nails.

Lubricating oil comes in handy for easing stiff nuts, bolts and screws, curing stiff locks and squeaking hinges, and maintaining tools. A small jar of grease is also useful, for protecting tools from rust.

Nails and screws. You will need a selection of *nails, screws* etc. *Round nails* have small round flat heads; *ovals* are neater with smaller heads, and *panel pins* are neater still for fiddly work. *Annular* or *screw nails* have rings round their shanks to use for fixing, for example, hardboard to a wooden floor. Use *clout nails* with large heads for securing roofing felts, and *sprigs* for holding glass in a window frame. *Masonry* nails are specially toughened for making fixings into brick, stone, etc. In general however *screws* make better fixings than nails; they come in various gauges according to thickness. The larger the screw the larger its number, from 4 to 20. Ordinary *steel screws* will rust unless protected by primer and paint, but *chromium-plated* or *zinc* screws will not rust; *brass* and *black japanned* screws are available for more decorative work and to match particular fittings. Ordinary screws have a *countersunk* head, designed to be driven flush with the surface of the wood; *round-head* screws stand proud of the surface and should be used for attaching metal fittings to wood; and *dome-headed* screws have an additional metal cap which is screwed on at the end of the job to give a neater finish on mirrors, for example.

Pliers. An absolutely vital household tool: you will find it difficult to manage for any length of time without a pair. You can use them to grip, pull and cut.

Sandpaper (more correctly called glasspaper) is useful for smoothing off surfaces; have handy coarse, medium and fine grades, and use wrapped around a small wooden or cork block specially designed for this purpose.

Saw. Avoid large carpenters' saws as they are rather difficult for a beginner to use. A small all-purpose saw with stiffened blade and small teeth will easily cope with most small jobs around the house.

Scissors. Keep a general purpose pair in your tool box, to save borrowing from the kitchen or blunting your dress-making shears. 'Tin snips' are particularly useful for cutting sheet metal.

Screwdrivers. There are many types of screwdrivers, and it is helpful to build up a selection in your tool kit. Screwdrivers with chubby handles are for screws in inaccessible places, and screwdrivers with insulated handles are useful for small electrical repairs.

Screwdrivers with flat heads will turn ordinary wood screws which have a single slot across their handle; but cross-slotted heads are also found on many screws, such as those fitted into many household appliances, and toys. For these you will need a screwdriver with a cross-pointed head. A number 2 Pozidriv screwdriver will suffice for all the most popular sizes of screws. Another type of screw which you may come across is the 'Phillips screw'. This has a plain cross-cut head and although now obsolete, it may still crop up around the home on appliances and so on. For this type of screw you may need a Phillips screwdriver as well.

Steel tape. Don't try to make do with a school ruler or a cloth dressmaking tape – which will stretch with use. Buy yourself a proper steel tape, preferably with metric measurements along one edge and imperial along the other.

Sticky tape is obviously useful for mending torn paper and doing up parcels etc. *Double-sided* tape can also be useful. *Sticky cloth tapes* give a firmer but more visible mend, and you can use them for bookbindings, repairing carpet edges etc. *Insulating tape* is used to protect the ends of bare wires, and temporarily to bind a fraying flex (but get this replaced as soon as you can). *Weatherproofing tapes* in various widths are useful for making repairs to outside gutters, skylights, roofs and so on. Transparent types are available for repairing cracked glass.

Spanner (adjustable). Another essential, this allows you to undo and tighten a wide range of sizes of nuts and bolts.

Trimming knife. Again, you will almost certainly need one of these. Always keep a packet of spare blades handy, and use for a whole host of small cutting jobs. Special blades are available as necessary: for example, hooked blades for cutting sheet vinyl.

Wall plugs. Keep a selection of these. Remember that when you make a fixing into a masonry wall (stone, brick, concrete, etc.) you should not put a screw in directly. First make a hole with your drill, using the correct bit, and put in a plug, then insert the screw. Size of the drill bit, plug and screw must all correspond. Fibre plugs make excellent fixings and come in sizes to match the screw exactly. But the inexperienced may find plastic plugs easier, because one size will cope with a range of screw sizes (see packs for details).

Specialized tools. You will need separate tools for household decorating, but *stripping* and *filling knives*, and general purpose *fillers* come in handy for general repair work.

For repairs outside, you may require these additions to your standard tool kit: a *trowel* for pointing, or applying cement rendering etc. A *hawk* (board on a stick), useful for holding mortar etc. and a *float* for smoothing off large areas of plaster or rendering. A *cold chisel*, specially toughened and shaped for chipping away masonry; hit this with a *wooden club hammer*. A *bolster*, which is a special version of a cold chisel, with a wide flat blade used for cutting bricks etc.

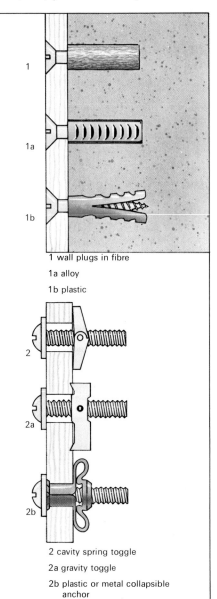

1 wall plugs in fibre

1a alloy

1b plastic

2 cavity spring toggle

2a gravity toggle

2b plastic or metal collapsible anchor

Right: You can cope with many small household repairs yourself if you have the right tools for the job, so it is well worth acquiring a good set.

1. Toolbox; 2. Rubber torch; 3. Adhesives; 4. Screwdrivers, several sizes; 5. Ratchet screwdriver; 6. Retractable steel measure; 7. Pliers; 8. Wall plugs; 9. Spanners; 10. Saw; 11. Hacksaw; 12. Sandpaper: fine, medium, coarse; 13. Oilcan (with oil); 14. Lightweight pin hammer; 15. Claw hammer; 16. Trowel; 17. Scraper; 18. Electric drill and chuck key; 19. Stanley knife

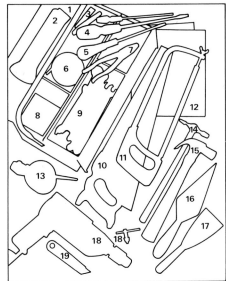

EXTERIOR UPKEEP

It is vital to maintain the outside of your house in a good condition. All the money and time you spend on inside decorations will soon be wasted if damp starts to penetrate, or – worse still! – the fabric of the building starts to rot and/or crumble.

It is unlikely that you will want to carry out all of the maintenance jobs and repairs listed below yourself. Nevertheless, it is important to be able to spot trouble areas, and to have sufficient knowledge intelligently to discuss possible remedies with a builder.

Do not wait for exterior faults to make their presence known internally. Regularly check the exterior of your property so that you can put defects right before they become serious problems. Building faults never go away of their own accord. They may *seem* to disappear in fine weather. But they always return, and ultimately get worse.

If you tackle the various parts of your house systematically, using the notes below as a check list, an exterior inspection will not seem such an impossible and alien task.

ROOFS AND CHIMNEYS

Start with an inspection of the roof, because it is essential that this is kept in a good state of repair. It is inadvisable for an amateur to tackle roof repairs, especially when these involve working at a considerable height, unless he or she feels absolutely confident about the task in hand. Nevertheless, you will need a knowledge of roof faults and roof 'language' when talking to your builder.

Pitched (sloping) roofs built before the second world war are usually covered with slates or clay tiles. Modern roofs usually have concrete tiles. Check regularly for cracked, slipped or missing ones. Ideally, you should spot these before water coming through a ceiling makes them obvious and causes additional damage. If you have (or can borrow) a pair of binoculars, you can inspect your roof from the ground, front and back.

Follow up with an excursion into the loft. If your roof is unlined (i.e. does not have a layer of felt below the tiles), on a bright day you will be able to see tell-tale

chinks of light where tiles are cracked, have slipped or are missing.

If your roof has a felt-lining below the tiles, look for water stains as a sign of leaks. Better still, visit your loft when it is actually raining and see for yourself where the water is coming in . . . a depressing experience! Bear in mind that water often starts dripping some distance from the actual leak, because it tends to run down inside the roof first. As a temporary measure, place a large bucket or basin in the loft – rest this on boards supported across the joists – to catch the drips and stop them coming through the ceiling. Then consult your builder.

Flat roofs are usually covered with layers of bituminous felt or with asphalt which is spread while hot. Small areas of damaged roofing felt can sometimes be repaired with bituminous mastic (from a builders' merchant) but if the felt is badly cracked and brittle, arrange for all of it to be replaced. Never use a flat roof as a sunroof or as a balcony without first checking with a surveyor or builder that the roof can take the extra weight; its surface will then need

Above: chimney pots, roofs and gutters must be kept in a good state of repair or damp will penetrate into your home and possibly lead to rot. Regularly check chimney pointing and the concrete 'flaunching' at the top of the stack into which the chimney pot is set. Flashings waterproof the gaps where two angles of a roof, or roof and chimney stack, meet. Keep them well-maintained. Check regularly for cracked, loose or missing tiles or slates. Make sure that gutters are well fixed, slope correctly and are free from obstruction
Left: brush-on bituminous mastic will seal small areas of damaged roofing felt
Right: clean out all gutters at least once a year – but first read carefully our points on ladder safety

protecting with tiles, which are usually made of asbestos and set into bitumen.

Flashings or 'sealing strips' are an important part of a sound roof, because they waterproof the gaps where two angles of the roof meet or where the roof meets with another part of the house, such as the chimney stack. Flashings can be made from a wide variety of materials, including strips of mortar, felt, lead, zinc, or an asbestos bitumen compound. Torn, cracked or missing flashings will allow damp into the house, so it is essential to keep them in good repair. You may be able to carry out small repairs with special waterproof tapes sold for this purpose at builders' merchants. Alternatively you can use several coats of a proprietary bituminous compound (also from the builders' merchant). However, flashings which have badly deteriorated must be replaced completely: consult your builder.

Chimneys should not be ignored merely because they are so far away and inaccessible! At best they may be porous and allow in damp; have them sealed with a coat of silicone water repellent. Or there may be minor cracks which need filling with mastic. Or the pointing (mortar) between the bricks may be crumbling; in which case it will need raking out and replacing. At worst, the brickwork of the chimney itself may be crumbling, in which case the chimney must be re-built, as this could be extremely dangerous.

Your chimney pots may be set into concrete at the top of the chimney stack; this is called 'flaunching', and should be kept in a good state of repair, with no cracks or crumbling areas that may let in the damp. Also, fit wire netting over the top of the chimneys to stop birds from nesting in them.

Chimneys which are not in use can be sealed off but it is important that the flue remains ventilated. You can use a half-round tile or a special capping pot to seal the chimney; these allow ventilation but keep out the rain. Inside the house, where fireplaces are sealed off, fit an airbrick or ventilator into the chimney-breast to stop damp being caused by condensation inside the flue.

RAINWATER GOODS

Guttering and downpipes are sometimes called 'rainwater goods'.

Gutters run around the bottom edge of your roof, to collect the rainwater, and prevent it from spilling over on to roofs

and walls to cause damp or even rot. Modern gutters are commonly made of plastic, but older ones may be cast iron. Plastic gutters need little maintenance, but cast-iron gutters need painting inside and out from time to time. First remove any rusty patches with a wire brush, and then prime with a metal primer and allow to dry before applying paint. In general you should use oil-based gloss paint – you can use up left-overs from other jobs on the insides of the gutters, since they will not be seen from the ground. But if the gutters have been painted previously with bituminous paint, you will have to use this kind of paint again, because bitumen 'bleeds through' (works its way to the surface) of any subsequent gloss coating. If you are not sure whether bituminous paint was used before, do a small test area to find out. Apply a little square of white gloss, allow to dry and see if any colour works its way through to the surface after a day or two.

Periodically check the slope of your gutters too, to make sure they are carrying the water to the downpipes (see below). Check for cracks and sagging, and also for cracked joints between sections. You may be able to make small repairs with waterproof tape or to repair damaged sections with a glass-fibre kit from your builders' merchant. However, it may be necessary completely to replace a damaged section.

Blocked gutters are a common cause of damp patches on adjacent walls. At least

twice a year (autumn and spring), check that your gutters are clear of leaves, twigs and other debris. As much debris as possible should be scooped out and removed (otherwise it may block the downpipes, see below). Then the gutters can be flushed through with clean water from a hosepipe. But place a small basin at the bottom of the drainpipes to stop twigs etc. from entering the drains where they might eventually form a blockage. When your gutters are clean and running freely, protect them from further blockage with wire mesh sold specially for the purpose.

Gutters are attached to wooden 'fascia boards' which run around the bottom edge of the roof. Check these at the same time as you check your gutters, and repaint them from time to time to prevent rot. Any rotten sections must be replaced, and the brackets that hold the gutters should be checked for firm fixings.

Downpipes carry the water from the gutters to the drains and it is just as vital to keep them in good repair. A leaking downpipe is not necessarily as obvious as a leaking gutter, but over a period of time can cause considerable damage to the fabric of the building. Watch out for telltale damp patches or green mouldy areas around downpipes and *do not* ignore them; they are the symptoms of a prime cause of dry rot (see *Damp*).

Repair downpipes in the same manner as for gutters. Downpipes are fixed to wooden plugs inserted into the brickwork of the house; if these have started to work loose, replace them with larger plugs.

Birds often nest in the tops of downpipes. If this happens, carefully lift out the nest with a piece of hooked wire. Don't try to wash the nest away with water because it may simply get stuck farther down the pipe. You may be able to clear other minor obstructions in downpipes with a long cane with a piece of rag tied to its end to

You can hire a set of drain rods to clear a blockage in your outside drains. Here, the blockage is between the two inspection chambers. Different attachments will cope with various types of blockage. Always turn the rods clockwise: if you turn them the other way, the sections will unscrew and you will be worse off than before

make a pad. If your downpipe becomes badly blocked, you can tell where the pipe is obstructed because just above the blockage, water will be flowing out of the joint between sections of the pipe. The downpipe will have to be taken to pieces section by section as far as the blockage.

Open gullies at ground level collect the water from the downpipes (and possibly also the waste water from your sink, basins and baths). Check that downpipes do indeed empty into a gulley and not on to the ground or against a wall. If necessary, correct the positioning, or lengthen the downpipes. If water persistently splashes up against the walls, fit downpipes with a curved 'shoe' section to divert and lessen flow. From the gully, an underground pipe flows into a brick-lined inspection chamber close to the house, covered by a removable, metal man-hole cover. Gullies may be fitted with their own 'traps' – an extra underground bend of pipe, the purpose of which is to stop smells – and even rats! – entering the house from the sewer.

Carefully remove any accumulated debris such as leaves and twigs from the tops of gullies; don't push them down into the drain where they could cause a blockage. When gullies are cleared, flush them through with clean water from a hose pipe. Keep gulley gratings clean by washing with hot water and soda, or place metal gulley gratings in a fire for a few minutes (e.g. a bonfire). You can fit a kerb in brick or cement around the top of a gulley and fit with a removable cover to prevent further blockages.

WALLS

Despite the large areas involved, walls too must be inspected regularly for faults.

Porous walls may be allowing rainwater to pass through to cause patches of 'penetrating damp' (see *Damp*) inside the house.

This is a common problem with older solid walls. It can even happen with cavity walls (walls which have an outer and an inner layer, and a gap in between) when the steel ties that hold the two sections of the wall together become bridged by, for example, droppings of mortar.

Coat porous walls with a clear silicone water repellent, available from a builders' merchant. Apply on a dry day, after carefully reading the directions on the can. This treatment will also protect your brickwork from frost.

Rising damp is another common problem for walls. Most houses built after the 1870s have a 'damp-proof course' or d.p.c. This is a line of waterproof material a few bricks up from the bottom of your outside walls. It can be made of slate or bituminous felt, or an extra thick band of mortar running through the brickwork. Its purpose is to protect the building from rising damp which otherwise might pass up through the brickwork from the soil foundations.

If your house does not have a d.p.c., you should have one installed by a specialist. Various methods are used – these include cutting the walls to insert a layer of slate, metal or fibre materials; injecting the walls with damp-repelling liquid; installing hollow tubes of clay to act as airbricks, or fitting a band of copper to get rid of damp by an electrical process known as 'electro-osmosis'. Get estimates from several firms before making up your mind on the right kind of treatment for your property. Choose a reputable company.

Even if your house is provided with a d.p.c., trouble can arise if the d.p.c. is defective – it must be kept completely clear or it cannot work properly. Dig away any soil that has collected against the walls below the level of the d.p.c. In the same way, you should make sure that any paths are at least 15 cm (6 inch) below the

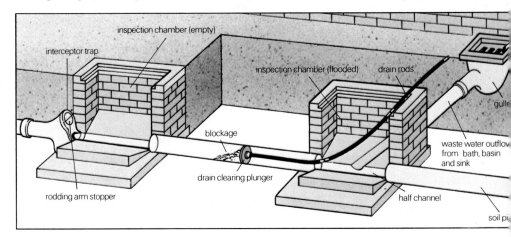

level of d.p.c. Adjoining outbuildings or walls should also have damp-proof courses at the same level as the d.p.c. for the house walls. Any concrete rendering covering the d.p.c. should be hacked away. If, even when cleared, your d.p.c. still appears to be defective, consult a reputable, specialist damp-proofing company.

Airbricks provide vital ventilation for suspended floors and prevent dampness from condensation. You will find them set low down in an outside wall looking like an ordinary brick with small round holes or a small grating. Keep your airbricks clear of piled-up soil, leaves and rubbish. Damaged airbricks should be replaced, as they may allow birds or vermin into your property. There are two types of airbrick: for a solid wall, there is an airbrick with holes for the outside of the wall, and a louvre to fix to the inside; a cavity wall airbrick extends right through the wall.

Pointing is the mortar (sand and cement mix) holding the bricks together and it may crumble after a period of time.

You can attempt small areas of repointing yourself. You will need a small sharp cold chisel and a wooden club hammer for chipping out the old mortar. Also a 'hawk' (board on a stick) to hold a small amount of mortar while working, and a pointing trowel. Ready-mixed pointing can be bought in small bags – simply add water as directed on the pack. The mix should be neither too stiff, nor too runny – aim for a 'buttery' consistency.

Chip out the old mortar to a depth of 1 cm ($\frac{1}{2}$ inch). Brush out all dust, then wet the cavities with water using an old paintbrush. Use your trowel to cut slices of mortar off the hawk and to press the mortar into the cavities. Cover 1 sq. m. (1 sq. yd.) at a time, doing the upright joints first, then the horizontal ones.

The joints should be finished off to match the surrounding brickwork. If the bricks are to be painted, then the joints can be left flush (flat). Simply draw the trowel smoothly across the mortar.

Hollow or rubbed pointing is shaped when the mortar is partially dry. Use a piece of timber or metal rod about 8 mm ($\frac{3}{8}$ inch) in diameter. Draw this along the joints to leave a concave impression. A piece of pipe is easy to use because it can be slightly bent to make it easier to handle.

Weathered joints are the trickiest to master. Shape them with the edge of the trowel, cutting away the face of the mortar at the top of the crevice by about 1 cm ($\frac{1}{2}$ inch) to prevent rainwater from collect-

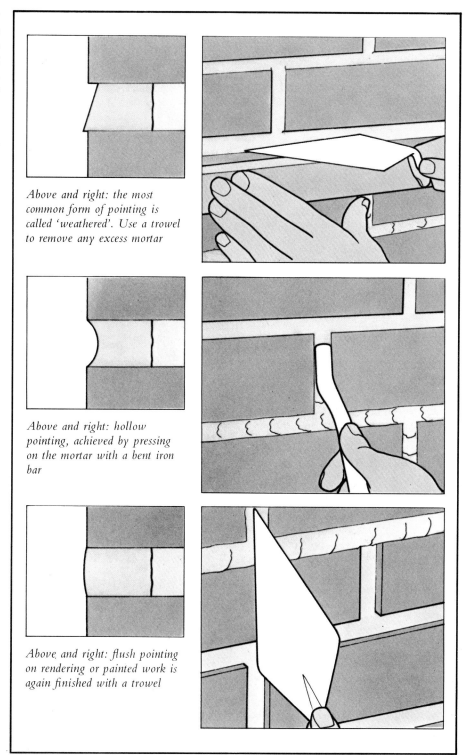

Above and right: the most common form of pointing is called 'weathered'. Use a trowel to remove any excess mortar

Above and right: hollow pointing, achieved by pressing on the mortar with a bent iron bar

Above and right: flush pointing on rendering or painted work is again finished with a trowel

ing. To make the vertical joints, draw the trowel back towards the right-hand bricks, while keeping a steady pressure inwards with the left-hand side of the trowel. Press inwards with the upper edge of the trowel to shape the horizontal joints.

If any mortar drops on to the front of the bricks, leave it to dry before attempting to clean up. When dry, you can lightly scrape it away with a trowel, then finish off by lightly brushing with a wire brush.

Damaged bricks which have weathered ('spalled') can be cut out and replaced. Work very carefully: on solid walls, it is easy to damage the internal brickwork and the inside plaster layer, making further repairs necessary. On cavity walls, you must be careful not to allow any brick or mortar fragments to drop on to the steel ties between the outer and inner layers of the walls where they could act as 'bridges' for damp to cause trouble later on.

You may be able simply to turn a brick around to present a fresh undamaged face. Otherwise, you must replace the brick with one that matches if possible; ask your builders' merchant for a used brick of the same type.

Spread pointing (mortar) around the new brick and slide it into the cavity; then match up the pointing with the rest of the wall (see above).

On bricks with only a small amount of damaged surface, it is sometimes possible to make a repair by patching up with mortar, coloured to match the surrounding brickwork.

Rendering is a layer of cement applied to external walls and usually painted. It is important to repair cracks and missing patches quickly as water can collect behind the rendering and cause damp inside. Fill small cracks with an exterior grade filler: first undercut the cracks with a scraper so that the crack is wider at the back than at the front, clean out the cavity with a wire brush and then dampen it before applying the filler.

Big cracks and holes, and bulging areas must be cut back with a sharp cold chisel and club hammer until sound rendering is reached. (If you suspect that rendering is defective tap it lightly with a hammer; if it needs replacing it will either crack or sound hollow). It is not economical to use proprietary fillers for large-scale repairs; use a mortar mix (ready-mixed sand and cement can be bought in small packs, and you just add water). For repairs of any depth, apply the mortar in layers, giving each layer a chance to dry. Smooth off the final coat with trowel, or with a block of wood.

Small hairline cracks on cement rendering can usually be effectively disguised with a proprietary stone or masonry paint which contains mineral particles (e.g. crushed stone or rock).

Pebbledash is trickier to repair as the aim is to match the surrounding surface. Use a mortar mix to make repairs as described for rendering above, but while this is still wet throw on matching pebbles and if necessary press them in lightly with a piece of board. If you cannot get a good match, consider painting the whole of the pebbledash area with a masonry paint. Apply paint with an old worn brush and a sharp dabbing action to 'punch' the paint well into the surface of the wall.

Wall tiles should be firmly fixed, as loose ones can allow damp to enter. They are usually nailed to battens which in turn are nailed to the wall. Give each tile a sharp tug to make sure that it is secure. If tiles seem loose, this may be caused by corroded nails, or by rotten battens. Tiling must be stripped off until the defective tile is reached. Then this should be re-fixed, replacing the battening if necessary. Then the rest of the tiles must be re-fixed using new nails.

Wood cladding should have rotten sections replaced. Old paint should be stripped off: use a scraper and paint stripper if necessary. New coats of paint should consist of at least a primer, an undercoat and two coats of oil-based gloss paint. Old varnish can be removed with abrasive paper, scraper or paint stripper, and then the surface should be rubbed down well with wire wool and water plus a little ammonia. Rinse well and allow to dry. Use a proprietary wood restorer if necessary to return wood to its original colour. Then revarnish, carefully following directions on the can.

A large jagged crack down the outside of a building indicates a serious fault, usually in the foundations of the house, and it is important to consult a surveyor or experienced builder as to its cause quickly.

Mouldy patches on walls indicate a damp problem of some kind (e.g. leaking gutter or downpipe, see above). Find and cure the cause of damp, then wash down the whole area with a solution of one part ordinary domestic bleach to four parts water. Repeat a day later, then leave to dry for two days. Rinse off with clear water.

Windows and doors. Gaps between frameworks and walls should be filled; if left they will allow the passage of damp. Use a non-hardening mastic available from your builders' merchant. This type of filler allows for the contraction and expansion of the wooden frames. If you have a lot of repairs to make you can use an applicator 'gun', which can be bought or hired. Very large gaps can be plugged first with rolled up rags, rope or fine mesh wire then finished off with mastic.

Renew all cracked sections of putty on window frames.

Timber sills must be protected with paint or varnish, but these coatings should only be applied to sound, clean, dry wood. Scrape or plane away any defective areas and use exterior grade filler for small cracks or holes; allow to dry thoroughly, then sand smooth and use a knotting compound to seal resinous knots before painting. Large areas of rotten wood must be cut away to leave a wedge-shaped cavity. Cut a piece of new wood to match the gap and use a waterproof glue and rustless nails to fix this in place, then prime before painting.

MIXING CONCRETE

Concrete is made from Portland cement, mixed with sand (fine aggregate) and/or stone particles (coarse aggregate), plus water. Mortar is a mix of cement, sand and water without any larger stone particles.

Cement is usually grey, but white cement can be used for coloured mixes or for a light coloured mortar required for pointing.

Bags of pre-packed dry mixes for concrete and mortar, with suitable proportions of cement and aggregate for most small jobs around the house and garden, are stocked by builders' merchants and D.I.Y. shops. These are probably easiest for the amateur.

Use a bucket for measuring quantities or 'parts', and a clean dry shovel or spade for turning the mix. (A board is preferable because you can dispose of it afterwards; wet cement adheres to paving for quite a long time before rain finally removes all trace.) First measure out the sand and coarse aggregate and tip into a heap. Measure the cement powder, tapping the bucket to compact the powder, then tip this on to the top of the heap. Use the shovel to turn the heap, always from the bottom, until the mixture is a uniform colour throughout. Even pre-mixed materials will need mixing in this way, as they tend to separate out in the bags while being stored. Make a crater in the top of the heap and very gradually add tap water, preferably from a watering can, and just sufficient to make the concrete stand up in a stiff pile. Continue to turn the heap until the mix is even; add more water if need be. Never try to dispose of leftover cement mix by sluicing it down a drain; it will cause a major blockage.

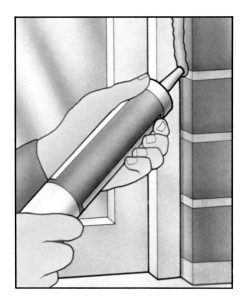

A 'drip groove' runs underneath sills parallel with the front edge to keep water clear of the wall underneath; check that all drip grooves are unobstructed and not blocked, for example, by dirt or paint.

On *concrete sills*, you can use an exterior grade filler for small cracks or holes. However, if the sill has crumbled away, you will need to build it up again with a concrete mix of one part cement to two parts fine sharp sand. Chip the crumbling sill away to a sound surface using a cold chisel and a wooden club hammer, and carefully brush away all debris and loose dust. Then give the surface a coating of cement grout: cement and water mixed to a thick creamy consistency. This improves the bonding of concrete.

Use a trowel to apply the concrete mix; a straight plank of wood is helpful for shaping right-angled edges. If necessary, you can fix a wooden framework around the sill as a support for the new concrete. Smooth off the repair with a steel float using a circular motion. Protect the repair from rain, hot sun or frost by covering it with damp sacking or polythene and do not use until concrete has completely hardened.

The same techniques can be used for repairing door sills and door steps.

PATHS

When cracks appear in concrete it is best to leave them for a few months to settle. When they do not seem to be getting any worse, you can carry out repairs as follows.

When dealing with very fine hair-line cracks, first brush the path well to remove surface dust. Then make a cement grout: cement and water mixed to a creamy consistency. Pour this over the surface of the path and allow it to settle and harden.

Top left: a mastic gun used to seal exterior gaps between walls and windows or doors
Top: cut out rotten sections of outside window sills and insert wedge-shaped new timber, fixed in place with exterior grade woodworking adhesive, then nailed
Above: a wooden framework will help support a concrete repair to a crumbling sill
Right: the blob method of applying mortar

Larger cracks can be repaired with a concrete mixture of one part cement to two parts sand. Use a bolster chisel and club hammer to chip out the crack until it is wider at the back than at the front. Brush out all loose debris and dust. Then apply a coat of cement and water, mixed to a creamy consistency, to improve the bond of concrete to concrete. While this is still wet, trowel on the concrete mix, and smooth off with a steel float.

Repair broken edges with a concrete mixture of one part cement to three parts all-in aggregate. If necessary, support with a board held firm with timber stakes while the concrete dries.

Larger defective areas (e.g. 'spalling' which is frost damage), or depressions, should first be chipped away to make a neat square or rectangle, with a uniform depth of about 1 cm ($\frac{1}{2}$ inch). Remove all loose particles and brush out well. Then wash out thoroughly with clear water, and apply to the moist surface a creamy consistency mix of cement and water, to improve the bond of concrete to concrete. Apply generously a concrete mix made from one part cement to two parts sharp sand. At first let the mix stand about 1 cm ($\frac{1}{2}$ inch) above the surrounding surface, so that you can 'tamp' it well down (i.e. compress and compact it) with a stout wooden board used on edge. Use the wooden board to level off the surface. If necessary, use a brush to texture the surface to match the surrounding concrete. Cover the repair with a piece of damp sacking, or a piece of polythene (e.g. a plastic bag cut open). While the surface is still very wet, hold the covering away from it with, for example, blocks of wood. Keep the repair covered for two or three days.

Paving stones that have sunk below the level of surrounding stones can sometimes simply be levered up with a bolster chisel

and relaid. But if the stone is cracked or if it cannot easily be removed intact, break it up with a club hammer and cold chisel working from the middle of the slab outwards. To put in a new slab, or to relay the old one, make a mortar mix of one part cement to five parts sand and, after cleaning out the hole, apply a blob in each corner and one in the middle, or a full bed of mortar. Place the slab in the hole, and tap down gently with the handle of the club hammer until flush with surrounding slabs.

Check the level with a straight piece of wood. If necessary, lift out the slab again and adjust the level of the mortar mix. Finally, brush a dry mix of sand and cement into the edges and point the joints to match the surrounding stones.

Replacement bricks in brick paving should be laid on a bed of mortar made from one part cement to three parts sand. To remove the old brick, break it up from the middle outwards with a bolster chisel and a wooden club hammer. Then clean out the hole and apply a layer of mortar – 'butter' mortar around the edges of the new brick and place it in the hole. Use the handle of the trowel to tap the brick down level with the surrounding bricks. If the brick sinks too far, or if it will not go down far enough, take it out and adjust the level of the mortar bed as for paving stones. Finally, point the joints.

FENCES

Timber fences should be treated with wood preservative once a year, carefully following the manufacturer's instructions. Or you can use creosote (if there are no plants close by), but this will darken the wood noticeably. The timber should be dry when you apply the creosote.

Inspect fences regularly as damage noticed at an early stage can usually be easily and simply repaired. But wooden fences can quickly deteriorate if left neglected, and then your only option may be a costly replacement.

Gravel boards are often fitted horizontally along the bottom of fences, to prevent damp from rising up and damaging the fence boards themselves. Try to keep gravel boards free from soil and plants and replace rotted boards immediately. If you dig a small trench, it is easier to fit the new board into position. New boards may be slotted into grooves in the fence posts or nailed to wooden blocks which have been screwed to the fence posts. Gravel boards should fit flush with the front of the fence. To fit new gravel boards to concrete fence posts, first drive pegs into the ground so

that at least 30 cm (1 ft) of each peg is below the ground. Then nail the new gravel boards to these pegs.

Fence posts can be prevented from rotting by digging away the soil around the base of the post occasionally, and applying a couple of coats of wood preservative or creosote.

Sound fence posts sometimes work loose. Dig away the soil round the bottom of the post and pack out the hole with, for example, bricks and gravel, then top off with well-rammed soil.

However, if the fence post has begun to rot away, you can strengthen it at the bottom by bolting on a concrete spur (a support with pre-drilled fixing holes) which you can buy at a builders' merchant or garden centre. The spur should be set in the ground to a depth of about 75 cm (2 ft 6 inch) and should be fixed to about 45 cm (1 ft 6 inch) of sound post with galvanized bolts.

Make a temporary support for the fence post with a couple of timber struts. Dig away around the bottom of the post, and saw off the rotten part, leaving only sound dry timber. Soak the end grain of the post in wood preservative.

Enlarge the hole sufficiently for the spur and put it in to see exactly how it will need to fit against the post. Mark the position of the spur fixing holes on to the post. Take out the spur, and drill holes in the post to receive the bolts from the spur. Now put the spur back in the hole again and pack rubble around to hold it upright (check it with your spirit level); fix the spur to the post and tighten the bolts. Then fill the hole with a dryish concrete mix made

from one part of cement to five parts of all-in aggregate. Again, use your spirit level to make sure that the fence post is vertical.

Sometimes, posts rot from the top downwards, in which case saw off the tops at an angle, then treat them with wood preservative. A piece of aluminium or zinc folded around the edge of the post and fixed with galvanized nails will protect the post tops more thoroughly. Alternatively, you can cut off the posts square, then fit capping pieces which have been soaked in preservative (also soak the post tops). Fix the caps with galvanized nails or screws).

Gates. Sagging gates may be caused simply by screws loosening in their hinges, so try tightening these. If the screws fit so loosely in their holes that they cannot be tightened, remove the hinges and fill the holes with timber plugs before refitting hinges and screws. If the gate post is weak, strengthen it with a concrete spur as described for fences, above.

There are several possible remedies for loose joints in a wooden gate. You can fit a brace (strip of wood) diagonally across the gate, secure it with glue and screws and paint to match the rest of the gate. Or you can use galvanized metal brackets fixed to the gate with screws and painted. Or you can take the gate to pieces and reglue the joints. Use waterproof adhesive, and cramp securely until adhesive is dry.

Protecting against rust is the top priority for metal gates. Once rust gets a hold, it can eat its way right through the metal. So inspect your gate regularly. Using a wire brush or emery paper, scrape away any spots of rust back to the bright metal and then clean with white spirit and prime at once with metal primer. Give metal edges a second coat of primer as they are particularly vulnerable to knocks and bangs; make sure that you brush primer well into screws, rivets and bolts, and around hinges. When dry touch up to match rest of paintwork.

Left: temporary support for a timber post while the concrete spur sets hard
Below: protecting wooden fence post tops

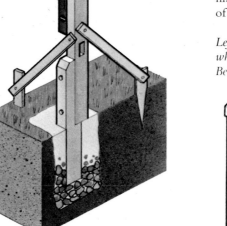

INTERIOR MAINTENANCE

ELECTRICITY

In general it is not advisable for the inexperienced to attempt electrical repairs. The dangers to life and to property are too great. Additions to wiring and most repairs should be carried out by the manufacturer's approved service agents, or by a qualified contractor from the Electricity Board or one who is listed on the roll of the N.I.C.E.I.C. (National Inspection Council for Electrical Installation Contracting) or is a member of the E.C.A. (Electrical Contractors' Association), or both. You can see a list of approved contractors at your local library or electricity showroom.

Tasks which you may be able to tackle yourself, provided you feel sufficiently competent include:

Wiring a plug
Shortening a flex and putting the plug back on
Checking the wiring connections within a plug
Replacing the fuse in a plug
Mending a fuse in the mains fuse box

Before investigating or repairing any electrical wiring or appliance, *always* turn off the electricity at the mains. The mains switch will usually be fixed close to your meter and fuse box. You may have more than one if, for example, you have a separate circuit for night storage heating. Make sure that all switches remain accessible.

Flexes. Always keep these as short as is practical. Long flexes trailing on the floor may trip people up; on a work surface, they can be pulled at by a child, or could get in the way of a hot surface such as a cooker; they could also dangle into the sink. You can shorten a flex yourself if you know how to put on a plug correctly – see next page. You should *not* try to lengthen a flex: have this done by a qualified electrician.

Never tape two flexes together with insulated or plastic tapes. Do not wind flexes tightly around appliances, in particular those that are still hot, such as an electric iron or electric fire.

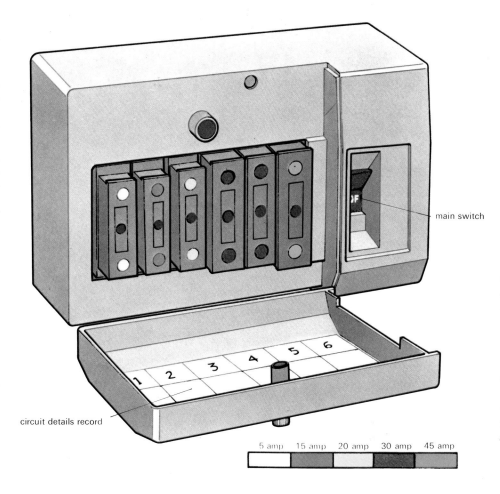

main switch

circuit details record

5 amp   15 amp   20 amp   30 amp   45 amp

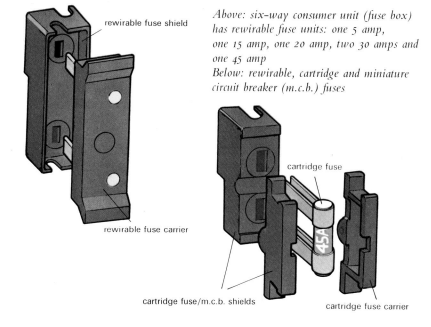

rewirable fuse shield

rewirable fuse carrier

cartridge fuse

cartridge fuse/m.c.b. shields

cartridge fuse carrier

Above: six-way consumer unit (fuse box) has rewirable fuse units: one 5 amp, one 15 amp, one 20 amp, two 30 amps and one 45 amp
Below: rewirable, cartridge and miniature circuit breaker (m.c.b.) fuses

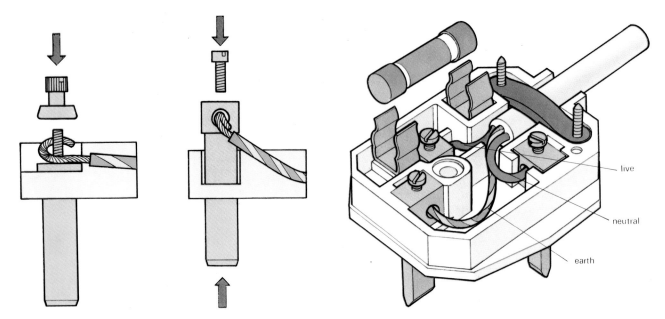

live

neutral

earth

Different makes of plug require different methods of attaching the wires to the pin ends, as shown and explained in the text Above: correctly wired three-pin plug

The conductor wires in the flexes of appliances bought after June 1970 are coloured as follows, according to an internationally-agreed code:

brown for Live
blue for Neutral
green/yellow twist for Earth

Learn this colour code: it is vital when you come to put on a plug, see below.

Old appliances may still have flexes coloured according to the old wiring colours:
red for Live
black for Neutral
green for Earth

Putting on a plug. Don't try to do this seemingly simple task unless you know that you can do it correctly. You must feel completely confident. A survey by a leading manufacturer of electrical fittings has revealed that around a quarter of the plugs in British homes are likely to be incorrectly wired. A plug that is not properly connected is potentially dangerous to you and your family, and will affect the working of the appliance to which it is fitted. Always buy plugs marked with the letters/numbers BS 1363. This refers to the relevant British Standard for quality and safety. Cheap foreign imports may save money initially but could overheat, causing a fire or even costing a life.

To put on a plug you will need a pair of pliers, an electrical screwdriver and a sharp knife. This is what you do:
1. Unscrew the back of the plug, put the back of the plug on one side; place the screws in it so they do not get mislaid.
2. If necessary, carefully cut away 5 cm (2 inches) of the covering (sheath) from the end of the flex, to reveal the inner coloured wires (two or three, depending on the appliance). If the flex is of the braided type, wind insulation tape around the cut braiding to prevent it fraying.

Cut away 1 cm ($\frac{1}{2}$ inch) of insulation from each of the wires in turn, working very carefully so as not to damage the thin strands underneath, then twist each set of exposed wire strands into a neat spiral – ensuring that no wire strands escape.
3. At the bottom of the back of the plug you will find two large screws that control the cord grip. Loosen these sufficiently to allow you to push the flex through, under the grip. The flex must penetrate the plug sufficiently for the cord grip to clamp down onto the outer covering of the flex, *not* onto the inner wires. In some plugs, there is simply a nylon safety grip, into which you push the flex (sheath) firmly.
4. Run the brown wire to the Live pin on the right with the cartridge fuse, marked L. Run the blue wire to the Neutral pin on the left marked N.

Run the two-coloured green/yellow wire to the Earth pin at the top of the plug, and marked E or with the Earth sign: ⏚. NOTE. Some appliances are double-insulated and do not have or require an earth connection. Typically, these include vacuum cleaners and hairdryers. They will be marked on the rating plate with the double-insulated sign, which is a box within a box.
5. Different makes of plugs have different ways for you to attach the wires to the pin ends. If the pin ends have holes with little screws, bend the ends of the wires back on themselves; loosen the screws, push each wire through its terminal in turn, tightening each screw as you go. If the pin ends

have washers held down by screws, twist the bared strands tightly together and wrap each one in turn clockwise once around the screw of its terminal underneath the washer, then tighten the screw. Always make sure that there are no loose bits of wire, and that the fuse is of the correct rating, see above.
6. Finally, replace the back of the plug, and secure with the screw(s) previously removed.

You can lengthen the flex of an appliance by using an *extension lead* (bought from an electrical shop); this will have a plug fitted on one end and a socket on the other. Always use an extension lead rather than trying to join on lengths of new flex; better still, have extra power points installed so that you do not need to use a lead. Never leave an appliance permanently connected to a socket by means of an extension lead.

If you must use *adaptors* to make electrical connections between plugs and sockets of different types, be sure that these have proper earthing connections, and fuses. Better still, change the outlets to 13 amp 3 pin pattern.

Do remember that if you still have sockets in your house with round holes, it is likely that your wiring is now unsafe and you should have it checked, with the view to having your house rewired.

An adaptor will also allow you to connect two appliances to one socket. But – and this is a very important safety point – the total electricity in watts used by the two appliances together must not exceed the rating of the socket into which the adaptor has been plugged. The wattage of each appliance is marked on its rating plate. A 13 amp socket outlet can supply up to 3,000 watts. If you exceed this figure you could start a fire through overheating of the socket and the adaptor. As with extension leads, you should aim to install extra socket outlets rather than rely upon the use of adaptors.

Changing a light bulb. Before changing a bulb *always* turn the light off at the switch. Be particularly careful with bathroom pullcords. When the bulb has failed you know that the switch is 'on' and you should give the cord a single tug to turn it 'off'. However, if you start tugging indiscriminately, you will have no means of knowing whether the switch is off or on; in which case it is safest to turn the electricity off at the mains.

If the bulb has recently failed, remember it will still be very hot: protect your hand with a thick cloth or wear gloves. Domestic light bulbs (called 'lamps' in the lighting trade) are usually of the *bayonet* type: two small projections on the bulb fit into the slots in the bulb holders. To free the failed bulb, carefully push slightly upwards and turn anti-clockwise. Press in the new bulb, and turn clockwise until you can feel that the bulb is fitting securely. If the old bulb has broken off inside the holder you must first turn off the electricity at the mains. Protect your hands with thick gloves, and use a blunt piece of wood (e.g. end of a wooden spoon) to prove the bulb base and ease it free. Or push a cork up on to the bulb base and use that to twist the broken bulb free.

There are now so many different types of bulbs (lamps) on the market that you may find it easiest to take your old bulb with you when shopping for a replacement. Buy two or three bulbs at a time if you find you have a type difficult to get locally. Never replace a bulb with one of a higher wattage than the maximum specified as to do so could create a fire hazard.

Occasionally, fittings may require *ES (Edison Screw)* bulbs which are screwed into place clockwise and removed anti-clockwise. This type of bulb is commonly fitted into refrigerators. Turn off appliance at the wall, before unscrewing the failed bulb and taking it to the shop to buy a replacement of the same type.

Fluorescent tubes should last for three years or more. Buy the colour marked *warm white de luxe* for normal domestic use. Tubes starting to blacken at the ends will shortly fail: you should also replace tubes that glow red at the ends or flicker. Replacing a tube is very simple. Turn off the switch. At one end, carefully ease the tube inwards to disconnect the two pins at its end from the plug in the fitting which holds them; then repeat for the other end. Fit the new tube in similar fashion.

The starter, a small round plug on the top of the tube holder, may need replacing if the tubes start to glow white at each end without lighting up, or if a newish tube flickers or keeps switching itself on and off. To remove the starter, turn off the light, then twist the starter anti-clockwise. Take it to an electrical shop and buy a replacement of the same kind. This is fitted simply by inserting it into the tube holder and twisting clockwise.

SIMPLE PLUMBING

Again, do not attempt to meddle with your plumbing unless you feel confident in what you are doing. Plumbers often complain that householders only make things worse by initially trying to cure a fault themselves.

Cleaning a blocked sink. First try boiling water plus a small bowl of washing soda crystals; solidified grease is a common cause of sink blocks, and this may do the trick. Or you can buy branded drain-cleaning liquids from a hardware store. A rubber plunger, which you can buy from a hardware store, is a good standby. Get one now: don't wait for your sink to be blocked on a Sunday morning! (Although

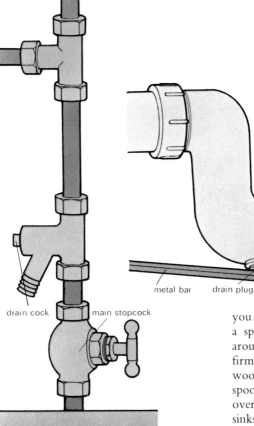

bottle trap

cap removal for draining

metal bar   drain plug   conventional U-trap

drain cock   main stopcock

Above: in an emergency such as a burst pipe, turn the mains stopcock clockwise to cut off the water before carrying out repairs Above right: if the U-bend beneath the sink becomes seriously blocked, you may need to empty the trap. Place a screwdriver or a spanner between the two lugs on the plug at the bottom of the U-bend and twist anti-clockwise. However, modern plastic bottle traps unscrew by hand. Place a bucket underneath to catch water and debris

you can make an emergency plunger from a sponge, folded in half then wrapped around with a dishcloth or flannel and firmly tied to the end of a longish piece of wood such as the handle of a wooden spoon.) Use a wet dishcloth to block the overflow of the sink; if you have double sinks, put the plug in the other sink and also block its waste with a damp cloth.

Place the plunger over the sink outlet and add water to cover the plunger cap. Press the plunger up and down vigorously, and listen for a gurgling noise to indicate that the blockage has freed itself. A new, and very effective, gadget for unblocking sinks is like a little bicycle pump, and shoots a powerful jet of water down the drain; but it is more expensive.

If the plunger method fails, you must empty the trap, a U-shaped piece of piping underneath the sink. First put a bucket or bowl in position to catch the dirty water. Then place a wooden batten between the two sections of the U-bend to hold them steady. Use a screwdriver or spanner placed between the two lugs on the plug at the bottom of the U to twist it anti-clockwise and open. If the plug has a six-sided bolt head, use a spanner or pliers to undo it. Modern plastic plumbing can be unscrewed by hand. Extract the blockage with tweezers, scissors, flexible curtain wire, or a piece of wire bent to make a hook at the end (e.g. a coat-hanger). When the U-bend is clear, screw the plug back in again.

Clearing a blocked lavatory. You may be able to shift minor blockages with a long piece of springy wire (e.g. a piece of curtain wire) pushed up and around the U-bend. Otherwise use a special plunger fitted with a metal disc. Push this as far as you can down inside the pan, and work it up and down. It may take some time to clear the blockage, so persevere.

Stopping a cistern overflow. Remove top of cistern, and tie the lever arm which operates the ball valve to a piece of wood placed across the top of the open cistern. A faulty ball valve is often the cause of the overflow, and if this is the problem, unscrew the ball from the lever arm, take it to a plumbers' merchant and buy a replacement of the same type. Sometimes, it is simply the level of the ball float that needs adjusting, and this can

be done by bending the lever or arm slightly downwards.

Clearing blocked drains. If the blockage is at all serious, it is wisest to call your plumber or drain clearance specialists, at the outset.

A gulley (open drain) at ground level collects rainwater from downpipes, and waste water from sinks, baths and basins. From this gulley, a pipe with a bent section called a 'trap' leads to your first manhole (underground inspection chamber with metal cover). But lavatories are connected to this manhole directly through an underground pipe.

If water is not running away through the gulley, first remove the grating over the drain and see if you can clear away any debris, but be careful because you could push obstructions farther into the drain where they may block the trap. The trap itself may need clearing, and you can try using a spoon tied on to the end of a stick for this.

If the water continues to overflow you can try lifting the manhole cover, but be careful because it will be heavy; you may need to scrape away earth from around its edges and use a lever to lift it safely; lift from one side. You will see two pipes coming into the chamber, one from the gulley and one from the lavatory. There will also be an outlet pipe leading to another manhole.

If the chamber is clear of water, you can assume that the blockage is in the pipe leading from the gulley, and you can try

using a garden hose with as strong a jet of water as possible to flush out the blockage. It is also possible to hire sets of drain rods which screw together to make a long thin probe with a hook or brush at the end. Push them down the drain and turn them with a clockwise action: if you turn them anti-clockwise they will unscrew and add themselves to the blockage! It is *not* a good idea to try and improvize with any other tools.

If the manhole chamber is full of water, the problem lies somewhere along the length of pipe that connects the chamber with the next manhole. Again, you can try flushing out the blockage with a garden hose, or using drain rods.

Changing a tap washer. Taps drip because the ring-like washer is no longer making a watertight seal inside the tap. Buy a black synthetic washer, which will be suitable for hot or cold taps. The most common sizes are 1 cm ($\frac{1}{2}$ inch) and 1.5 cm ($\frac{3}{4}$ inch), and you should keep a couple of spares in both sizes. But large bath taps may need a 2.5 cm (1 inch) washer.

Before you proceed any further, you *must* turn off the water supply to the tap. For the kitchen tap, turn off the mains stopcock which may be under the sink, or in the cellar if you have a large old house. For other cold taps, there should be a stopcock to turn off the supply near the cold water cistern (tank) in the roof. A stopcock for the hot water tap will be near the hot water cylinder, possibly in the airing cupboard. Turn off any heaters or

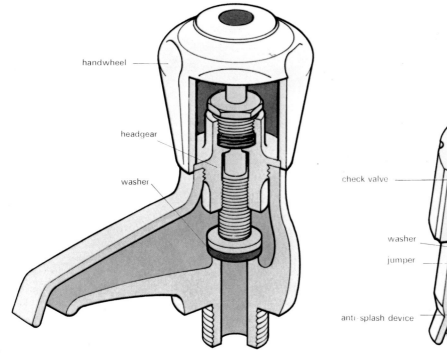

handwheel

headgear

washer

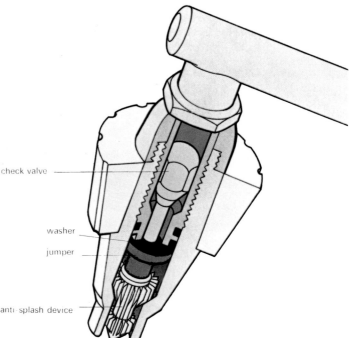

check valve

washer

jumper

anti-splash device

boilers that might burn out without a water supply. Open the tap until all water has run out. Then put the plug in the basin to safeguard against any tiny parts falling down the drain.

Unscrew the little grub screw in the side of the handle and then, using an adjustable spanner over a rag, unscrew the domed cover plate below the tap handle. Modern taps may have handle and cover all in one piece, with a small screw holding them on at the top (possibly secured by a cap) or the side. Some modern handle/covers simply pull off.

When you have removed the tap handle/cover, use a small spanner or adjustable pliers to undo the large hexagonal nut inside. This will enable you to lift free the inside of the tap, called the 'head gear'. Pull the bottom part – a brass stem called the 'jumper' – away from the top part and

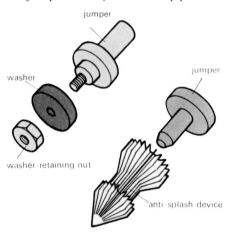

Far left: the inside workings of a pillar tap of the modern type, with handle and cover all in one piece. Before replacing a washer, turn off the water supply to the tap
Left: the inside workings of a Supatap. For this type of modern tap it is not necessary to turn off the water supply before fitting a new washer
Above: how a washer is fitted into an ordinary pillar tap (left) and a Supatap (right)
Right: to patch a damaged piece of wall vinyl, cut out the new patch and the damaged area at one and the same time, using a sharp knife. Wallpapers should not be cut – tear them to feather the edges and make them less obvious

you will find the washer on the bottom part, held in place by a retaining nut which can be undone with a spanner. Remove all the bits of old washer, and fit a new one of the same size. Re-assemble the tap and open the stopcock.

Supataps are a modern design which can be rewashered without turning off the water supply. The handle and nozzle are in one piece, pointing down into the sink.

To change the washer on a Supatap, loosen the locking nut above the nozzle with a spanner. Then hold the nut and unscrew the whole nozzle anti-clockwise. Any water coming out will stop as soon as you remove the nozzle. Now turn the nozzle upside down, and gently knock it up and down on a flat surface. The washer and its mounting will fall out attached to the finned anti-splash device. Prise out the combined jumper and washer and fit a new Supatap washer, then reassemble tap.

To *cure a dribbling tap*: in this case there is no need to turn off the water supply. Open the tap fully and remove the cover of the tap (see changing a washer, above) to expose the gland nut that holds the headgear onto the body of the tap. Tighten this gland nut a little bit, using an adjustable spanner. Now open and close the tap a little, to see that it works easily, and slightly loosen the gland nut if it seems too stiff. Then re-assemble the tap.

WALLS AND PAINTWORK

Always keep in a safe dry place any oddments of paint and paper etc. left over from decorating. They are invaluable for small repairs and 'touching up'.

Cracks in painted walls and ceilings should be scraped out first to clear all loose material, then filled with a proprietary filler, using a flexible filling knife. When the crack is dry, sand it smooth and repaint to match the existing decoration. Larger holes should be filled in layers, allowing each to dry before applying the next. If a hole is very large, you may first have to plug it with some dampened crumpled newspaper or rag. You may find that the best way to conceal cracks between the top of the wall and the ceiling is to add a coving made from polystyrene; this is simply glued in place and painted to match the existing decoration.

Repairs to paintwork. Fill small chips with a proprietary filler and then sand smooth before touching up to match the surrounding surface. You may find that you have to paint a whole section of woodwork, as a touched up area can show

up as rather noticeably bright, particularly if the original shade was white, which tends to yellow after a while. Blisters in paintwork can be cut out with a sharp knife; then you should prime the wood beneath before filling, allowing to dry, sanding and repainting.

Knots may show up as brown marks under a paint film, and resin may start to seep through. Sand or scrape away the paint film, then paint the surface of the knot with a branded shellac knotting liquid to seal in the resin. When dry, repaint to match the surrounding area.

Patching wallpaper. First tear away the paper around the damaged area, then cut a matching piece of paper slightly larger than the damaged area. Tear around its edges to 'feather' them, which makes the patch less noticeable. Stick the patch in place over the damaged area using wallpaper paste and taking care to match the pattern, then press down edges well using a clean dry cloth or wallpaper seam roller.

Patching vinyls, wallfabrics etc. These cannot be torn. So cut a piece slightly larger than the damaged area, and place it over that area, taking care to match any pattern – this is very important. Now use a sharp knife (e.g. Stanley knife) to cut through the replacement piece close to its

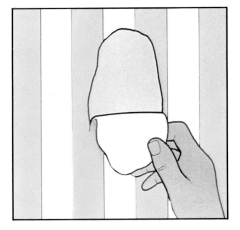

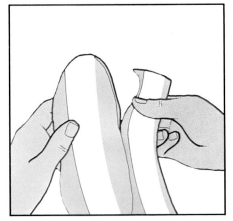

Above: tear away damaged area of wallpaper. Then, from a spare piece, cut a new section slightly larger than the damaged area, matching the pattern carefully. Tear around the edges of the new patch to 'feather' them and make joins less noticeable. Stick down the patch over the damaged area, matching the pattern
Above right: where seams are lifting loose, ease a little wallpaper paste underneath with a slim paintbrush and smooth down with a seam roller or small, clean sponge. Vinyls will not stick to themselves, so vinyl overlaps must be stuck down with latex adhesive

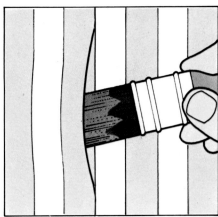

edges *and* through the original wallcovering. Then remove the patch, peel away the damaged wallcovering, and fix the new patch exactly into place with the appropriate adhesive.

Replacing a damaged walltile. Rake out the grout around the damaged tile, using a screwdriver or a metal skewer, then gently break the old tile, using chisel and hammer, and working from the centre outwards (it helps first to drill a hole in the middle with a masonry bit). Work very carefully to avoid damaging any other tiles surrounding the damaged one. Remove all remnants of the old tile adhesive, and fix a spare matching tile into position with tile adhesive. Make sure that the level is the same as that of the surrounding tiles. If you do not have a matching spare tile, try replacing several tiles with ones of the same size, to give a random pattern effect. When the adhesive is dry, regrout the whole area.

If it is merely the tile grouting that is stained and worn, rake it out and replace with new.

DOORS AND WINDOWS

Sticking doors. First of all, simply try tightening the hinges. If the trouble persists, take some carbon paper and use it

to find exactly where the door is sticking. Place the carbon paper between the door and its frame, with its carbon side against the door. Open and close the door, each time moving the paper until you have worked all round the door, so that smudges from the carbon will show where the sticking occurs. Rubbing these spots with candle grease may prove effective, or you can try rubbing the door edge with a coarse sandpaper. If the door is sticking badly you may have to plane the edge slightly, but first wedge it steady with a card or a thin sliver of wood.

Rattling doors can sometimes simply be cured with self-adhesive draught-proofing tape, from any good D.I.Y. or hardware store. Or you can try filling the gap between the door and its stop: i.e. the wooden frame against which the door closes. Make a little pencil mark on the door frame to show its normal closed position. Now, from the *outside* of the room press the door hard against its lock or catch and mark then measure carefully the distance between this and its normal position. Now fix with panel pins and hammer a thin wooden strip around the face of the stop, to fill the gap.

Broken window panes. You can often make a short-term repair over a crack with a clear adhesive tape from a builders' merchant. Or, if the glass is shattered, you can nail polythene sheet across the frame after removing any fragments of glass (see below). Strengthen the polythene with wooden strips nailed around the edge to the window frame.

Be very careful when you take out the remains of the old glass. Wear heavy gloves and use a hammer to tap out the pieces from the frame, starting at the top. You may have to cut away the putty to release all the pieces. As you go, wrap all the fragments in several layers of newspaper and put them in a box; warn the dustmen.

You can try fitting a small pane of new glass yourself; but if the window is large, call in a glazier. Most glass merchants also offer a glazing service.

Before you go to buy new glass, measure up using a steel tape and taking the dimensions on the outside from rebate to rebate (wooden edge to wooden edge). Then take away about 3 to 4 mm ($\frac{1}{8}$ inch) from these measurements to ensure a good fit. Take a small piece of the old glass with you so that you can ask the glazing shop to supply the same weight and thickness.

Before you fit the new glass, clean away all the old putty from around the frame

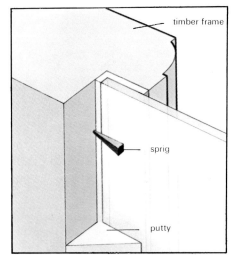

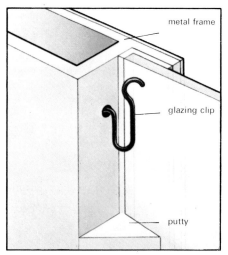

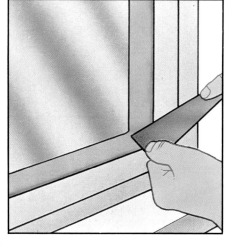

edges; use an old chisel or screwdriver. Also remove any small nails. Metal windows have small retaining s-shaped clips. These should be carefully taken out, marking their position on the frame as you go, and saving the clips for re-use.

The next step is to prime the rebates (edges of the frame) with wood or metal primer, as appropriate. Now spread a thin roll of putty around the rebate, using your fingers, and dipping them in water if the putty seems to stick. Use linseed oil putty for wooden windows, and metal casement putty for metal ones. Gently press the glass into place against the putty, pressing only at the edges and corners, *never* in the middle. Tap in glazing sprigs at 15 cm (6 inch) intervals around a wooden frame to hold the glass in place: slide your hammer gently over the glass to avoid breaking it.

In metal windows, simply replace the clips. Roll another strip of putty and press this around the edges of the glass, then trim off to a neat 45° angle (copy the shape from a nearby window), using an angled putty knife. Trim off any excess putty from inside the window. Leave putty seven to

Above left: glass is held in timber frames by sprigs; in metal frames by glazing clips
Top: gently press the new pane of glass into place in a thin roll of putty spread around the rebate (see text). Press only at the edges and corners, never in the middle
Centre: put in sprigs or clips, as appropriate then roll another strip of putty and press this around the edges of the glass
Above: trim putty to a neat 45° angle

14 days to harden, then paint to match frame, taking the paint about 3 mm ($\frac{1}{6}$ inch) on to the glass to give a waterproof seal.

FLOORS AND FLOORING

Squeaking or loose floorboards. These can sometimes be cured by dusting talcum powder down between the edges of the boards. Boards that are noticeably loose however, should be screwed through to the joist underneath to pull them tight. If you cannot get a good fixing at the end of a board, nail a small piece of wood to the side of the joist on which it rests and screw the board to this instead. Be careful not to pierce pipes or wires that run underneath.

Gaps between floorboards can be filled with papier maché made from shredded newspaper and wallpaper glue, with added wood stain if necessary. Force between the boards with a filling knife. When dry and hard, this mixture can be sanded smooth. To fill large cracks, cut fillets (strips) of wood to size, glue into place and plane flat. Fill gaps between floorboards and skirting with a branded filler, or nail quadrant (quarter round) moulding around the edge. Use panel pins at 15 cm (6 inch) intervals, and mitre the corners neatly.

If a wooden floor is *very* uneven and full of gaps, you could consider covering the whole surface with sheets of hardboard. Small sheets are easier to handle than large ones. Before you lay the hardboard sheets, spread water on the mesh side of the boards with a large old paintbrush and leave them to dry for 48 hours stacked flat back to back in the room in which they are to be laid.

Use 15 mm ($\frac{3}{4}$ inch) annular nails to fix the boards; these have rings around their shanks to stop them working loose. The boards must be nailed down at 15 to 23 cm (6 to 9 inch) intervals all over their surface, working from the centre of the board outwards. Punch the nail heads slightly below the surface of the board. The boards can then be sealed with a minimum 3 coats of polyurethane sealant, or covered with a flooring to your choice.

Uneven solid floors of, for example, quarry tiles or concrete can be levelled with a 'self-levelling compound' available as bags of powder from D.I.Y. shops or builders' merchants. Mix this with water and spread it over the floor, where it will settle to form a smooth level surface. But do not use these compounds for wood or wood-block floors.

Patching a carpet. If your carpet is worn through in part(s): or if it has suffered a burn, or a stain which is impossible to remove, consider making a carpet patch. For this reason, always keep any off-cuts or spare pieces when fitting a new carpet. If you do not have a suitable off-cut, take your patching material from a place which is usually hidden by furniture: e.g. under a sideboard or a settee.

Loose-laid carpets or rugs can be repaired from the back. There is a special technique for making sure that the patch fits exactly. Lay the new piece over the face of the damaged area, making sure that the pile slopes in the same direction. Now cut through both layers around the damaged area with one cutting action, using a sharp knife. Smear latex adhesive around the inside of the hole and around the edges of the patch, to about half-way up the pile: leave this to dry until the thick white liquid has turned semi-transparent.

Turn the carpet over and put the patch in from the back, then cut a piece of hessian slightly larger than the repaired area. Stick this over the underside of the patch, to hold it in place on the back of the carpet. Check that the edges are well stuck down, and then tap all over with a hammer for a really good bond.

For *fitted carpets*, of course, you will have to work from the front. First cut your patch, as described for loose-laid carpets, above, and coat its edges with latex adhesive. Place on one side. Now cut a piece of thick paper larger than the patch and put it through and under the hole so that it lies flat on the floor or underfelt. Cut a piece of hessian a little smaller than the paper, but still slightly larger than the patch and push this through the hole so that it lies on top of the paper. Coat the hessian and inside edges of the hole with latex adhesive, and then insert the patch and tap around the edges with your hammer.

Alternatively, you can use carpet seaming tape to fix the patch in place for fitted carpets. Cut the patch as already described. Cut four pieces of seaming tape slightly longer than the sides of the patch. Apply adhesive to one side of each piece and insert them through the hole to lie on top of the underlay or floor, forming a frame around the edges of the neatened hole, sticky sides up. Apply adhesive to the edges of the back of the patch, place it in the hole and tap around the edges with a hammer so that the two sticky surfaces bond together.

Worn edges of carpets, rugs and mattings can be bound with cloth binding tape, about 7.5cm (3 inch) wide. First trim the edges removing loose threads etc., and then vacuum to remove as much loose dust

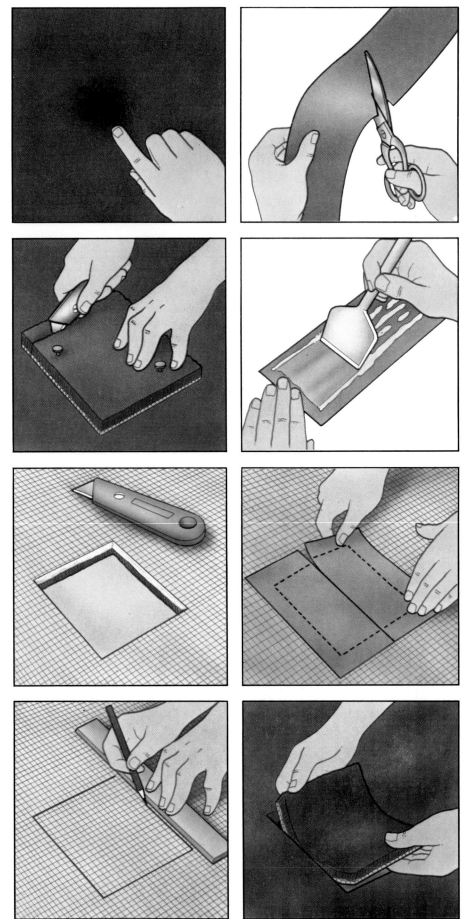

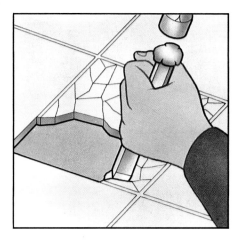

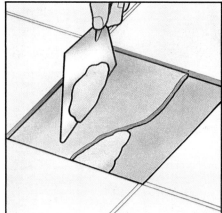

Left: loose-laid carpets can best be patched from the back. First decide how much of the worn or stained area you wish to replace. Then lay your spare piece of carpet over the damaged area, taking care that both piles run in the same direction and, if possible, that any pattern matches. Cut through them both with a sharp knife. Then smear latex adhesive around the inside of the hole and the edges of the patch, to halfway up the pile, and leave to dry until semi-transparent. Turn the carpet over and put the patch in from the back; cut a piece of hessian to reinforce the patch, slightly larger than the repaired area. Stick in place with latex adhesive. Alternatively, cut two pieces of carpet seaming tape and glue them into place from the back to reinforce patch. Fitted carpets, of course, must be patched from the front. Cut out patch as shown above. Reinforce the back of the carpet as described in the text, opposite, then insert patch from the front as shown here

Above: always keep spare tiles after completing any wall or flooring job. To replace a damaged ceramic floor tile, gently break up the damaged tile with a hammer and cold chisel, working from the centre, outwards. Wear safety goggles to protect your eyes from flying fragments. Pick out the pieces, prising them up with a chisel if necessary. Spread a new layer of ceramic floor tiling adhesive, then bed down new tile, making sure that it is the same level as the surrounding tiles. Scrape away any excess adhesive using a trowel

Right: metal repair brackets come in various sizes in three basic shapes: right-angled, flat L-shaped and flat T-shaped. They can be used to repair a variety of wooden structures, including furniture, window frames and gates (see overleaf)

as possible from the edges. Cut tape to length and apply latex adhesive to half its width; then brush on adhesive to the same width on one side of the carpet. Wait until the adhesive is nearly dry and then press the tape down on to the carpet edge taking care to position it neatly without wrinkles. Turn the carpet over and repeat the technique on the other side. Finally tap down along both sides with a hammer to ensure good adhesion.

Curling rug edges can sometimes be cured by coating the back with latex adhesive and allowing this to dry. Or you can try backing the rug with underfelt, stuck on with latex adhesive. If the curl is really persistent try backing that area with a thin piece of card. Foam underlay is available for rugs that creep on top of carpet, and rubberized netting can be bought to stop rugs from slipping on polished floors.

When patching vinyl and lino, place spare piece over damaged area and cut through both layers to obtain a patch which is an exact fit. Fix patch to floor with heavy-duty double-sided adhesive tape. Clean the floor as well as you can before sticking down the tape, to get a good bond.

Damaged ceramic and quarry tiles can be replaced provided you have a spare tile of the same design. Keep a few spare tiles after any new installation. Gently break up the damaged tile with a hammer, working from the centre outwards, and taking care not to damage surrounding tiles in the process. Pick out the pieces, prising them out with a chisel if necessary. Scrape away all the old adhesive, and stick down the new tile using the appropriate adhesive. Renew grout as necessary.

You can also replace *damaged cork and vinyl tiles*, provided once again that you have a replacement to match. Ease away the damaged tile with a broad-bladed

stripping knife: you may find that it helps first to heat the tile with a fan-heater or hairdryer to soften the adhesive. Scrape away as much of the old adhesive as you can. Then fix the new tile in place with the appropriate adhesive. If the problem is simply that the corners of the tiles are curling upwards, restick them, and weigh down (e.g. with cans of foodstuffs such as fruit) until set.

FURNITURE

You can make small running repairs to your furniture, but furniture of any value (e.g. antiques) should be repaired by an expert. Many manufacturers will take furniture back for repair: ask at the shop where you bought the furniture, or write to the manufacturer direct.

Loose joints, legs etc. Sometimes these can be rectified simply by tightening up existing screws or nuts on bolts, so examine the furniture carefully to see how it is made. If screws have worked loose because their holes are now too big, take out the screws (anti-clockwise), fill the

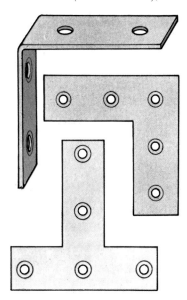

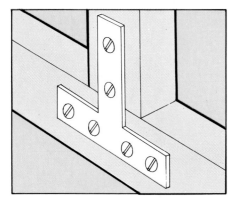

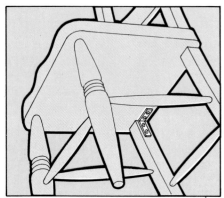

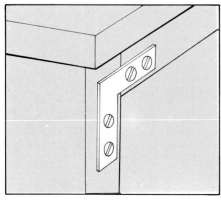

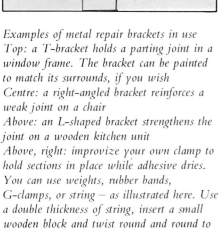

Examples of metal repair brackets in use
Top: a T-bracket holds a parting joint in a window frame. The bracket can be painted to match its surrounds, if you wish
Centre: a right-angled bracket reinforces a weak joint on a chair
Above: an L-shaped bracket strengthens the joint on a wooden kitchen unit
Above, right: improvize your own clamp to hold sections in place while adhesive dries. You can use weights, rubber bands, G-clamps, or string – as illustrated here. Use a double thickness of string, insert a small wooden block and twist round and round to increase the tension, then wedge in place to hold firm

hole with a fibre plug or pack out with matchsticks and woodglue, and rescrew. Alternatively, you can sometimes use a thicker screw to solve this problem. Or you can use metal repair plates, available from hardware shops in a wide variety of shapes, to pull together a loose joint. These can also be used to mend a break in, for example, a leg (see diagrams for bracket shapes and ideas). On a more ambitious scale, you may want to take the furniture apart completely, scrape out the old glue, and then reglue with pva woodworking adhesive. Use clamps or string to hold the wood in place while the glue sets.

Castors that squeak are often cured with a few drops of oil, but do wipe carefully afterwards, or you will stain your carpet or flooring. Sometimes the screws which fix the castors to the furniture legs work loose; try unscrewing the castors, and turning them round a little, so that you can rescrew into fresh wood (make a starting hole first with a gimlet). If wood at leg ends has become damaged you may be able to replace plate castors with a cup type that fits around the bottom of the leg and is screwed in from the sides; or, if this would not lower the chair height too dramatically(!) you could shorten all four legs by *exactly equal* amounts to give fresh wood for the castor fixing. Castor holes that have become enlarged can be packed out with matchsticks and woodworking glue before replacing the screw(s).

Hinges. Where hinge holes have become enlarged, pack them out with matchsticks and glue, as for castors, above. A few drops of oil will usually cure squeaking hinges. If hinges have been set too deeply (to cause, for example, a cupboard door continually to spring open) use a thin piece of card to pack out the recess into which they fit. First fit card behind the hinge on the cabinet side: if problem continues, pack out the hinge on the door side as well.

Handles that have worked loose may simply need screws or nuts tightening up. But if there is a screw holding the handle that has worked loose, pack out the hole with matchsticks and pva woodworking glue. Alternatively, wind cotton thread around the thread of the screw attaching the handle, then dip in glue or gloss paint, and re-insert into the furniture.

Sticking drawers may be jammed because something is sticking up inside, in which case, open the drawer a little way if possible and dislodge obstruction with a piece of hooked wire. Or you may be able to get to one drawer by taking out the drawer above or below.

Sometimes drawers jam because the wood has swollen: try drying the furniture out with a fan heater placed about 90 cm (3 ft) in front for an hour or two, but do not attempt this method with antique furniture. When drawers stick during opening and closing, it sometimes helps to swop their order around. Or try rubbing their runners with soap or a candle but *do not* use oil or grease.

Patching upholstery. Usually you have to patch from the front. Find a fabric to match as near as possible. Sometimes it is possible to cut a small piece from an out of sight place. To patch a small tear, snip off any loose threads, and cut fabric just slightly longer than the tear. Lift up the edges of the tear and slide in the patch, easing it flat with the blade of a knife. Then use the knife to smear latex adhesive underneath fabric edges to hold patch in place: wait until adhesive is nearly dry, then press edges together and hold down for a few minutes. Carefully wipe off any excess adhesive before it sets.

A hole can be patched in the same manner – cut the patch a little larger than the neatened hole all round and use pvc adhesive.

CHINA AND GLASS

In china, odd chips can sometimes be satisfactorily touched in with matching gloss paint; or try filling them with epoxy resin, mixed with titanium dioxide for white china (a powder from artists' supply shops) or with artists' powder colours to match other shades. Finish off with a coat of varnish if necessary.

Breaks can be mended with epoxy resin adhesive, carefully following the directions on the pack. First work out how the pieces fit together, and clean away all traces of any old adhesives with a solvent such as methylated spirits or nail-varnish remover. Rinse well and allow to dry. You will need to support your work while it dries and you should plan in advance how you are going to do this. There are various possibilities. You can gum dampened brown paper sticky strip crossways over the break: this is better than ordinary sticky clear tape because it contracts as it dries to pull the pieces tightly together. Sometimes the broken pieces can be supported in a box or bowl of sand, or held with plasticine, or a broken plate can be held in a drawer; or a bowl can be supported by another bowl. If glueing several pieces, tackle only two pieces at a

time and let them dry completely, before going on to fix the next whole piece. Continue in this way until the item is wholly repaired. Carefully remove all traces of glue before it finally sets: leave it for a few hours until it is tacky then peel it off with a sharp craft knife, unless it is of the fast-setting type, in which case the surplus must be removed more quickly.

Chips around the edges of glasses can sometimes be ground down by a professional glass and china repairer. Breaks can be repaired in the same way as for china, see above, but the joins will always show to some extent. There are, however, special clear adhesives now sold for mending broken glass.

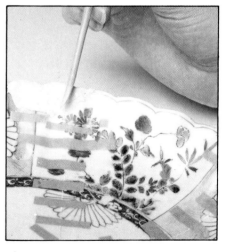

Above: mend china one piece at a time, waiting until each dries before adding the next. While the adhesive dries, the mended piece can be supported with plasticine, or in a box of sand. Use brown paper sticky tape crossways across joints. As the paper dries, it will shrink, pulling the sections together. Sometimes, small chips around edges can be touched in with matching gloss paint and a fine brush

DEALING WITH PESTS

Today, domestic pests should not prove an enduring problem. You can buy from chemists and hardware stores a wide range of effective pesticides, to deal with most infestations, provided you read carefully the directions on the pack. If you *do* find you have a pest attack which seems outside your control, contact the Environmental Health Department.

SAFETY PRECAUTIONS

Chemicals available for pest control come as aerosols, powders (often in 'puffer' packs), and baits. Take safety precautions in all cases. Read all directions carefully, and store out of reach of children and animals. Keep products in their own containers: do not transfer to those which have held food or drink. Get rid of excess products by washing them down the drain with plenty of water. Always wash your hands after use, and wash away any splashes on the skin. When using aerosols, do not breath the vapour, and do not spray food, working surfaces or utensils. Keep the room well ventilated.

NOTE: excess products should not be washed down the drain if there is a septic tank, as to do so would destroy the bacteria.

CONTROLLING MEASURES

Ants. Trace black ants back to their nest, and pour boiling water over entrance hole. Then puff insecticidal dust containing lindane or carbaryl into hole but do not use near food. Baits are also available, and aerosols for spraying skirting etc. Treat red ants with jelly baits.

Bedbugs. Wingless brown flat insects which feed on human blood. Spray all haunts with an aerosol insecticide containing malathion, lindane or pyrethrum.

Booklice. Tiny, soft-bodied, off-white insects that run over furniture and paper. Ventilate and dry affected areas and items as well as you can and heat to as high a temperature as possible. Then spray with an aerosol for crawling insects.

Carpet beetles. Small golden brown 'wooly bear' insects which lurk in airing cupboards, lofts, carpet felt, etc. and even-

tually turn into small mottled oval beetles. Spray affected areas with an aerosol marketed especially for treatment of this pest; protect other clothes and furnishings with crystals sold for mothproofing.

Cockroaches. Black insects which love warm moist places around pipes, cookers, boilers and sinks. Use an insecticide spray for crawling insects and sprinkle their haunts with a powder containing carbaryl or lindane. If the problem still persists, contact your Environmental Health Department.

Earwigs. On the whole, these cause no real damage to a house; dust woodwork with an insecticidal powder, or use an aerosol for crawling insects.

Fleas. Treat pets with flea powder or with a spray from your vet or pet shop. Always buy a spray especially intended for your type of pet: do not use sprays for one type of animal on another, as you could make your pet ill. Follow directions carefully and avoid spraying in your pet's eyes in particular. Treat your home with a suitable powder or aerosol at the same time. Burn infected animal bedding, and use a cardboard box and newspapers renewed nightly until the infestation is cured. Vacuum often and thoroughly to remove eggs, which can lurk in any kind of crevice: e.g. down sides of upholstery, and in edges of carpets and skirtings.

Flies. Keep your kitchen and any other part of your home where food is stored meticulously clean. Never leave food uncovered, and throw away all waste immediately, wrapped in newspaper. Scrape plates clean and put to soak, and throw away empty tins and bottles. Make sure that your refuse bin has a tight-fitting lid, and use an insecticidal spray during summer. Use an insecticidal powder in your dustbin. Kill the insects with an aerosol spray, or use fly strips that give off a slow-release fly-killing vapour.

Mice. The signs are small dark droppings around food, plus scratching noises at night. They contaminate food and carry food poisoning. Buy from your chemist or

hardware store one of the rodenticides designed specifically for killing mice; these send mice to sleep and they die painlessly without waking up. But take care that you keep these poisons away from your toddlers and pets.

Mosquitoes. Use an aerosol to give immediate clearance; a drop of paraffin in a water-butt, for example, will stop larvae developing into adults.

Moths. Keep clothes clean: moths prefer soiled fabrics. They do not like synthetics, preferring wool, but will feed off the wool in fibre mixtures. Store clean woollens in sealed polythene bags or closely wrapped in newspaper, in cool rooms. Add moth repellent sachets, discs or tablets. Protect wool upholstery with repellents down the sides and backs. Hang repellents in cupboards and wardrobes. Clean wool carpets regularly, and twice a year spray edges of fitted carpets and areas under furniture with a good moth proofing aerosol.

Rats. You can buy rat bait poisons from your chemist or hardware store, or you can contact your local Environmental Health Officer who will come and deal with the problem free of charge.

Silverfish. A wingless silver-grey insect about 1 cm ($\frac{1}{2}$ inch) long which does very little actual harm. Use an aerosol or puffer pack for crawling insects.

Woodworm. This is the grub of the furniture beetle. Look for the tell-tale signs in old furniture and woodwork: a series of little holes (the flight holes) slightly larger than a pin head. If the holes are very fresh, you may see a little wood powder as well. Treat small infestations in furniture with a branded woodworm-killing fluid, used exactly according to directions on the can. Remember that woodworm in furniture could soon spread to the surrounding timbers of your house. If you do see signs of woodworm in the house timbers, it is advisable to call in a specialist timber firm who will survey the damage free of charge, and estimate for professional eradication under guarantee.

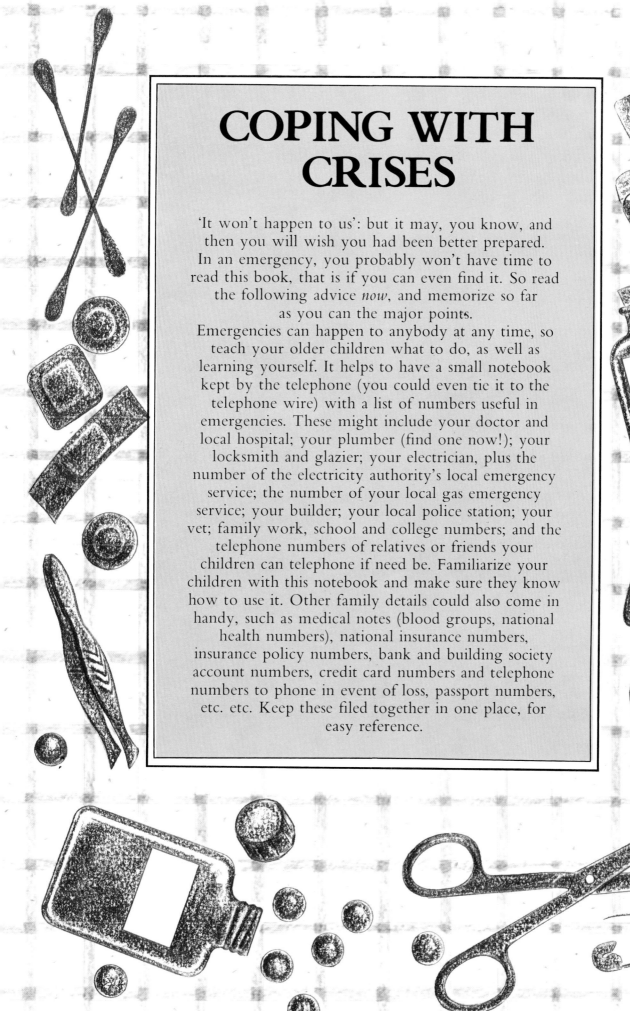

COPING WITH CRISES

'It won't happen to us': but it may, you know, and then you will wish you had been better prepared. In an emergency, you probably won't have time to read this book, that is if you can even find it. So read the following advice *now*, and memorize so far as you can the major points.

Emergencies can happen to anybody at any time, so teach your older children what to do, as well as learning yourself. It helps to have a small notebook kept by the telephone (you could even tie it to the telephone wire) with a list of numbers useful in emergencies. These might include your doctor and local hospital; your plumber (find one now!); your locksmith and glazier; your electrician, plus the number of the electricity authority's local emergency service; the number of your local gas emergency service; your builder; your local police station; your vet; family work, school and college numbers; and the telephone numbers of relatives or friends your children can telephone if need be. Familiarize your children with this notebook and make sure they know how to use it. Other family details could also come in handy, such as medical notes (blood groups, national health numbers), national insurance numbers, insurance policy numbers, bank and building society account numbers, credit card numbers and telephone numbers to phone in event of loss, passport numbers, etc. etc. Keep these filed together in one place, for easy reference.

HOUSEHOLD EMERGENCIES

FIRE

If you suspect a fire in your home, don't delay, take action immediately. Always investigate at once any strange smell or noise that could be the start of a fire. Teach your children to come and find you at once if they smell anything odd.

You should only try to tackle a fire yourself if it is a small fire in its early stages. The appropriate action varies according to what is burning; see different headings below. But in all cases the first thing you should do is to shut the door of the room where the fire is, and the windows as well, if you can reach them safely.

Major fires. If a fire breaks out which is beyond your control, here is what to do:
1. Get everybody out of the room *at once* and tell them to leave the house immediately. Do not use lifts.
2. Leave the room yourself and shut the door.
3. On the way out, alert other people so far as is possible, and shut other doors and windows if you can do so without risk.
4. Go yourself and telephone the fire brigade. Don't assume someone else has done this already. Simply dial 999: you do not need money for an emergency call from a public call box. State the location of the fire as clearly as you can, giving the full

address. Otherwise the fire brigade may loose precious minutes trying to find you.

If you suspect that there is a fire behind a closed door, **never** open it, because the fire will simply sweep out and engulf you. Get everybody out of the house and call the fire brigade just as quickly as you can.

Always remember that life is infinitely more important than property, and **never** take risks to rescue your valuables.

If you are trapped in a room by fire, don't panic, but try to follow this basic drill (teach it to your children, too).

Close the door of the room as quickly as possible, and close any other openings,

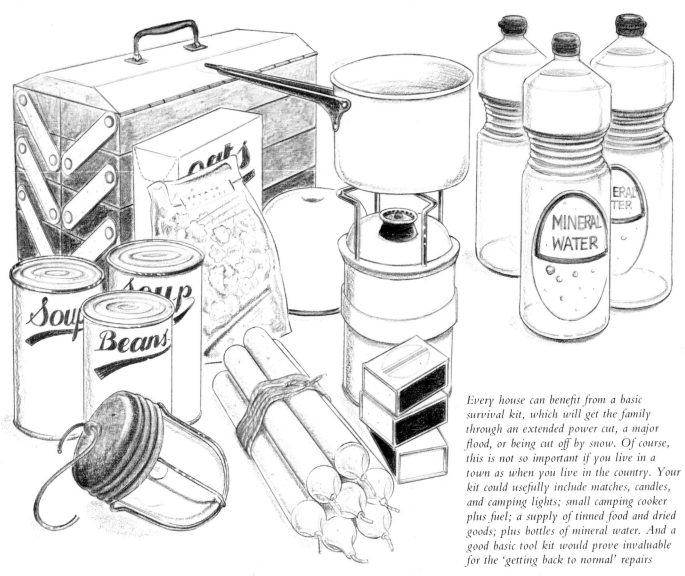

Every house can benefit from a basic survival kit, which will get the family through an extended power cut, a major flood, or being cut off by snow. Of course, this is not so important if you live in a town as when you live in the country. Your kit could usefully include matches, candles, and camping lights; small camping cooker plus fuel; a supply of tinned food and dried goods; plus bottles of mineral water. And a good basic tool kit would prove invaluable for the 'getting back to normal' repairs

such as fanlights, skylights, ventilators, etc. Seal up the gap along the bottom of the door with rolled up clothes or bedding.

Go to the window and try to attract the attention of someone outside. Make a lot of noise, or wave something very brightly coloured.

Don't try to get out unless you are forced to; many people are injured unnecessarily by panicking in this way. If the room starts to fill up with smoke, try not to become alarmed. Tie a handkerchief or scarf around your mouth, and lean out of the window to breathe. But if this is not possible, crouch down near the floor, because the heat and smoke will be less there.

Climb out of the window only if you absolutely have to. If you have to break a window, use your shoes to kick it out, or use a chair leg or something else that is heavy: **do not** try to break the glass with your hands. Try to clear jagged glass from the lower edge, and if you can, place a blanket over the sill before escaping. If possible, make a rope for yourself by tying together sheets or curtains and knotting them to a bed or a heavy piece of furniture. Make certain that all the knots are tied securely and that the rope will bear your weight.

If you cannot make a rope, throw down cushions or bedding to break your fall. Get through the window feet first, lower yourself to the full extent of your arms and drop: this reduces the distance you have to drop, and helps to keep your limbs relaxed.

Chip-pan fires. These are among the most common causes of fire in the home.

Do not use water, earth or sand on a chip pan fire, or you will spread particles of burning fat all over the kitchen.

Do not try to move the pan: you could spread the fire and badly burn yourself.

If it is possible to do so safely, turn out the heat under the pan.

Smother the pan with a lid, plate, tin tray, large board or damp cloth (e.g. towel wetted under the kitchen tap). Keep the fire covered until the fat has cooled, or the fat will simply re-ignite. A fire blanket could be very useful in an emergency of this kind: keep it close to the cooker but not where it will be obscured by any flames.

Whatever you use to smother the flames, hold it at an angle of 45°. If you hold the lid, tray, damp towel or blanket flat the flames can lick out from underneath and could badly burn your arms.

If you find you cannot control the fire,

Top: if you are trapped in a room by fire, close the door without delay and seal the gap along the bottom with rolled-up clothing, towels, curtains or bedding
Centre and above: using a fire blanket to extinguish a chip pan fire

do not attempt any further action, but follow the basic fire precautions described opposite (get everyone out of the room, close the door, etc.).

Upholstery fires. These have received a lot of alarming publicity recently. Modern foam upholstery cannot set fire to itself: follow basic fire precautions. But once upholstery is burning, you should remember that very large amounts of poisonous fumes can be given off in as little as two minutes. It is therefore absolutely vital to clear the room of people *at once* and to close the door. There is not time to collect together possessions: just get everyone out, and call the fire brigade as soon as you can.

Electrical fires. If possible, switch off at the socket and pull out the plug. Provided you have been able to do this, you can then use a bucket or jug of water, or water from a hosepipe, to put out the fire. But if you cannot disconnect the appliance from the electrical supply, it will remain live, and you must not use water, or you could get a shock.

If the fire is still small, smother the appliance with a heavy towel or blanket, but if the fire seems out of control, leave it, get everyone out of the room and house, shut the door and call the fire brigade. Throwing a blanket on a large fire will only fuel the flames. You can use a dry powder or carbon dioxide fire extinguisher, provided you are absolutely sure of how it works. If you have one of these, make sure you know how to use it *before* a fire occurs.

Chimney fires. Keep your chimney regularly swept to avoid fire.

If the chimney does catch fire, call the fire brigade at once. If possible, place a finely meshed guard around the fire. Move furniture and carpets away from the fireplace. Close down ventilation to the fireplace and keep the windows of the room closed.

Keep an eye on the other rooms through which the chimney passes. If the walls are getting hot, it is sensible to move furniture away from them.

Don't try to put out the fire yourself: you could hurt yourself, and make things worse. Wait for the fire brigade, who know exactly what to do.

Clothing fires. If your clothing catches fire, the most important thing to do is to lie down immediately and roll over and over to put out the flames. If you can, whilst rolling, wrap yourself in any large piece of fabric that comes to hand, such as a rug, dressing gown, curtain or so on. But *do not* delay lying down to look for this, and do not smother smouldering clothes for longer than necessary because the hot fabric will be held against the skin and cause extra damage.

If another person catches fire, push them onto the floor and smother the flames with whatever fabric is available, as above. Take care to protect the casualty's face from the flames.

FLOODING

Sooner or later an emergency will happen for which you need the services of a plumber: find your plumber *now* before disaster strikes. If you do find your home becoming engulfed in a flood of water, as always, try not to panic.

Action! Turn off the electricity at the mains. Then find out what is causing the flood and, if possible, turn it off: for example overflowing washbasin or bath, overflowing washing machine or dishwasher, etc.

However, if a simple action will not stop the flow of water, you must turn off the water at the mains. In newer houses the stopcock for your mains water supply is probably under the kitchen sink. In older houses, it could be in the cellar. Some old houses may not have an inside mains stopcock: the stopcock may be outside the house under a small metal flap, reached with a special turnkey.

To turn a stopcock off, turn it clockwise as far as it will go, like a tap. Make a habit of opening and closing your stopcocks twice a year to stop them getting stiff. Check *now* that you know where your

stopcocks are and that you can turn them easily.

Turn off any appliance that heats your water, such as boiler, immersion heater, washing machine, etc.

If water continues to flood out, if possible, turn off the stopcock on the supply pipe from your cold water cistern. But if you cannot reach this easily, open cold taps and flush cisterns to empty the tank as quickly as possible. If water is coming from the hot water supply system, turn off the stopcock adjacent to the hot water cylinder, on its supply pipe.

Drying out. Once you have checked the flow of water, assess the damage. If ceiling plaster seems to be bulging under the weight of water from above, make a small hole with a skewer, screwdriver or knitting needle, and put a bucket underneath to catch the water.

Mop up the water as thoroughly as you can. Start by scooping it up with a shallow bowl, then finish off with old towels or cloths, wringing out the water as you go. When you have got the floor as dry as you can, turn on extra heat in rooms affected and·open windows.

Stand mattresses and foam cushions on their edge as seepage is slower on a vertical

Push burning casualty to the floor and smother the flames with any available non-flammable fabric. Take care to keep the flames away from casualty's face

surface. Take up wet carpeting and looselaid flooring: carpets should be professionally cleaned.

Wait until any area containing electrical wiring has dried out before you turn the electricity back on. You may however be able to isolate the power and lighting circuits concerned by taking out the relevant fuses from your fuse box, so that you have power for the rest of the house.

You should not replace furniture and heavy appliances until you are sure that the floor has dried out completely; this may take several weeks.

Contact your insurance company as soon as any kind of flood has happened.

Major flooding. If you live in an area where major floods are likely from overflowing rivers, get in touch with your local authority who will advise on appropriate flood precautions and action. For your own comfort, organize your own supplies of tinned and dried food, and bottled water, in case your house is isolated for any length of time. Have some means of heating and lighting that are not dependent on the mains electricity supply, such as an oil stove, and candles or camping lights. A small camping cooker could also be useful: even a single burner is enough to boil a kettle and heat a can of beans! If flooding does occur, move your family and whatever possessions you can to the upper floors and wait for the local authority relief service to tell you what to do next.

Remember that flood water is almost certainly contaminated, and **do not** use any utensils which have been flooded without disinfecting them. Your water supply is likely to be contaminated after flooding, so **do not** drink from it until you hear from your local authority that all is well. In the meantime, use bottled water and canned drinks.

Frozen and burst pipes. If your pipes are frozen, first turn off your water at the mains. Then turn off your water heating and your central heating boiler. Inspect the frozen pipe(s) and try to determine whether they have burst: you may see ice glistening in the pipe, or you may be able to feel a split.

If the pipe does not seem to have burst, take gentle steps to try to thaw it. Working back from the frozen tap, use a hairdryer, a hot water bottle, or even hot cloths to try to thaw the pipe. But **never** use a naked flame.

However, if the pipe has split, bind rags tightly around the leak and place a bucket underneath to catch the water as the pipe thaws. Call your plumber. If possible, turn off the stopcock on the outlet to the cold water tank. If it is a hot water tap that has burst, turn off the stopcock controlling the supply of water to the hot water cistern. If escaping water *cannot* be controlled, open all cold taps and flush cisterns in order to drain the system as quickly as possible (save some water in the bath and in jugs or bowls to use until the plumber comes).

GAS

Everyone in the family should know how to turn off the gas supply at the mains. If you do not know where your gas tap is ask your meter reader next time he calls. The gas supply tap is usually a small lever on the gas pipe near your meter.

Turning off at the mains. To turn the main gas supply OFF, turn the lever until the notched line on the spindle points ACROSS the pipe. If your tap seems stiff, don't attempt to loosen it up yourself – call your local gas service centre who will come and loosen it for you safely, free of charge.

Before turning the gas on again, make sure that all appliances and pilot lights are turned off. The gas tap is ON when the notched line on the spindle points ALONG the pipe. After turning the supply back on, be sure to relight all pilot lights.

If you smell gas you should at once open all doors and windows and put out any naked flames, including cigarettes.

Do not turn electrical switches on or off.

Make sure that a gas tap has not been left on by mistake and that all pilot lights are still burning.

If the smell persists, you must turn off the mains supply, then telephone the gas service at once: look under Gas in the telephone book.

Never look for a gas leak with a naked flame.

ELECTRICITY

It is dangerous for unqualified, inexperienced people to meddle in any way with electrical wiring or repairs, except for matters of a very minor nature. However, mending fuses is within the competence of most householders.

The fuse box. The electricity supply cable for your home passes through your meter to a small box containing a large switch which turns the supply on and off

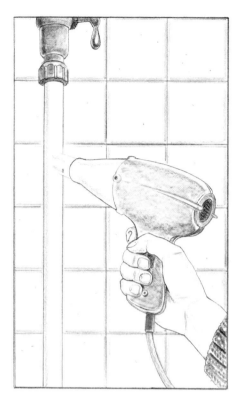

To defrost a frozen pipe use a hairdryer, hot water bottle or hot cloth; never use a naked flame for this purpose

for the whole house. This box also contains the fuses for the various wiring circuits that take the electricity around the home, and is commonly called 'the fuse box', although officially it is known as the 'consumer unit'. Make sure you know the whereabouts of your consumer unit, and that the individual fuses inside are labelled.

Repair kit. To deal with minor electrical repairs, you should have a small electrical repair kit, kept apart from your other tools, in its own small bag or box, preferably adjacent to your fuse box. You will need a torch that works, so check the battery every now and then. A rubber-cased torch copes with knocks and bangs, but a small metal-cased torch is also useful for testing fuses, see below. You will also need an electrical screwdriver, a card of fuse wire (or cartridge fuses, see below) and a selection of 13A and 3A fuses for your plugs. You could also include some candles, and a box of matches.

Mending a blown fuse. A fuse is simply a deliberately weak spot in the wiring of your home designed to blow (break) if there is a fault in an appliance or in the wiring of the house itself, or if the circuit is overloaded because too many appliances are being used at any one time.

Fuses in your fuse-box may be of two types: they may be thin lengths of wire, called *rewirable fuses*. Or (less common) they may be small tubes sealed at both ends with metal caps, called *cartridge fuses*. In both cases, it is essential to carry out repairs with a fuse correctly rated for the circuit which it is protecting. Cartridge fuses are clearly labelled and coloured according to their rating (for more details, see below): and fuse wire is labelled on the packaging card.

Never try to replace a cartridge fuse or fuse wire with a fuse of a higher rating, or with any kind of makeshift substitute. You should not do this even as a temporary measure. When you lose the protection of the fuse (by making the weak link stronger in some way) you expose yourself and your family to the dangers of fire or shock.

To replace the fuse in the mains consumer unit (fuse box), you must first turn off the electricity for the whole house at the mains switch. But if you have an old wiring system, you will have several switches, all of which must be switched off until you can see which circuit is affected.

To mend a rewirable fuse: after turning off the electricity, and using the light of a

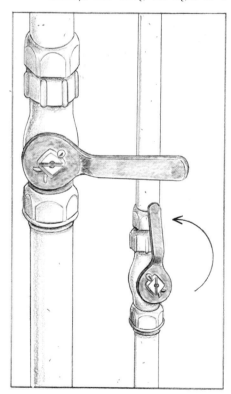

Above left: to turn off the main gas supply, turn the tap until the notched line is pointing across the pipe, as shown
Above right: in the 'on' position, the notched line should point along the pipe

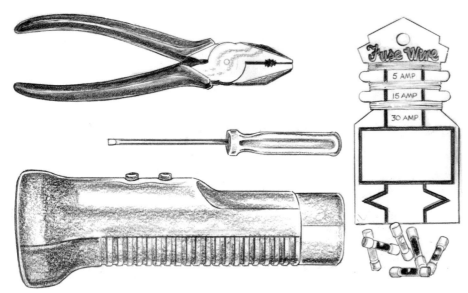

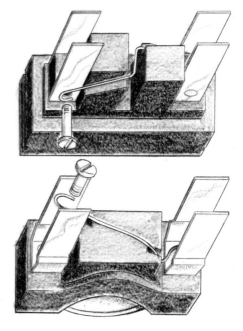

torch or candle if necessary, take out (i.e. unclip) each fuse holder in turn, and look at the thin length of wire which it holds. The faulty fuse is the one in which the wire has broken or melted. But before you mend the fuse, try to work out why the fuse blew in the first place. If the wire seems simply to have parted, suspect overloading; i.e. using too many appliances at once. Unplug some of your appliances before mending the fuse and switching back on again. But if the fuse wire has virtually disappeared, suspect a fault in an appliance. See if you can locate the faulty appliance, and unplug it before going any further.

Loosen the screws on the fuseholder (anti-clockwise) and clear away the bits of broken or melted wire. Then cut a long enough piece of fuse wire to wind around the screws at each end. The fuse wire must be of a correct rating (thickness) for the circuit which it is protecting: 5 Amp (thin) for lighting circuits; 15 Amp (medium) for heating circuits; and 30 Amp (thick) for ring mains or large fixed appliances. Circuits for cookers may require fuse wire rated at 45A or 60A. Wind the new wire clockwise around the screw terminals in the fuseholder at each end (clockwise, because otherwise the wire tends to unwind as the screw is tightened). Do not stretch the wire too tight.

Then you can replace the fuseholder in the box, close up the box, and turn on the main switch.

To mend a cartridge fuse: first turn off the electricity at the mains. Fit new fuse of correct rating in circuit affected. You cannot tell simply by looking which fuse has blown, as you can with rewirable fuses. You can find out either by trial and error or proceed as follows: take a small metal-cased torch, take off its end, and switch it

on. Test each fuse in turn by holding it across the end of the torch, with one end resting on the battery and one on the torch casing. The sound fuses will light the torch. But first try to work out why the fuse blew (see above).

Cartridge fuses for mains fuse boxes are rated 5 Amps coloured white for lighting circuits; 15 Amps coloured blue for immersion heaters; 20 Amps coloured yellow also for immersion heaters; and 45 Amps coloured green for cookers.

Instead of rewirable or cartridge fuses, as described above, some modern fuse boxes may be fitted with 'miniature circuit breakers'. Instead of a fuse blowing, there is a switch which automatically turns itself off. First find out the cause of trouble (overloading, faulty appliance) as before. Then simply turn the switch back on again.

If a mains fuse continues to blow, even though you have mended it correctly, it is essential to call in a qualified electrician. Never try to replace the fuse with one of a higher rating. And if all your lights and power should fail, first check with your neighbours whether there is a power cut. If there is not, call the Electricity Board's 24-hour emergency service; it will be listed under Electricity in the telephone book.

Power cuts. Make sure that you have in your home torches and candles and/or camping lights where you can find them easily and safely even in the dark. But take particular care when using candles for they are, of course, a dangerous fire risk. Put candles well out of reach of children and when the power comes back on again, make sure that all candles are extinguished. Preferably, use heavy-based candle holders rather than a makeshift arrangement of candles in saucers; if using bottles,

weight them with sand, or they could be toppled over. Non-electrical heating (e.g. open fire, gas fire or oil heater) and a small cooking appliance (e.g. a camping ring or stove) are useful in extended power cuts.

As soon as you have organized some light (if necessary) turn off those electrical appliances which might prove dangerous if left unattended or forgotten when the power comes back on again: these include cookers and hobs, cooking appliances such as deep fat friers, electric fry pans, irons, electric blankets, fires and so on.

Fridges and Freezers. Leave your fridge and freezer switched on. Check to see that the fridge drip tray is in position, then keep the fridge door closed. *Do not* open your freezer; its contents will remain unharmed for about eight hours. The more food you have in the freezer the longer the contents will keep without thawing. However, food which has started to thaw should not be refrozen but should be removed and eaten as soon as possible. Uncooked thawed food such as meats and vegetables can be cooked into various dishes (pies, casseroles, etc.) and then refrozen.

When the power is restored, check all candles as already mentioned. Also reset electric clocks including those that control your central heating and the one on your cooker.

Above left: keep a small electrical repair kit conveniently near the fusebox. Include a rubber torch, pliers, screwdriver, fuse wires and spare fuses
Below: fitting new fuse wire in two different types of rewirable cartridge fuse

FIRST AID

First aid is the immediate care of a person who has been injured or suddenly taken ill. The treatments are simple and can be learned by anyone, young or old.

The main aim of first aid is to keep a casualty alive until more experienced and better equipped help – ambulanceman, nurse or doctor – is available.

Often the first aider is the most important person in the passage from injury to recovery. Someone who has suffered serious injury can die within four minutes – far less time than it takes for an ambulance to arrive. So prompt and effective first aid is a life saver in serious injury or illness.

Here we concentrate on life-saving techniques and measures to prevent injuries becoming worse and to reduce the time taken for a casualty to recover. Throughout we have specifically referred to the casualty as either 'him' or 'her' – but of course, all the techniques and treatments described apply equally to both sexes.

First aid is not the elaborate and precise bandaging of wounds, nor should it be thought of as being entirely the province of voluntary organizations such as St John Ambulance or the Red Cross. These bodies provide an excellent service, but they are not immediately available when your child is accidentally burnt or an elderly relative suffers a heart attack.

Ideally, everyone should know how to perform life-saving first aid. Every day thousands of people are injured or taken ill suddenly, many of them while they are at home. There are one million home accidents in Britain each year where the casualty needs hospital treatment. More than 5,000 people in England and Wales die each year as a result of home accidents.

The elderly and the very young are particularly vulnerable.

The need for all adults and older children to know how to cope with serious injury and illness is obvious, but there is a second less obvious reason why everyone should know first aid. Research has shown that people trained in first aid, even through emergency first aid courses lasting only four hours, are less likely to be involved in accidents.

The reasons for this are not yet fully understood, but it seems probable that trainees become more aware of potential danger and are also more determined to avoid injury.

If the whole family becomes more aware of potential danger in the home it is likely to become a safer place.

GENERAL POINTS TO REMEMBER

At all times consider first the safety of the casualty and of yourself. You cannot help an injured person if you become the second casualty. This is particularly important when dealing with electric shock, smoke filled rooms and road accidents.

A first aider should aim to do as little as possible but all that is essential to maintain life. Elaborate bandaging should be avoided because time will be wasted at hospital removing it again. Wherever possible the first aider should do no more than summon help, reassure the casualty and, by careful vigilance, try to prevent more serious conditions developing.

Moving someone with a damaged limb will cause pain, increase shock and possibly cause further damage. **Wherever possible wait for experts to move the casualty.**

Summon expert help as quickly as possible. Ask another responsible person to ring for the doctor or an ambulance so that you can remain with the injured person. Rescue services are called by dialling 999 and asking the operator to send an ambulance. Remember to give the full address of the place where help is needed. This must include the village or part of town as well as the street and house number. State the nature of the injury and the number of casualties who need help.

Keep the number of your doctor near your telephone for quick reference. **If help is required urgently, always ring for an ambulance first – it should arrive more quickly.**

See also **General Aspects of First Aid** and **Summary of Life-saving First Aid**.

FIRST PRIORITY – OXYGEN

The most important system of the body is that which provides oxygen to the brain and other vital organs. Anything which prevents oxygen reaching the brain will lead to death in a very short time.

When we breathe, oxygen enters the lungs where it passes into the bloodstream. The blood is pumped round the body by the heart and so delivers oxygen to all the organs, the most important of which is the brain. The heart is very efficient, pumping about 4.75 litres (10 pints) of blood a minute.

The brain can be deprived of oxygen in four main ways:

1. The path from the mouth to the lungs is blocked.
2. Breathing stops.
3. The heart stops beating.
4. There is not enough blood to take the oxygen to the brain.

Life-saving first aid concentrates on preventing or correcting these problems when they occur.

LIFE-SAVING TECHNIQUES
1. Keeping an open, clear airway from the mouth to the lungs.
2. Restarting breathing or breathing for the casualty.
3. Preventing further loss of blood or other body fluids.
4. Placing casualty in recovery position.

A further life-saving technique is restarting the heart or using external pressure on the heart to pump blood round the body. Unfortunately, this last technique cannot be taught by a manual, it requires good personal instruction and practice on dummies.

SHOCK

Shock follows every serious injury or illness and, without proper treatment, can lead to death. The treatment of injuries discussed later is largely concerned with preventing further shock.

Cause. Shock is caused by the loss of body fluid in the form of whole blood, blood plasma, vomit or sweat. Here, we are primarily concerned with the loss of whole blood or blood plasma.

Red blood cells carry oxygen round the body. Plasma is the liquid part of the blood and is usually lost following burns or crush injuries. Loss of plasma is just as serious as loss of whole blood.

Once blood has been lost from the circulation, the body changes in an attempt to make up for the blood loss. (These body changes are described under BLEEDING). If the body fluid loss continues, the body becomes unable to compensate and death may occur.

Treatment. The treatment of blood or plasma loss can only be carried out in hospital, because lost blood has to be replaced with a transfusion. The first aider must deal with the cause of the blood loss, reassure the casualty and arrange for transport to hospital as quickly as possible.

Unconscious. If the casualty has lost consciousness, is semi-conscious or is vomiting, place him in the recovery position. (See UNCONSCIOUSNESS).

Conscious. If the casualty is conscious he should be kept warm with a light blanket, reassured that he will be all right and made comfortable by loosening tight clothing at the neck, chest and waist.

Because shock means that the brain is being deprived of oxygen, the blood supply to the brain should be increased by lying the conscious casualty on his back with the head low and the legs raised.

Fainting is a less serious form of shock. It can be caused by the sight of blood, bad news, pain, heat or infection. While blood is not actually lost from the body, it stagnates in the muscles and gut, temporarily reducing the volume of blood available for transporting oxygen to the brain. As a result the patient will look ill and may appear to be having a fit.

The casualty usually recovers very quickly because falling down automatically increases the flow of blood to the brain. This recovery can be aided by placing the casualty in the feet high position shown and by loosening all tight clothing.

If the faint is the result of an infection the patient may not make a quick recovery. In such cases a doctor should be called.

DIARRHOEA AND VOMITING

These conditions are usually the result of infection and lead to a large amount of fluid loss from the body and hence to shock. The condition of patients, particularly children, may deteriorate rapidly.

Treatment is mainly by controlling diet. Solid foods should be avoided, as should fruit juices. The patient should be given plenty of fluids to minimise shock – milk and water are most suitable. The patient should be kept at rest and warm.

If symptoms continue for several hours a doctor should be called – particularly in the case of a young child.

UNCONSCIOUSNESS

Unconsciousness is the result of injury to, or interference with, the function of the brain. States of unconsciousness can vary from drowsiness to coma, where the casualty cannot be roused at all.

POINTS TO REMEMBER ABOUT SHOCK:

1. Shock will follow every serious illness or injury.

2. The only treatment for shock caused by blood loss is a transfusion.

3. Summon an ambulance as quickly as possible.

4. Treat external bleeding and make sure the casualty is breathing.

5. If the casualty is unconscious, put him in the **recovery position**.

6. If the casualty is conscious, make him comfortable, loosen any tight clothing, keep him warm but not too hot, and lie him down with his legs raised higher than his head. Remember to talk to the patient and to give lots of reassurance.

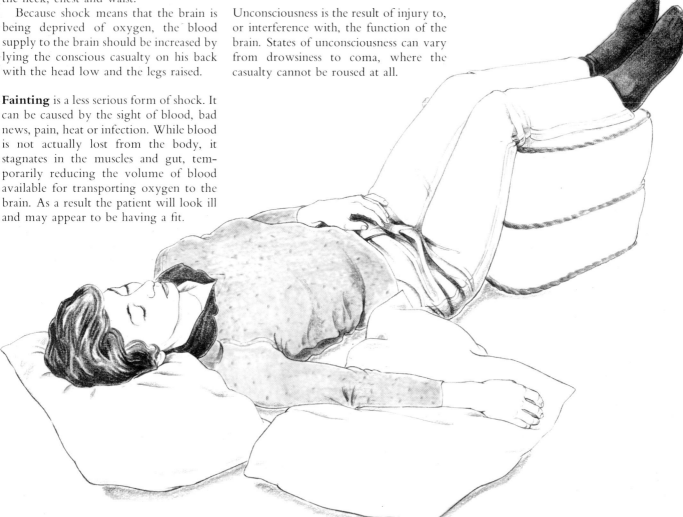

In general, if a casualty cannot answer your questions coherently she should be treated as unconscious.

The immediate cause of unconsciousness may not always be obvious, but the treatment is always the same. Many people who become unconscious die unnecessarily because they do not receive the correct first aid.

When someone loses consciousness, her brain loses its ability to control many of

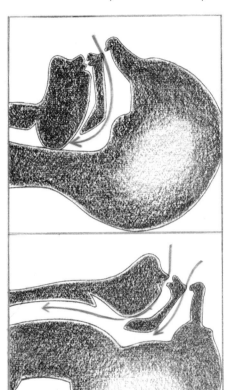

the body's muscles – including those which position the tongue. If the casualty falls to the ground on her back, the tongue will tend to move to the back of the throat, cutting off the supply of air to the lungs. **If this happens the brain, deprived of oxygen, will be damaged within four minutes and death will quickly follow.**

The aims of first aid treatment for the unconscious casualty are to ensure that she can breathe and will continue to breathe and to get her to hospital as quickly as possible. Trivial injuries must not be treated before you have dealt with unconsciousness.

The first priority is to open the airway, which is done by tipping the head back. This has the effect of pulling the tongue away from the back of the throat, allowing air into the lungs (see diagram). This process is helped if the lower jaw is also pulled forward.

If this procedure does not lead to the casualty's breathing restarting then **artificial respiration** will be necessary (see *Artificial respiration*).

A second threat to the life of the unconscious casualty is the possibility that she may vomit, so reblocking her airway. Breathing may also be cut off by broken false teeth, or blood or saliva at the back of the throat. These blockages must be cleared, if necessary with your fingers, in order to allow the casualty to continue breathing.

If the casualty is breathing she should be turned into the **recovery position**, which

is **also called the unconscious, coma, or semi-prone position**. This position keeps the tongue away from the back of the throat, because the head is tilted back, and at the same time allows anything in the mouth or throat – such as vomit, blood or saliva – to drain out through the mouth.

If possible, the lower body should be raised to increase blood flow to the brain. Make sure that the casualty's mouth and nose are not covered by whatever she is lying on. Also, remember to loosen all tight clothing.

Recovery position. It does not matter how you put someone into the recovery position, but the following method is the easiest – with practice even children can use it to turn an adult over. The casualty should be turned onto a blanket if one is available.

Kneel by the side of the casualty, who has collapsed onto her back, and position yourself level with her hips. Place her arms alongside her body, the nearer arm tucked slightly under the body, and cross the far leg over the near one. By grabbing the clothing at the far hip (and the far sleeve as well, if possible) pull towards you until the casualty is lying across your knees. If you are able to pull the casualty over using only one hand, use your other hand to protect her head as she is pulled over.

When the casualty is lying across your knees, slide out allowing her to come to rest on the ground. Bring the casualty's nearest knee up towards her chest. The arm on the same side should be positioned at right angles to the body, and the

Above: in unconsciousness, the tongue is likely to fall to the back of the throat, cutting off air from the lungs. Tilting the head back lifts the tongue, clearing air passage
Left: feet high position for faint or shock
Below: the life-saving 'recovery position'

forearm should then be bent up parallel with the casualty's head. The far leg can be slightly bent and the far arm pushed a little way from the body. Tip the casualty's head slightly back so that she is in the position shown in the illustration.

In the **recovery position** it is impossible for the unconscious casualty to roll over on her own. But never leave an unconscious person alone. She may recover slightly and move back into a dangerous position or she may stop breathing. Send a responsible person to call for an ambulance.

Things to check. Check that the casualty continues to breathe and take her pulse regularly, making a note of its speed and strength. Check for bleeding and, if necessary, treat it – but do not leave the casualty in order to look for dressings.

Never try to revive the casualty by slapping or shaking her. **Nothing should be given by mouth to an unconscious casualty: she is incapable of swallowing**.

Any person who has been unconscious, even for a short time, must always be seen by a doctor. The only exceptions to this rule are people who have fainted; and known epileptics who have suffered a fit but recovered normally with no injury to the person.

No head injury should ever be ignored. The damage caused may not become apparent until some time after the injury, and then it may be too late to help. Anyone who has suffered a head injury should go to hospital or see his doctor.

POINTS TO REMEMBER ABOUT UNCONSCIOUSNESS

1. Make sure the airway is open and clear of obstruction.

2. If the casualty is not breathing, start artificial respiration immediately.

3. If the casualty is breathing turn her into the **recovery position**.

4. Never leave an unconscious casualty alone. Send another responsible person to call for an ambulance.

5. Never give an unconscious person anything to drink.

6. Get the casualty to hospital as quickly as possible.

Practice turning people into the recovery position. It is the easiest way in which you can save a life.

BLEEDING

The importance of blood in carrying oxygen to the organs of the body – particularly the heart – has already been explained. The average adult has between 10 and 12 pints of blood. Children have less – about 1 litre per 13 kg (1 pint per stone) of bodyweight.

Blood is kept circulating by the pumping of the heart, which beats at a rate which can vary considerably from person to person. However, the heart of an adult who is relaxing will normally beat between 60 and 80 times a minute. Children tend to have a faster heart rate.

The heart rate will increase at times when the body requires extra oxygen – for instance, following physical exercise or when lifting heavy weights. However, an increased heart rate can also be a sign that something is wrong.

Blood loss. Blood passes through the body in a vast system of pipes or blood vessels. If any of these is cut, blood will escape and be lost. Shock will develop, its severity depending upon the amount of blood lost. Blood loss can be external and internal.

External bleeding will follow cuts in the skin. Deep cuts can be caused by glass or knives, or the skin can be torn by catching on sharp objects such as barbed wire. Bruises are another form of blood loss. Extensive bruising can indicate a large loss of blood from the circulation.

Internal bleeding is less obvious simply because the blood is not immediately visible. It can follow injury to the internal organs of the body – as a result of a fall or head injury, for example. Fractures where the skin is not broken are also likely to cause internal bleeding. The sharp ends of the broken bones may cut through blood vessels, allowing blood to leak into the muscles and hollow parts of the body. Certain medical conditions can also lead to internal bleeding, one example being a burst ulcer.

Effects. The effects of internal and external bleeding are the same. If a person loses 20 per cent of his blood, that is, 1 litre (2 pints) in an adult, he is ill and will look it. Changes in the body make it relatively easy to identify a victim of blood loss.

Symptoms. Because the brain, heart and lungs must be kept supplied with blood, other organs may be starved of their normal supply when blood loss is heavy. The skin normally contains a large amount of blood which gives the body a normal healthy colour. When the volume of blood is reduced, the supply to the skin is withdrawn to keep the brain, heart and lungs functioning. So the first sign of blood loss is *pallor* of the skin.

Blood circulating through the skin keeps it warm and evaporates the large amount of fluid which passes through the skin as sweat. When blood is withdrawn from the skin, it becomes *cold* and *clammy* to the touch.

When the body is losing blood, it is less efficient at taking in and circulating oxygen. In order to compensate for this, it will try to grab more oxygen from the air. The casualty starts to breathe more quickly and each breath is shallower than the last. So breathing becomes *fast*, *shallow* and may sound *laboured*.

The victim of blood loss will become *anxious*, particularly when suffering from internal bleeding where there may be no obvious sign of injury. The lack of oxygen to the brain will lead to *irritation* and *restlessness*.

Finally, in order to move oxygen around the body as quickly as possible, the heart will beat *faster* but each beat will be weaker.

SUMMARY OF SYMPTOMS OF BLOOD LOSS

1. The skin becomes pallid, cold and clammy.

2. Breathing becomes fast and shallow.

3. The casualty becomes anxious and restless.

4. The heart beats faster but less strongly (this can be measured by taking the pulse).

With serious blood loss, unconsciousness and death may follow if condition remains untreated.

Taking the pulse. When a casualty has no obvious injuries and the signs of blood loss or shock are detected it is reasonable to assume that there is internal bleeding. The surest sign is the pulse rate which continues to get faster and weaker as blood is lost. Because the pulse is such an important indication of blood loss it is essential that all first aiders are capable of measuring and recording it accurately. With practice the technique is quite simple.

At the wrist. The illustration of a hand will help you to find the pulse. Place your middle three fingers on the bone, which can be felt quite easily. The fingers should be placed in a straight line, directly below the base of the thumb. The fingers should then be pulled over the skin in the direction of the arrow. By pressing the fingers in between the bone and the next ridge of the wrist, the pulse should be felt.

Practise finding the pulse on yourself or on other people until you can find it with ease.

At the neck. If the pulse is too weak to detect at the wrist, it may be possible to feel it at the neck. This point is nearer the heart, so the pulse should be stronger.

Place two or three fingers in line from above to below the Adam's apple. Slide the fingers sideways into the hollow on either side. Press the fingers in and you should be able to feel the pulse. Again, practise finding this pulse on yourself.

Whenever you are taking a pulse **remember never to use your thumb**. This is because the thumb has quite a strong pulse of its own and you might find yourself measuring your own pulse instead of that of the casualty.

Recording the heart beat. Each beat felt is one beat of the heart. Using a watch with a second hand, count the number of beats in 30 seconds and multiply by 2 to find out how many times the heart is beating in a minute. The strength of the heartbeat can be judged by how difficult it is to feel the pulse.

When treating a casualty, keep a note of the pulse each time you take it. This will show how the heart rate has changed over a period of time – useful information for doctors estimating the extent of blood loss. Even without the help of a watch, you should be able to judge whether the heart rate is increasing or not and whether the beats are getting weaker.

First aid for internal bleeding. Internal bleeding leads directly to shock. There is no treatment a first aider can give. The patient must be sent to hospital as soon as possible for a blood transfusion.

If the patient is unconscious he should be placed in the recovery position (see UNCONSCIOUSNESS).

If the patient is conscious he should be made comfortable, placed in the legs higher than head position described under SHOCK, reassured and kept warm. His pulse should be taken and recorded regularly, and you should check that he remains conscious and continues to breathe.

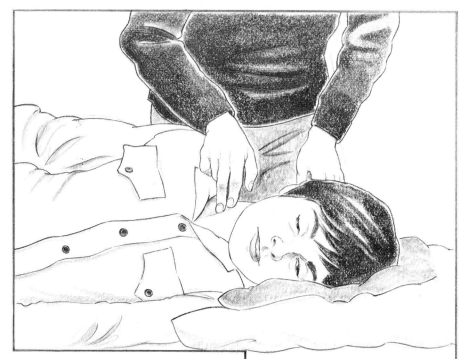

There is no excuse for a casualty to be allowed to die from internal bleeding just because the symptoms go unrecognized. Always assume that a casualty is suffering from internal bleeding until you are satisfied that he is not. Watch for the signs of blood loss to develop for at least 20 minutes and monitor the pulse carefully.

First aid for external bleeding. External bleeding is generally easy to detect. But sometimes blood can collect in the hollows under the body or be soaked up by the casualty's clothes, so be sure to check carefully for such signs of bleeding. The signs of serious blood loss are the same as those for internal bleeding – pallid, cold and clammy skin; fast, shallow breathing; casualty becomes anxious and restless; the heart beats faster but less strongly. The casualty may become unconscious and death may follow.

Most cases of bleeding from wounds are minor and the blood flow will stop naturally with the help of the clotting process. This seals up the hole in the blood vessel. When bleeding is severe, clots may not be able to form and help is needed for the natural process to work.

Control of external bleeding is achieved in three ways: rest, elevation and pressure.

Rest is essential for a casualty who is bleeding. Make him lie down before you do anything else and try to keep him from moving. Movement will disturb blood clots which are forming and will also increase the amount of blood flow, leading to even more bleeding.

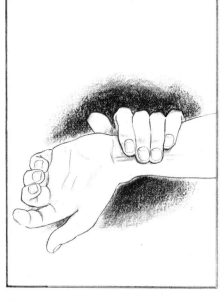

The pulse rate is an important indicator of blood loss. All first aiders should be able to measure it, particularly so that they can recognize internal bleeding. The pulse at the neck can be found in the hollow on either side of the Adam's apple. It may be possible to detect the heart beat here if the pulse is too weak to be felt at the wrist. The wrist pulse is found below the base of the thumb by pressing into the hollow between the bone and the next ridge of the wrist. Practise finding both pulses until you are confident – and remember not to use your thumb

179

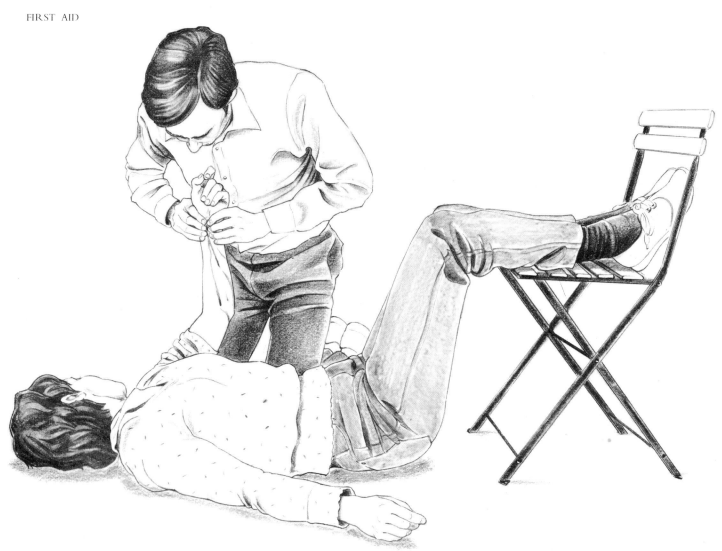

Elevation. When the casualty is lying down raise the part of the body which is bleeding above the level of the heart. This will reduce the flow of blood to the wound because it is harder for the heart to pump 'uphill'.

Pressure. Remove clothing from around the wound and press with your fingers or hand directly onto the bleeding point. If you can, press over a sterile dressing or any clean, absorbent material – but do not waste time. If nothing is quickly available just press with your hand. This pressure must be maintained for at least 10 minutes, to reduce or stop the blood flow and allow clotting to take place.

A dressing should be placed on the wound as soon as possible – pressure can be applied more effectively with a dressing than with the hand.

Any pad may be bandaged onto the wound, but sterile (germ-free) dressings are best. These consist of a thick pad of cotton wool topped with a layer of lint stitched to an open weave bandage. The pad should be placed directly onto the wound and the longer end of the bandage

should be wound firmly over the pad. The knot should be tied directly over the wound to provide extra pressure.

If the wound continues to bleed do not remove the dressing as this would only disturb any clotting which has occurred. Instead, a second dressing should be applied firmly over the first.

It is important to check that the blood flow to the injured limb below the wound has not been cut off by too tight a dressing. Compare the injured limb with the good one, checking that the colour is the same and that the blood vessels do not appear more pronounced. If the blood flow has been cut off, the dressing must be loosened and re-tied.

Serious bleeding. When dealing with serious bleeding, speed is essential: stopping the blood loss reduces the level of shock which will develop. Do not waste time washing your hands, cleaning the wound, or searching for sterile dressings. Do not bother how neatly the bandage is tied as long as it stays in place and provides sufficient pressure on the wound without causing too much distress to the circulation

of the lower limb.

After bandaging the wound take the pulse and look for the signs of shock. A casualty who looks ill, feels weak and has a pulse which is fast and weak must be taken to hospital.

Tourniquets must NEVER be used to stop bleeding. They can lead to the loss of a limb.

Bleeding can always be stopped by simply applying direct pressure to the wound area.

Foreign bodies such as glass or sharp blades should be left in a wound, to be removed at hospital. Often if left in place they will reduce or prevent bleeding. Moving them might well cause damage.

Dressings can be built up round the foreign body. For example, a rolled bandage on each side of the object can be used to apply pressure. A further bandage can then be used to cover the wound, the foreign body and the rolled bandages. The outside bandage should be tight enough to apply pressure to the sides of the wound but care must be taken not to press down on the foreign body as you bandage.

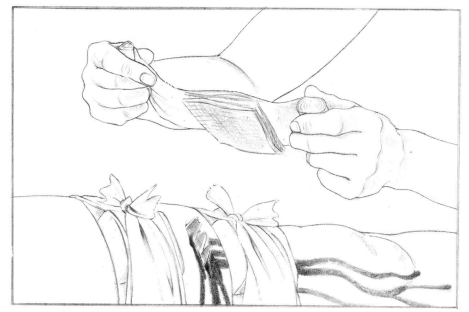

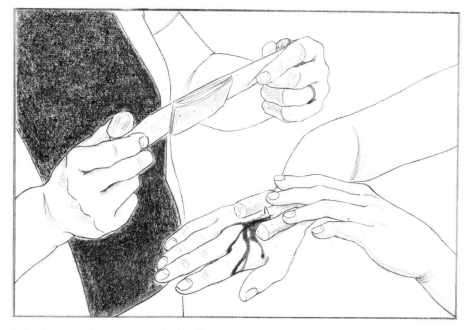

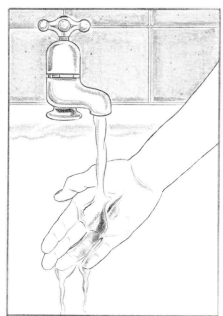

Left, above: apply pressure to the bleeding point and maintain pressure for at least 10 minutes to allow blood clot to form
Above: foreign bodies such as glass are normally best left in the wound until removed at hospital. Removing them yourself could cause further damage, whereas they may actually lessen bleeding if left in place. For large wounds (top) use two standard wound dressings to apply pressure to the sides of the wound and stem any bleeding. then bridge the two pads with a third dressing applied so that it does not press down on the foreign body. Smaller wounds (above) can be dressed in a similar way, using rolled bandages to form bridge
Top right: treatment for a nosebleed
Above right: wash small wounds under running water, and clean with cotton swabs

Nose bleeds. Nose bleeds are quite common but they can be alarming, nevertheless. As in all cases of bleeding, a small amount of spilt blood can cover a large area. However, nose bleeds are generally quite easy to stop.

The casualty should sit over a basin or bowl with his head inclined slightly forward. This will allow any blood which runs down the back of the nose to escape from the mouth and not be swallowed.

The casualty should breathe through the mouth, and the fleshy part of the nose should be pinched closed between finger and thumb. The pressure must be maintained for at least 10 minutes and the casualty should not blow his nose for several hours afterwards.

If the bleeding continues or recurs, the casualty should see a doctor or be taken to hospital. Never attempt to plug the casualty's nose.

Minor cuts and bruises. Unlike cases of serious bleeding, speed is not essential when dealing with minor wounds. Blood loss is minimal and shock will not be a problem. The main aim of this first aid treatment is to prevent infection and to protect the injury.

Before starting treatment wash your hands carefully, preferably in hot running water. Stop the bleeding by putting a sterile dressing over the wound and applying firm pressure. At the same time elevate the injured limb.

If the wound area is dirty, wash it under running water and use cotton wool

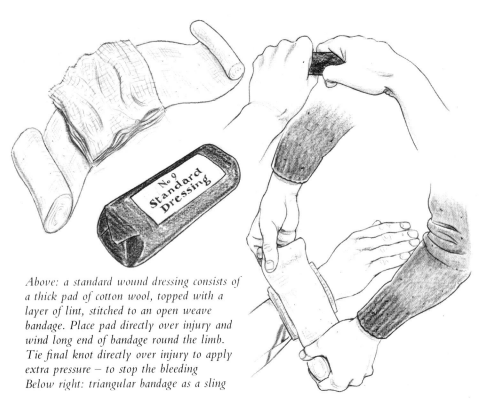

Above: a standard wound dressing consists of a thick pad of cotton wool, topped with a layer of lint, stitched to an open weave bandage. Place pad directly over injury and wind long end of bandage round the limb. Tie final knot directly over injury to apply extra pressure – to stop the bleeding
Below right: triangular bandage as a sling

swabs to clean the wound. Use each swab once only and work in towards the wound, but wiping *away* from the injury. When the wound is clean and free from grit or other dirt, dry the skin with more cotton wool.

Puncture wounds can be caused by animal bites, stabbing or by treading on a nail. Such wounds may not appear very serious as bleeding may be slight and easily controlled. However, there is a danger that nerves or muscles may have been damaged and that dirt may have been introduced deep into the body. Similar problems may also occur with jagged cuts such as those caused by the sharp edges of opened tins.

Bleeding from deep wounds should be controlled as described under **Serious bleeding** and a dressing applied. Such casualties should see a doctor and hospital treatment may be required to ensure the wound is properly cleansed. Often, the casualty will be given an injection to prevent the possibility of tetanus developing.

Widespread cuts or grazes can be covered with a sterile dressing to keep them clean. For **small wounds** a porous fabric plaster should be used to cover and protect. This type of plaster allows air to circulate around the wound and promotes healing.

Waterproof plasters should be used only when the wound is likely to be exposed to dirty water. Afterwards the waterproof

plaster should be replaced with a fabric one.

Generally it is better not to apply any ointments or lotions. A diluted antiseptic lotion may, however, be used to clean the wound. Remember that with minor wounds the main concern is to prevent infection.

Slings. In cases of minor bleeding from arm or hand it is useful to keep the limb elevated in a sling when it has been dressed. With other injuries, too, the comfort of the casualty can be improved by supporting the arm across the chest with a sling.

SLINGS CAN BE IMPROVIZED IN THE FOLLOWING WAYS:

1. By supporting the arm inside a buttoned jacket or waistcoat.

2. By pinning the sleeve of a dress or shirt to the clothing.

3. By turning the lower edge of a jacket up over the arm and pinning it to the clothing.

4. By using scarves, belts or ties. However, the best sling is made from a triangular bandage.

Triangular bandage sling. Ask the casualty to support his injured arm across his chest as high above his heart as possible with the fingers pointing towards the shoulder on the uninjured side.

Place the triangular bandage across the forearm with the long edge hanging straight down and one short end parallel with the injured arm and with the point

well below the elbow (see figure). Ease the base of the bandage under the arm and around the casualty's back (making a cradle for the injured arm) onto the front of the sound shoulder. Tie the ends of the bandage in the hollow in front of the neck on the uninjured side. Fold the point across the front of the elbow and secure it with a safety pin. If you have no safety pin, simply tuck the point inside the sling. A pad can be placed under the knot to prevent it digging into the casualty's neck.

As long as the sling is comfortable and is capable of holding the arm securely in place, it does not matter how well it is applied. Remember to feel for the casualty's pulse and look at the colour of his fingers to check that blood is still circulating in the injured arm. It is a good idea to practise tying triangular slings if you can find a co-operative friend.

POINTS TO REMEMBER ABOUT BLEEDING

1. Blood loss is serious because it leads to shock.

2. After any injury always suspect, and check for, internal bleeding.

3. With **internal bleeding** treat for shock and send to hospital.

4. With **external bleeding** lie the casualty down and keep him at rest. Elevate the area which is bleeding and apply direct pressure to the wound for at least 10 minutes.

5. Maintain pressure by applying one or more dressings.

6. If signs of shock develop, send the casualty to hospital.

BURNS AND SCALDS

Burns are injuries caused by heat, cold, friction, electricity or chemicals. Scalds are caused by hot liquids. Burns and scalds have a similar effect on the body and the first aid treatment for both is similar.

Most burns happen in the home and children are most at risk. **The seriousness of a burn depends more on the extent of the body area injured than on the depth of the injury.** But for young children even small burns should be regarded as very serious and hospital help should be sought.

When the skin is damaged by burns, plasma – the liquid part of the blood – seeps from the nearby blood vessels and can form blisters.

It is important to be able to estimate what proportion of the body is affected in cases of burns. Anyone with burns over 10 per cent of his or her body needs hospital treatment urgently. Burns covering 10 per cent or more of the body can prove fatal, but hospitals can now save the lives of people who have up to 70 per cent of the body area burnt. In assessing the area of burns, it is useful to remember that the palm of the casualty's hand represents one per cent of his or her body area

Losing plasma is equivalent to losing a similar volume of blood, so, as with bleeding, a major problem with burns is shock. Extensive burns can be fatal because of the shock produced.

A burn which affects 10 per cent of the body area produces a loss equivalent to 1 litre (2 pints) of blood. Someone who loses that much blood is quite ill and will need hospital treatment.

Estimating area of burns. It is important to estimate what proportion of the body has been burnt. For instance, a burn to the whole arm or both forearms will cover about 10 per cent of the body area.

A good way of estimating the extent of a burn is to remember that the palm of the casualty's hand is one per cent of her body area.

With scalds it is possible for several separate areas of the body to be affected. Remember that it is the total area injured

that matters – whether one, two or more areas are burnt.

Burns are unlike bleeding in that the loss of fluid from the body is slow and insidious. Shock may not become apparent until one or two hours after the injury and because of this it may be difficult to convince a burn victim that he is seriously ill – especially where serious burns have destroyed the pain-sensitive cells.

But first aid measures should not be sacrificed in an attempt to rush the patient to hospital. Prompt first aid treatment for burns can dramatically reduce shock.

Although burns covering more than 10 per cent of the body area can prove fatal, hospitals can now save the lives of people who have up to 70 per cent of their body area burnt.

Anyone who receives a burn larger than a five pence piece should be seen by a doctor. Similarly, anyone with burns on the hands or face should be sent to hospital for expert attention, as scarring or other damage can occur.

THE AIMS OF TREATMENT FOR BURNS:

1. To prevent further damage.

2. To prevent infection.

3. To minimize the effects of pain and fluid loss from the burnt area.

4. To reassure the casualty.

5. To transport the casualty to hospital.

Cooling the injury. The first priority in the treatment of burns is to cool the injured area as quickly as possible. This reduces the pain and lessens the severity of the burn. Often a major part of the burn damage occurs *after* the actual contact with heat. Quick cooling can reduce the amount of tissue damage.

The burnt area should immediately be held under the nearest cold running water and the treatment continued for at least 10 minutes. If after this time no further pain relief is achieved by cooling or the pain does not return when cooling stops, the next stage of the treatment can begin. Otherwise cooling under running water should continue.

Extensive burns. If there are extensive burns, or if the burns are on parts of the body which are awkward to place under running water, cooling of the injuries by immersion in a cold bath should be used.

If burnt clothing is attached to the skin leave it there. It will have been made sterile by the heat and pulling it away may tear the skin. **However, if the area has been scalded, the wet clothing should be stripped off** because it will retain the heat. **Scalding will cause the injured area to swell, and so it is important that anything constrictive** such as tight clothing, rings or bracelets **should be removed as quickly as possible.** If they are left in place they may have to be cut off in hospital – a sometimes difficult and possibly painful procedure.

Preventing infection. After cooling, the next priority is to prevent infection. The burnt or scalded areas should be covered with loose, clean, dry dressings. For example, a clean pillow case will make an excellent covering for a burnt arm. Never apply pressure to burnt areas, simply cover them entirely.

When burns require hospital treatment, on no account should any creams or ointments be applied to the injuries. This will only delay treatment while the wounds are cleaned – a painful process.

Never prick or burst blisters. If this is done a closed wound becomes open to infection. The blisters may well be removed at hospital but sterile instruments will be used in sterile conditions.

Relieving shock. Once the burns have been covered, the casualty should be treated for shock. She should be kept calm and be reassured that she is going to be all right. An ambulance should be called for transport to hospital.

Burns are one type of injury where the conscious casualty may be given drinks. In fact, seriously burnt patients should be given water which they may sip slowly. They should be discouraged from drinking too much too quickly as this may cause them to vomit. But a sensible amount of drinking will help replace some of the lost body fluid.

Treatment of minor burns. Virtually all burns should be seen by a doctor – even if hospital treatment is not necessary.

If the skin is broken, no ointment or cream should be applied but the burn should be covered with a non-adherent dressing.

If the skin is not broken, cream can be applied to the burnt area. This should then be covered with lint (fluffy side up) and a layer of cotton wool over the top. The burn will produce a discharge which the cotton wool will absorb. The discharge

forms a crust over the burnt area and protects the wound while healing occurs.

Do not change the dressing frequently. Often it will have stuck to the wound and removing it may pull away the protective crust, causing bleeding and retarding healing. If the dressing must be removed, it should be soaked off.

Even with small wounds infection is a danger. But there is no need to remove the dressing to check the wound for infection. Simply trim the dressing so that it covers the burnt area but leaves the skin immediately around the burn uncovered. If infection occurs the area round the wound will become red, swollen and painful. If this happens consult a doctor.

Sunburn can destroy skin tissue in the same way as any other type of burn, so the same treatment – cooling and covering – should be given. If blistering occurs, medical help should be sought. If the skin is red but not blistered, calamine lotion will give some pain relief.

Cold burns. If the skin is kept in contact with the frost in a deep freezer for too long it may stick to the frost and the casualty may tear the skin while trying to free herself. A burn of this type should not be treated by cooling. The injured area should be cleaned and covered with a non-adherent dressing.

Electrical burns. Electrical burns are caused by contact with live current and anyone who suffers such a burn should see a doctor. Although only a small area of the skin may appear burnt, the electricity passing through the body travels along the

Washing chemicals from an eye. Make sure that contaminated water does not run into other eye, causing further injury

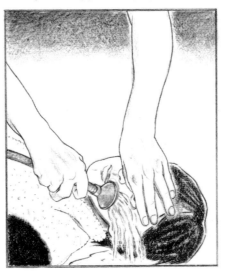

blood vessels and will damage structures under the skin, such as muscles, nerves and tendons.

All electrical burns are deep, and often surgery is necessary to repair the damage caused. Electrical burns should be covered with clean, dry dressings and the casualty should be sent to hospital.

Chemical burns should be treated in the same way as scalds. The affected areas should be showered with cold water for 10 to 20 minutes. All contaminated clothing should be removed while the water is being applied, but take care not to burn yourself in the process.

The treatment should be immediate and continue until you are sure that all the chemical has been washed off and the injury cooled. This time will be well spent – the initial first aid measures being more effective than quick removal to the hospital.

After washing and cooling the burn, cover it with a clean, dry dressing and send the casualty to hospital with a sample of the offending chemical.

Chemical burns to the eye. Turn the affected eye towards a basin or bowl (to prevent the chemical from running into the other eye), and wash or, preferably, shower the injured eye with plenty of water for at least 20 minutes – check the time on a watch or clock. Then cover the eye with a clean, dry dressing and send the casualty to hospital.

Summary of types of burn likely to be received in the home or during leisure activities.

Dry heat burns may be caused by contact with fires, irons, hot plates or hot water bottles.

Dry cold burns may be caused by contact with the frost in deep freezes.

Sunburn can follow over-exposure to natural sunlight or sunray lamps.

Friction burns can be caused by grabbing fast moving ropes or through the skin coming into contact with surfaces at high speed – for example, when sliding on gravel after falling from a bicycle.

Electrical burns can be caused by poor wiring or do-it-yourself accidents.

Scalds can be caused by hot water from kettles or saucepans, or by hot fat.

Chemical burns can result from contact with bleaches, cleaning agents and caustic soda.

Precautions against burns. All parents are aware of the risks to children of hot objects or liquids and yet thousands of youngsters suffer burns each year. Do remember to take care when cooking – never leave children unattended in the kitchen. Guard all fires and put matches and cleaning agents well out of the reach of young children, preferably in locked cupboards.

POINTS TO REMEMBER ABOUT BURNS

1. Burns should be cooled with running water as quickly as possible after the injury.

2. Cooling should be continued for at least 10 minutes or until no further pain relief is being achieved.

3. The cooling process should not be rushed – it is the most important part of the treatment for burns.

4. The injured area should be covered with a loose, clean, dry dressing.

5. The casualty should be treated for shock and sent to hospital.

ARTIFICIAL RESPIRATION

Artificial respiration, or artificial breathing, is necessary when a casualty is unable to breathe for himself. A person who has stopped breathing will be unconscious because the brain is deprived of oxygen.

Breathing failure. There are many ways in which breathing can fail.
1. Loss of blood leads to shock and unconsciousness and breathing failure may follow in serious cases.
2. Drowning is caused through water entering the airway and obstructing the passage of oxygen to the lungs.
3. Children can be smothered by plastic bags blocking their nose and mouth, so preventing them from getting the oxygen they need.
4. Scalds, stings or infections can cause the throat to swell – again blocking the airway.
5. An electric shock may disturb the heart's natural rhythm or paralyze the muscles in the chest to prevent breathing.
6. Pressure on the chest can, similarly, prevent breathing.
7. Exposure to harmful gases, such as carbon monoxide (produced in car exhausts), and overdoses of drugs often found in the home, such as aspirin or prescribed medicines, can prevent the body from using oxygen efficiently and so cause breathing to fail.

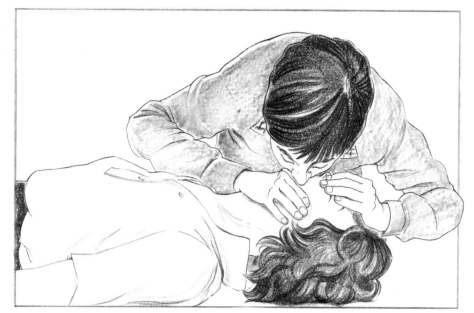

Signs of breathing failure. It is usually easy to tell if someone has stopped breathing. He will appear pale and the face, lips and finger nails will be tinged blue-grey, indicating a lack of oxygen in the blood.

Watch for the chest rising and falling. Listen for breathing, with your cheek (which is very sensitive) close to the casualty's nose and mouth where you should be able to feel exhaled breath on your skin.

If it is clear that the casualty is not breathing, mouth-to-mouth or mouth-to-nose resuscitation should be started immediately.

Applying artificial respiration. The aims of artificial respiration are to get the casualty to begin breathing again on his own or, if this is not possible, to provide

If a casualty is not breathing, start artificial respiration immediately. Make sure that the mouth is clear of obstructions, then tilt the head back to lift the tongue from the back of the throat. Support the jaw with one hand and pinch the casualty's nose with the other. Then cover the victim's mouth with your own and blow into it, watching for the chest to rise – indicating that air is reaching the lungs. Give four quick 'blows' without allowing the casualty's chest to fall completely between each one, then start breathing into the victim at the normal respiration rate of about 12 times a minute. Remove your mouth after each 'blow' and watch for the chest to fall. If the casualty does not begin to breathe on his own, keep up artificial respiration for at least an hour, or until a doctor says 'stop'

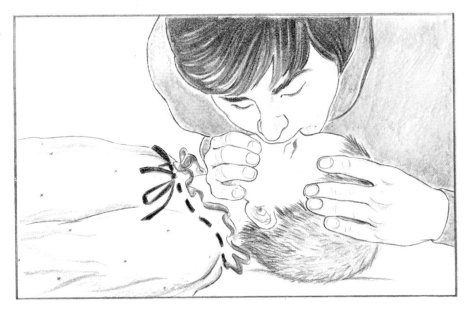

him with oxygen until more expert and better equipped help arrives.

Giving artificial respiration means breathing air into the lungs of the casualty who cannot do this for himself. We use only about one quarter of the oxygen that we breathe, so when we breathe out we expel about 15 per cent oxygen – more than is needed by a casualty to survive.

1. In order to receive artificial respiration the casualty should be placed on his back.

2. Check that nothing is blocking the mouth or throat. If there is any obstruction it must be removed or allowed to drain out by turning the head to one side.

3. When obstructions have been cleared, the head should be tilted back in order to open the airway as wide as possible. Sometimes these actions alone may be enough for the casualty to start breathing again. If he does start to breathe, he should be turned into the recovery position (see UNCONSCIOUSNESS).

Mouth to mouth. If the casualty does not begin to breathe, keep his head tilted back by pushing up on the lower jaw and use your other hand to pinch his nostrils closed, thus preventing air from escaping through the nose. Then completely cover the casualty's mouth with your own and blow into him, watching all the time for his chest to rise.

If the chest rises oxygen is successfully reaching his lungs. If the chest does not rise check that the head is tilted far enough backwards and that the seals at the nose and mouth are not allowing air to escape.

Start by giving four quick, full 'blows' without allowing the casualty's chest to fall completely between each one. This will quickly saturate the lungs with oxygen. After the first four inflations,

respiration should continue at the normal breathing rate – about 12 times a minute. After each 'blow' remove your mouth and watch the chest deflate.

Mouth to nose. The mouth-to-nose method should be used when there is difficulty or danger in using the casualty's mouth, for example when the mouth is injured, when corrosive chemicals are present or when the mouth is too big. The technique is the same except that the lips should be sealed and the nose left open.

When performing artificial respiration on a very young child or a baby, cover both his mouth and nose with your mouth. More gentle blowing will be needed to fill his lungs, but the rate of breathing should be faster than that for an adult.

Continue with artificial respiration until the casualty begins to breathe on his own or until someone else takes over for you – it is a very tiring procedure. When carrying out mouth-to-mouth resuscitation, do not stop immediately when an ambulance or doctor arrives. Wait until the expert tells you he/she is ready to take over. It may be necessary for him/her to obtain equipment or oxygen supplies before actually taking over treatment. Any interruption in the treatment could have serious results. If the technique is working, the colour of the casualty's skin will change from blue-grey to pink.

If the casualty does not begin to breathe on his own DO NOT GIVE UP; **you should try to continue giving artificial respiration for at least an hour or until you are told to stop by a doctor.** Normally, expert help will have arrived long before the hour is up.

When the casualty is breathing on his own, he should be turned into the

recovery position and then watched carefully to ensure that breathing continues. If he stops breathing, turn him onto his back and start **mouth-to-mouth resuscitation** again. Do not move the casualty unnecessarily. Make sure that someone has called for an ambulance.

If there is no improvement in the colour of the casualty's skin and no pulse can be felt at the neck, it is likely that the heart has stopped beating. But continue with artificial respiration because the heart may still be working, though less efficiently than normal.

Heart failure (stoppage). The heart may stop beating following a heart attack, an electric shock or simply through lack of oxygen because the casualty has stopped breathing.

POINTS TO REMEMBER ABOUT ARTIFICIAL RESPIRATION

1. Check whether or not the casualty is breathing.

2. If the casualty is not breathing turn him on to his back.

3. Check that nothing is blocking the airway. If there is a blockage, remove it.

4. Tilt the head backwards to open the airway as wide as possible.

5. Seal the nose and cover the casualty's mouth with your own.

6. Give four quick 'blows' without waiting for the chest to deflate completely.

7. Continue to 'blow' at a normal rate, removing your mouth between each one and watching the chest fall before blowing into the casualty again.

8. Continue artificial respiration until the casualty begins to breathe on his own, or until expert help can take over, or until you are told to stop by a doctor.

9. If the casualty begins to breathe on his own, turn him into the **recovery position**.

10. Transport the casualty to hospital as soon as possible by ambulance.

Left, above: mouth to mouth and nose respiration
Right: treatment for a choking baby
Right, above: the Heimlich Manoeuvre

Artificial respiration will not work if the heart has stopped completely because oxygen in the lungs will not be circulated via the blood stream to the vital organs.

There is a technique for 'massaging' the heart back into action, and maintaining artificial circulation of the blood, which trained first aiders can perform. But the technique cannot be taught through the printed word. Good tuition and extensive practice on life-like dummies are essential because **damage can be caused if heart massage is carried out incorrectly.**

Almost anyone can learn the technique with practice and we strongly recommend that you seek out a local centre where tuition is available. Imagine the distress of being the only person available to help a dying casualty and not having the necessary skills to provide that help.

A second reason for attending such a course is the need to practice the techniques of **mouth-to-mouth** and **mouth-to-nose resuscitation**. These must never be practised on people who are breathing normally, only on life-like dummies. As with all first aid techniques, practice will

give you greater confidence to use the techniques if a real emergency arises.

RESPIRATORY EMERGENCIES (BREATHING)

The title 'respiratory emergencies' sounds very daunting. It refers to conditions which can cause difficulty in breathing – the most urgent of which is choking.

Choking on food is the sixth most common cause of accidental death in the U.S.A., and in 1978 about 560 people in Britain choked to death.

If a sweet or a piece of food lodges in the airway, stopping breathing, the victim will die in a short time unless the obstruction is removed. Fortunately, most people who start to choke manage to clear the obstruction by coughing it out.

Recognising choking. Foreign body obstruction of the airway usually occurs while the victim is eating. However, in the case of young children choking may also happen during play when a small object or toy becomes lodged in the airway.

A choking victim may well bring his hand to his throat. Ask anyone who gives this sign whether they are choking and look for a nod of the head in response.

There are three stages of choking: inability to speak or breathe; pallor of the skin and a blue tinge to the lips (a sign of lack of oxygen); loss of consciousness and collapse. By the time a victim becomes unconscious he is very close to brain damage and death.

There is a danger that choking could be confused with a heart attack. The setting provides a clue – sudden death in restaurants is nearly always caused by choking. Age may also be an indicator – heart attacks are relatively rare occurrences below the age of 30.

The conventional treatment for choking is a series of sharp slaps on the back and an attempt to remove any firmly lodged obstruction with the fingers. In the case of babies it is better if they can be held upside down, and a young child can be bent face-down over your knee. Giving the casualty a drink is dangerous.

If the methods described do not remove the obstruction, a new technique known as the Heimlich Manoeuvre may be tried. There is still some question over how effective the technique is and further damage to the victim may result from its use. **For this reason the technique should be used only as a last resort.**

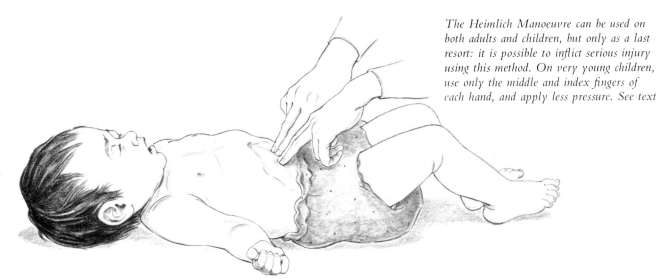

The Heimlich Manoeuvre can be used on both adults and children, but only as a last resort: it is possible to inflict serious injury using this method. On very young children, use only the middle and index fingers of each hand, and apply less pressure. See text

The Heimlich Manoeuvre. The object of the Heimlich Manoeuvre is to produce a pressure of air from the victim's lungs, forcing the obstruction out of the airway.

If the victim is standing or sitting, you should stand behind him and wrap your arms round his waist. Place your fist slightly above his navel and below the rib cage, with your thumb against the victim. Grasp your fist with your other hand and press into the victim with a quick upward thrust. The action should consist of a sharp flexion of the elbows rather than a 'hug' – with the emphasis on your hands. This may be repeated several times if necessary.

If the victim has collapsed to the floor and you cannot lift him, place him on his back, kneel astride him and place the heel of one hand just above the navel and below the rib cage. Place your other hand on top of the first and again give a quick upwards thrust, repeating it several times if necessary.

The Heimlich Manoeuvre for infants. Most choking incidents in young children can be dealt with by a slap on the back. But the Heimlich Manoeuvre may prove necessary and the rescuer should use the same method as for adults but apply less pressure. **With very young children sufficient pressure can be applied using only the middle and index fingers of both hands.**

Remember that the Heimlich Manoeuvre should only be used when survival depends on clearing the airway quickly. The victim should see a doctor immediately after a rescue.

FITS OR CONVULSIONS

Fits and convulsions can often appear more dangerous than they really are. Generally a person having a fit or convulsion should not be restrained unless in danger of injuring himself. If restraint is necessary, gentle force only should be used because the victim may be aware of what is happening and could become more violent in his actions.

Move any objects which could cause injury out of the victim's way. When the fit has finished lie the victim in the recovery position (see UNCONSCIOUS-NESS) and send for medical help.

If a *baby* has convulsions, he is often easier to handle if wrapped in a blanket.

Convulsions in *young children* often result from high temperatures caused by infection. It is therefore important that the child should see a doctor.

EPILEPSY

There are many different kinds of epilepsy and they vary considerably in severity. About 2,000 new cases are diagnosed each year, many of them the result of head injuries.

Anyone witnessing a major epileptic fit is likely to be alarmed because death may appear imminent. The patient will lose consciousness and become intensely rigid, with teeth and fists clenched. The breathing muscles may be affected causing the face colour to become livid. The eyes will stay open and fixed and appear to roll upward.

The convulsion stage follows, during which muscle contractions can become extreme with violent jerkings of the body and limbs. As this stage passes, jerky breathing is restored preventing any danger of death. The convulsions eventually cease and breathing returns to normal.

Return to consciousness may or may not be quick. A patient who regains consciousness quickly will look exhausted and will have a pale, sweating skin. He may not be aware of his surroundings and should be encouraged to sleep if he wants to. A patient who does not recover consciousness quickly may enter a coma which gradually changes into natural sleep.

Treatment is restricted to preventing injuries occurring during the attack. If there is time before the convulsions start, loosen tight clothing and use something soft to support and protect the head.

Try to keep onlookers out of the way and reassure them that the patient is not seriously ill. Do not put anything into the victim's mouth – it could cause damage and epileptics rarely bite their tongues. Do not restrict the patient's movements during the convulsion stage, but move furniture or other hard objects out of the way if possible.

When the fit has finished and the patient is sleeping, treat him as though you had found him unconscious: clear the mouth of any excessive saliva and mucus and turn him into the **recovery position**. When he wakes, stay with him and offer him a drink. Do not leave him alone until he is totally aware of his surroundings.

As long as the patient is known to be epileptic there is no need for him to go to hospital and he may return to work as soon as he has completely recovered from the attack. But make sure that the patient is fully recovered and capable of answering questions.

On recovery the patient will be aware of any injuries which may have occurred and some minor first aid may be necessary.

There are rare cases where fits recur without recovery between attacks. If attacks continue for longer than 15 minutes, either a doctor or an ambulance should be called urgently.

DIABETES

Diabetes is a disease affecting one per cent of the population and it is estimated that a further 60,000 people in the UK are undiagnosed sufferers. Although the disease cannot be cured, it can be controlled – allowing sufferers to lead full and active lives.

Diabetes is caused by the inability of the body to produce sufficient insulin. The action of insulin is not fully understood, but it is known to reduce the amount of glucose (a form of sugar) in the blood and make it available as a source of energy to the body.

It is important that the amount of glucose and insulin in the blood are balanced. The patient must maintain this balance by careful diet and often by injecting himself with extra insulin. Emergencies arise when an imbalance occurs.

Too much insulin. The most common imbalance is one in which the patient has too much insulin. This may result from an overdose of insulin which the patient has given himself by mistake, or following excessive physical exercise, worry or when a meal has been missed – all of which will reduce the amount of glucose available to the body.

The condition is relatively easy to diagnose, particularly if the patient is a known diabetic. However, it is quite common for a diabetic going into a coma to be mistaken for a drunk. The patient becomes aggressive, with a pale sweating skin. He will appear confused, mentally agitated and may start shouting. Speech can be affected and the patient becomes unsteady on his feet before eventually losing consciousness and entering a coma. Changes will occur in the breathing and the pulse will become weak and fast.

A diabetic coma is a life threatening condition so correct diagnosis and first aid are essential. First priority is to prevent the patient losing consciousness. The immediate treatment is to give five teaspoonfuls of sugar in a warm drink to the patient. He may be unco-operative, but persist and make sure it is swallowed.

If there is any doubt about the onset of an insulin reaction do not hesitate to give sugar – it is better to err on the safe side as no harm will result.

Recovery is usually quite rapid. When the patient has recovered, tell him how much sugar he has taken so that he can make adjustments to his diet.

If the patient is not given sugar before he lapses into a coma, no treatment by the first aider is possible. The patient should be treated as unconscious and urgent medical aid should be sought. If the patient is sent unconscious to hospital, it is important to inform staff that he is a diabetic and that you believe he is in a diabetic coma.

Too little insulin. In cases where a patient has insufficient insulin for the body's needs, the onset of symptoms will be much slower and hospital treatment should be sought – particularly in the case of undiagnosed diabetics. Giving sugar to a diabetic in this state, while not improving the condition, will not cause serious damage.

Many diabetics carry a 'medic alert' card to warn of their condition. They may also carry sugar for use in case of emergency.

POISONING

A poison is any substance which when taken into the body in sufficient quantity is capable of causing damage or death. About 3,000 people in Britain die of poisoning every year. Children under five are most at risk – about 40,000 of them are treated for poisoning in hospital each year.

Poisons may be solid, liquid or in gas form.

Common solid poisons include aspirin, paracetamol, prescribed tablets and poisonous foods such as some fungi, berries and plants – particularly laburnum and belladonna (deadly nightshade).

Liquid poisons include household cleaning materials, which may be corrosive; petrol and oil-based liquids; weedkillers, and alcohol if taken in excess.

The most common imbalance suffered by diabetics is one in which the patient has too much insulin. It is essential to stop the sufferer losing consciousness by giving him five teaspoonfuls of sugar in a warm drink without delay

Common poisonous gases are fumes from fires or stoves and motor exhaust fumes.

Different poisons can affect a victim in different ways. The following signs may be noticed: excitability, loss of coordination of movements, changes in breathing – this may become faster or slower – or convulsions. The combination of the effects that occur will depend on the poisons involved.

Treatment. The first priority is to ensure that the victim's airway is kept open and that breathing is maintained. If the victim loses consciousness, turn her into the **recovery position** (see UNCONSCIOUSNESS). If breathing fails, start **artificial respiration** immediately. If the victim remains conscious, keep her still and reassure her that she will be all right.

Avoid causing extra stress to the victim as this will cause the poison to be absorbed more quickly. You may have seen films in which someone who has taken a drug overdose is kept awake and made to walk about. This method must *not* be used. Nor should poison casualties ever be given any form of stimulant such as black coffee.

The second priority is to get the victim to hospital as quickly as possible. Although 3,000 people die from poisoning each year, of the 120,000 poisoned casualties who reach hospital only about 600 die – that is one death for every 200 casualties. **These figures emphasize the vital importance of prompt hospital treatment.**

Left: store medicines and tablets in a locked cabinet, out of reach of children
Below: a checklist of household products that can be poisonous
Below right: place a conscious stroke casualty in a comfortable position and reassure

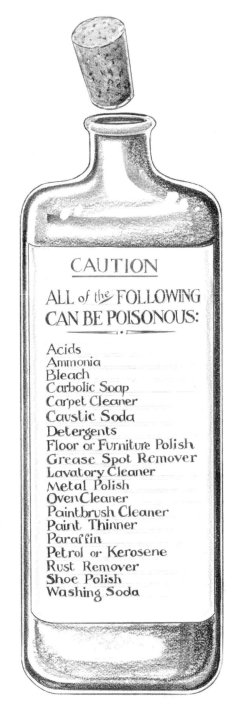

If the victim is conscious and unlikely to vomit, and if you have your own transport, take her to hospital yourself. If there is a danger of unconsciousness, vomiting or breathing failure ring for an ambulance.

Apart from coping with the emergencies which may follow poisoning, the best course is to do nothing. If the casualty is conscious, ask her what the poison was and how much she has taken. This should be done quickly in case the victim loses consciousness. For the same reason the casualty should never be left alone.

In almost every case the casualty should not be made to vomit. This might cause further damage. On no account should salt water drinks or any other emetic be given.

The only occasion on which you should try to make the conscious casualty vomit is following a drug overdose when you know there will be a delay before the victim can reach hospital. Induce vomiting by pushing fingers (either your own or the casualty's) down the victim's throat.

The only time when a drink may be given is when the casualty complains of lips, mouth or throat burning – an indication that she has swallowed something caustic. Even in this situation, if quick access to hospital is possible, it is better not to give a drink. But if there *is* some delay and you are sure that the casualty is fully conscious and unlikely to vomit, she may be given milk or water to sip. This should dilute the poison and reduce further damage.

Take a sample of the poison to hospital with you if possible. This could be in the form of tablets, empty or part-filled bottles, or berries you suspect of being poisonous.

When a victim has vomited, a sample of this vomit should also be taken to hospital. In order to pick up a sample, put your hand into a plastic bag, grab a handful of vomit and turn the bag inside out. Then seal the top of the bag. If possible, let the hospital know when the poison was taken and how much was consumed.

Precautions. Awareness of the dangers of poisoning in the home is very important. Children love to put things in their mouths – particularly if they are colourful, as so many drugs are these days. The only safe way is to keep anything poisonous out of the reach of children. Medicines and household cleaners should be locked up.

Always keep poisons and medicines in properly labelled containers and preferably the ones they were bought in. Never take medicines in the dark and always dispose of old tablets and other medicines by flushing them down the lavatory.

CAUTION

ALL of the FOLLOWING CAN BE POISONOUS:

Acids
Ammonia
Bleach
Carbolic Soap
Carpet Cleaner
Caustic Soda
Detergents
Floor or Furniture Polish
Grease Spot Remover
Lavatory Cleaner
Metal Polish
Oven Cleaner
Paintbrush Cleaner
Paint Thinner
Paraffin
Petrol or Kerosene
Rust Remover
Shoe Polish
Washing Soda

POINTS TO REMEMBER ABOUT POISONS

1. Make sure the casualty's airway is not blocked and that she is breathing.

2. Arrange for transport to hospital as quickly as possible.

3. Keep the conscious casualty still and reassure her.

4. Never leave the casualty alone.

5. Do not make the casualty vomit. Never use salt water drinks – they are dangerous.

6. Drinks of milk or water should only be given to conscious casualties who have swallowed an acid or caustic substance – burning round the mouth is a tell-tale sign. But do not give drinks even in this situation if the casualty can be transported to hospital quickly.

STROKES

Strokes are caused by a bursting artery or a blood clot in the brain. They occur most commonly in elderly people and can vary considerably in severity.

Symptoms. At the onset of a stroke the patient becomes confused and dizzy and may have a headache. He may have trouble controlling his limbs and muscles, find talking difficult and will usually dribble saliva from one side of his mouth. The patient will look extremely ill, his skin will appear blue and breathing will be loud and harsh.

Treatment. If the patient is conscious he should be placed at rest in a comfortable position and given a lot of reassurance. A doctor should be called straight away. If the patient is unconscious he should be placed in the **recovery position** and treated as an unconscious casualty (see UNCONSCIOUSNESS).

HEART ATTACKS

The role of the heart in pumping blood containing oxygen round the body to the brain and other organs is discussed earlier. We have also recorded that the heart may fail soon after breathing fails or following an electric shock. However, it is more common for the heart to fail as a result of disease.

Heart disease is a major cause of death. The term 'heart attack' is used to describe many different types of sudden illness involving the heart, but it is not important for the first aider to know exactly what has gone wrong. As in all emergency first aid the priority is to maintain life until expert medical aid can take over.

A person who has suffered a heart attack will be in a state of shock. He will look ill, his skin will be pale, cold and clammy, and he may feel giddy. He will be very anxious and restless, his breathing will be laboured and his pulse will be weak and irregular.

Treatment. If the victim is conscious, he will probably complain of severe pain around the chest, down his left arm and in his neck and jaw. Do not move him unnecessarily but put him into the sitting position. This will give him maximum relief and comfort and will allow him to breathe more easily.

Loosen any tight clothing at the neck, chest and waist. Reassure the casualty that he is going to be all right and arrange for an ambulance to come as quickly as possible.

If the casualty loses consciousness, he should be turned into the **recovery position** (see UNCONSCIOUSNESS) and his breathing and pulse should be checked frequently.

Following a serious heart attack, the heart may fail. If this happens **heart massage** and **artificial respiration** will be necessary to maintain life until help arrives.

Again we must encourage you to attend a course where you can learn to perform external heart massage and have the opportunity to practise mouth-to-mouth resuscitation. These skills are particularly important if you have elderly relations living with you.

POINTS TO REMEMBER ABOUT HEART ATTACKS

1. Summon an ambulance as quickly as possible.

2. If the victim is conscious place him in the **sitting position** and give him reassurance.

3. If the victim is unconscious place him in the **recovery position** (see UNCONSCIOUSNESS) and check frequently that his airway is clear and that he is still breathing.

4. If the heart fails, **external heart massage** and **mouth-to-mouth resuscitation** are required to maintain life.

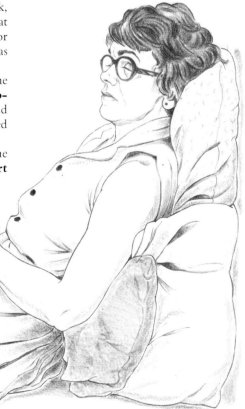

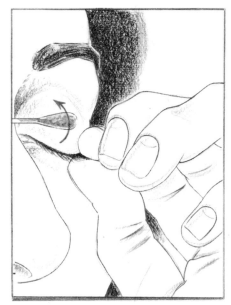

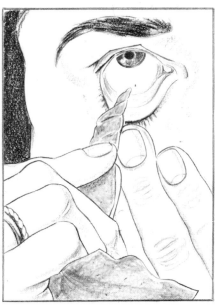

Top: small pieces of dirt can float on the surface of the eye and cause discomfort and pain. Locate the foreign body by systematically searching the eye, asking the casualty to look up, to the right, to the left and then down (top). If the object is still not found, the top lid can be turned back on itself by holding the lashes and pulling gently up and out to fold the lid over a cotton bud (above). Then try removing the foreign body with the corner of a clean handkerchief or tissue; but if it does not move easily, cover the eye with a pad and take casualty to hospital
Right, above: closed and open fractures
Right: position for chest wound casualty – half-sitting, inclined towards injured side

EYE INJURIES

All serious injuries to the eye and the skin immediately around it require urgent medical attention. When a casualty has an eye wound, she should be made to lie down and be kept still. The eye should be closed and covered with a sterile dressing, and she should be sent to hospital as soon as possible.

Black eye. A black eye is a bruise of the eye socket and lids, and the colour and swelling are due to bleeding underneath the skin. Swelling can be reduced with ice packs if they are used quickly after the injury.

Beef steaks are *not* recommended – they provide no relief and are rather expensive! A black eye may be associated with eye damage and even a fractured skull, so it is essential that the casualty be sent to hospital for assessment.

Foreign bodies. Small foreign bodies such as grit, loose eyelashes and fragments of metal or glass can float on the surface of the eyeball, causing considerable pain and distress to the casualty. The casualty should be discouraged from rubbing her eye as this will only cause more discomfort.

Such floating foreign bodies can be removed with the corner of a paper tissue or a clean handkerchief.

Seat the casualty facing a good light and stand behind her. Ask her to lean her head back until it is against you. Search the eye systematically for the foreign body. The casualty should be asked to look up, to the right, to the left and then down so that you can see the different parts of the eye.

If you still cannot find the object, grasp the lashes on the upper eyelid and pull it down. This may loosen the foreign body, but if not the upper lid can be turned back on itself to expose more of the eye. To do this, ask the patient to look down, pull the upper lid down, place a cotton bud across the lid and gently pull the lid out and up to fold it over. If you have friends who are not squeamish, practise this technique on them.

Once the offending object has been found, it should be removed with one gentle wipe of a paper tissue. **If the object does not move or come out with the wipe, then it is probably stuck to the eye and no further attempt should be made to remove it.** Cover the eye with a pad and send the casualty to hospital.

An alternative method of removing a foreign body from the eye is to blink her eye under water. However, this method is less likely to be effective.

If no foreign body is found but the casualty continues to suffer discomfort, she should be sent to hospital for closer examination of the eye.

FOREIGN BODIES IN NOSE OR EAR

It is quite common for children to stick beads, food such as beans or peas, or other small objects into their ears or nostrils. Do not attempt to remove objects which are stuck (you may push them farther in), nor pour water or oil into the ear. The child should be taken to hospital where the object will be removed. There is generally no immediate danger of injury by a foreign body – unless it is sharp.

FRACTURES

A fracture is a broken or cracked bone, and can be either closed or open.

A closed fracture is one where there is no break in the surface of the skin.

An open fracture is one where there is a wound leading down to the break or where the broken end of a bone protrudes through the skin.

Fractures usually occur in accidents involving force, such as car crashes or falls. Falling is the most common cause of death in the home – more than 3,000 people die in the home each year because of a fall. A common home accident is caused by people standing on chairs and stretching to reach high cupboards or to hang curtains. Always use a pair of steps for such jobs.

INDICATIONS OF A POSSIBLE FRACTURE ARE:

1. Pain in or near the injured part.

2. Tenderness on gentle pressure.

3. Swelling around the injured part (with later bruising).

4. Loss of control over the injured part and loss of power – for example, an inability to put weight on a leg.

5. Deformities such as:
   (a) irregularity of the bones;
   (b) shortening of the injured limb;
   (c) depression of a flat bone such as the skull;
   (d) the ability of the limb to move in abnormal ways;
   (e) the sound of grating when the limb is moved.

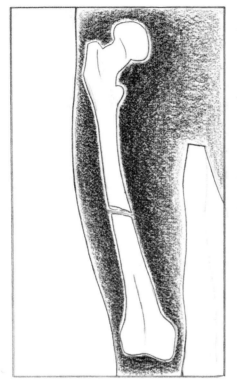

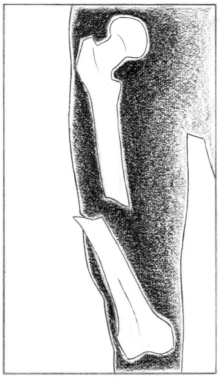

Dangers. Fractures themselves are not generally life-threatening injuries – even though they can be extremely painful and incapacitating. The immediate danger for the casualty is blood loss and the resulting shock.

The ends of broken bones are very sharp and can cause considerable damage to the soft tissues around them. They can also cut through blood vessels. Such internal bleeding may be seen as swelling around the site of the fracture.

It is not unusual for certain fractures to cause the loss of as much as 1 litre (2 pints) of blood. Multiple fractures may cause an even greater loss. As we have already seen, the loss of two or more pints of blood means that a casualty will be seriously ill.

Fractures to the skull and spine are particularly dangerous.

Skull, or base of skull fractures. A casualty who suffers such an injury is likely to be drowsy or unconscious. Such an injury can sometimes be identified because of bleeding from the nose or ear. If a skull

Elderly people are particularly prone to fractures. This is because their bones become brittle with age and they may be unsteady on their feet and more likely to fall in consequence.

Diagnosing a fracture. A casualty often knows when she has suffered a fracture because she hears the bone snap. However, the way to be sure that a fracture has occurred is by an X-ray. If there is any uncertainty about whether a casualty has a fracture or not, always assume she has broken a bone and send her to hospital for an X-ray and expert medical treatment.

Never test for (d) and (e) as this will cause unnecessary pain and probably further damage as well.

Not all these indications will be present with a fracture. In fact, sometimes the victim of a fracture will continue as normal without realizing that her injury is so serious. A good way of checking for a fracture is to compare the injured limb with the uninjured limb. Differences may well make the fracture obvious.

fracture is suspected, the casualty's head should be kept absolutely rigid. The bleeding should be allowed to continue, the blood being soaked up by cotton wool or any available absorbent material.

Fracture of the spine. When such an injury has occurred, a conscious casualty may complain that she is unable to feel or move her legs. An unconscious casualty may be discovered in a grotesque twisted position. **If a fracture of the spine is suspected, the casualty must not be moved because of the danger of causing further damage.**

The only times when a casualty with a fractured skull or spine should be moved are when the casualty is in danger of further injury – for example, when a fire is threatening her life – or if her breathing fails. In this latter case, **artificial respiration** becomes the first priority.

Chest and rib injuries. Ribs are commonly fractured in falls, through being crushed against the steering wheel in a car crash, or when playing sports. They can even be broken by a severe coughing fit. The casualty will complain of a sharp pain in the region of the fracture on breathing or coughing. She will take shallow breaths in order to reduce the pain. If a lung has been damaged by the broken rib, she may cough up blood and her breathing will be very distressed.

Muscles attached to the ribs provide adequate immobilization, and first aid treatment is limited to dealing with any complications and making the casualty comfortable.

A conscious casualty should be placed in a half-sitting position inclined towards her injured side. This allows the uninjured lung to continue working normally and ensures that any blood flow will be restricted to the already damaged lung.

Arrangements should be made to send the casualty to hospital as quickly as possible, preferably by ambulance.

A chest wound caused by a fractured rib coming through the skin is a serious complication as it may allow air to be sucked into the chest cavity. Other puncture wounds caused by a knife or bullet create a similar problem.

The wound should be covered at once with a sterile dressing covered by an adhesive dressing. A polythene bag can also be used to prevent air being sucked in. Again the patient should be inclined towards the injured side. If the patient is conscious, she can be transported to hospital in a sitting position or a half sitting position inclined towards the injured side.

Arm and leg fractures. Although it is generally best to do as little first aid as possible when dealing with fractures, there are occasions when some treatment may be helpful.

A conscious casualty who has suffered a fractured arm can be transported to hospital by car: it is not necessary to call an ambulance. It will aid the comfort of the casualty if the damaged limb is put into a sling; use a folded newspaper to provide a rigid support.

A casualty with a broken leg must be taken to hospital by ambulance and in most cases it is best simply to ensure that she is as comfortable as possible until the ambulancemen arrive. Support the injured leg in the most comfortable position with pillows or cushions, and try to prevent movement of the injured limb. **Do not attempt to straighten or splint a broken limb – leave this to the ambulancemen.** They will have special inflatable splints and anaesthetic gas to relieve the pain.

Sometimes, however, it may be necessary to move the casualty; for example, when she may be in further danger. Before you move the casualty, immobilize the

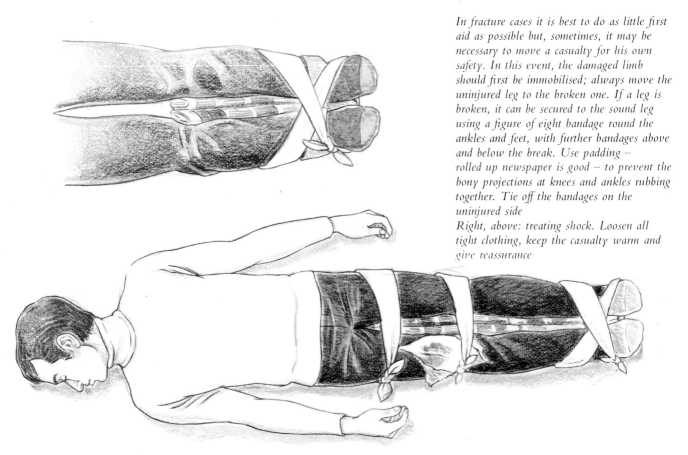

In fracture cases it is best to do as little first aid as possible but, sometimes, it may be necessary to move a casualty for his own safety. In this event, the damaged limb should first be immobilised; always move the uninjured leg to the broken one. If a leg is broken, it can be secured to the sound leg using a figure of eight bandage round the ankles and feet, with further bandages above and below the break. Use padding – rolled up newspaper is good – to prevent the bony projections at knees and ankles rubbing together. Tie off the bandages on the uninjured side

Right, above: treating shock. Loosen all tight clothing, keep the casualty warm and give reassurance

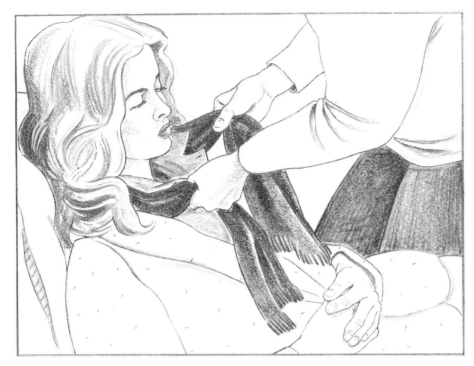

injured leg by securing it to the sound leg. Remember, this technique should be used *only* when the injured leg is not severely deformed.

Always bring the uninjured leg towards the injured one, moving carefully and slowly – there is usually no need to rush. Watch the casualty to make sure you are not causing too much pain. Use some padding – towelling or sweaters for example – between the knees and ankles to prevent these bony projections rubbing against each other and secure with triangular bandages, folded into broad bandages. **Do not** remove the casualty's shoes – they will make the bandaging more effective and comfortable.

The first bandage, which should be applied in a figure of eight around the ankles and feet, is best tied on the edge of one of the shoes. Unless the knee is fractured, the second bandage should be placed around the knees and tied at the side of the uninjured leg. Two more bandages may be used, one above and one below the site of the fracture – again tied on the uninjured side.

The bandages should be tied firmly enough to prevent one leg moving without the other. But watch for swelling around the fracture. If this occurs it will be necessary to loosen one or more of the bandages.

Once the fractured leg is immobilized in this way the casualty will be more comfortable while being moved. However, this form of immobilization is likely to cause pain to the casualty and **should only be used when it is really necessary to move her.**

General treatment. The best treatment for fractures is to do as little as possible. Unnecessary movement will only cause further distress and damage. Usually a conscious casualty will adopt the most comfortable position automatically. Once she has done this there is no point in moving her.

Open Fracture. If the fracture is open there may be external bleeding. There is also the danger that infection will enter the wound or even the bone. The wound should be covered carefully with a sterile dressing but pressure should not be applied as bleeding will probably be minor. If pressure is required to stop the bleeding, the method of dressing wounds containing foreign bodies should be used (see BLEEDING).

Arrange for an ambulance to come as quickly as possible. While waiting for it to arrive, treat the casualty for SHOCK. Reassure her that help is on the way and that she will be all right. Loosen all tight clothing and cover with a blanket. Do not leave the casualty alone, and check her breathing and consciousness. Keep a record of her pulse rate as this will help doctors to estimate the amount of blood lost and to decide whether a transfusion is necessary.

If the casualty loses consciousness, she should be moved gently into the **recovery position**. If breathing fails, **mouth-to-mouth resuscitation** must be started at once. Never give the casualty anything to eat or drink as she will probably need an anaesthetic when she reaches hospital.

Sprains and dislocations. Sprains and dislocations are both injuries which affect joints such as the shoulder or ankle. In *a sprain* the soft tissue around the joint is stretched or torn. *A dislocation* is the displacement of one or more bones at a joint.

Both types of injury appear similar to fractures and often occur at the same time. Usually an X-ray is required before an accurate diagnosis of the injury can be made. It is not necessary for the first aider to be able to tell the difference between fractures, sprains and dislocations. The casualty should be treated in the same way for all three conditions.

POINTS TO REMEMBER ABOUT FRACTURES

1. Move the casualty as little as possible, just help to make her comfortable.

2. Quick transport to hospital should be arranged.

3. The casualty should be treated for shock as internal bleeding will occur. Reassure the casualty.

4. Open fractures should be covered with a sterile dressing to reduce the risk of infection.

5. Check carefully for possible fractures of the skull or spine. If such fractures are suspected, the casualty must not be moved unless it is absolutely essential in order to preserve life.

HEAT EXHAUSTION/STROKE

Heat exhaustion or heat stroke may occur when a person is exposed to too much sun and high temperatures – most likely to be encountered when on holiday abroad – but it *can* effect you in your own garden if you don't time sun-bathing sessions sensibly, or if you fall asleep in full sun.

In *heat exhaustion* the casualty will suffer dizziness, nausea, headache and muscle cramps. He will also have the symptoms of shock – pale colour, cold clammy skin and a weak pulse.

The casualty should be moved to a cool place and *if conscious* given cool drinks to sip. Large amounts of salt should not be given as this may increase nausea.

Heat stroke is a very serious condition;

Above: elderly people are particularly prone to hypothermia when they have insufficient heating in their homes during the winter. The body temperature falls to a dangerously low level and death can follow. First aid treatment is to warm the body gradually, by putting the casualty into bed and covering with a blanket. Do not use direct heat, such as a hot water bottle, but a warm drink can be given. Call a doctor
Right: always give as little first aid as is necessary. Where urgent medical attention is required, dial 999 and ask for an ambulance. Be as precise as you can about the nature of the illness/accident and always give the full address clearly

the casualty may lose consciousness, his face will be flushed, his skin will feel hot and dry, his pulse will be strong and fast and his temperature may be very high. He should be treated as an unconscious patient (see UNCONSCIOUSNESS) and the doctor called as soon as possible.

HYPOTHERMIA

This is a serious condition in which the body temperature falls dangerously low. This can occur because of exposure to severe weather and is also likely to affect elderly people because of insufficient heating at home during the winter, or babies inadequately clothed for an unexpectedly cold day.

Treatment. If conscious, the casualty should be placed in bed and covered with warm clothing so that he warms *gradually*. Direct heat – such as a hot water bottle – should not be used, but the casualty can be given warm drinks. Call a doctor.

If the casualty is unconscious he should

again be put in bed – in the **recovery position** (see UNCONSCIOUSNESS) – and covered with warm clothing. An ambulance should be called without delay and a careful check should be kept on the patient's breathing.

GENERAL ASPECTS OF FIRST AID

Approaching a casualty. Your approach to a casualty should be calm, reassured and unhurried, as this will help to allay the anxiety that any casualty will have. It will also help you to overcome your own anxiety. Announce that you are a first aider and reassure the casualty and others present that the situation is under control and that further help will arrive soon. Never rush into treatment. Check first whether there is danger of further injury and whether it is necessary to move the casualty.

Be careful not to waste time treating obvious injuries such as minor bleeding when more serious, life-threatening problems may exist.

The priorities. Make sure the casualty is breathing, that there is no serious bleeding and that the casualty is conscious before doing anything else.

If there is more than one casualty, deal with the one who is in the most serious condition first. Responsible onlookers can be told how to care for the casualties who are less seriously hurt. The first aider must assume leadership unless a doctor or more qualified first-aider is present.

Sending for help. Send a responsible person for help as soon as possible. Generally it is best to send for an ambulance. The person requesting it should give the exact location of the emergency, the cause, the number of casualties involved, and brief details of extent of injuries, if known. As far as possible *never* leave a casualty unattended. Always send someone else to phone for help.

One point to remember when calling for help is that if the injury was caused more than 24 hours earlier, a hospital may refuse treatment without referral from a doctor. Therefore, if the effects of the injury do not appear until 24 hours after the accident which caused it, a general practitioner should be summoned in the first instance.

When to give drinks. The general rule is that no food or drink should be given to a casualty, for the following reasons:

1. Unconscious patients are unable to

swallow and will choke on anything given by mouth.

2. Many casualties will require an anaesthetic on arrival at hospital. An anaesthetic can only be given to a patient whose stomach is empty, again because of the danger of his choking or vomiting while unconscious. If a casualty has been given something to drink, treatment may be delayed for several hours until the stomach empties.

Only conscious casualties suffering from burns, or who have swallowed acids or caustic substances, may be given drinks. However, there is always the danger that these drinks may cause the casualty to vomit; so, if the casualty can be transported to hospital quickly, avoid giving him a drink. If you know that there will be some delay in getting the casualty to hospital, then a drink should be given.

Offer the casualty water and allow him to take sips rather than forcing him to take the whole drink quickly – which could cause the patient to vomit.

A person who is recovering from a faint may be given a drink – but on no account must this ever be alcohol.

Keeping the casualty warm. Following injury or sudden illness, the casualty should be kept warm but not overheated. One blanket will generally be enough cover, and as most heat is likely to be lost if his body is in contact with a cold surface, the blanket should be placed under the casualty if possible.

Never use a lot of blankets or any form of artificial heating, such as a hot water bottle. If the skin is overheated, blood will return to the skin to help cool the area and this will only increase the casualty's shock.

How to handle a casualty. Casualties should always be handled gently and carefully. Rough handling will increase pain and anxiety, and can make injuries worse or increase bleeding. If it is not essential to move a casualty, do not do so.

A *conscious casualty* will generally put himself into the position which he finds most comfortable, so nothing will be gained by moving him. Casualties with fractures or dislocations should not be moved unless they are in danger or have more serious complications such as bleeding or unconsciousness. Wait for the ambulance to arrive and let the ambulancemen take responsibility for moving the casualty – they are experts.

Distance from emergency services. The advice in this book has been to give as little first aid as is necessary at all times. This is because we are dealing with accidents in the home and most people live near enough to ambulance services and hospitals for expert help and treatment to be given reasonably quickly.

However, a large number of people live in more isolated places where help may not arrive for some time. More elaborate first aid treatment may be appropriate in such cases, and people living in isolated areas are advised to attend a full 16-hour first aid course. These are offered by the St John and St Andrew's Ambulance Associations, the British Red Cross and other organizations. It may also be worthwhile to attend a home nursing course.

Also, in isolated areas it may be better to call a doctor to the scene of an accident before sending for the ambulance. If you know the ambulance will take a long while to arrive, a doctor will probably be able to ease the casualty's pain and certainly offer more advanced first aid.

Transporting casualties. After receiving first aid, many casualties need to be quickly transported to hospital where more expert attention and equipment is available. In most cases where urgent medical attention is required, it is best to dial 999, give relevant information, and ask for an ambulance.

But there are times when transport by ambulance is inappropriate or even anti-social. Sometimes it may be quicker to take a casualty to hospital by car – either your own or a neighbour's – and at other times treatment may not be required or a doctor's visit may be sufficient 'second aid'.

Naturally, it is better to err on the side of safety and obtain hospital treatment as quickly as possible if serious injury or illness is suspected.

An ambulance must be called to any casualty whose life is threatened: for example, casualties who are unconscious, have uncontrolled internal or external bleeding, are not breathing or are in severe shock. An ambulance will also be needed for a casualty who can be moved only by stretcher.

Casualties may be taken to hospital by car in certain instances: for example, following a fracture of the arm or shoulder, where a poisoned casualty is conscious, following a blow to the head where the casualty is conscious and co-operative, when bleeding is controlled but stitching is required, or following burns.

When driving a casualty to hospital try to have a third person in the car who can ensure that the injured person does not deteriorate and that he remains conscious.

Where life is not threatened and hospital treatment does not appear necessary, the best course is to ask the casualty's GP to call as soon as possible. However, always bear in mind that anyone who has been injured or has suffered an acute illness could develop symptoms over a period of time: for example, where there is internal bleeding. So it is important not to leave the casualty alone and to check his condition – particularly his pulse – for some time after the injury.

SAFETY AND THE FIRST AIDER

A casualty is usually found at the place where she was injured, so the possibility of a second accident is very real. Before attending to a victim's injuries stop to consider what has caused those injuries. If the hazard still exists it must be removed before treatment begins.

Above everything else the first aider must ensure that he or she does not become a second victim. This will not help the original casualty and may make rescue even more difficult.

The second consideration is the danger of further injury to the casualty. Where such danger exists the first aider must decide whether to move the casualty to a safer place.

Car accidents. There is great danger in treating a casualty at the site of a road accident and this applies even if the site happens to be outside your own front door, in a normally peaceful street. People should be sent in both directions to warn approaching traffic if the casualty is not to be moved.

If two or more vehicles have collided, there is a danger that petrol may ignite. Engines should be turned off and keys removed from the ignitions before starting any first aid treatment.

Do not allow smoking near a road traffic accident.

Electricity is another potential danger. If the victim of an electric shock is still in contact with live current she must not be touched by anyone. If you can locate it quickly, switch off the electricity supply at the main, otherwise switch off at the plug, then remove the plug before attempting any treatment.

Fire or poisonous gases. Even when you are sure there is a casualty in a room filled with smoke or poisonous fumes, **do not** enter alone unless you are wearing some form of breathing apparatus. If you have

an assistant, tie a rope round your waist and cover your mouth with a damp cloth. Keep close to the ground because smoke and poisonous gases will rise, leaving more oxygen near the floor.

The assistant should be instructed to pull you out by the rope if you do not return within a couple of minutes.

When giving first aid to someone who has been in contact with poisonous substances or gases, take care not to be affected yourself while removing contaminated clothing from the casualty. If **artificial respiration** is required, start it only after the casualty has been moved into the fresh air and move your head well away from the casualty as she exhales. **Where there are signs of burns around the mouth do not use mouth-to-mouth resuscitation use mouth-to-nose instead, if safe to do so.**

Before treating a casualty who is bleeding:
1. Remove any source of further potential injury, such as broken glass, and switch off any unattended machinery.
2. If the casualty has been injured by falling stones or bricks, move her to safety before starting treatment.

Commonsense. Such matters may seem simple commonsense when considered at leisure. But when confronted with an injured person, your first reaction is likely to be a mixture of shock, confusion and a desire to help as quickly as possible.

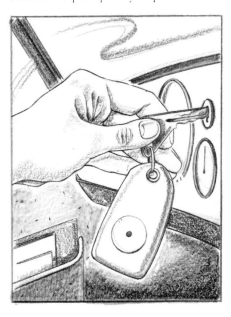

Before treating anyone injured in a road crash, make sure car ignitions are turned off and keys removed to prevent the possibility of the petrol igniting and creating more casualties

Do not rush in without thinking. Stop to consider what has happened and whether there are still potential dangers. This few seconds delay will also give you a chance to overcome your initial nervousness.

Too many cases are reported of one or more rescuers dying while the first casualty survives. However good the intention, this is not good first aid. **Remember: the first priority is safety – your own safety and the safety of the casualty.**

THE HOME FIRST AID BOX

Every home should have a First Aid Box, because accidents can happen – even in the most highly organized of households. You can either buy one already equipped, from main chemist shops and stores, or you can improvize one and stock it up as recommended below. All members of the family should know where the box is kept – and how to use the contents. But it must, of course, be kept well out of reach of young children.

Any box in which first aid materials are to be kept should be clearly labelled 'First Aid'. A biscuit tin or an empty ice cream container will serve the purpose as long as it is properly cleaned and labelled.

The following contents are recommended for home treatment:
Standard wound dressings – numbers 8 and 9.
1 crepe bandage
Triangular bandages
Cotton wool
Lint, gauze or melolin squares
Plaster strip
A selection of porous fabric plasters
Antiseptic cleanser
Antiseptic cream
Calamine cream
Wasp-eze spray
Burn spray
Soluble aspirin BP
Paracetamol
Milk of magnesia
Safety pins
Scissors, 13 cm (5 inch) stainless steel with blunt points
Tweezers – spade ended

Wound dressings. The standard wound dressings are the type with a pad stitched to the bandage. They are sold in various sizes, but Numbers 8 and 9 are the most handy for home use.

Crêpe bandages can be used to give additional pressure over a dressing if bleeding is hard to control. The bandage should not be stretched to more than two-thirds of its capacity when applied. This will allow for the limb swelling, but remember to check that blood circulation is not affected.

Triangular bandages are particularly useful because besides making slings they can be folded and used as ordinary bandages. You can make your own triangular bandages by cutting a 90 cm (36 inch) square of cotton diagonally from corner to corner.

Cotton wool is useful for cleaning wounds and for absorbing discharges when used over a non-adhesive dressing.

Lint, gauze and melolin squares are used to cover small wounds. Melolin squares are small, sterile, non-adherent wound dressings. They are reasonably inexpensive and particularly useful for covering grazes and small burns.

Plaster strip, cut into short lengths, is useful for fixing small dressings to the skin. Porous fabric plasters are recommended because they promote better healing than waterproof plasters, which do not allow air to circulate. When the injured parts are likely to be exposed to dirty water, waterproof plasters may be used, but afterwards they should be replaced with the fabric variety.

Antiseptic creams and lotions. Generally it is best to leave a clean, dry dressing. However, if the wound is likely to weep, an *antiseptic cream* can be used to provide a greasy surface which will prevent a dressing from sticking to the wound. *Liquid antiseptic* can also be used to clean small wounds, and antiseptic cream to treat gravel grazes or very small burns. When using an antiseptic cleanser be sure to follow the manufacturer's directions, otherwise healthy skin tissue may be damaged or skin reactions may occur.

Cold compresses. In the case of a twisted ankle or bruising in which the skin is not broken, swelling can be reduced and comfort provided by the application of a cold compress or ice pack. However, it is important first to check that no serious injury, for example a fracture, is present.

A cold compress can be made by soaking a clean, folded handkerchief or a folded triangular bandage in cold water. Place the compress over the injury without wringing it out. This dressing can then be secured with a firm bandage. Alternatively, a No 8 or 9 bandage can be soaked

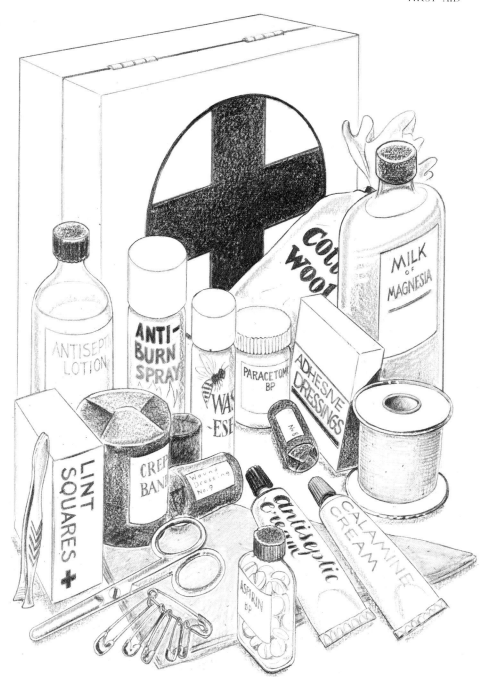

and applied directly over the injury. The bandage should be kept wet with more cold water.

Always check that the bandage is not tied too tightly, preventing blood flow.

An ice pack can be made by wrapping ice cubes in a towel and crushing them with a hammer. The pack can then be placed on the injury.

Calamine cream is useful for the relief of sunburn, itchy bites, heat spots and other minor skin irritations. It has the benefit of cooling the affected skin area.

Wasp-eze spray reduces the swelling and pain associated with wasp or bee stings.

Burn sprays are also very effective in reducing pain but they must be used with caution – only on minor burns and **never** on burns where the skin is broken.

Any wound or burn which requires hospital attention should have nothing other than a sterile dressing applied.

Soluble aspirin BP is effective in relieving pain and cold symptoms. It also tends to lower temperatures. Aspirin should not be given to people with upset stomachs or with a history of stomach trouble.

Paracetamol is also effective in relieving pain and is less likely to cause upset stomachs.

Milk of magnesia should be used for minor stomach upsets.

Other items such as tablets for indigestion may be added if considered necessary.

Remember that minor problems such as headaches, stomach upsets and indigestion should be referred to a doctor if they recur frequently or last for more than 24 hours.

Scissors. It is worth investing in a good pair of scissors for cutting dressings, but make sure they stay in the first aid kit.

Safety pins are particularly useful for fixing dressings, especially where triangular bandages are used as slings.

Tweezers are useful for removing splinters and stings.

SUMMARY OF LIFE-SAVING FIRST AID

The following chart illustrates the order in which events can happen following serious injury. Good first aid should help to prevent the casualty reaching the next stage in the chain. In fact, the casualty can be helped to progress back up the chain: for example, if breathing is restored or consciousness regained. Full details of each first aid technique appear earlier in this chapter under the relevant heading e.g. UNCONSCIOUSNESS, BLEEDING, etc.

A casualty need not pass through every stage. Heart attacks, electric shocks and head injuries can lead directly to **unconsciousness** or to **heart failure**. Very occasionally, following serious injury, death may be almost immediate.

Bleeding. Prevent further blood loss by lying the casualty down, using direct pressure, elevation and rest.

Burns. Reduce plasma (=blood) loss by cooling the affected area and cover with a loose, clean, dry dressing.

Fractures. Do little more than reassure the casualty. Check for fractures of the skull and spine.

Shock. Reassure the casualty, make him comfortable, lie him down and raise the lower part of the body, loosen tight clothing. Check the pulse frequently and keep a written note of the rates, for the information of the doctor/ambulancemen.

Unconsciousness. Ensure that the airway is clear. Turn the casualty into the recovery position. Check frequently that breathing

continues. Note the pulse frequently, and keep a written record as above.

Breathing failure. Turn the casualty onto his back. Check that his airway is clear and tilt his head back. Start **mouth-to-mouth** or **mouth-to-nose resuscitation** immediately.

Heart failure (stopped). Lie the casualty on his back. Make sure the airway is clear. Start heart massage and mouth-to-mouth resuscitation at once. Heart massage can be learnt only by attending a first aid course.

Remember: Never leave a casualty unattended. Arrange for transport to hospital as quickly as possible – but do not delay first aid treatment.

FIRST AID PRIORITIES

The first priority is to maintain a clear airway at all times and to keep the casualty breathing. The second priority is to stop serious bleeding. The third priority is to turn the casualty into the recovery position. Remember the priorities as follows:
A–Airway
B–Bleeding (serious)
C–Consciousness

If the casualty is breathing normally, serious bleeding has been checked, he is in the **recovery position** and an ambulance has been called, attention can be given to treating less serious injuries. But always remember to check breathing and pulse rates regularly until the ambulance arrives and you are relieved of responsibility for the casualty.

Reading about first aid techniques cannot take the place of practical experience. This can only be obtained by attending a first aid course. Most people

enjoy learning first aid, and facilities will probably be available for practising the techniques of **mouth-to-mouth resuscitation** and **heart massage**, which cannot be practised at home.

First aid is the simple appliance of common sense, but many casualties still die unnecessarily every day and a widespread knowledge of life-saving techniques would prevent many of these deaths.

However advanced your knowledge of first aid the simple priorities must never be ignored – that way you should always deliver a live casualty to hospital.

USEFUL ADDRESSES

Further information may be obtained from the following organisations, which also provide training in first aid:

St John Ambulance Association
1 Grosvenor Crescent
London SW1X 7EF

British Red Cross Society
9 Grosvenor Crescent
London SW1X 7EJ

In Scotland first aid training is offered by:

St Andrew's Ambulance Association
Milton Street
Glasgow G4 0HR

For local addresses consult your telephone directory.

DEVELOPMENT OF SERIOUS INJURY

Conditions	Necessary actions
Bleeding, Burns, Fractures and Other Injuries	
LOSS OF BODY FLUID →	Prevent further loss of body fluid
SHOCK →	Lie casualty down. Raise lower part of body. Give reassurance.
UNCONSCIOUSNESS →	Turn into recovery position. Check breathing.
BREATHING FAILURE →	Use mouth-to-mouth resuscitation. Check pulse.
HEART FAILURE →	Use heart massage and mouth-to-mouth resuscitation.
DEATH	

Transport to hospital as quickly as possible.

INDEX

ACKNOWLEDGMENTS

Abbey National Building Society 11, 36, 39 above; Allmilmo 66; Bissell Appliances Limited 109 above, 115; Blue Circle Enterprises 42, 151; John Cook 81, 85 above, 93 right, 95, 96, 97, 103, 146; Eastham Burco 109 below, 122; Kleeneze 107, 130; Bill McLaughlin 58, 76, 117; Octopus Picture Library 22, 50, 55, 56–7, 80, 150; David Prout 93 above and below left, 99, 116; Rex Features 31; Rentokil Limited 145; Rowenta Limited 141; Sandersons 110; Shaftesbury Society Housing Association 39 below; Spectrum Colour Library 23, 30, 35; Lee Story 114; T.I. Creda Limited 129; Thorn Domestic

Appliances Limited 141; Elizabeth Whiting and Associates 4–5, 8, 26–7, 56, 70, 71, 74, 75, 77, 78, 85 below, 86, 124; Paul Williams 41, 67, 73, 79, 87, 105, 113, 119, 123, 131, 138, 143, 149; Zefa Picture Library (Corneel Voigt) 34.

The publishers would also like to thank the following for their help in preparing, or permission to reproduce charts: Nairn Floors Limited 63; Wallpaper Marketing Board 87, 91; Crown Paints Limited 88–9